The Oxford Introductions to U.S. Law

Torts

The Oxford Introductions to U.S. Law

Torts

JOHN C. P. GOLDBERG
BENJAMIN C. ZIPURSKY

Dennis Patterson, Series Editor
The Oxford Introductions to U.S. Law

OXFORD
UNIVERSITY PRESS

Oxford University Press, Inc., publishes works that further Oxford University's objective of excellence in research, scholarship, and education.

Oxford   New York
Auckland   Cape Town   Dar es Salaam   Hong Kong   Karachi   Kuala Lumpur
Madrid   Melbourne   Mexico City   Nairobi   New Delhi   Shanghai   Taipei   Toronto

With offices in
Argentina   Austria   Brazil   Chile   Czech Republic   France   Greece   Guatemala
Hungary   Italy   Japan   Poland   Portugal   Singapore   South Korea   Switzerland
Thailand   Turkey   Ukraine   Vietnam

Library of Congress Cataloging-in-Publication Data

Goldberg, John C., 1961–
   The Oxford introductions to U.S. law. Torts / John C.P. Goldberg, Benjamin C. Zipursky.
      p. cm.—(The Oxford introductions to U.S. law)
   Includes bibliographical references and index.
   ISBN 978-0-19-537397-4 (pbk. : alk. paper) 1. Torts—United States.
I. Zipursky, Benjamin Charles, 1960- II. Title. III. Title: Torts.
   KF1250.G645 2010
   346.7303—dc22   2010002666

Printed in the United States of America on acid-free paper

Note to Readers
This publication is designed to provide accurate and authoritative information in regard to the subject matter covered. It is based upon sources believed to be accurate and reliable and is intended to be current as of the time it was written. It is sold with the understanding that the publisher is not engaged in rendering legal, accounting, or other professional services. If legal advice or other expert assistance is required, the services of a competent professional person should be sought. Also, to confirm that the information has not been affected or changed by recent developments, traditional legal research techniques should be used, including checking primary sources where appropriate.

(Based on the Declaration of Principles jointly adopted by a Committee of the American Bar Association and a Committee of Publishers and Associations.)

For Homer and Bette Goldberg ✹ J.C.P.G.

To my father, Alvin Zipursky, and to the memory
of my mother, Freda Zipursky
for nourishing love and the love of learning ✹ B.C.Z.

Acknowledgments

WE ARE GRATEFUL TO Julie Faber, Homer Goldberg, Sam Issacharoff, Ken Levy, Antonia New, and Damian Treffs for commenting on the manuscript, as well as to the participants in a faculty workshop discussion held at Fordham University School of Law. Our research has been generously supported by Dean William Michael Treanor and the Fordham University School of Law, Deans Elena Kagan and Martha Minow and the Harvard Law School, and Dean Ed Rubin and the Vanderbilt Law School. Chris Collins, Jessica Picone, Erica Woods Tucker, and Lori Wood patiently guided us through the production process. Finally, we thank Dennis Patterson and Oxford University Press for inviting us to undertake this project.

Contents

CHAPTER 6 **Negligence: Advanced Topics** 113

Note to Readers

THIS BOOK AIMS TO provide a comprehensive yet accessible account of tort law, including its history, its practice, and the political debates that surround it. Chapters 5–10 and 12 analyze in depth the judicial decisions and doctrines typically covered in first-year Torts classes. Law students may wish to focus particularly on those chapters.

ONE

Introduction

※ 1.1 What is a Tort? What is Tort Law?

The word "tort" was borrowed by English-speaking lawyers from French. It means "wrong." A tort is a wrong. To commit a tort is to do wrong to another.

Although every tort is a wrong, not every wrong is a tort. A tort is a special kind of wrong. Most important, a tort is a legal wrong—a wrong recognized by law, as opposed to wrongs that are exclusively violations of moral rules. As we will see in a moment, torts are distinctive in other ways: they form a special subcategory within the category of legal wrongs.

The concepts, rules, and principles of tort law are usually spelled out in opinions written by judges in the course of resolving particular lawsuits. They are also contained in statutes and agency regulations. These concepts, rules, and principles define what sort of interaction with another will count as a tort. They also establish the terms on which a victim can respond to a wrongdoer for having been wronged. The standard form of response authorized by tort law is a lawsuit that, if successful, results in a wrongdoer, or "tortfeasor," paying compensation to the victim. The term "liability" refers to a tortfeasor's obligation to pay compensation to the victim(s) of her tort. A person who commits a tort is usually subject to liability, although courts sometimes provide tort victims with other kinds of relief.

As there are many ways to mistreat another, so there are many torts. A manufacturer of a dangerously defective lawnmower that injures its user may be subject to liability under the branch of tort law known as *products liability*. A local television station that airs a news story falsely suggesting that a particular person is a pedophile risks liability for *slander* or *libel*. If a bar patron intentionally attacks another, the victim may be able to recover for the tort of *battery*. If a store owner detains a customer in a back office on unfounded suspicions of shoplifting, the owner may be committing *false imprisonment*. A doctor who treats a patient incompetently so as to injure or kill the patient may be liable for *medical malpractice*. A scam artist who tricks an elderly person out of her savings has probably committed the tort of *fraud*. A property owner who maintains a mulching operation that constantly emits foul odors that nauseate his neighbors when they are in their yards may be liable for a *nuisance*. A person who drives a truck across farmland owned by someone else may have committed a *trespass to land*.

What do the foregoing examples have in common? Most fundamentally, all are wrongs. Each involves *the violation of a norm of conduct*. Tortious action thus tends to give rise to the same sort of sentiments—guilt, shame, or denial on the part of the injurer and anger, resentment, or vengefulness on the part of the victim—as behavior that would tend to be adjudged morally wrongful independently of the law of torts. To understand tort law, one must appreciate that torts are "wrongs" of the same general character as moral wrongs: each tort involves the violation of a norm that specifies how one must treat others in light of certain important interests, such as the interest each person has in bodily integrity.

Still, the wrongs identified by tort law have special attributes that set them apart as a distinctive species of wrong. First, as noted above, torts are *legal wrongs*. They are defined by judicial decisions and statutes. While it may be wrong to annoy your neighbor by blasting loud music at a school graduation party, the law does not recognize this as a "nuisance" because judicial decisions define that wrong as an *ongoing* interference with another's enjoyment of her property. Conversely, a manufacturer that sells a product that injures someone because of a hidden defect—even though the manufacturer has taken great care to make the product safe—may not have acted in a blameworthy fashion, but may have committed a tort. To be sure, there is plenty of overlap between blameworthy conduct and torts. The inquiry into whether a tort has been committed will call for the application of legal concepts—such as the concepts of duty and intent—that bear a close relationship to counterpart concepts found in ordinary morality. This is hardly surprising. When jurors, judges, and legislatures apply or make the rules of tort law—rules that determine when one person has wronged another—they rely to some extent on ordinary moral sentiments. Still, as the examples of the annoying party and the defective product attest, the law of torts stands apart from ordinary morality in certain ways. Throughout this book we will have occasion to consider when and why tort norms depart from moral norms, either by being less demanding or more demanding.

In addition to being legal wrongs, torts are also *relational wrongs*. Each tort identifies forms of conduct that are not merely wrongful in the sense of being antisocial or undesirable, but wrongful *toward* a person or set of persons. In turn, that person or those persons are usually the only ones who will be entitled to invoke the tort system to respond to the wrongful conduct. For example, to libel someone is, roughly speaking, to publish in writing a statement about that person that is false and of a sort that tends to cause reputational harm. Suppose a newspaper knowingly smears John Doe with a false story asserting that he has funded terrorist activities. Suppose also that the story emphasizes that Doe joined a terrorist cell of his own accord, without the knowledge of friends or family. On these facts, only Doe has been libeled, and only he has the legal right to demand damages from the newspaper. This is so even if some of his friends and family members have been harassed by readers who ignore or dismiss the part of the story exonerating the family and friends. They cannot prevail on a libel claim against the newspaper because *they have not been defamed*; rather, they have been harmed by the defaming of another. This same relational structure is present in all other torts. As we study various torts in greater detail, we will have occasion to consider what the relational aspect of torts does and does not entail.

Third, torts are *injurious wrongs*. Other branches of law, including criminal and regulatory law, recognize and respond to victimless wrongs. There are no victimless torts. Illegal drug possession or a failed conspiracy to bomb a building might constitute victimless crimes. Likewise, if a lawyer co-mingles personal funds with funds that a client has placed in her custody, she has probably violated a code of professional conduct, even if her client suffers no financial loss. None of these wrongs are torts because none involves injurious misconduct. By contrast, a bombing that succeeds in destroying property is a tort as to the possessors of the property. And if a lawyer's violations of professional rules result in harm to her clients, those violations may amount to the tort of legal malpractice. In sum, torts always involve acts that are not only *wrongful toward* another (the relationality requirement) but also *injurious to* that other (the injury requirement).

Finally, torts are *civil wrongs*. To say that torts are civil wrongs is partly to say that they are *not* criminal or regulatory wrongs. The commission of a tort, precisely because it is a relational, injurious, legal wronging of a victim by a tortfeasor, has the special consequence of generating in the victim the power to respond to the wronging through a civil lawsuit. The lawsuit and its outcome, if it is successful, constitute a form of recourse or satisfaction to which the victim is entitled. Misconduct can be both a crime and a tort: an intentional killing can be both the crime of murder and the tort of battery. However, the commission of a tort does not of itself render the perpetrator subject to incarceration or criminal fine. Rather, it renders her vulnerable to a suit brought by the victim(s). Thus, it is up to the victim to decide whether to invoke tort law as a means of pursuing civil recourse against the wrongdoer. Likewise, it is the victim who stands to obtain a remedy that is typically meant to provide her with a measure of satisfaction as against the wrongdoer.

When wrongful conduct is addressed as a crime, it is treated as a wrong full-stop, or a wrong against the state or "the people." Therefore, a representative of the public, such as a district attorney, decides when and how to prosecute the case, and the victim usually has relatively little say in how the prosecution will proceed.

▓ 1.2 The Politics of Tort Law

Today more than ever, tort law is in the public eye. Sometimes, it is particular lawsuits that garner attention, as when thousands of consumers sue the manufacturer of a prescription drug alleging that it caused them to experience harmful side effects. More generally, since about 1980, *tort reform*—that is, the adoption of measures such as caps on damage awards that are designed to discourage tort suits—has been a powerful political movement, particularly in the United States.

Proponents of reform decry tort law as a system of "jackpot justice" in which undeserving claimants and greedy plaintiffs' lawyers reap windfalls while penalizing and discouraging socially beneficial activities. They also argue that tort suits are emblematic of, and partly responsible for, a "compensation culture" in which citizens too readily cast themselves as victims owed something by others. Defenders of the tort system deny that it is especially arbitrary, that it significantly impinges on economic productivity, and that it has eroded notions of personal responsibility. More affirmatively, they defend tort law as one of the few mechanisms by which ordinary individuals can hold powerful political actors and multinational corporations accountable for the harms that their actions cause.

This book has something to say about these debates, although it will approach them indirectly. Its primary aim is to give the reader a better understanding of what tort law is and how it operates. Once one grasps in detail what it means for torts to be legal, relational, injurious, and civil wrongs, one can come to a clearer understanding of the strengths and weaknesses of this body of law.

This appreciation, we argue, will reveal that the positions staked out by reformers and defenders of the tort system are caricatures. Tort law empowers victims to obtain recourse against those who have wronged them. As such, it fits comfortably within Anglo-American liberal democratic traditions and their emphasis on the rule of law, the protection and vindication of individual rights, and the importance of interpersonal obligations to the maintenance of civil society. Yet like any legal and political institution, tort law is subject to manipulation and dysfunction. And the modern tort system—unlike its historical predecessors—operates as part of a bureaucratized regulatory and welfare state that can attend to events such as accidents in ways other than by empowering victims to sue. The real political question today for tort law is its proper place alongside other bodies of law (e.g., contract and criminal law) and other institutions, particularly insurance mechanisms and public assistance programs.

1.3 Can Tort Law Be Given a Meaningful General Description?

Tort law is capacious. It covers a wide range of human behavior and injuries. Moreover, it has been and is being shaped by jurors, judges, and legislatures operating on the basis of an array of considerations ranging from concerns for the integrity of the legal system to concerns for economic growth. Fastening on these features of tort, many law professors have expressed skepticism that one can give a general description of the subject that is both substantive (nonvacuous) and yet faithful to the diversity of the phenomena for which it purports to account. According to them, about the most that can be said about tort law at a general level is that it provides occasions for one person to haul another person into court, thereby conferring on judges and juries a power to attempt to accomplish one or more of a number of possible objectives by denying or granting relief to the person who has brought suit.

These objectives might include compensation of victims; deterrence of undesirable conduct; reinforcement of social norms; expression of political protest; and redistribution of wealth. By contrast, they regard approaches such as ours, which attribute a unifying substance and structure to tort law, as unrealistic.

Tort law is wide-ranging and has been and is shaped by an array of forces and considerations. Moreover, it presents many issues over which reasonable people can and do disagree. Yet to acknowledge these points is by no means to concede that tort law is an *ad hoc* assemblage of decisions made by judges and juries with a hodgepodge of goals in mind. Tort law hangs together in its content, character, and structure. As a law of wrongs and redress, it is distinct in form and substance from other bodies of law, such as regulatory law, insurance law, or tax law. Disagreements among judges and other legal actors about tort law are disagreements about something in particular, not all-things-considered discussions of everything and anything. They are disagreements about what should count as the sort of wrong that entitles its victim to pursue recourse against her wrongdoer through the courts. By grasping and articulating the concepts of wrongdoing, legality, relationality, injuriousness, and civil recourse, among others, one can simultaneously acknowledge the complexity and protean nature of tort law while still providing a meaningful general characterization of it.

⚸ 1.4 Plan of the Book

The materials that follow aim to provide an introduction to the history of tort law, the workings of the legal institutions that make and apply tort law, the current state of tort doctrine, and academic and political critiques of tort law. To help keep the discussion grounded, and to help law students connect our analysis to materials that they are likely to encounter in an introductory torts course, we will make frequent reference to influential judicial decisions and other legal materials pertaining to tort law. Although the focus throughout will be on U.S. tort law, we hope that our treatment will shed light on tort as it operates in other common law jurisdictions and perhaps even in civil law systems as well.

Chapters 2 through 4 canvas the history of tort law, the range of conduct that it identifies as wrongful, and the basic procedures through which claims of wrongdoing and injury are adjudicated. Chapters 5 and 6 offer a detailed account of the particular tort of negligence. Chapters 7 and 8 discuss torts that are quite different from negligence in that they do not demand care or vigilance, but instead prohibit certain 'boundary crossings'—intentional violations of one's person or one's property rights. These include the torts of battery, assault, false imprisonment, trespass, nuisance, and conversion. In discussing these wrongs, we will also have occasion to mention related wrongs such as sexual harassment and fraud. Chapters 9 and 10 focus on the concept of "strict" or no-fault liability, discussing its application and rationales as applied to "abnormally dangerous activities" and the sale of products containing dangerous defects. Chapter 11 addresses the defamation and privacy torts. Chapter 12 sets out the rules by which tort damages are determined, including both compensatory and punitive damages, as well as rules by which damages are allocated between or among multiple wrongdoers. Finally, Chapter 13 offers some thoughts on current trends in tort law.

TWO

A Brief History of Tort Law

THE HISTORY OF TORTS is equally one of continuity and discontinuity. As far back as 1250 AD English law recognized the right of a victim of an unjustified physical attack to sue his attacker for damages. By 1500, it recognized torts ranging from medical malpractice to defamation. In so doing, it embraced the idea that the law's fundamental tasks include the defining of wrongs and the empowering of victims to initiate court proceedings as a form of recourse. Yet in terminology, substance, and the context in which it operates, tort law has also undergone enormous changes. Courts and legislatures have created new torts and abolished existing ones. The procedures used to litigate tort claims have changed markedly. As recently as 150 years ago, now-standard mechanisms for financing litigation and for protecting against ruinous liability did not exist. Until the mid-twentieth century, tort law was often the legal system's only mechanism for regulating unsafe conduct. Today it operates against a backdrop of extensive federal and state safety regulation.

✹ 2.1 1250–1800: 'Tort' Law Under the Writ System

Although it was not known by the name "tort" until the mid-1800s, tort law has been a part of English law (and later American law) for centuries. Starting in the late 1200s, the Chancery, an office of the English royal government, began making available a document called the *writ of trespass vi et armis*. Issued in the name of the king, it was provided (for a fee) to persons who alleged they were victims of beatings, robberies, and other wrongs involving force. As issued, the writ would contain a very brief description of the alleged wrong and the damages suffered by the victim, and would order a local sheriff to produce the wrongdoer before a judge so that the wrong-doer could defend himself against the accusations. A victim who successfully pleaded and proved the alleged "trespass" stood to recover damages from the wrongdoer.

The name of the trespass writ conveyed the type of victim to whom recourse was being provided. Although today the term "tres-pass" refers to interferences with another person's land or posses-sions, for much of English history, it was used more broadly as a synonym for "wrong" or "transgression." (This is the sense of the term employed in the familiar petition from the Lord's Prayer that our "trespasses" be forgiven.) And yet the use of the phrase *vi et armis*—"with force and arms"—at the same time confined the writ's availability to transgressions that involved *the direct application of force by the wrongdoer to the victim*. The category of forcible, direct wrongs was in turn broken down by lawyers into subcategories. For example, the victim of a physical beating would seek a writ of tres-pass *vi et armis* for battery. By contrast, a property owner whose land had been physically invaded by another would ask for the inclusion in his trespass writ of the phrase "*quare clausum fregit*" (literally, a breaking of the plaintiff's boundaries) to clarify that the wrong he was complaining of was a direct, forcible interference with his property rights—what we would today call a trespass to land.

Because the trespass writ was defined in terms of directness and forcibleness, and *not* in terms of any intention to do harm on the part of the defendant, many *accidental* physical injurings were actionable under the writ as batteries. (As we will see, the term "battery," like the term "trespass," means something different today.) For example, in the 1616 decision of *Weaver v. Ward*,[1] the defendant

---

1. (1616) 80 Eng. Rep. 284 (K.B.).

and plaintiff were participating in a military training exercise when the former accidentally shot the latter. When the plaintiff sued in trespass for battery, the defendant argued that he should not be held liable because he was engaged in a lawful activity and had acted without any intention of harming the plaintiff. The English Court of Common Pleas rejected this argument, explaining that the writ of trespass covered forcible harms committed accidentally. However, the court also identified a potential defense for trespass defendants, stating that a forcible injuring would be excused if the defendant could establish that the injury to the plaintiff was an "inevitable accident" that occurred "utterly without his fault." Here the court seemed to have in mind a situation in which a defendant could prove that he was exceedingly careful in taking steps to prevent the accident in which the victim was hurt, yet nonetheless caused an injury because of circumstances entirely outside of his control—e.g., the victim of the shooting 'came out of nowhere' and stumbled in front of the gun just as it was discharging.

The limitation of the reach of the trespass writ to direct and forcible wrongs was largely driven by jurisdictional considerations. Under medieval conditions, central royal government had only limited authority, and the royal courts competed for litigation business with local and church courts. Accordingly, the royal judges initially confined their attention to disputes of a sort that had potentially broader ramifications. Beatings and physical invasions of land, by threatening to undermine civil order ("the king's peace") cried out for the ministers' attention.

In response to victims' demands for access to the royal courts, and because the royal government was interested in expanding its authority, the common law's reach over what is today called tort law soon expanded. Indeed, by about 1400 AD a new writ had been recognized. Because it was crafted to cover instances of wrongful injury that somewhat fit the mold of the original trespass writ, yet did not involve the application of force by the defendant to the plaintiff, it was dubbed the writ of "*trespass on the case*"—a generic name befitting the miscellaneous collection of wrongs that it covered.

In its early years, trespass on the case was invoked by owners of goods against transporters (carriers) for losing or destroying the goods while in transit, by homeowners against neighbors for carelessly permitting fire to spread to the homeowner's property, and by patients and animal owners against doctors and veterinarians for incompetent medical treatment. Although many of these actions arose out of a pre-tort relationship between defendant and plaintiff (e.g., owner and carrier), the case writ could sometimes be invoked by a victim to hold a stranger liable for wrongfully injuring him. An early example of such a claim is provided by the eminent historian J. H. Baker. In *Loghton v. Calys*,[2] a woman was seriously injured when a pile of logs, which were situated as land adjacent to a public way and carelessly maintained by the defendant, collapsed onto her as she passed by. The allegations contained in the writ, Baker reports, were sufficient to make out a claim for trespass on the case. Later, in the 1500s, the case writ would be expanded to permit other actions, including by those seeking damages for having been libeled or slandered by another.

Although the division of personal injury actions into the categories of 'trespass' and 'case' was an artifact of the royal courts' initially limited jurisdiction, English lawyers would come to insist that it marked a conceptual line between two distinct forms of wrongdoing. They struggled, however, to articulate the precise nature of the distinction. By the early 1700s, the prevailing formulation suggested that the *vi et armis* writ was available only for injurings that involved the *direct* application of force by the defendant to the plaintiff, whereas the case writ was available to remedy injuries caused nonforcibly and *indirectly*. Thus, it was said that a man who, while working on a house, carelessly dropped a plank on a passerby would be subject to liability for a battery via the writ of trespass (direct and forcible harming), whereas the same man would be subject to

---

2. *See* J.H. BAKER, AN INTRODUCTION TO ENGLISH LEGAL HISTORY 409 n.40 (4th ed. 2002).

liability under the case writ if he were to carelessly drop the plank harmlessly into a public street, only to have a passerby later suffer harm by tripping over it (indirect, nonforcible harming).

Even as judges purported to maintain a sharp distinction between trespass and case, the distinction was being undermined in practice by plaintiffs' lawyers who increasingly sought to frame the claims of certain clients as claims for trespass on the case. These clients were the victims in so-called running-down accidents, e.g., instances in which someone was run over by a horse or a horse-drawn cart, or injured in a collision of vehicles. The lawyer for this sort of victim was confronted with a dilemma because the procedural rules required him at the outset of litigation to frame the client's claim in terms of one of the two writs. Yet he often had to make this choice without knowing critical information that would tell him which writ to use. And if he ended up choosing the wrong writ, the suit could be thrown out of court.

For example, suppose a lawyer invoked the writ of trespass *vi et armis* to sue the owner of a horse-drawn carriage that allegedly ran down his client. If the evidence later revealed that the defendant's horse bolted when unexpectedly spooked, a judge might rule that the suit should have been brought under the 'case' writ because the arguably autonomous intervening action of the horse had rendered the defendant's running-down of the plaintiff indirect rather than direct. Moreover, even if the running-down were conceived as a direct injuring of the victim by the driver, if the driver turned out to be the *servant* of the owner rather than the owner himself, the plaintiff who sued in trespass would find himself with an action only against the likely impecunious servant—the direct injurer. While the law would sometimes permit this sort of victim to *impute* a servant's wrong to his deeper-pocketed master, any claim against the master would be for an *indirect* injuring and thus would have to be brought in 'case.'

In reaction to these and other potential litigation traps, plaintiffs' lawyers argued that all running-down cases—even those that technically fit the definition of a trespass *vi et armis*—should be actionable in case. After some initial resistance, English common law courts in the 1830s endorsed this line of argument, permitting any claim of *accidental* injury to be brought under the case writ, regardless of whether the injury involved the direct or indirect application of force. In doing so, the courts fundamentally realigned the way that lawyers and judges classified the wrongs we now know as torts. Instead of dividing the world of torts into direct, forcible wrongs and indirect, nonforcible wrongs, the new division was between wrongs that could be committed entirely inadvertently and wrongs that could not be committed completely by accident. This difference would later give rise to the modern divide between "intentional" torts and "unintentional" torts.

2.2 1800–1870: The Emergence of "Torts" as a Legal Category

The collapse of the direct/indirect distinction in the early 1800s was followed in short order by the rejection of the entire writ system and the notion that injury victims should be required to fit their complaints into the mold of one of the two trespass writs. As a result, lawyerly usage of the term "trespass" to refer to an array of transgressions largely faded by the turn of the twentieth century. At the same time, lawyers were increasingly inclined to place into a separate category legal obligations defined by voluntary agreements as opposed to obligations that accompany activities and occupations irrespective of agreement. The former sorts of obligations were assigned to the new category of "contracts." (Previously, breaches of contract had been sued upon primarily under the writ of trespass on the case.)

These developments paved the way for the adoption in the late 1800s of the old but sparsely used term "torts" to refer to wrongs involving the breach of obligations not to injure others, apart from obligations determined by agreement. In turn, the domain of torts was subdivided into the distinct wrongs that we still recognize by name today. For example—in a marked departure from the older writ-system usage described above—"battery" became the name for the wrong of *intentionally* causing a harmful or offensive touching of another. Defamation actions were grouped under the headings of libel (written defamation) and slander (spoken defamation). Physical interferences with land were deemed trespasses to land.

2.3 1870–1980: Modern Tort Law

The shift from the categories of "trespass" and "case" to the new category of "torts" probably did not reflect major substantive changes in the law. The wrongs recognized by the tort law of 1870 were not dramatically different from those actionable under the trespass writs in 1770. But as the twentieth century approached, tort law was beginning to undergo a series of important changes in substance, significance, and the context in which it operated. Four developments are particularly worthy of note here.

2.3.1 Accidents, Negligence, and Products Liability

The first set of significant changes in tort law involved an interrelated set of economic, technological, sociological, and doctrinal changes. Simply put, *accidents* became the most economically and politically salient source of tort suits. The operation of railroads and later motor vehicles produced an unprecedented spate of accidental deaths and injuries. Industrial workplaces were likewise frequently loci of injurious mishaps. Not far into the 1900s, mass-marketed consumer products would begin taking their toll. To be sure, conduct amounting to batteries, nuisances, libels, and frauds remained common enough. Yet in volume and political and economic significance, accidents causing physical injury emerged as the dominant tort scenario.

Corresponding to these developments was the emergence of "negligence" as a tort in its own right. Prior to 1825, one rarely finds lawyers using the term "negligence" as the name of a legal wrong. Rather, as we have seen, when accidents gave rise to tort claims, they were actionable via the writs of trespass and trespass on the case. Yet, as we have also seen, just prior to the demise of the writ system, judges had extended the reach of 'case' to cover harms caused by accident, whether directly or indirectly. By placing accident litigation under the heading of the case writ, judges invited lawyers to think about accident law as a unitary field. And they did so by identifying a generic accident tort defined in terms of the qualities of actions that render unintended or accidental injuries wrongful—qualities such as *carelessness* and *incompetence*. Thus was born the idea that there existed, or ought to exist, a cause of action named "negligence," which would be defined generically as the breach of a duty to exercise ordinary care so as not to cause harm to those to whom the duty is owed.

In U.S. tort law—which is principally constituted by the appellate decisions of state courts—the judicial opinion that would come to stand as one of the first to recognize negligence as a tort in its own right was written in 1850 by Chief Justice Lemuel Shaw for the Massachusetts Supreme Judicial Court in *Brown v. Kendall*.[3] While trying to stop a fight between his own dog and Brown's dog, Kendall raised a stick over his head, striking and partially blinding Brown, who was standing behind him. There was no evidence that Kendall intended to strike Brown. The trial judge framed the litigation in terms of the old notion of trespass as a direct and forcible injuring. Thus he concluded that the plaintiff could recover unless the defendant was able to convince the jury that he had acted with "extraordinary care." (Note that the trial judge's analysis follows that

---

3. 60 Mass. 292 (1850).

of *Weaver v. Ward*, discussed above, which held that any direct, forcible injuring counts as a trespass but then allowed for an "inevitable accident" defense.) Reversing the trial court, Shaw's opinion held that, henceforth, all accident litigation in Massachusetts—whether for forcible or nonforcible, or direct or indirect injurings—would proceed under the heading of negligence. An accident victim's right to recover would therefore hinge on his ability to prove that his injuries resulted from the defendant's breach of a duty to use ordinary care to prevent injury to another. Thus, if in *Brown* itself, the plaintiff could not establish to a jury's satisfaction that Kendall was *careless* in the way he went about separating the fighting dogs, he could not recover.

Historians have vigorously debated what significance to attribute to the emergence of the tort of negligence. Some have argued that judges like Shaw were aiming to make it more difficult for plaintiffs to recover under the new negligence law than it had been under the old writ system, in part to protect nascent American industry and thereby promote economic growth. (In providing this analysis, these historians suppose that the number of injurers who could avoid liability under the old trespass writ by establishing that the victim's injury was an "inevitable accident" was smaller than the number who could avoid liability in negligence on the ground that they had acted with ordinary care.) Others argue that this change in terms and concepts involved mere nomenclature, not substance. Regardless, it is clear that by the late 1800s, "negligence" was regularly being invoked as the name for a generic cause of action applicable to a vast array of accidentally caused injuries.

Many of the most important developments in tort law that occurred between 1870 and 1980 were developments in the law of negligence. The tendency of courts in this period was to expand the reach of negligence. One way this expansion took place was through judicial recognition of expanded duties of care—the identification of new classes of persons toward whom one was obligated to act carefully or the identification of new classes of harms against which certain actors were obligated to take care not to cause. Other doctrinal changes that helped fuel the expansion included the modification or elimination of certain affirmative defenses that had been available to negligence defendants. Many of these developments are canvassed in Chapters 5 and 6, below.

Although the expansion of negligence was probably the most important doctrinal development in substantive tort law during the period from roughly 1870 to 1980, we should mention here for completeness's sake another doctrinal development of nearly equal importance that would come later. In the 1960s and 1970s, U.S. judges and commentators would develop the doctrine of strict products liability. Under this doctrine, a consumer injured by the use of a product in the ordinary course can recover from any seller of the product, including both manufacturer and retailer, without proving that the seller was careless or inattentive to the danger in question. Instead, the consumer need only prove that the product was "defective"—less safe than it ought to be—and that the defect caused her injury. As explained in Chapter 10, there is a lively dispute today as to whether liability under the products liability doctrine is radically or only subtly different from liability under a regime of negligence. Regardless, it is clear that, with the recognition of "products liability" as a distinct genre of tort liability, suits by consumers against manufacturers and sellers for product-related injuries have come to account for a significant portion of the torts landscape.

2.3.2 Lowered Barriers to Suit, New Claimants, and Deeper Pockets

The second set of changes affecting tort law occurred at the turn of the twentieth century and concerned the elimination or relaxation of rules that had blocked or restricted certain claimants' access to the courts, or limited the resources that might be available to satisfy a successful tort claimant's judgment.

For example, prior to 1850, evidence law treated plaintiff and defendant as "interested parties" who were barred from testifying at trial because their testimony was presumed to be biased. The lifting of this ban allowed for claims that would otherwise have been doomed simply for lack of third-party witnesses or other evidence. Another barrier to suit consisted of the expenses associated with obtaining legal representation. Lawyers, of course, charge for their services. Moreover, there are other expenses associated with suits, including court costs and perhaps expert witness fees. By law in the United States, fees and costs associated with initiating a tort lawsuit are usually borne by the plaintiff, regardless of the outcome of the litigation. Likewise, the defendant is responsible for his legal costs. The pay-your-own-way approach is dubbed the "American Rule" because it contrasts with the English Rule, under which the losing party—whether the plaintiff or the defendant—pays the litigation costs of *both* litigants.

For much of English history, and in the early years of American history, the expenses associated with litigation probably rendered the tort system unavailable to many persons of modest means. However, during the nineteenth century, access to civil justice was significantly enhanced as states authorized the use of *contingent fees*, which quickly became the dominant method of financing civil lawsuits. Under a contingent fee arrangement, the plaintiff does not pay her lawyer for his services during the litigation. Instead, the lawyer receives compensation in the form of a percentage— typically about 33 percent—of any recovery, whether in the form of a judgment or a pretrial settlement. Although English law still prohibits contingent fees, it now generally permits *conditional fees*, whereby the plaintiff's lawyer and the client agree in advance that if the plaintiff prevails, the lawyer will be paid at a higher-than-normal hourly rate. Note that, under the English Rule, this amount will be paid to the lawyer of a successful tort plaintiff by the defendant.

The reach of tort law was further extended by the enactment of *Wrongful Death Acts*. Under the old common law, if the victim of a tort died prior to or during litigation, his claim simply vanished—it could not be brought on his behalf by anyone else. This rule rested on a particular application of the more general idea, discussed in Chapter 1, that torts are relational wrongs. A tort victim sues for a wrong done *to her* by the defendant. Given the personal nature of the wrong, the remedy is conceived by the law in equally personal terms—i.e., as belonging to the victim and no one else. The courts reasoned that if the victim died prior to judgment, then the only person entitled to press the claim had disappeared. Wrongful death legislation changed this by authorizing close family members of deceased tort victims to press the claims that the decedent would have been able to press had he survived. In other words, these statutes did *not* create new torts, but rather gave new classes of persons the right to press claims for already-recognized torts. Surviving family members with viable wrongful death claims typically can recover not only the losses that their decedent suffered prior to her death (e.g., medical expenses, lost wages, and pain and suffering experienced from the time of the tort to the time of the decedent's death), but also compensation for certain losses that *they* (the family members) have suffered as a result of the tortfeasor's harm to and killing of the decedent, including lost economic support and loss of companionship. Thus claims for battery, negligence, and other torts that once would have 'died with the victim' became viable.

Nineteenth- and early-twentieth-century law expanded the universe of tort claimants in another way. Early American law, like traditional British law, was patriarchal. To oversimplify, the husband/father was deemed the sole rights-bearer in the family. Thus, if his wife or one of his children suffered a tortious injury, it was he who would sue, and the gist of the claim would be for interference with *his rights* to enjoy the company and services of his spouse or child, as opposed to *their* rights to bodily integrity, etc. Through legislation primarily enacted in the late nineteenth and early twentieth centuries, married women were finally deemed independent persons with standing to bring claims in court to vindicate their own interests in bodily integrity, property ownership, and the like. Claims for injuries to a minor child are today recognized as claims to vindicate the child's own interests rather than the father's, although they are still typically brought by parents or guardians acting on the child's behalf. Likewise, with the abolition of slavery and the enactment of the Fourteenth Amendment's guarantee of the "equal protection of the laws," former American slaves were recognized as persons whose interests were protected by the law, and hence as persons who enjoyed (at least in principle) the power to sue when those interests were wrongfully infringed.

Each of the foregoing developments opened courthouse doors to plaintiffs who previously lacked access to them. Other developments improved tort plaintiffs' prospects for obtaining meaningful relief upon prevailing. In both the United States and Britain, the courts' reaffirmation and expansion of the doctrine of *respondeat superior* has made meaningful recoveries possible for a vast array of tort plaintiffs who might otherwise not be able to collect on their tort judgments. Under this doctrine—which translates literally, as "let the master answer [for his servant]"—employers are held liable for injuries caused by carelessness committed by their employees *in the course of employment* regardless of whether the employer authorized the action or was careless in failing to prevent it. So, for example, if a driver for a shipping company, while on a delivery route, drives carelessly and hurts a pedestrian, the pedestrian can sue the company and satisfy her negligence judgment against the driver out of the company's assets, even if management was entirely careful in hiring, training and supervising the driver.

The emergence of robust markets for liability insurance has been another enormously significant source of tort law's increased prominence. Until the late nineteenth century, few insurers issued policies that would reimburse the costs associated with the payment of a tort judgment. Indeed, it was usually *illegal* to sell this form of insurance, in part because it was considered immoral for a person to pass off to others his obligation to pay for his own wrongs. By the early twentieth century, however, liability insurance policies had been legalized and were becoming common. Today, they provide a standard source by which successful tort plaintiffs are compensated for accidentally caused injuries. Indeed, as discussed in Chapter 3, lawyers employed by and representing the insurers themselves, rather than the insured tortfeasor, often take the lead role in defending against the plaintiff's suit.

2.3.3 Tort Law's Place in the Administrative State

The fourth set of changes that has significantly affected the contours of modern tort law concerns the emergence of new political institutions that either by design or in effect have supplemented or supplanted tort law in responding to wrongful and/or injury-producing conduct.

The most notable effort in Anglo-American law at replacement of the tort system with an alternative scheme occurred in the early decades of the twentieth century with the enactment by all U.S. jurisdictions of *workers' compensation systems*. The deployment of these schemes was advocated by both workers and employers: workers because of dissatisfaction with the uncertainty and delays associated with efforts to recover compensation for workplace injuries via negligence suits against employers; and employers because of frustration over the uncertainty and variability of jury awards for successful negligence claims by injured workers. Although workers' compensation schemes vary significantly, they generally relieve injured workers of the burden negligence law places on them of having to prove *fault* on the part of their employer. Instead, the worker need only establish that he or she has suffered a genuinely work-related injury. Moreover, the claim for compensation is processed through simplified and speedier procedures. In exchange, workers give up their right to pursue negligence claims in court before a jury and the right to obtain certain kinds of compensatory damages that would ordinarily be available to them were they to prevail in a negligence suit, particularly damages for pain and suffering. Instead, workers' compensation schemes usually limit recovery to the cost of medical treatment and a fixed fraction of their lost wages.

The adoption of workers' compensation schemes has significantly reduced what once was, and would surely today be, a huge domain of tort litigation. However, it is important to emphasize that workers' compensation laws operate as a substitute only for claims brought by workers *against their employers* for on-the-job accidents. Thus it is still open to workers who suffer on-the-job injuries to sue *third parties* for their injuries. For example, if a factory worker is injured while operating machinery, she may have a claim both for benefits under a workers' compensation scheme and a tort claim sounding in negligence or products liability against the machine's manufacturer and/or seller. Workers' compensation schemes also do not cover workplace injuries caused intentionally, rather than accidentally.

Other features of the modern state have reduced overall reliance on the tort system. For many centuries after its birth, tort law operated within a legal and political regime that lacked professional police forces and prosecutors. Since about 1800, the growth of these offices has caused criminal law partially to eclipse tort law with respect to certain classes of serious offenses. To be sure, the victim of a vicious beating or a rape can sue in tort even apart from any criminal prosecution, but some victims find it sufficient that the perpetrator has been subjected to fine and imprisonment. Moreover, many criminal defendants do not have assets adequate to justify undergoing the hassles and expense of a tort suit.

The emergence in the 1930s, and then again in the 1960s and 1970s, of executive-branch and independent agencies such as the federal Food and Drug Administration and the Securities Exchange Commission has also had a significant impact on the operation of tort law. One of the core functions of these agencies is to issue regulations that set standards of conduct backed by the threat of fines or other governmentally imposed sanctions. For most of the century, agency-generated safety regulations were treated as a complement to tort law. Thus, a manufacturer's compliance with agency regulations as to the sort of safety equipment or warnings that must accompany its products, even if sufficient to satisfy its regulatory obligations, would not preclude a determination in the course of a tort suit brought by an injured consumer that the manufacturer had acted carelessly or produced a defective product. Regulations, in other words, generally were understood to set safety floors instead of ceilings. However, at least in the United States, that view is now facing pressure from the opposing view that compliance with safety regulations should *prevent* judges and jurors from finding the regulated entity at fault in a tort suit. As discussed in Chapter 13, one engine for this apparent shift has been a series of U.S. Supreme Court decisions holding that an actor's compliance with federal administrative safety regulations bars the imposition of tort liability for compliant conduct.

Finally, in Britain and Canada, the adoption of nationalized health care, by addressing at least to some degree the immediate health care needs of injury victims and reducing the economic dislocation associated with injuries, has reduced reliance on the tort system. To a lesser extent, federally funded health-care assistance to the poor and the aged in the United States under the Medicaid and Medicare programs, as well as privately purchased health insurance, have somewhat reduced injury victims' reliance on the tort system as a source of compensation for their injuries.

If, in all the foregoing ways, the growth of the modern, regulatory state has limited or reduced the significance of the operation of the tort system, the same development has in one respect expanded the domain of tort liability, particularly in England and commonwealth countries. This is because, as government has taken on additional welfare functions, it has subjected itself to certain forms of tort liability for performing them badly. For example, one has seen in the last seventy-five years the growth of suits against government entities such as borough councils insofar as they act in the capacity of landlords. By and large, governmental liability is less common in the United States, both because state and local governments play smaller roles than their European counterparts and because they benefit from certain tort immunities.

✺ 2.4 1980–Present: The Modern Tort Reform Era

As the foregoing thumbnail sketch demonstrates, tort law has by no means been standing still over the centuries. Instead, it has been substantially reshaped by both judges and legislatures. In this sense, tort reform is as old as tort law itself. And yet, in current usage, the phrase "tort reform" refers not to the general phenomenon of tort law being changed by judicial or legislative initiative. Rather, it is the name for an influential anti-tort movement that sprung up in the late 1970s. Founded by businesses and business-friendly interest groups, the movement claims that, thanks to many of the expansionary trends described above, the modern tort system is 'out of control.' Among other things, tort law is said to reward claimants who press frivolous claims, to undermine notions of personal responsibility by attributing fault to others where there is none, and to permit biased juries to engage in illicit redistributions of wealth from business owners to claimants. Assertions such as these are often bolstered by colorful anecdotes of patently undeserving claimants obtaining large jury verdicts. Some of these anecdotes have turned out to be exaggerated or just false. Regardless, reliance on them is suspect. By their nature they tend to be unrepresentative of tort litigation. Also, counter-narratives—anecdotes of deserving claimants who gain access to appropriate remedies—cannot hope to compete for public attention. (A story about a tort claimant pressing a reasonable claim and receiving a reasonable verdict is hardly likely to be circulated on the Internet.)

The tort reform movement has been a remarkable success. Its victories include the enactment at the state level of legislation that erects new procedural hurdles for claimants (e.g., heightened pleading requirements that make it easier for judges to throw out tort claims at the outset of litigation) as well as caps on damages awards. Also, many courts at the state and federal level—including formerly 'progressive' courts such as the California Supreme Court as well as the U.S. Supreme Court—have been substantially influenced by the movement, as evidenced by the issuance of decisions over the last quarter-century that have tended to make it more difficult for certain classes of tort claimants to recover, decisions often justified in terms of the need to fend off frivolous claims and protect business from ruinous liability. Many of these developments will be considered in later chapters.

THREE

Tort Law's Gallery of Wrongs

※ 3.1 Wrongs and Recourse

Tort law contains a series of proscriptions that address actors before they act. Thus, it is not difficult to imagine a person being counseled against interacting with another in a certain way because it might constitute a tort: *"That would be an invasion of privacy."* *"That would be malpractice." "That would be fraud."*[1] At the same time, because torts are injurious wrongs—because they consist of misconduct that has certain consequences for another—they also are quite naturally described in retrospective terms. Thus, we can also easily imagine an injury victim declaring: *"It's your fault that you ran into me!" "You defamed me!" "You trespassed on my land!"*

The juxtaposition of these two ways of thinking about torts vividly demonstrates the tight linkage between the relational and injurious aspects of torts on the one hand, and what we referred to in Chapter 1 as their "civil" character on the other. To commit a tort is

---

1. As these examples may suggest, tort law is evidenced as much by torts that do *not* happen as those that do. A bar patron who refrains from physically retaliating for a perceived insult, a publisher who decides to omit names from a story rather than risk defaming others, a motorist who drives carefully, a manufacturer's adoption of quality control measures—each of these can be and often is a testament to the degree to which the norms of conduct embedded in tort law are routinely heeded because they have been marked out as obligatory and because committing them renders one vulnerable to suit by the victim.

not only to act wrongfully toward someone so as to injure them, but it is also to open oneself up to a response by that person. The point is not merely that the victim's sense of being aggrieved is what typically prompts a civil suit that aims to determine if an actor has committed a tort. It is that tort law's recognition of a special species of wrong— wrongs that have victims—goes hand-in-hand, conceptually and practically, with the notion that victims of these kinds of wrongs deserve a legal mechanism by which to respond against those who have victimized them. Tort is in these particular senses *a law of wrongs and recourse.*

Chapters 3 and 4 focus, respectively, on the forward- and backward-looking aspects of tort law. This chapter provides a brief overview of types of conduct that count as torts. Chapter 4 describes more precisely the way in which the legal system empowers victims to seek and obtain recourse against wrongdoers.

ℳ 3.2 Touring the Gallery: Protected Interests

It is an unhappy fact of life that there are many different ways to wrong another person. Many of these are torts. Deliberately punching someone in the nose or shooting him is battery. Communicating to a third party that someone else is a charlatan or a pederast is a slander or libel, although such a communication is permissible if true. Torts can be committed through the touching of another, the publication of pictures, and the completion of financial transactions.

There is no generic tort underlying these diverse forms of wrongdoing. Rather, there are many distinct torts. Tort law is a gallery with many rooms, in each of which hang portraits of certain legal wrongs. (Or to switch to a scientific analogy, tort law is more like chemistry than physics in that a classificatory inquiry is an important starting point for the subject.) This chapter provides a whirlwind and incomplete tour of the gallery. Subsequent chapters will address particular 'rooms' and 'portraits' in greater depth.

Why would lawyers and judges have organized tort law in this way? Why not have, as some legal systems do, a single legal norm stating that a person is subject to liability to another for wrongfully injuring her? One reason has to do with the ways in which law can most effectively speak to the persons whom it governs. Although radical critics of tort law have sometimes argued that its directives are so vague as to violate requirements of fair notice, the division of tort law into particular torts goes part of the way toward meeting this concern. At least in their central applications, each tort prohibits conduct that citizens already know to be wrongful (beating another, defrauding another, stealing from another, etc.). And each tort admits of many clear examples. Anyone who drives a car can readily call to mind examples of what it would mean to do so negligently. (No one will be surprised to learn that a drunk driver who runs down a pedestrian will face the prospect of negligence liability.) The division of tort law into particular torts that correspond to familiar forms of mistreatment provides meaningful guidance as to how we must act or refrain from acting.

Some ways of wronging another are not legal wrongs and for that reason not torts. A man who seduces his best friend's wife is wronging his friend, but in most jurisdictions today, he is not committing a tort. (Interestingly, at one time this sort of conduct *was* tortious. The items on display in the gallery include portraits that have been around since English tort law first got underway and some that were added later, even much later. Other items have been taken down and put into storage.) It is also wrong, but not a tort, for a mother to stunt her child's development by not permitting the child to play with other children and for a gas station owner to gouge its customers in response to a local natural disaster. The foregoing are all moral wrongs committed against others; all of them would be recognized as violations of accepted norms of how to treat others. Yet the law does not recognize them as conduct that would justify a court in permitting a plaintiff to obtain redress.

So which wrongs-to-others are torts? We have noted that torts are, among other things, *injurious wrongs*. Thus, one way to begin answering questions about the kinds of wrongs that count as torts is to work backwards from certain basic interests that individuals (and entities) have. Then we can turn to the kinds of conduct that are deemed invasive of those interests (injuriously wrongful conduct) and which tort law enjoins. Proceeding in this manner will give us a rough picture of the categories of wrongs that comprise torts. In following this approach, we will also have occasion to consider interests and invasions—such as conduct that violates the interest in not being subjected to race, age, or gender discrimination—that are recognized and protected through modern statutory schemes that occupy distinct departments of law, such as civil rights law or employment law. We do so because one of our aims in this book is to explain how tort law connects to the legal system more generally. These statutorily defined legal wrongs are torts in structure and function.

※ 3.3 Battery, Negligence, Defective Products, and Strict Liability for Abnormally Dangerous Activities (Bodily Integrity)

Along with trespass to land (discussed below), the tort of *battery* has a respectable claim to being the most basic tort. As indicated in Chapter 2, back when legal wrongs were organized around the writs of "trespass" and "case," battery was the name given to any direct and forcible injuring of another, whether intentional or accidental. Today, however, the term is reserved for *intentional physical touchings of another's body* that are harmful or offensive. Battery law enjoins people not to hit, kick, stab, or shoot others. It further enjoins people from spitting on or fondling others. Note that each of these verbs connotes a conscious rather than accidental touching of another's body. A battery involves one person intentionally (or in some cases knowingly) making contact with another person's body in a certain way. The sense of intentionality required for the commission of a battery is discussed in Chapter 7.

An obvious justification for prohibiting acts such as the foregoing is that each of us has an interest in bodily integrity, and acts
such as these invade or threaten that interest. This is a part of why
we say they may not be done. Another reason these sorts of acts are
treated as wrongs and earn our opprobrium is that they are in certain respects intentional. This means both that refraining from
them tends to be relatively easy, and that enabling victims to hold
wrongdoers accountable to them for these acts seems to be an
entirely plausible response.

A special branch of battery law that also overlaps with the law of
false imprisonment, discussed below, concerns wrongs perpetrated
by government actors such as police officers. Although police enjoy
a special leeway to use physical force in the furtherance of law
enforcement, their privilege to do so is limited. The relevant constraints derive not from 'mere' judge-made law but from the U.S.
Constitution, which grants citizens a right against "unreasonable
searches and seizures" and against being "deprived of . . . liberty . . .
without due process of law." Persons against whom state or federal
governmental officials use excessive force (as well as persons unjustifiably confined) are empowered by statute and by the Constitution
itself to bring "constitutional tort" claims that stand to vindicate the
right to bodily integrity (and freedom of movement) as against invasions by governmental actors.

Although battery is among the most basic torts, it no longer
occupies the main room in the gallery of torts. Rather, as discussed
in Chapter 2, that room is presently filled with portraits of the tort
of *negligence*. The principal wrong identified by negligence law is
the wrong of *carelessly inflicting physical injury upon another person*.
In some instances, negligence protects other interests. Most prominently, it protects the physical integrity of personal possessions
(chattels) and real property. A truck driver who carelessly runs off
the road and through a shop window has committed the tort of
negligence by damaging the shop owner's property. In a few settings,
invasions of interests in emotional well-being and wealth are also
actionable under the rubric of the tort of negligence. A mortician

who carelessly loses a corpse entrusted to him for burial will be deemed to have wronged the devastated family members. An accountant who causes economic loss to a client through failure to follow proper accounting procedures may be subject to liability for malpractice. ("Malpractice" is a term for negligence in the carrying out of a profession or skilled trade such as medicine, law, accountancy or architecture.) By and large, however, the core applications of the tort involve cases of bodily injury and property damage. The point is not that physical injuries are always more serious than, say, emotional injuries. Rather, both numerically and as a matter of legal doctrine, negligence is most often encountered and shaped by courts in cases in which the injury complained of is physical in nature.

Like battery law, negligence law rests on a norm that identifies certain kinds of conduct as wrongful. And, like battery law, the principal interest (though not the exclusive interest) protected through these norms is bodily integrity. Because we value bodily integrity, the law recognizes, in addition to the norm against harmful and offensive touchings, a norm enjoining people to take care not to inflict physical injury upon others accidentally. This latter norm is violated when a person carelessly causes bodily injury to another. As we shall see, it is a delicate question why the violation of this norm is treated as a wrong roughly of the same order as a battery. By definition, the conduct in question is not intentional and indeed is frequently inadvertent.

A third kind of wrong that pertains primarily to the interest in bodily integrity is the infliction of bodily injury through the sale of a *defective product*. Selling someone a diet drug that, because of its defects, causes the drug's user to develop heart disease is a tort. Similarly, it is a tort to sell hair dye that destroys a person's scalp during ordinary use and to sell a snow-blower that chops off the fingers of someone using the product in an appropriate manner. The norm of conduct is not to injure people through the circulation of dangerously defective products. Over the past several decades, this set of norms—known typically as *products liability law*—has become one of the most active areas of tort law pertaining to the protection and vindication of physical integrity.

We discuss below the doctrinal issues that have arisen in determining what counts as a "defective" product. Although it is tempting at first blush to think a product is defective insofar as it poses a danger of physical injury, this understanding is too broad. A careful cook who cuts herself with a knife cannot sue its seller even though the knife, simply by virtue of being a sharp instrument, poses a significant risk of physical harm. The challenge, then, is to determine what sort of dangers, when present in a product, render it not merely dangerous but defective. As we will see, modern tort law recognizes as potential defects both the physical characteristics of a product and the information provided or not provided to potential users via instructions or warnings. Many products have been deemed by judges and juries to be defective because their sellers failed adequately to warn users of the risks of harm posed by their use.

Fourth and finally, in a handful of instances, tort law has imposed strict liability—liability without regard to fault—for activities that cause physical injuries to passive bystanders. For example, a firm that uses explosives on a construction project has traditionally been held strictly liable for property damage or personal injuries to bystanders caused by flying debris. To be subjected to a rule of strict liability is to be held to account irrespective of how careful one has been. One may fairly ask whether it makes sense to think of liability imposed on these terms as liability for a wrong. If there is no intent on the part of the actor to injure the victim, and the actor took extraordinary care to avoid injuring others but nonetheless unfortunately did injure someone, in what sense has she committed a wrong? We take up this question in Chapter 9.

✺ 3.4 Assault, False Imprisonment, Intentional Infliction of Emotional Distress, and Workplace Harassment (Personal Space)

Some of the oldest and best-established torts involve wrongs that do not require personal injury or property damage. Indeed, this is true of the tort of battery itself. Battery requires an intentional touching that is harmful *or* offensive. A kiss, if unwelcome, can be a battery.

The ancient tort of *assault*—which is a discrete wrong, even though it is often paired with battery in the phrase "assault and battery"—does not require any touching whatsoever. An assault occurs when a person intentionally acts toward another person in a manner that causes her to *anticipate* an imminent harmful or offensive touching. A punch to the head that just misses, and of which the intended victim is aware, is an assault. And this is so *not* because an assault is an attempted battery. (In fact, there are no attempt torts even though there are attempt crimes.) Rather, it is because a completed wrong has occurred even without the fist's making contact. In today's parlance, one might say that the defendant has interfered with plaintiff's personal space. The wrong consists of an interference with one's ability to go about one's life free from being exposed by others to certain kinds of fears or apprehensions.

Closely related, and also of ancient vintage, is the tort of *false imprisonment*. A defendant commits this tort when he intentionally *confines the plaintiff* or causes her reasonably to perceive herself as being confined. The interest protected is that of liberty of movement. A police officer or store security guard who baselessly locks up another has committed this tort.

Historically, false imprisonment has been linked with battery and assault as among the most basic torts. And it is not difficult to see why they have been thought to be similar. Although there is a divergence in the type of interest protected—bodily integrity versus freedom of movement—we are inclined to see all three torts as protecting a set of autonomy-based rights to be able to go about one's life unmolested, a right quite fundamental to interactions among human beings.

The tort of *intentional infliction of emotional distress* through outrageous conduct is sometimes called the tort of "outrage." This synonym identifies the most important and difficult-to-satisfy element of the tort: the sheer outrageousness of the defendant's conduct. Even one who succeeds in 'freaking out' another will not usually be deemed to have committed this wrong, for it is limited to cases in which the defendant's conduct goes beyond any sense of decency, so as to induce a reasonable observer to exclaim "outrageous!" A vicious jokester who arranges for the public humiliation of a victim whom he knows to be gullible and frail is subject to liability for intentional infliction of emotional distress if the plot succeeds and causes the victim to suffer serious emotional distress.

Concern for the combination of bodily integrity, personal space, and liberty figures in at least some instances of a large category of misconduct that has been rendered unlawful by federal and state statutes, namely, *employment discrimination*. These statutes, an outgrowth of the modern civil rights movement, prohibit discrimination on the basis of race, religion, and gender, as well as age and disability. To focus on but one form of employment discrimination: it is a recognized statutory wrong for an employer to engage in sexual harassment of an employee; harassment of this sort is a form of workplace gender discrimination. Some conduct that might be described as harassment fits the definition of recognized common law torts such as battery or intentional infliction of emotional distress. But there are also instances that fall outside the scope of these wrongs because, for example, they do not involve inappropriate physical contact or outrageous conduct. An infringement of a person's sense of autonomy—her ability to go about her job free from untoward interference—can occur when an employer creates or tolerates a work environment that is pervasively sexist (e.g., in permitting constant sexist remarks, displays of pornography in workspaces, etc.). Sexual harassment of this sort is a legal wrong, and harassment victims are statutorily empowered to obtain redress for it.

※ 3.5 Trespass, Nuisance, and Conversion (Possessory Interests)

We have seen that careless damaging or destruction of real property and chattels can be actionable negligence. The interest in ownership is also protected by other tort causes of action. One of these—*trespass to land*—is on a par with battery in terms of its ancient pedigree. A trespass to land is a physical invasion of another's real property. The interest being protected is not the physical integrity of the land per se but the land-possessor's *right to exclude* others from it. To dump garbage on another's land is to commit a trespass to land. So too is it a trespass to build a fence or a shed on someone else's property. It is even a trespass for someone who has been permitted on another's property to overstay his welcome or enter portions of the property that are off-limits, as when a store customer walks into an 'employees only' area. In these and many other ways, tort law enjoins us to refrain from physically invading or occupying another's land. Similarly, the tort of *trespass to chattel* enjoins us to refrain from physically interfering with another's ownership of personal possessions.

Unlike negligence law as it pertains to damage to property, the trespass torts do not enjoin actors *to take care* to avoid *harming* another's land or possessions. Instead, they prohibit physical invasions that interfere with the possessor's right of exclusive possession and use. Like battery, trespass can be accomplished only through an intentional touching. And like battery—think of the spitting and caressing examples mentioned above—there can be trespass without tangible damage or destruction. For example, if a

truck driver uses a dirt road on a possessor's property as an unauthorized shortcut, his driving on the road will constitute a trespass
even if the property is in no way damaged or diminished. Parallels
between battery and trespass to land will occupy us in Chapter 8.
For now, note that both bodily integrity and property are protected
by twin categories of tort: a form of trespass in the broad sense
(battery and trespass) and a form of negligence law.

Closely related to the modern trespass torts is the tort of
nuisance, which identifies wrongs to landowners that are less direct
and tangible—but frequently more grave—than trespasses to land.
A nuisance is an *unreasonable interference with a landowner's right
to use and enjoy his property*. The ongoing production of loud noises
or nauseating stenches constitutes the sort of activities that spoil
another person's ability to enjoy his own land. Conversely, a person's
interference with a property-owner's possessions may go beyond
interference with exclusive use, and may consist in a temporary or
permanent seizure of the property of another. In common parlance,
this is theft or stealing. In tort law, it is called the wrong of *conversion*.

"Intellectual property"—copyrighted works, patented technologies, trademarked products—is among the most important form of
property in modern economies. There has accordingly been an
explosion of interest in the subject among law professors, lawyers,
and students. Although copyright infringement is part of "intellectual property law" rather than tort law, it is a wrong that bears a
close resemblance to trespass to land and trespass to chattels. All
are interferences with a right of exclusive possession. For all, a critical aspect of the right of exclusive possession is that others may not
avail themselves of the property without the owner's consent.
Copyright law, like trespass law, affords the owner a private right of
action against the infringer; money damages and injunctive relief
are available remedies. However, copyright (as well as patent and
trademark) are protected principally by federal statutory law, not
by state common law. This is one of the reasons that these wrongs
typically are not considered to be torts. But the parallel is worth

noting, for these are also wrongs, the commission of which empowers the victim to seek redress in court against the wrongdoer.

⁊⁊ 3.6 Fraud and Tortious Interference (Freedom of Choice and Contract)

A range of torts protects an individual's interest in making choices free from the taint of bad information or certain pressures. The oldest of these is the tort of deceit, more commonly known today as *fraud*. This tort enjoins people from *deceiving others into detrimental transactions* of various forms. Where a defendant has intentionally made representations that he knows to be false, and lured a plaintiff into relying upon those misrepresentations, thereby causing the plaintiff to lose something of value, the defendant has defrauded the plaintiff. Typically, fraud involves deceptions that generate economic losses, though it is at least arguable that it is also fraud (or perhaps some other tort) to induce transactions that result in physical or other harms. For example, if a pet store owner induces a customer to buy a pet snake by knowingly misrepresenting that the animal is harmless when it is poisonous, he might be liable for fraud if the victim is later poisoned by a bite from the snake.

As noted above, the tort of negligence sometimes identifies the careless invasion of economic interests as wrongful. One way it does so is by rendering actionable certain instances of *careless* rather than knowing misrepresentation. For example, if an accountant carelessly conducts an audit of a company on behalf of a potential investor, erroneously reports to the investor a rosy picture of the company's finances, and thereby causes the investor to lose his investment, the investor may be able to sue the accountant for *negligent misrepresentation.*

Closely related is *tortious interference with contract* (or with economic expectancy). As with fraud, this tort protects individuals' arrangements against outside interference. Here, though, the interference consists of conduct toward a third party. Imagine a person who, purely out of spite for the plaintiff, convinces a supplier to break his existing contract to supply needed equipment to the plaintiff's business (say, by threatening to harm the supplier if he does not do so). In so doing, he has wrongfully interfered with the plaintiff's entitlement to the benefit of his transaction with the supplier. The interest in having and carrying through business transactions is regarded as worthy of protection by our legal system. The willful interference with it, under certain limited circumstances, is a tort.

A very broad range of legally wrongful conduct is defined by federal and state statutes, including federal and state antitrust law and consumer protection law. Some of this law, while defining impermissible conduct, does not define wrongs to individuals, but rather kinds of conduct that, cumulatively, will harm consumers generally. Other parts plainly resemble tort law. Most notably, the federal regulations that prohibit *securities fraud*—that is, knowing misrepresentations that are intended to induce and do induce the purchase or sale of stock in a company—offer what is essentially a variation on common law fraud. Many statutory antitrust violations also amount to torts in that they involve wrongfully targeting a specific competitor and through unfair means undercutting its ability to compete.

⅏ 3.7 Defamation and Privacy Torts (One's Standing in the Eyes of Others)

A good reputation is valuable and is certainly an interest that tort law protects. The common law defines two kinds of wrongs that involve interference with reputation: *libel* and *slander*. Both wrongs involve reputational attacks. To commit the wrong of libel against someone is to *defame that person by written word*, depiction, or scripted broadcast that is transmitted to a third party. To commit the wrong of slander is to defame that person by spoken word that is transmitted to a third party.

Historically, the common law of defamation (referring to both libel and slander) has tended to resemble trespass law more than it does negligence law. Indeed, until quite recently in our history, defamation law's commitment to the protection of reputation generated norms of conduct that were in some respects very onerous. For example, if a newspaper article identified a particular person as a convicted thief, and the article turned out to have mistaken that person for the actual thief because the two shared the same name, the publisher might have been subject to liability for libeling the plaintiff. And liability in principle could sometimes attach even if this sort of mistake was made despite the fact that the publisher was careful in trying to identify the plaintiff correctly.

For reasons discussed in Chapter 11, this feature of defamation law is less pronounced today, particularly in American tort law. However, its presence in older incarnations of libel and slander reveal the connection to doctrinal 'cousins', such as trespass to land. The latter is prepared to hold liable as a trespasser even someone who enters another's land with the reasonable belief that the land is open to the public. Also like trespass (and unlike negligence), libel and slander require the defendant to have voluntarily undertaken a certain kind of invasive act against the plaintiff. In libel and slander, one must intentionally write or speak statements about another that are of a sort that tends to cause reputational harm. In trespass, one must intentionally tread upon certain real property. A third commonality is that the torts of slander and libel, like the tort of trespass, have historically permitted plaintiffs to recover without proof of harm flowing from the commission of the wrongful act itself. In this respect too, these torts differ fundamentally from the tort of negligence.

Since the mid-1960s, the reach of the American law of defamation has been substantially curtailed by a series of decisions issued by the United States Supreme Court. The Supreme Court does not normally occupy itself with defining the contours of tort law. However, the Court determined that traditional defamation law was in some applications so onerous as to violate the free speech guarantee contained in the First Amendment to the United States Constitution. The threat of defamation liability, the Court reasoned, was unduly discouraging journalists, broadcasters, and others from speaking or writing forthrightly about political events, government officials, and even ordinary citizens. Accordingly, the Court has cut back significantly on the reach of defamation torts.

We pointed out above that some contemporary legal wrongs—such as infringements of copyright or sexual harassment—have not been categorized within the common law of tort because they derive from statutory schemes usually understood to form separate departments of the law. By contrast, the new-to-the-twentieth-century legal wrong of *invasion of privacy* was principally developed by courts using common law reasoning, although some jurisdictions enacted privacy protection statutes. Whether actionable by common law or statute, invasion of privacy is usually considered a tort and is frequently coupled with the torts of libel and slander. As discussed below, today there are many state and federal statutes addressing specific matters within the realm of privacy, such as the privacy of personal data or medical records.

Among the first to theorize about the recognition of a distinctive wrong dubbed "invasion of privacy" were attorneys Samuel D. Warren and Louis Brandeis in a famous article from the late 1800s.[2] They worried that, in modern mass societies characterized by anonymous interactions among strangers, norms and practices discouraging others (especially the media) from snooping into people's private affairs were breaking down. In this situation, they argued, tort law ought to be used by courts at the behest of litigants to reestablish and reinforce norms of privacy. In other words,

---

2. *The Right to Privacy*, 4 HARV. L. REV. 193 (1890).

they argued, courts ought to respond by identifying interferences with privacy as legal wrongs to which victims ought to have a right to recourse through the legal system.

A few decades later, Dean William Prosser, perhaps the most influential tort scholar of the mid-twentieth century, published an article arguing that, even though they had not fully realized it, courts were already recognizing four kinds of privacy torts.[3] Prosser dubbed the first of these *intrusion upon seclusion*. The gist of the wrong is one person's gaining access through non-physical (and therefore non-trespassory) means to another's private life. The classic example of an intrusion upon seclusion is that of a Peeping Tom who peers through a bedroom window without actually trespassing on anyone else's property. The second of Prosser's privacy torts is *public disclosure of private facts*. An example of this form of invasion of privacy would be a local newspaper story that merely for sensational effect describes in lurid detail a private citizen's recent sexual activities. The third privacy tort, *appropriation of likeness*, involves using the name or likeness of an individual for trade or advertising without consent. If for example, the owner of a start-up business happens to find a picture of an attractive person on a Web site and then uses that image in ads for its products without the consent of the person depicted, that use would amount to an appropriation of likeness. Finally, there is the tort of portraying another in a *false light*: publicizing a statement about (or depiction of) another that, although not defamatory, falsely assigns to her a highly embarrassing or offensive act, experience, or attribute. For example, a television broadcast that falsely identifies a private citizen as suffering from an embarrassing medical condition may be subject to liability for false light invasion of privacy.

Overlapping with these now generally recognized causes of action for invasion of privacy, federal and state statutes identify a

---

3. *Privacy*, 48 CAL L. REV. 383 (1960).

number of more specific privacy-related wrongs, such as those of wiretapping someone's phone or disclosing someone's private medical information without his or her consent. Often these statutes arm victims with a tort-like right to redress.

✸ 3.8 Conclusion

We conclude our hurried tour with some reflections about our initial choice of metaphor. In conjuring up the image of a gallery, we intend first to convey that tort law, like many other areas of law and of human enterprise, is most easily grasped through prototypes. There is a finite number of torts, but the number is large and the types of torts are various. Each has a somewhat distinctive look and shape, even though they are all part of the same legal family. The diverse wrongs of tort match some of the many forms of wrongdoing familiar to people from their everyday lives. A non-lawyer can easily grasp what it means for someone to be the victim of a libel or a fraud or a dangerously defective product or medical malpractice. Each is its own particular kind of wrong, and yet there is no reason to suppose that this feature of torts makes the subject ungainly rather than intuitive.

Having emphasized the separateness of the different torts, however, we should be careful not to overstate the point. It is certainly the case that one course of conduct can sometimes meet the description of two or more torts. For example, an actor who gratuitously and viciously terrorizes and tortures another may have at one and the same time committed the torts of assault, battery, false imprisonment, and intentional infliction of emotional distress. In such a case, the victim will allege each of these wrongs in her lawsuit. Alleging and proving that a wrongdoer's conduct constituted more than one wrong usually will not change the amount of compensation to which the victim is entitled, but it may bring other procedural advantages.

Another message that is being signaled by our use of the metaphor of the gallery of wrongs is that we are interested in viewing torts 'horizontally', rather than as part of a hierarchical structure in which a fundamental idea is presented first and then various applications of that idea are developed in a pyramidal manner. Although there is a great deal to be learned from comparing the various torts, and although understanding them requires understanding much about what they share, a horizontal spectrum—a gallery—is a more useful way to think of the structure of the field. Like the Ten Commandments or the Seven Deadly Sins, torts are several.

The metaphor of a gallery also holds together two admittedly opposing ideas about the intended objectivity of our inquiry. In some respects, to view one's subject matter as akin to artwork hanging in a gallery is to suggest that the observer is able to detach himself from the object of inquiry and scrutinize something quite concrete that exists independently of him. And yet one should not get carried away with the aspiration to objectivity, for while art work hanging on a wall is in one sense a physical object, it is of course the prototype of a cultural artifact and a human creation, and it is clear that the ability to see a work for what it is depends heavily upon the experience, socialization, perspective, and education of the person who is looking at it. To depict tort law as a gallery of wrongs is in part to suggest a similar duality in objectivity. As lawyers and scholars who specialize in this area of the law, we believe there is a great deal in our books, our courts, and our history that is really there. However, what is there is a human creation, and our own capacity to see it, to understand it, and to help others see what is there depends to some degree on our own participation and education in the law.

Finally, stepping back, one might fairly ask of tort law's gallery: Why these injurious wrongs? Why not others? Here again, one can appreciate the sense in which the law of torts that we have inherited and developed is historically contingent, yet not entirely haphazard. Our legal system could have recognized a different set of torts or perhaps no torts at all. Still, it is hardly surprising to find in today's gallery (and galleries of past eras) wrongs such as battery, negligence, trespass, fraud, and libel. As we have noted throughout this chapter, each of these wrongs involves an interference with a basic or important human interest.

Civil Recourse

THIS CHAPTER HAS THREE SECTIONS. It first discusses how the legal system has traditionally processed claims by victims of alleged wrongs seeking recourse for them. It then notes important changes to the ways in which claims are made and resolved in modern litigation. Finally, it steps back to consider why law should be in the business of defining wrongs that generate in victims a right to respond to the wrongdoer through a lawsuit.

✿ 4.1 Recourse: The Trial-Centered Account

A longstanding maxim of English common law reads *ubi jus ibi remedium*: where there is a right, there shall be a remedy. If the law has proscribed conduct as wrongful toward others—if they have a right not to be so treated—and if another is injured by virtue of such conduct, the law will grant the victim the right to respond to the injurious wrongdoing. Tort law, by providing an avenue of response to certain wrongs, is one of the chief mechanisms through which the law fulfills the dictates of this maxim.

But are all the legal wrongs that count as torts in fact wrongs to which a victim has a right to respond through the legal system? The answer is "yes and no." "No," because, as discussed in subsequent chapters, there are many defenses and immunities that can defeat victims' claims to relief, even where the victim has proven that she has suffered a wrong as defined by the law. In other words, the law—sometimes for policy reasons—lets some tortfeasors off the hook. The answer is also "no" for more mundane reasons. The time and effort required to pursue a lawsuit, the various hurdles that a claimant faces in proving her case, and the challenge of actually securing the relief to which one is entitled can be daunting, sometimes insurmountable. Thus, being candid, one must acknowledge that a victim of a genuine tort may not always be able to obtain recourse as against the person who wronged her, whether as a matter of legal principle or practical reality.

With these very substantial qualifications acknowledged, the answer to the above question is, "yes: torts are wrongs to which a victim has a right to respond." A person libeled by his town newspaper as a sex offender has a right to exact damages from the newspaper to compensate him for the injury to his reputation. A person rendered paraplegic by a surgeon's malpractice has a right to exact damages from the surgeon. A person whose enjoyment of his rural home is spoiled by a recently opened sewage plant next door has a right to have the sewage plant closed. A person defrauded into purchasing a supposedly authentic piece of art has a right to a court's aid in undoing the transaction. Any act that is a tort grounds a right of response in the victim against the tortfeasor. The jurisdictional, evidentiary, procedural, and doctrinal obstacles to relief can be, and often are, substantial. And the remedies available to a given victim may or may not be satisfactory, but if these obstacles are surmounted, a remedy will be available to the victim.

How do victims actually respond to torts through the legal system? In this section, we describe a *simple trial-centered account* of tort litigation, which is the account of the tort system's operation traditionally provided by law professors to new law students. In this account, a single plaintiff files suit against a single defendant, and pursues that claim all the way through to a verdict, which is typically rendered by a jury in the United States and by a trial judge in England. Following the verdict, the trial judge will ordinarily enter judgment for the prevailing party, after which an appeal of that judgment may or may not occur. If it does, appellate courts may be asked to review the judgment and either affirm it, thereby finalizing it, or reverse it, which typically entails that the case is remanded for further proceedings in the original trial court.

For most plaintiffs, the first step in responding to a perceived tort is the hiring of a lawyer. *Pro se* lawsuits—lawsuits in which an individual represents herself—are permitted and happen frequently in certain settings (for example, by prison inmates claiming constitutional rights violations). But the overwhelming majority of tort claims (by non-prisoners) are brought by a lawyer on behalf of a client. The means by which most plaintiffs' lawyers are paid—the contingent fee—is discussed in Chapter 2.

To bring a tort suit requires that a *complaint* be filed against a defendant in a courthouse and delivered to the defendant or her lawyer. The complaint, usually a very short document, accomplishes several things. It marks the commencement of the tort suit, which is important because there are statutory limits on the time period within which a victim may bring a tort claim. It states succinctly what the defendant allegedly has done to the plaintiff and what has happened to the plaintiff as a result. It categorizes the defendant's misconduct as fitting the legal definition of one or more torts. And it requests that the court enter a judgment against the defendant. The request for judgment may be stated in terms of a compensatory payment (e.g., "plaintiff requests that the court enter judgment in an amount to be specified") or in terms of an order from the court directing the defendant to refrain from acting in a certain way (e.g., "plaintiff requests that the court permanently enjoin the defendant from operating its sewage treatment plant").

A defendant—again, usually through a lawyer—will normally respond to a complaint with a document called an *answer* that speaks both to the facts alleged and the legal categorization of the defendant's conduct as a wrong. The defendant will also typically assert in its answer substantive *defenses* (for example, that the defendant is not liable because the plaintiff consented to the defendant's conduct), as well as procedural *defenses* (for example, that the plaintiff exceeded the time period set by the legislature within which a person alleging having been wronged must file her complaint). He may also bring *counterclaims* against the plaintiff—for example, allegations that the plaintiff in fact committed some torts against the defendant and that the defendant therefore has a claim against the plaintiff—or bring additional actors into the litigation (third-party joinder).

Instead of submitting an answer, a defendant may sometimes submit a *motion to dismiss*. (A motion is a request for a ruling from the judge presiding over the case.) A motion to dismiss asserts that there is something so patently defective on the face of the complaint that the judge ought to dismiss it without any further effort to figure out what happened. Because at this point there has been no fact-finding, when ruling on motions to dismiss, the trial judge assumes that everything the plaintiff alleges in her complaint is true. Thus dismissal motions are usually only granted for complaints containing a facial defect—for example, those that quite clearly indicate the suit is time-barred under an applicable statute of limitations because the plaintiff waited too long to bring her suit.

If the defendant fails to file either an answer or a motion to dismiss in a timely manner, the plaintiff is entitled to a default judgment, with damages to be determined by a judge or jury.

Assuming the litigation proceeds past the filing of a complaint and a responsive pleading from the defendant, the process of trial preparation begins. By means of this process, which can take months or years depending on the complexity of the case, each side seeks access to information that the other side has control over, as well as information from third parties. Lawyers refer to this information-gathering process as *discovery*. Discovery can include the taking of witness testimony through under-oath depositions, as well as the exchange of documents and other materials such as electronic records or videotapes. Discovery is a critical feature of civil litigation. Without it, many who have been injuriously wronged would lack access to the information and evidence needed to prove their allegations. Likewise, many alleged tortfea-sors would be unable to secure information that supports their exoneration.

On the simple model, the parties and the judge presiding over the case will set a timetable for completing discovery and a tenta-tive date for trial, at which the evidence gathered through discovery would be presented by the lawyers for each side through witness testimony or the introduction of physical evidence. In England, most tort trials are presided over by a judge who both applies gov-erning law and plays the role of fact finder by, for example, assessing the credibility of witnesses and drawing inferences from circum-stantial evidence. When the judge plays this role at trial, the pro-ceeding is referred to as a *bench trial.* In the United States, either litigant in a tort suit can demand a jury trial. If this right is waived by both, there will be a bench trial. If the right to a jury trial is exercised, as it usually is, six to twelve jurors will be selected and charged with the job of fact-finding. The jury will also be asked to apply certain legal standards that the trial judge will explain to them by means of jury instructions given at the close of the trial, just prior to their deliberations.

The trial of a simple tort case might last only a day or two, whereas a complex case could involve weeks of witness testimony and other evidence-presentation. The burden is usually on the plaintiff to prove that defendant acted in the way that she alleges and that she did in fact suffer the injuries she alleges she suffered. If the fact finder determines that the plaintiff has proven her allegations—and if the defendant fails to sustain a valid defense—it will then decide the amount of compensation the plaintiff is entitled to receive from the defendant given how the defendant acted toward her and the injuries that resulted.

If the jury rules for the plaintiff, the trial judge will usually enter a judgment in that amount for the plaintiff and against the defen-dant. However, there is an additional step prior to the entry of judg-ment. A defendant who loses at trial can file a motion inviting the trial judge to overturn the jury's verdict and throw out the plaintiff's claim *as a matter of law*—that is, on the ground that no reasonable jury could have found for the plaintiff given the governing law and the evidence presented at trial, even interpreted favorably to the plaintiff. Alternatively, the defendant can ask the trial judge to order a *new trial*—a 'do-over'—on various grounds. For example, she can seek a new trial on the ground that the jury's damages award was so excessive as to demonstrate juror bias against her. (In the event of a defense verdict, a plaintiff is are also entitled to ask for a judgment as a matter of law or for a new trial, although it is much more common for post-trial motions of this sort to be filed by defendants against whom a verdict has been entered.)

Assuming the trial judge enters judgment on the jury's verdict, it will be open to the defendant to appeal. Appellate courts generally do not second-guess fact finders' conclusions as to whether the defendant acted in the manner alleged by the plaintiff or whether his actions caused injury to the plaintiff. Instead, they look for "mistakes of law"—misapplications of governing legal standards, such as a trial judge's erroneously denying one of the parties the right to introduce a key piece of evidence or instructing the jury incorrectly on the definition of the tort the defendant was alleged to have committed. Assuming the defendant has exhausted all appeals, the judgment against the defendant and for the plaintiff now stands.

What does such a judgment accomplish? If it is a money judgment, ordinarily the defendant—particularly institutional defendants such as government entities or large businesses—will pay it. Sometimes, however, defendants decline to pay. Because of this possibility, the legal system makes available to plaintiffs various avenues of post-judgment relief. For example, a plaintiff with a tort judgment can sometimes place a *lien* on the defendant's house, which means that if the house is sold, the proceeds must be used to pay the defendant's tort debt to the plaintiff before the remainder (if any) can be put to certain other uses. Or the plaintiff can obtain a court order *attaching* the defendant's bank accounts or other assets such that they must be turned over to the plaintiff. Or the plaintiff can, again via a judicial order, *garnish* a portion of the defendant's wages, which means that the defendant's employer will be required to pay a certain percentage of defendant's wages to the plaintiff. If injunctive relief is sought, then the judgment will consist of an *injunction*—an order from the court that the defendant refrain from engaging in the tortious conduct in question (e.g., requiring a defendant to close down its sewage treatment plant). Defendants who fail to heed orders such as these risk being fined or imprisoned for contempt of court.

In the foregoing ways, plaintiffs may seize an uncooperative defendant's assets. Defendants, however, may have at their disposal certain legal protections against tort judgments. For example, they can sometimes place assets in hard-to-reach offshore trust accounts. They can also file for bankruptcy. Under federal bankruptcy law, defendants cannot protect themselves by strategically filing for bankruptcy on the eve of a tort judgment. However, a good faith filing that occurs prior to the entry of judgment—which triggers a process by which a bankruptcy court sets priorities among the debtor's various creditors for the collection of debts—often results in the debtor's assets being paid out to other creditors (such as banks that have loaned money to the defendant) before it is the victim's turn to collect on her tort judgment against the defendant.

Before turning to consider other forms of response and dispute resolution, it is worth noting some of the burdens that our system places on tort plaintiffs. Some are psychological. The person who believes she has been victimized must be prepared to accuse another of wrongdoing and to follow through on the accusation, knowing that it will probably generate hostility and counterattacks, including investigations through discovery of many facets of her personal life. The handling of lawsuits by lawyers helps to deper-sonalize the conflict to some degree, but there is still plenty of room for conflict and hard feelings, especially if the suit is between persons in some sort of a preexisting relationship.

Other burdens take the form of economic costs. Even a client who hires a lawyer on a contingent fee arrangement will usually have to front some money for court costs and fees. And the lawsuit will take time and attention away from other pursuits. Note, too, that both of these types of cost are incurred in the name of a project that usually carries with it a great deal of uncertainty, which might itself be treated as a third category of cost. A plaintiff with a strong legal claim might end up losing for reasons having nothing to do with its merits. For example, a key witness might testify in a manner that alienates the jury. Alternatively, the plaintiff will lose if the jury concludes, on the basis of the evidence presented, that the plaintiff's account of what happened is possibly what happened, but the defendant's account is equally likely. This is because the plaintiff in a tort suit typically carries the *burden of proof*, which means that she must provide evidence sufficient to establish that her account of what the defendant did to her is *more likely than not* what actually happened. On certain issues—such as whether a defendant was actually driving carelessly at the time he struck the plaintiff or whether a certain pharmaceutical product actually caused the plaintiff to suffer a heart attack—this burden can be difficult to meet.

The challenges facing tort plaintiffs are often amplified—and at times exploited—by defense lawyers, particularly lawyers for wealthy entities. It is often in the interest of such defendants to drag out the litigation and thereby increase its costs, the cost of litigation in order to discourage the plaintiff and her lawyer from pursuing the claim. (Some large businesses adopt a policy of not settling even simple meritorious tort claims in order to send a signal to others that litigation against them will always be drawn out and expensive, thereby discouraging the filing of claims.) Rules of civil procedure set certain limits on the degree to which a defendant can avoid responding to discovery requests or inundate a plaintiff with requests of its own. However, their enforcement requires a vigilant trial judge who is committed to pushing the litigation forward. When it comes to disputes over discovery, many trial judges prefer to take the 'work-it-out-yourselves' stance of a parent dealing with squabbling children.

On a related note, there is the question of what the plaintiff stands to gain for her troubles. First, if a claimant has relatively modest injuries and therefore can expect relatively modest compensation, one-third of which will be paid to her lawyer, the lawsuit may not be worth the time, effort, and expense. Second, juries have broad discretion to determine how much compensation a successful plaintiff will receive, which means that even a plaintiff with a strong case and serious injuries cannot be sure of what damages she will recover. And even if everything goes right at trial, there is the prospect of appeals that will delay recovery and possibly result in the case being re-tried or even dismissed.

Obviously these problems are not so grave as to discourage all tort litigation. Some putative victims are fully motivated to accuse another of wrongdoing, and contingent fee arrangements do significantly reduce up-front costs. Moreover, a good plaintiff's lawyer will be able to make reasonably accurate predictions about how the case is likely to proceed, the approximate odds of various possible outcomes. On the other side, defendants themselves face uncertainties, including the risk of facing a huge damages award (and perhaps attendant bad publicity) in cases where there is evidence of serious injuries or grave misconduct. Still, in light of the foregoing, it is perhaps no surprise to learn of studies suggesting that many persons—perhaps most persons—who have colorable (nonfrivolous) tort claims do not bother to bring them.

4.2 Recourse Today: Settlement, Insurance, Vicarious Liability, Remote Actor Liability, and Aggregate Litigation

The realities of modern litigation add to or diverge from simple, trial-centered litigation in ways that have generated new law school courses and curricula and extensive academic debate. This section will examine a few of the more important of these features of contemporary tort litigation.

The first and perhaps main lesson to absorb is that, at least in the United States, jury trials of tort cases are exceedingly rare. Indeed, statistics suggest that *less than five percent* of tort suits filed are resolved by trial. Some are abandoned voluntarily by the plaintiff, others are thrown out prior to trial based on a determination by the judge that there is some fatal defect in the plaintiff's case, and sometimes plaintiffs win a default judgment—a judgment entered for the plaintiff because the defendant has not bothered to respond to the complaint. Most suits generate a certain amount of discovery, some motion practice (for example, a motion to dismiss that is denied by the trial court), and then settle.

A settlement is a contractual agreement. Typically, when a settlement is reached, the defendant—or, as discussed below, an insurance company that has issued a liability insurance policy to the defendant—agrees to pay a certain amount of money to the plaintiff without any admission of liability, and the plaintiff signs a document releasing the defendant from any and all claims in connection with the conduct complained about in the lawsuit. Often the parties further agree to keep the settlement terms confidential, a practice that has drawn criticism for depriving the public of important information about matters such as the safety of a mass-produced product. When a plaintiff responds to a wrong by filing a lawsuit against a defendant, if the plaintiff ends up obtaining relief, it will probably be because the plaintiff on the one hand, and the defendant and/or his liability insurer on the other, has or have decided to settle the case to avoid the costs and risks associated with proceeding to a jury trial.

As indicated, in many instances when a settlement is reached, it is an agreement between the plaintiff and an insurance company. This pattern is a consequence of the widespread availability of liability insurance, discussed in Chapter 2. Often, perhaps typically, the defendant in a tort suit will have purchased insurance to cover the cost of certain tort liabilities that he might encounter. For example, automobile insurance policies typically include provisions that will cover (up to a specified amount) a liability incurred as a result of careless driving by the persons covered under the policy. Likewise, doctors and lawyers are protected by policies that provide insurance for malpractice liability.

Overwhelmingly, policies such as these apply only to tort liabilities arising from events that, from the perspective of the insured, are *accidental* rather than intentional. This is because insurers have little ability to predict and therefore accurately price coverage for the incidence of intentional wrongdoing. They are also wary of the 'moral hazard' that is created by providing insurance on terms that give the insured the ability to choose to act in a manner that stands to generate liability and, with it, a claim under the policy. A standard liability policy might provide that in the event the insured (the driver, the doctor) is subject to tort liability for an accident covered by the policy (careless driving, shoddy medical care), the insurer will *indemnify* the defendant—i.e., cover the cost of the liability—up to a stated amount. The insurer will also typically promise to undertake the legal defense of the insured, which means that a lawyer or lawyers hired by the insurance company—rather than by the driver or the doctor himself—will manage the defense of the tort suit, decide whether to settle with the plaintiff, and so forth.

Note that when an insurance company pays for a settlement or a judgment under a liability policy, the payment is still predicated on the plaintiff's having a viable or potentially viable claim against the defendant—the insured—for having committed a tort against the plaintiff. The insurer's obligation to pay is *derivative* rather than primary. For this reason, when an insurer takes over the defense of a tort suit against one of its insureds, it will naturally want to argue that the defendant did not in fact commit any tort against the plaintiff. If the argument prevails, the insurer will not be obligated to indemnify the defendant, since there will be no losses for which the defendant is liable. (However, given the American Rule for court costs and legal fees—see Chapter 2—the insurer will still have incurred the costs associated with defending the lawsuit.)

Another significant feature of modern tort litigation that departs from the simple trial-centered account is that it often involves multiple parties, particularly when the claim is for negligence or products liability. In many instances, a single plaintiff complaining of a single injury will allege that more than one actor is responsible for that injury. In other scenarios, a single suit will be brought on behalf of multiple plaintiffs.

One longstanding and vitally important basis for adding an additional defendant to a tort suit is the doctrine of *vicarious liability*. Under this doctrine, certain actors other than the tortfeasor can also be held liable because of their relationship to the tortfeasor. Most significantly, under the doctrine of *respondeat superior* (mentioned in Chapter 2), employers are held vicariously liable for negligence committed by their employees *in the course of their employment*. Thus, if a driver working for a freight company carelessly crashes his truck into another's car, both he and the company will be subject to liability, a happy fact for the plaintiff given the likelihood that the company will have more assets by which to satisfy her tort claim than will the driver. Respondeat superior is the most important form of vicarious liability, but it is not the only one. (Owners of vehicles who lend them to other drivers are often subject to liability for injuries caused by the driver's carelessness.) The relationship between partners in a business partnership, like the employer–employee relationship, generates vicarious liability.

Vicarious liability attaches by virtue of either the relationship of the vicariously liable actor to the person who wrongfully inflicts injury on the plaintiff or that actor's ownership of property. A car owner who is held liable because the person who borrowed her car carelessly ran down the plaintiff is not subjected to liability for herself having acted carelessly, but for being the owner of a car who has lent it to another. The management of an employer subject to vicarious liability may not have been the least bit careless in hiring, training, and supervising its employees, yet will still be subject to liability if one of them injures someone carelessly while acting within the scope of her employment. By the same token, vicarious liability will *not* attach if the requisite relationship or ownership is absent, or if the immediate tortfeasor is acting outside the terms of that relationship. A homeowner who hires a carpenter to do some work on her home will not be held vicariously liable to a third party who is injured if the carpenter carelessly drops a beam on that third party during construction. This is because the carpenter is an *independent contractor* rather than an employee. Likewise, an employer is not subject to respondeat superior liability if one of its employees carelessly causes a car crash while driving his own car on a weekend getaway: the driving will be deemed outside the scope of employment. Whether a given employee's tortious act was committed within or outside the scope of employment is often a pivotal and contested issue in accident litigation.

Finally, it is worth noting that, although vicarious liability is relationship-based or ownership-based rather than fault-based, if there is evidence of carelessness on the part of an employer or owner that has contributed to a plaintiff's injury, that carelessness may provide a separate ground for holding the employer or owner directly liable to the victim. If an owner of a car *carelessly* entrusts his car to a visibly intoxicated person who proceeds to crash it into another person, the owner is liable for negligent entrustment—a form of "primary" rather than vicarious liability. Likewise, if a trucking company knowingly hires a driver whose license has been suspended because of repeated moving violations, and if the driver carelessly injures a third party in the course of driving for the company, the company can be held liable for negligence in hiring. Note that where there is evidence of negligence in hiring or supervising employees, the range of conduct for which management might be held liable is potentially broader than it is for instances of vicarious liability. A recent example that attests to this fact is the imposition of substantial liability on Catholic archdioceses for failing to monitor and control priests who were sexually abusing young parishioners. Heinous employee misconduct of this sort would ordinarily be deemed to fall outside the scope of employment and hence would not provide a basis for vicarious liability. Yet evidence that church higher-ups knew of a priest's abusive acts, yet turned a blind eye toward them, provided grounds for victims to bring negligent supervision claims. (Of course, the abusers themselves would also be subject to liability for battery.)

Just as tort suits can sometimes involve claims against multiple defendants they can sometimes involve multiple plaintiffs. In principle, though now relatively rarely in practice, tort plaintiffs can take advantage of the formal aggregation device known as the *class action*. In a class action, one or a few plaintiffs are authorized to represent the interests of a larger class. Imagine that thousands of users of a drug manufactured and marketed by Drug Co. claim that the drug has caused them to experience serious harmful side effects that would have been avoided had the drug been accompanied with better warnings. A lawyer representing only one or a few of these claimants might make a motion to the trial judge to have the litigation *certified* as a class action. Were the judge to grant the motion, the litigation would no longer be on behalf of just the claimant(s) before the court (the "lead plaintiff(s)"), but instead on behalf of a much larger set of persons complaining of similar injuries deriving from the same wrongful conduct by Drug Co. For instance, the class might be defined as all persons who, while residents of the jurisdiction in which the court sits, allege to have suffered certain specified injuries from taking the drug. The lead plaintiff(s) would be said to represent the interests of all other members of this class. If the suit prevails, relief will be provided not only to the lead plaintiff(s) but to all members of the class. If the suit fails, that failure will also bind all members of the class, thus blocking them from suing separately for the same alleged wrongs.

Because the resolutions of class actions are binding on class members not present before the court, and thereby depart from the norm of permitting each person with a grievance to pursue his claim individually, trial judges are permitted to certify classes only if there are substantial commonalities in terms of the legal and factual issues raised by the claims of each class members. The lawyer for the lead plaintiff(s) will in addition be required to undertake substantial efforts to notify class members that their rights are being adjudicated through the class action. Class members in turn are usually given the right to opt out of the class action in the event they wish to pursue their own claims.

Particularly in the 1970s and the early 1980s, the class action device seemed as if it might revolutionize tort litigation. Among the pioneering mass tort class actions was a suit brought on behalf of Vietnam veterans against the manufacturers of Agent Orange, a defoliant used in the war. The veterans claimed that exposure to it had caused them to suffer various physical ailments. Eventually the litigation produced a settlement that earned exposed veterans a relatively modest set of payments. Nonetheless, the suit seemed to provide a model for how to resolve efficiently mass torts involving injuries to hundreds or thousands of alleged victims.

However, by the late 1980s, appellate courts in the United States were expressing skepticism as to whether the class action device really was suitable for the resolution of tort claims. In part, they have worried that even if a number of plaintiffs are all complaining about the same allegedly wrongful conduct—for example, a manufacturer's having defectively designed or mislabeled its drug—the question of what harms, if any, the drug has caused and the question of whether users have misused or mishandled the drug are highly individualized fact issues that cannot be resolved on a class-wide basis. These sorts of concerns have tended to go hand-in-hand with the emergence of a more conservative mood in the American judiciary, and a sense that the certification of class actions in tort cases might be handing plaintiffs' lawyers the power to 'extort' excessive settlements from defendants, given that the stakes of litigation on behalf of thousands of claimants can be so enormous as to make it very difficult for defendants to take the risk of not settling.

Lawyers also have various informal means by which they may aggregate claims. Suppose dozens of residents in a town believe that emissions from a nearby chemical plant have caused them to suffer respiratory illnesses of varying severity. It would not be surprising if all of them ended up being represented by a single lawyer who is able to convince them that she has the necessary expertise and experience to best represent each of them. Her efforts to obtain discovery from the defendant would, as a practical matter, be on behalf of all of her clients, and it is likely that any settlement discussions between her and the defendant's lawyers would seek a package deal, whereby all the claims would be settled at once, with the amount that each claimant stands to receive being calculated in part by reference to the amounts that others will receive.

In recent years, informal aggregation of the sort just described has occurred in response even to mass torts that are alleged to have caused widely dispersed harms. For example, consider the case of Drug Co. mentioned above in connection with the discussion of class actions. Although today it is unlikely that a court would certify a class consisting of all those in a given jurisdiction who allegedly suffered a certain kind of side effect from a given drug, it is quite possible that persons who believe they have been tortiously harmed by one of Drug Co.'s products might contact a local lawyer, who in turn might refer them to a mass tort specialty firm. Lawyers for Drug Co. will generally be happy to have the opportunity to enter into settlement negotiations with a single plaintiffs' firm or a few such firms if those negotiations promise to resolve all or almost all claims against the defendant in a single master agreement. Again, it is likely that if a settlement is reached, it will include grids or point systems that establish different recoveries for different categories of plaintiffs depending on factors such as age, pre-tort income, and health impairment.

※ 4.3 Why Have a Law of Wrongs and Recourse?

We now have a better understanding of the ways in which tort law empowers victims of torts to respond to tortfeasors through the legal system. This understanding will prove important as we move to a discussion of the substance of particular torts because these wrongs have been shaped by judges and legislators with an eye toward the remedial consequences that will follow from recognizing particular conduct as tortious. Before leaving this topic, however, it will be worthwhile to step back and consider what is being accomplished by a body of law that connects the identification of a special type of wrong to the provision of redress in the way that tort law does.

The right of the tort victim to exact a remedy is, obviously, a creation of the legal system. As we have seen, the exercise of that right can be costly both to victims and to alleged tortfeasors and, in the long run, to consumers of goods and services that cost more because their providers build the cost of liability insurance into their overhead costs (at least so far as market pressures on prices allow). The public also incurs the modest expenses associated with maintaining the court system. The system operates in a way that invites parties to adopt an adversarial stance toward one another rather than reconcile. And the process is time-consuming. Certainly, if the sole point of the exercise is to get compensation promptly to needy victims in the manner of effective disaster relief, the tort system is itself a disaster. So why should the law recognize such a right? What is its point? Would it not be better for the law instead to set up a scheme that grants victims of wrongs a right to obtain reimbursement for their medical costs and certain economic losses via a governmental fund financed by general tax revenues? With just this sort of question in mind, ambitiously programmatic reformers have sometimes dismissed tort law as a crude and outdated way by which primitive governments first responded to injurious wrongdoing. "Perhaps in the year 1300 this was the best that could be done," the reformer might say, "but today we can do much better by replacing tort with some combination of criminal law, regulatory law, and compensation schemes."

Although this sort of view is commonly expressed in academic circles, it fails to come to terms with what tort law aims to do. The provision of redress to victims of wrongs was not set up as, and is not today, a system for getting compensation into the hands of needy victims. Nor is it a system of deterrence through threats of liability imposition. Instead, it embodies a basic political commitment to the idea that a person who has been wronged by another should be able to *respond to* the wrong and the wrongdoer, and that an actor who is deemed properly subject to this sort of response should be held *responsible to* the victim of the wrong. This is no mere coincidence of words. Through the tort system, the defendant's responsibility for having wronged another takes the form of his being properly the object of a victim's response. Tort law is at its core a scheme that empowers victims of wrongs to respond to them, and in so doing holds wrongdoers responsible to their victims.

Why have such a system? John Locke, the great English political philosopher, observed long ago that modern states largely deny individuals an entitlement to take self-protective and self-restorative acts against those who injure them. This is for a good reason: outlawing 'self-help' remedies is an important means by which civil order is maintained. Yet precisely because the state disempowers its citizens in this way, Locke argued, government is obligated to provide them with an alternative avenue of recourse against wrongdoers. To cut off all possibility of response is to deprive individuals of one of a cluster of rights associated with standard liberal rights to life, liberty, and property. Government, by providing an avenue of legal recourse to victims against those who have wronged them, empowers citizens to vindicate their rights as against those who have wrongly interfered with them. The legal right to redress wrongs recognizes a residual private privilege to act against others, even within a constitutional democracy in which the state has a monopoly on the legitimate use of force. From past centuries to the present, both English and American political systems have treated the right to respond to wrongs as fundamental, which is why tort is one department of law among several that forms a basic pillar of our legal systems.

To be sure, as a body of law that embodies a commitment to the recognition of individual rights, tort can and does accomplish many things. As already indicated, it can have a *pacifying* effect. Absent the recognition of lawsuits as a permissible means for responding to wrongs, individuals would probably more frequently engage in the sort of self-help that often characterizes premodern and lawless societies. In identifying various redressable wrongs, tort law by the same token reinforces the fabric of *civil society*—the idea that, although we enjoy a great deal of liberty to live in accordance with our own designs, we nonetheless owe duties to others that require us to act with vigilance as to their interests. The redressability of wrongs can also have a *deterrent* effect. Legal actors know that if they do commit torts upon others, they may be sued and held liable for them, and thus have an incentive to refrain from committing those torts. The system of private lawsuits also at times provides *compensation*, permitting those injured by legal wrongs to recover for losses stemming from them. Typically, defendants who engage in activities that have a high risk of leading to litigation obtain liability insurance, and so stand ready to provide compensation to those who seek it.

Effects such as these are often described by lawyers, judges, and scholars as "functions" of tort law, and there are long-standing arguments about which of them is most basic or important. This use of the term "function" is in our view misleading. Tort is not a system for deterring antisocial conduct, or a system for providing funds to needy injury victims, or a system for achieving civil peace. It is a system for the identification of wrongs and for the provision to victims of an avenue of recourse. Of course, tort law in its operation often accomplishes other things and tends to jibe with and reinforce other values that we deem important. But neither the achievement of these things nor the realization of these values is properly described as a "function" of tort law.

Aside from worries about whether tort or some alternative body of law can or should embody other values or more directly pursue other ends, one might legitimately ask how well tort law in practice lives up to the ideal of a law for the redress of wrongs. After all, as we noted above, the rules under which civil lawsuits operate raise significant barriers that both inhibit some would-be claimants from pursuing redress and burden in various ways those who do pursue such claims. If tort law is designed to empower victims, why does it make the task of responding to wrongs so difficult and cumbersome? There are no doubt several explanations. For one thing, even though government may be doing right by its citizens by providing an avenue of redress or recourse, it may also be doing right by setting up barriers that encourage victims to do so thoughtfully rather than rashly and to consider whether what has been done to them really warrants the elaborate response of a lawsuit. Many wrongs are, in the scheme of things, minor affairs that are better resolved informally or through alternative mechanisms such as insurance. Alleged wrongdoers also have rights, and to the extent that the barriers placed in the way of tort claimants are part of an effort to preserve those rights, they may well be justified. When a complaint is filed, it will often be unclear whether a wrong has been committed, and much of the point of procedural and evidentiary rules is to ensure, as much as possible, that allegations of wrongdoing are adjudicated fairly and with relatively full information.

There is a different way in which attention to the "realities" of modern tort litigation might be taken to suggest that there is something contrived about discussing the subject of torts in terms of redress being obtained and wrongdoers being held responsible. Such an account—the argument continues—might accurately characterize tort when it is thought of in terms of the simple trial-centered model discussed above. Yet as we have seen, today's tort suits usually end in a private settlement in which money changes hands without any admission of responsibility. Settlements are often negotiated and paid not by the alleged tortfeasor, but by a third party—the defendant's liability insurer. And when multiple claimants allege injuries from the same wrongful conduct, their claims tend to be resolved in coordination with each other rather than individually, suggesting that tort in these cases operates more like a bureaucratic claims-processing scheme rather than law that enables personalized redress.

There is something to these claims, but they can easily be overstated. Even if most tort litigation does not follow the path described in the trial-centered account, it is the availability in principle of that path that sets the benchmark against which insurers assess claims, and lawyers for both sides measure the value of alternative modes of proceeding. Moreover, depending on how they are arrived at, settlements can themselves empower victims and impose responsibility. A victim who, with proper legal advice from a lawyer, accepts a settlement is choosing one form of response over another. Of course she might prefer not to be faced with choosing between receiving a sum of money sooner or taking a chance on, and facing the delays of, a trial. And it may be that our system of litigation should be reformed in various ways to make the choice to proceed to trial a more realistic one for more claimants. Still, an informed, voluntary settlement agreement reflects the victim's (constrained) choice about how to respond to having been wronged.

Finally, what are we to make of the fact that it is often not wrongdoers, but their liability insurers who end up paying tort judgments or settlements? Again, there clearly is an attenuation of responsibility as compared to the alternative of the tortfeasor paying the entire judgment out of his own pocket. But it is hardly an abolition of responsibility. For example, most drivers are insured up to a specified amount against liabilities resulting from harms to third parties caused by their careless driving. Yet insured drivers hardly consider themselves freed from the responsibility to drive carefully. An insured driver who is actually sued in negligence for causing harm to another—even one whose settlement is paid for by his insurer— will not likely experience the episode as one devoid of any attribution of responsibility to her. If the litigation proceeds through discovery, she will likely be grilled about her actions in a deposition. She will also face increased premiums or perhaps even have her coverage cancelled. Also, liability insurance rather obviously confers a corresponding benefit on many victims of wrongs. Absent liability insurance, many wrongdoers would lack the means to satisfy judgments in cases involving serious injuries. The important question, then, is whether the advantage to victims of improved access to tangible redress is worth the weakening, in some instances, of what it means for a wrongdoers to be held responsible for a wrong.

We have explained that tort law in action typically involves settlement and payouts from insurance companies, not full-fledged adjudications and direct tortfeasor payments in satisfaction of victims' claims against them. These aspects of tort law in action at times generate justifiable complaints by plaintiffs that the law is giving short shrift to their right to recourse. Likewise, defendants subjected to weak or meritless claims who are nonetheless forced into draining and expensive litigation and settlements can justifiably complain that our system has departed from the ideal of holding wrongdoers accountable to their victims. To make these observations is to observe that tort law—like any complex institution—often falls short (sometimes significantly short) of the ideals it embodies, and to emphasize the importance of efforts to try to improve the system's performance. It is not to suggest that there is something erroneous about a depiction of tort law as a domain of wrongs and recourse, nor is it to suggest that this body of law ought to be sharply curtailed or abandoned. Indeed, litigants' understandable bridling at practical deficiencies in our system only makes sense when we see that our legal culture really does understand tort law as *aspiring* to achieve a certain sort of justice between private parties.

"Justice" is a word that we have not used much in this book. Readers should be aware that the wrongs and redress model put forward in this chapter—and that animates this entire volume— has emerged in part from an academic movement devoted to the idea that tort law is about achieving "corrective justice" between private parties. The leaders of this movement—Jules Coleman,[1] Richard Epstein,[2] Stephen Perry,[3] Arthur Ripstein,[4] and Ernest

---

1. JULES L. COLEMAN, RISKS AND WRONGS (1992).

2. Richard A. Epstein, *A Theory of Strict Liability*, 2 J. LEGAL STUD. 151 (1973).

3. Stephen R. Perry, *The Moral Foundations of Tort Law*, 77 IOWA L. REV. 449 (1992).

4. ARTHUR RIPSTEIN, EQUALITY, RESPONSIBILITY AND THE LAW (1999).

Weinrib[5]—have self-consciously constructed their views in opposition to those of scholars such as Guido Calabresi and Richard Posner who see tort law as a mechanism for inducing actors to take cost-efficient precautions against causing accidents. Our views on large-scale questions about the nature and purposes of tort law are much closer to those of corrective justice theorists than economists. And yet in emphasizing the two major themes of this chapter—wrongs and recourse—we are reaching back further into the Anglo-American roots of tort law—to William Blackstone and John Locke, and we are reaching out more broadly to the real world entrenchment of tort concepts in actual practice.[6] Tort law is at once more public and more private than many of the corrective justice theorists suggest. It is more public because it is about the role our legal system plays in identifying certain behaviors as "wrongs" to others; it contains legal rules that guide conduct rather than simply allocate losses after the fact. It is more private because, when tort law aims for justice, it does not aim for some objectively just redistribution of wealth. Instead, it alters the power relationship between private persons by empowering victims to assert claims against, and to obtain satisfaction from, tortfeasors: it offers civil recourse for wrongs.

---

5. ERNEST J. WEINRIB, THE IDEA OF PRIVATE LAW 134–35 (1995).

6. John C. P. Goldberg, *The Constitutional Status of Tort Law: Due Process and the Right to a Law for the Redress of Wrongs*, 115 YALE L.J. 524 (2005); Benjamin C. Zipursky, *Civil Recourse, Not Corrective Justice*, 91 GEO. L.J. 695 (2003); Benjamin C. Zipursky, *Rights, Wrongs and Recourse in the Law of Torts*, 51 VAND. L. REV. 1 (1998).

FIVE

Negligence
The Basics

IN 1980, A STUDENT ENTERING a U.S. law school could expect a five- or six-hour Torts course that toured many of the rooms in tort law's gallery of wrongs. Today, the standard introductory course is four hours, and at least half of it will probably be devoted to intensive study of a single tort—negligence.

That torts courses have grown shorter reflects, among other things, a need to shrink traditional common law courses to provide coverage of other subjects, including regulatory and international law. That they focus more intensively on negligence attests in part to the numeric dominance of the world of torts by negligence actions. Car accidents, professional malpractice, and slip-and-falls, which for the most part give rise to claims for negligence, form the bulk of contemporary tort litigation. Torts courses also tend to focus on negligence because twentieth-century academics are attracted to the view that tort law's distinctive role in modern legal systems (if any) is to deter or otherwise respond to *accidents*. And claims arising out of accidents are primarily, but not exclusively, framed as negligence claims.

As our "gallery of wrongs" metaphor suggests, we reject the notion that accidents and negligence form the conceptual core of modern tort law. Nonetheless, given negligence law's prominence in contemporary litigation and legal education, we acknowledge that it deserves special attention. Accordingly, we commence this part of our book with two chapters on it. This chapter provides an overview of the tort. Chapter 6 delves into advanced topics.

※ 5.1 One Tort, Many Iterations

Each tort can be broken down into component parts or elements that the plaintiff must establish in order to prevail. Elementally, the tort of negligence can be rendered as follows.

A commits negligence against *V* if:

1. *V* has suffered an *injury*;
2. *A* owed a *duty* to persons including *V* to take *due care* against causing an injury of the type *V* suffered;
3. *A breached* the duty owed to *V* by acting carelessly toward *V*;
4. *A*'s breach *actually* and *proximately caused V*'s injury.

If a negligence plaintiff can prove to the jury's satisfaction that all four elements have been satisfied, and if the defendant fails to offer a valid affirmative defense, then liability is established, and the plaintiff is entitled to a remedy, usually an award of compensatory damages.

Many textbooks and judicial opinions identify the elements of negligence slightly differently, defining it in terms of (1) duty, (2) breach, (3) causation, and (4) damages. This ordering and nomenclature is understandable. For one thing, it follows the chronology of an instance of negligence: a duty-bearer breaches a duty of care owed to a victim, thereby causing her to suffer damages. However, we have found that it aids the cause of clarity to list the "injury" element first rather than last, then to proceed through duty, breach, and causation. Doing so emphasizes that it is the happening of an injury that provides the necessary trigger for a valid negligence claim. Moreover, as suggested by our discussion of interests in Chapter 3, the rules that define torts and set the scope of liability often vary according to the type of injury suffered. Placing injury first thus helps to organize the treatment of different variations on the basic negligence tort. Finally, it is desirable to use the term "injury" rather than "damages" because the latter confusingly can refer both to the setback experienced by the plaintiff and the amount of compensation awarded to the plaintiff in light of the set-back. "Injury," by contrast, more clearly refers to the setback. For these and other reasons, we label the four elements of negligence as follows: (1) *injury*, (2) *duty*, (3) *breach*, and (4) *cause*.

In most negligence cases, there is nothing particularly mysterious about what each of these elements requires, even though there may be a great deal of controversy over whether some or all of them can be or have been satisfactorily proven. It will help orient the remaining analysis in this chapter to consider some simple examples.

Pedestrian versus Driver. Pedestrian crosses the street and Driver runs his car into her, knocking her down. Pedestrian suffers a serious spine injury that causes her chronic and debilitating pain. Under settled law, Driver owes a duty to other users of the roads to drive with ordinary care for their physical well-being. Pedestrian will need to show at trial that Driver breached this duty by, for example, speeding or driving inattentively. If Pedestrian proves that Driver was driving carelessly, and that doing so caused him to run down and injure Pedestrian, assuming there are no successful affirmative defenses, Pedestrian will have proven her case. If she prevails, she will be entitled to a payment of damages from Driver that in principle will compensate her for medical expenses, lost wages, pain and suffering, and other losses traceable to the tort.

Patient versus Doctor. Doctor performs minor surgery on Patient. Patient ends up a paraplegic. In providing medical care, doctors owe their patients a duty to meet the standard of care for their profession. Patient will attempt to establish that the doctor's treatment fell below this standard and that it caused his condition—i.e., that he ended up a paraplegic because of what would have been a harmless procedure had it been performed by a doctor complying with the standard of care. Patient will seek damages not only for his medical expenses and the trauma of becoming paraplegic, but also for additional support services that he will need going forward, and for any diminution in earnings that he suffers.

Merchant versus Factory. Merchant's retail store is burned down because Factory, located next door, experienced a massive fire traceable to industrial chemicals stored on site by Factory. Merchant will strive to show that the fire was caused by a failure on the part of Factory's managers or owners to exercise the sort of care in storing flammable materials that a reasonably prudent industrial entity like the defendant would use. If Merchant prevails, she can recover for the damage to her building, damage to her inventory, and lost business.

Camper versus Camp. Camper, aged 14, suffers a serious gash in his hand while whittling wood with a sharp knife, which is a Camp-sanctioned activity. Camp fails to provide first aid or to deliver Camper to a nearby hospital emergency room. Camper loses partial use of his hand, which is permanently disfigured. Assume that the initial happening of the gash was no one's fault. Camp nonetheless was under a duty to take steps to provide first aid to campers injured in ordinary camp activities. Camper (through a lawsuit brought by his parents) will argue that this duty required Camp to make reasonable efforts to provide or arrange for medical care for Camper and that there probably would have been a better health outcome (e.g., a small scar with no loss of function) had Camp done what it was obligated to do.

In each of these examples, we are supposing that the plaintiff can easily establish some elements (injury and duty) and may be able to establish the others (breach and causation). Note, however, that even where the elements are satisfied, a defendant will not always be held liable. This is because negligence law, like the law of every tort, recognizes certain *affirmative defenses* (discussed below).

Before turning to a discussion of each of the elements, as well as their need to 'align' properly to generate liability, it will be worthwhile to step back for a moment to appreciate the breadth of the negligence tort. As the four preceding examples perhaps already suggest, courts have defined the negligence tort capaciously to encompass a diverse array of wrongful and injurious acts. Indeed, some scholars writing at the turn of the twentieth century argued that the instances of actionable negligence are so diverse that it is a mistake to suppose there is a single tort of negligence as opposed to more particular torts, such as careless operation of a vehicle, medical malpractice, failure to maintain safe premises, and failures to provide assistance. Although history has resolved this debate decisively on the side of treating these and other forms of unintentional wrongdoing as instantiations of the single wrong of negligence, it is worth keeping in mind that efforts to find uniformity across the breadth of this tort inevitably generate a certain amount of conceptual strain.

✹ 5.2 The Injury Element

Part of what makes the examples of Pedestrian, Patient, and Merchant straightforward is that in each, the claim of the plaintiff to have suffered the sort of setback that counts as an injury is unassailable. To have damage done to one's spine or to experience permanent paralysis is to suffer a serious or catastrophic personal injury. Likewise, proof that one's land or possessions have been physically damaged or destroyed readily suffices to establish an injury in the eyes of negligence law.

There is another important lesson in the Pedestrian and Patient examples. A successful negligence plaintiff who proves that she has suffered *bodily harm* renders herself eligible to obtain compensation for other forms of harm flowing from that harm, such as pain and suffering or lost wages. (We use the word "successful" in the preceding sentence to emphasize that, to obtain any damages at all, the plaintiff must prove not just injury, but also the other elements of her negligence claim.) Compensation for attendant harms of this sort is often referred to as *"parasitic damages."*

The rules for recovery of parasitic damages in connection with property damage, as opposed to bodily harm, are slightly different. As indicated by the Merchant example, a business owner whose place of business is destroyed, and who as a result loses income that she would have otherwise received, can claim that lost income as damages parasitic on the destruction of her place of business. However, courts are probably less willing to recognize parasitic damages claims for emotional distress over losses of property (e.g., distress over the loss of one's home because of a fire carelessly caused by a neighbor). Parasitic emotional distress damages may in some courts be recoverable when the property in question is a beloved pet or otherwise of sentimental value.

What about careless conduct that causes *neither* bodily harm *nor* tangible property damage? In the absence of these sorts of injuries, a negligence plaintiff can still establish that she has suffered an injury by proving a different sort of setback, including emotional distress or loss of expected revenues. (Damages awarded for these sorts of nonphysical harms are no longer deemed 'parasitic' because we are now focusing on cases in which they do not piggyback on an underlying physical harm.) However, as is discussed in Chapter 6, there are special duty rules that substantially limit the occasions on which carelessness giving rise to one of these sorts of injuries will count as actionable negligence. In other words, to suffer emotional distress or loss of income *is* to suffer an injury, but in many instances, it will be an injury that the defendant was not under a duty to take care against causing.

Depending on one's view of it, the example of Camper arguably presents a special case of injury. Camper clearly experienced physical harm in the form of the gash, but the gist of his complaint against Camp is not that its carelessness caused the gash, but that it failed to respond to the gash and thereby allowed the condition of the hand to worsen into more severe, lasting damage. One could say that the claim of injury being raised against Camp would be the additional increment of physical harm suffered by Camper after Camp's failure properly to intervene. So characterized, the claim would be a straightforward claim for bodily harm. However, one might alternatively characterize the effect on Camper of the Camp's inaction as a failure to preserve the plaintiff's health or his prospects for health. We need not at this point settle on the best characterization of Camper's injury. The point for now is that there are special cases that fall under the heading of affirmative duty (discussed in Chapter 6), in which the injury suffered by the victim will not easily be captured by the idea of having suffered a loss or setback, rather than the idea of having been denied an opportunity or benefit.

5.3 The Duty Element

The examples of Pedestrian, Patient, Merchant, and Camper share another feature. They are all instances in which there would be no serious dispute as to whether a duty to exercise care was owed by the defendant to the plaintiff. The question of whether a person owes a duty of care to a certain category of potential victim is a *question of law*, which means that it is determined in the first instance by a judge without deference to the jury even when a jury has been or will be empanelled to decide other aspects of the case.[1] It is settled law in every Anglo-American jurisdiction that car drivers owe other users of the roads a duty to take care not to cause them physical harm. Likewise, physicians owe it to their patients not to physically harm them by providing care that falls below the standards of their profession; neighboring property owners owe

---

1. This is slightly overstated. Judges set the rules of duty, but the application of these rules sometimes turn on factual questions that, in a jury trial, a jury might need to resolve. For example, a property owner ordinarily does not owe a duty to maintain safe premises for the benefit of adult trespassers, but can incur such a duty if he knows that trespassers regularly traverse a particular portion of the property. As applied in a given case, the rule thus might require jury findings as to whether the defendant's property was routinely trespassed upon, and whether the owner knew of the trespassers.

each other ordinary care against causing property damage to one another; and organizations, such as sleepaway camps, owe the campers who have been entrusted to them various duties, including the affirmative duty to take reasonable steps to provide necessary medical care.

Speaking generally, negligence suits arising out of acts by a defendant that have caused physical injuries and property damage to a plaintiff—or at least have done so without the intervention of other actors' wrongful acts—tend *not* to raise difficult duty questions. This is because courts have fashioned the relevant duty rules quite broadly. For example, it is common for courts to say that any person who engages in a course of conduct—whether walking, driving, operating a machine, or providing a service—owes a duty to exercise due care against *physically harming* anyone whom he might *reasonably foresee* physically harming were he to perform that conduct carelessly. This notion of reasonably foreseeable victims—i.e., persons whom one can expect might suffer personal injury or damage to their property because of one's careless conduct—is today a standard doctrinal test for determining to whom a duty of care is owed.

Intuitive though it may be, the notion that one is under a duty to take care against causing physical harm to persons whom one can foresee physically harming by one's careless conduct emerged relatively recently—and only with the abandonment of older, narrower duty rules. In *Winterbottom v. Wright,*[2] the plaintiff driver, who was employed by the English Postmaster General to drive one of its horse-drawn mail coaches, was seriously injured when the coach he was driving collapsed under him. The driver sued the manufacturer of the coach, alleging careless construction and maintenance. The court held that, even if the manufacturer's carelessness caused the driver to be injured, the driver could *not* recover because the coach manufacturer owed a duty of care *only* to the immediate purchaser of the coach (the Postmaster General). In short, the court

---

2. (1842) 152 Eng. Rep. 402 (Exch.).

deemed the manufacturer at liberty to be careless toward third parties who used the product—even third parties who, like the driver, could readily be expected to use it at the invitation of the immediate purchaser.

The decision in *Winterbottom* was motivated in part by the judges' concern that a duty of care grounded in foreseeability was too expansive in rendering manufacturers vulnerable to actions by too many victims, including (in a case like *Winterbottom*) coach drivers, coach passengers, pedestrians and other bystanders. (Note that, as explained in Chapter 2, liability insurance was at this time largely unavailable to help defray the costs potentially associated with an expanded conception of duty.) The judges also seemed to suppose—perhaps unrealistically—that the safety of products could in many instances be adequately addressed in negotiations between purchaser and manufacturer, as well as between purchaser and ultimate victim. (Perhaps they imagined that, for self-interested business reasons, the Postmaster General could be expected to demand sound coaches, while drivers could likewise be expected to dicker with the Postmaster over employment terms, including the relative safety of working conditions.)

Winterbottom's so-called privity rule for duty—the phrase "in privity" refers to parties in a contractual relationship—was eventually undone in a series of important late-nineteenth- and early-twentieth-century decisions. One notable salvo against it was *Heaven v. Pender*,[3] an English decision holding that the supplier of a defective scaffold that collapsed could be held liable in negligence for physical injuries caused to workers using the scaffold even though the workers' employer, not the workers themselves, had contracted with the supplier for the scaffold. Although purporting merely to distinguish rather than overrule *Winterbottom*, Judge Brett's famous concurring opinion in *Heaven* maintained that the duty owed by the scaffold supplier to the workers rested on the fact

---

3. [1883] 11 Q.B.D. 503 (App. Cas.).

that the supplier must have foreseen that, if anyone was going to be injured by a carelessly made scaffold, it was the workers who would use it. Generalizing from this observation, he maintained that *an actor owes a duty of care to another if, at the time of acting, a reasonable person in the position of the actor would have in mind persons such as the plaintiff as among those who might be physically harmed were the actor to go about his conduct carelessly.*

Two subsequent landmark decisions from the early 1900s— *MacPherson v. Buick Motor Co.*[4] and *Donoghue v. Stevenson*[5]—finally killed off *Winterbottom*. In *MacPherson*, which established Benjamin Cardozo's reputation as a leading jurist, the owner of a car was injured when the car's wheel collapsed as he was driving it. Because he had purchased the car from a local car dealer rather than from Buick itself, Buick attempted to defeat liability by invoking the privity rule. Echoing *Heaven*, Cardozo's opinion for the New York Court of Appeals refused to let actors limit their duties of care simply by selling through middlemen. The duty to take care not to injure, he emphasized, is not something one chooses to accept. It is imposed by law for the protection of potential victims. Accordingly, the law asks of manufacturers, like other actors, that they take reasonable steps to ensure that their products not physically harm anyone whom they might reasonably expect to be so harmed if such steps were not taken, including most obviously users of the products in the ordinary course.

It is important to note that, in articulating the notion of reasonable foreseeability, both Brett and Cardozo had before them a certain kind of scenario; namely, one in which an actor, by virtue of his own careless actions, *irrespective of the prospect of wrongful actions by others*, risks causing *bodily harm or property damage* to another. To say the same thing in reverse, the allegation of wrongdoing against the manufacturers in *Winterbottom* and *MacPherson*

---

4. 111 N.E. 1050 (N.Y. 1916).

5. [1932] All E.R. 1.

was *not* that they should have taken steps to protect the plaintiffs *against wrongful conduct by an intermediary* (i.e., the Postmaster General or the car dealer). Instead, the assumption in each case was that the defendant was essentially acting directly on the victim, with the intermediary playing only the modest role of bringing the victim into contact with the defendant's carelessly made product. Likewise, the gist of each plaintiff's complaint was that the defendant had acted carelessly *with respect to the plaintiff's interest in physical integrity*, as opposed to his interest in economic well-being or mental tranquility. These sorts of scenarios still today constitute the heartland for the application of the reasonable foresight test for duty. As we will see in subsequent chapters, when intervening wrongful conduct by actors other than the defendant is part of what the defendant is being asked to take care against, or when the injury at issue is not a physical harm, foreseeability often will be *insufficient* to ground a duty of care.

It is also worth emphasizing that the concept of reasonable foreseeability contains both probabilistic and normative aspects. Part of what determines whether harm to a certain sort of person is foreseeable is an assessment of how likely it is that an actor's careless acts will hurt a person situated in relation to those acts as the plaintiff is situated. But this is only part of the inquiry. In addition, there is an evaluative judgment to be made about what sorts of harms to what sorts of persons an actor can *fairly be expected* to anticipate. Thus a judicial opinion that deems a certain kind of harm to a certain class of person to have been unforeseeable is typically supposing that the law would be demanding too much to ask the defendant to have anticipated causing such harm, even though there was some probability of causing it.

Finally we must emphasize that foreseeability of physical harm to others, though central to the recognition of duties of care in a wide array of scenarios, is not the only grounds for recognizing them. The duty of competent treatment that is uncontroversially owed by physicians to their patients is grounded as much in the physician's explicit or implicit undertaking to tend to the patient's health as it is in the foreseeability of harm to the patient. Likewise, in a variety of situations, the existence of a pre-tort special relationship such as camp-camper, school-student, hotel-guest, and airline-passenger will support the recognition of a duty of care owed by the one to the other.

Still, the fact that foreseeability is often sufficient to generate a duty of care against causing physical harm or property damage tells us that pre-tort relationships are not necessary to the generation of duties of care. Indeed, as Cardozo emphasized in *MacPherson*, one of the features of tort duties that separates them from contractual duties is that the former attach automatically to conduct and often cannot be undone, even by an explicit agreement between the defendant and the plaintiff. The duty to drive a car with care for the physical well-being of those around you derives from the law itself, not from any agreement, and it cannot be voided or rescinded, even if by some bizarre means a driver were able to enter agreements with those around him that purported to relieve him of this duty.

5.4 The Breach Element

As we have already seen through numerous examples, negligence law requires people not to injure others *through carelessness*. But what counts as carelessness? How much care must be used? This topic will occupy us for much of the rest of this chapter.

With respect to this issue, the problem long faced by courts has been how to articulate a standard that offers guidance to actors, while being open-ended enough to permit negligence to function as an all-purpose accident tort. One might dub this the problem of the "openness" of the breach standard. The courts' dominant solution to the openness problem has been to define carelessness with a series of phrases that ends, finally, with an image of an ideal type—the reasonably prudent person. For example, New York law, which is representative in this respect, requires judges to provide instructions to jurors who are about to deliberate on a negligence claim with the following definition of carelessness:

Negligence [i.e., breach or carelessness] is *lack of ordinary care*. It is a failure to use *that degree of care that a reasonably prudent person would have used under the same circumstances*. Negligence may arise from doing an act that a reasonably prudent person would not have done under the circumstances, or, on the other hand, from failing to do an act that a reasonably prudent person would have done under the same circumstances.[6]

To breach the duty of ordinary care is to fail to have been as careful as a reasonably prudent person would have been under the same circumstances. Of course this description invites a new question: What sort of care would a reasonably prudent person exercise? As we will see below, and again in Chapter 6, courts have fashioned rules that render relevant or irrelevant certain considerations that might bear on this question, yet still leave the fact finder—juries or, in bench trials, trial judges—broad discretion in applying the standard to particular cases.

Before proceeding further, we should point out that this model instruction, like most others, refers to the breach of the duty of care as "negligence." Although such usage is common among lawyers, it is very unhelpful, given that "negligence" is also the name for the entire tort. The overlap invites confusion by, for example, allowing one to say that an actor has *been negligent* yet has not *committed negligence*. (If a driver drives inattentively but manages not to hit anyone or anything, she has acted "negligently" but cannot be held liable for negligence given that her careless conduct did not cause injury to anyone). To avoid confusion, we will endeavor to use the term "negligence" to refer only to the whole tort—i.e., only to a breach of a duty of care owed to another that proximately causes

---

6. New York Pattern Jury Instruction: Civil 2:10 (3d ed. 2000) (emphasis added).

injury to that other. We will use terms like "breach" and "careless-ness" to refer to the failure to live up to the standard of care.

5.4.1 The Objectivity of the Standard of Care

Most torts classes will include a discussion of the 1837 English deci-sion of *Vaughan v. Menlove*.[7] The defendant, Menlove, stacked bales of hay on his property in a manner that caused the formation and release of gases that spontaneously combusted. The fire spread to Vaughan's land and burned structures on it. Vaughan sued Menlove for damages, claiming that Menlove was careless because he failed to stack his hay in a different manner that was known to reduce the risk of spontaneous combustion. Menlove's lawyer responded to this allegation with an interesting argument. He did not deny that his client failed to pile the hay in the safer way. Instead, he argued that Menlove had done his best—had acted as carefully as he was capable of acting, given that he was not a particularly thoughtful or prudent man. So long as one does the best that one can do in taking care, he argued, one cannot be *blamed* for failing to act differently, and thus ought not to be subject to liability to another for hurting him under such circumstances.

The court famously rejected this argument, holding that con-duct is to be assessed according to the care that a person of ordi-nary prudence would have used. The standard advocated by Menlove, the judges reasoned, would create a *subjective* standard that would vary among persons no less than their foot sizes. In part, the judges were acting out of concern for the litigation process. To accept Menlove's position would be to invite negligence defen-dants to feign obliviousness and to play games by introducing perhaps contrived evidence of their foolish natures while leaving

---

7. (1837) 132 Eng. Rep. 490 (C.P.).

fact finders to gauge the very difficult question of whether a given defendant had actually done his best.

In addition to practical concerns, the judges perhaps had in mind certain normative considerations. One emphasized by subsequent commentators, including future Supreme Court Justice Oliver Wendell Holmes, Jr., is that each of us is entitled to expect of others that they will go about their business as safely as an ordinarily constituted person would. Others have suggested that the law would not be asking enough of people if it instructed them to *try their best* to be careful, as opposed to telling them that they must *actually succeed in being careful.* Although the law does not necessarily address competent adult citizens paternalistically, one can analogize in this instance to the example of a parent speaking to a young child about the importance of taking care not to hurt others. Most likely, the parent will do better to say to the child, "you must take care not to hurt others," as opposed to saying "you must do your best to take care not to hurt others." The former is not only easier to communicate and more effective in making its point, it also has the advantage of not inviting the recipient to make excuses ("But I tried my best!").

Because it rejects the argument for a conception of carelessness tied to the characteristics of each individual defendant, *Vaughan's* conception of negligence has appropriately come to be known for establishing an *objective* standard of care. This objective standard is used by all Anglo-American courts today. To make clear what it means for the standard to be objective, we will begin with a slightly overstated account of its objectivity that we will later soften.

Negligence law's standard of ordinary care is objective in two different ways: it is both a *general* standard and an *external* standard. A subjective standard might particularize itself for different kinds of persons with different attributes and abilities. It might ask, for example, whether the defendant used the care that would have been used by a reasonably prudent man with roughly the same IQ as, and experience of, the defendant. This sort of particularism is rejected under the objective standard in favor of a more generalizing approach. As a rule, negligence law does not assign to the reasonably prudent person a set of more specific attributes (such as a particular level of intelligence, dexterity, etc.), but asks only what a reasonably prudent person under the circumstances would have done. Second, a subjective standard might focus on what was going on inside the mind of a defendant—on whether he or she was actually being mindful of the risk of harm to others at the time he or she was acting. By contrast, an objective standard focuses on the external conduct of the defendant. The question at hand is whether the actions undertaken by the defendant were the actions a reasonably prudent person would have performed.

Of these two dimensions of objectivity—generalizing and externalizing—the latter is in some ways easier to accept than the former. There are many advantages to tort rules that gauge liability on the basis of conduct rather than subjective state of mind. First, the inner mental state of an actor can be difficult for the fact finder to ascertain. Second, it is the defendant's conduct, not his state of mind, that hurts the plaintiff or invades her rights. Third, liability in a negligence case is civil, not criminal, which means that the defendant is not being blamed for his conduct in the strong sense of being branded an outlaw or pariah. Rather, he is being held responsible for the harmful results of his substandard conduct. The fact that he may have acted with a pure heart need not foreclose liability imposed on such terms. Finally, in reality, a jury or judge deciding a negligence case might well end up taking into account the full picture of the defendant's conduct. Indeed, it can be argued that by asking the jury or judge to look at what a reasonably prudent person would have done under the circumstances, our system invites fact finders to soften their potentially harsh judgments.

If negligence law's reliance on an external standard is relatively easy to grasp and defend, its willingness to generalize and thereby gloss over the particularities of a defendant's actual capacities is perhaps less so. Should a driver with two years' experience really be held to the same standard as a driver with twenty years' experience? Shouldn't a commercial hotel chain that charges business guests

$500 per night for a room and employs a trained staff be required to deliver safer premises than a person of modest means who permits an old college roommate to sleep on the couch in her run-down apartment? Should a blind man walking along a sidewalk be held to the same standard of careful action as a sighted one? It seems at least unfair and possibly irrational to overlook these sorts of fundamental differences in how various actors are situated. Indeed, even if judges and juries would somehow incorporate these differences, why should we leave such significant distinctions to the happenstance of what a judge or jury notices rather than building them into the legal standards themselves?

Were negligence law as nonresponsive to particularities as the foregoing questions presume, then there might be powerful grounds for complaining about its unfairness. In fact, it does not adopt so extreme a version of generalizing. Rather, it is selective about where it generalizes and where it particularizes. Physicians, and indeed most licensed professionals, are held to a standard of care that is particularized to their training, education, and specialization. A board-certified neurosurgeon will be held to the standard of care in neurosurgery of board-certified neurosurgeons. Conversely, a child will often be held to a standard of care that generalizes beyond her individual intelligence and agility but still particularizes as to her age level. Although in some jurisdictions children below a certain age (usually seven) are immunized from negligence liability, older children are expected to act with the degree of care with which a child of like age and intelligence would have acted under the circumstances. (However, minors are held to the general standard of ordinary prudence when they engage in "adult activities" such as driving a car.) Typically, commercial innkeepers are held to a higher standard of care with regard to their customers than are individual homeowners with regard to their friends; and a blind person is not expected to be as careful as a sighted person insofar as a blind person cannot be deemed careless for having failed to look where he was going while walking.

These partial concessions to particularization notwithstanding, the generalizing tendency of the standard of care is still a significant and demanding feature of negligence law in many situations. Inexperienced drivers are held to the same standard as experienced drivers; the frail and elderly are held to the same standard as the robust and vigorous; and the clueless are held to the same standard as the clever. Fear of line-drawing problems is undoubtedly part of the rationale for these rules. But so too is the normative consideration articulated in *Vaughan* itself; the norm of conduct to which we expect compliance for dangerous everyday activities such as driving should not vary with the ability to comply both because the right of others to safety does not vary with an individual's ability to conform her conduct to that standard and because there is value in having the law demand that citizens aspire to achieve ordinary levels of care, even if some are incapable of doing so on a consistent basis.

5.4.2 Ordinary Care, the Reasonably Prudent Person, and Levels of Care

What does the adjective "ordinary" connote in the phrase "ordinary care"? The answer given by negligence law has three interlocking parts. First, "ordinary care" is a phrase that invites a decision maker to define it and is particularly well suited to a system that uses non-experts as its decision makers. Be it juror or judge, the fact finder in a negligence case will often lack expertise or firsthand experience bearing directly on the conduct of the defendant. Instead, the fact finder will presumably draw upon daily experience to decide whether the defendant was being as careful as she should have been in driving a truck, storing dangerous chemicals, or handling a sharp surgical instrument. (In some cases—professional malpractice, for example—it is professional training and standards that are relevant, not daily experience, and the breach standard is accordingly quite different. *See* Chapter 6.)

Second, the significance of "ordinary" care is clarified by contrast with certain alternative standards of conduct that the law might adopt and sometimes does adopt. Although treated as part of "negligence" law, certain precedents require of actors not just ordinary care but *extraordinary care*. For example, late-nineteenth- and early-twentieth-century courts tended to require of common carriers (e.g., railways, bus companies, and cruise lines), innkeepers, and custodians of property (coat check rooms, parking lots, and repair shops) that they be extraordinarily careful with their passengers, guests, and guests' possessions. In some jurisdictions, defendants are still today held to this higher standard; in others, only ordinary care is asked of them. Ordinary care is not as fastidious as extraordinary care.

Conversely, the ordinary care standard sets a higher standard than is sometimes seen in other tort contexts. In these other settings, the defendant is subject to the less demanding requirement that he not act with *gross* negligence—an extreme and entirely inexcusable departure from ordinary care. To establish gross negligence requires proof of something more than an inadvertent slip or blunder that, depending on the circumstances, can constitute failures of ordinary care.

Third, the standard of ordinary care is defined by reference to the conduct of a prototype: the reasonably prudent person under the circumstances. It is notable that the phrase "reasonably prudent person" utilizes the term "reasonably" as an adverb to modify *just how prudent or how careful* this prototypical figure is. "Reasonably" in this context connotes a moderate degree. Negligence law, though demanding in ways discussed above, does not ask us to be takers of optimal precautions. It is enough to take adequate precautions. Sometimes the notion of the "reasonably prudent person" is glossed as the "reasonable person" or (in an older, sexist formulation) "the reasonable man." The non-optimizing, essentially moderate nature of this figure is famously described in *Blyth v. Birmingham Waterworks Co.*,[8] in which the English

---

8. (1856) 156 Eng. Rep. 1047 (Exch.).

Exchequer Court ruled that a waterworks company had not acted carelessly by failing to construct its pipes to prevent cracks and leaks in unprecedented cold temperatures. Said one of the judges:

> A reasonable man would act with reference to the average cir-
> cumstances of the temperature in ordinary years. The defendants
> had provided against such frosts as experience would have led
> men, acting prudently, to provide against; and they are not guilty
> of negligence, because their precautions proved insufficient
> against the effects of the extreme severity of the frost of 1855,
> which penetrated to a greater depth than any which ordinarily
> occurs south of the polar regions. Such a state of circumstances
> constitutes a contingency against which no reasonable man
> can provide.

5.4.3 Fault-Based Liability Contrasted to Strict Liability

There is another contrast that is closely related to the foregoing contrasts among standards of care, but worth separate mention because of the theoretical and practical significance attributed to it. This is the distinction between negligence law's ordinary care stan-dard and the idea of *strict liability*, also known as no-fault liability. (We alluded to this difference in Chapter 2 in discussing how the adoption of workers' compensation schemes had permitted employ-ees injured on the job to recover compensation without proof of employer fault.)

The basic distinction is easy enough to grasp. Under a regime of strict liability, an actor who causes harm to another is held liable simply by virtue of having caused harm. There is no further inquiry into whether the actor behaved with ordinary care; that issue is irrelevant. For example, by statute in many jurisdic-tions, a dog owner is held strictly liable if her dog bites and injures another person. Under this rule, the victim does not need to prove that the dog's owner failed to exercise care to control the dog. She needs only to show that the dog was in fact the owner's and that it in fact bit her. (The statutes recognize certain excusing conditions—e.g., if the victim was baiting the dog—but these are affirmative defenses, and the plaintiff need not prove their absence as part of her prima facie case.) Thus, even if in a given dog-bite case there is overwhelming evidence that the owner was extraordinarily careful, having spent thousands of dollars on restraining equipment and training, this evidence is legally irrelevant. She is held strictly liable.

It is difficult to overstate the attention that legal scholars have devoted to the distinction between strict liability and negligence. Economists have endlessly debated which rule is more likely to induce actors to take optimal precautions (those precautions, but only those precautions, that are cost-justified in the sense of being cheaper than the estimated value of the harms that will occur if they are not taken). Historians have likewise debated whether liability under the old writ system was essentially "strict" such that the emergence of negligence in the mid-1800s amounted to a broad shift toward a more defendant-friendly tort law. (*See* Chapter 2.) And philosophers have long argued about whether or when it is morally justifiable to impose liability without fault.

These are important and interesting debates, and we will address them in the materials that follow, particularly in Chapters 8–10. However, our view is that they tend to be framed simplistically. The conceptual difference between the idea of strict liability and fault-based liability is indeed real and sharp. But its sharpness is significantly blunted by both formal doctrine and informal practice. In terms of doctrine, one rarely encounters strict liability in its pure form—the dog-bite statutes mentioned above being an important exception. Rather, it is much more common to encounter torts that meld strict liability components, or occasional strict liability applications, with other components or applications that involve notions of fault or culpability. This is true of "property torts" such as trespass to land (discussed in Chapter 8) and even of "strict" products liability (discussed in Chapter 10).

5.4.4 The Openness of the Standard of Care

As we have seen, the concept of ordinary care is meant to be sensitive in application to the defendant's circumstances. This sensitivity, coupled with the inherent vagueness of the "ordinary care" concept, creates an open-textured standard by which to assess breach or fault. Is this openness a problem? The answer is "yes and no."

Many areas of regulatory law are intricate and fine-grained, spelling out with precision the particular obligations that a person in a certain situation has. This is the case, for example, with many tax codes. From the standpoint of those being subjected to legal regulation and legal penalty, it is desirable to have a checklist that permits them to determine with a high degree of confidence whether they have lived up to the law's requirements. But there is a downside to the checklist approach, which is that lawmakers cannot contemplate everything that it is important for someone to do or not do. In tort, new possibilities for injuries and new needs for precautions constantly arise. Moreover, it takes time to create new regulations and rules to meet new scenarios. Yet it is often critical that precautions be taken promptly.

Automobile airbags provide a good example. At a certain point, it became clear that a reasonably prudent manufacturer of cars would install passenger-side front-seat airbags. Doing so promised to save the lives of thousands of crash victims at a reasonable cost to consumers. A code of conduct enacted before this presumably would not have included the installation of airbags on its checklist of required actions. Moreover, once airbags became common features of cars, a new issue arose. Airbags are designed to work by punching against an average adult's chest with enough force to absorb the impact of a collision. But for a child or a person of short stature, an airbag's high-impact punch could cause a broken neck. With the emergence of this information, one might well suppose that a reasonably prudent manufacturer would be obligated to warn consumers of this risk and instruct them to keep children and persons of short stature out of the front passenger seat. By holding manufacturers to an open-ended standard of ordinary care, negligence law permits the recognition of this new obligation even without specific regulations.

An entirely different advantage of the openness of the negligence standard has to do with the kind of decision-making it leads to within trials. Openness entails room for discretion, which in many contexts is a desirable thing. The American legal system asks jurors to play a major role in resolving both criminal and civil disputes. (Even though few cases go to trial, the prospect of a trial by jury influences pretrial settlement negotiations and motion practice.) It does so out of certain basic democratic commitments. Tort trials call for judgments about rights and wrongs, and the American system is committed to a populist mechanism for making these judgments. The open question at the heart of negligence law—"what would a reasonably prudent person have done under these circumstances?"—invites jurors to engage in an inquiry in which they bring to bear their own values, judgments, and common sense about how people ought to behave with respect to the risk of injuring others. This is in part the significance of the law's treatment of breach as a question of "fact" to be answered by the jury rather than a question of "law" reserved for judges. (The label "fact" is not entirely helpful, since there is clearly a normative component to the judgment as to whether someone has acted with ordinary prudence. The jury has to determine how a person in the position of the defendant *ought to have* behaved.)

There are also downsides to having an open-ended breach standard. First, it makes litigation more costly as compared to a strict liability standard, since each side will have to present evidence as to whether the defendant did or did not act with ordinary care. Second, the discretion enjoyed by fact finders under the ordinary care standard is not always exercised wisely, a problem that might be controlled by a more sharply defined standard. Judges and jurors can sometimes be persuaded to impose liability on unpopular businesses that have done nothing wrong, and popular defendants can be spared liability when they have done something careless. Third, actors who are particularly likely to find themselves defending against negligence claims (e.g., manufacturers and retail store owners) often feel unable to predict what will count as lack of ordinary care. (In a skeptical moment, they and others might say that ordinary care is simply whatever a jury says it is.) Relatedly, they may also worry that judges' and jurors' judgments about conduct will be affected by "hindsight bias"—an after-the-fact inclination to suppose that the prospect of an event's happening (i.e., the injuring of the plaintiff) was clearer beforehand than it actually was. Problems of unpredictability and bias are only exacerbated when a suit is for serious injuries that can support a very large damage award. For reasons such as these, negligence law has at times, though not consistently, deployed doctrines that limit jurors' discretion in making findings on the issue of breach. Some of these doctrines are discussed in Chapter 6.

𝕸 5.5 The Cause Element: Actual Cause

After injury, duty, and breach, the last element of the negligence tort is causation. The causation element has two distinct components. One is known as "*actual cause*" (or "cause-in-fact"). The other is "*proximate cause*" (or "legal course" or "scope of liability"). This section will focus on the actual cause component of the element of cause. Proximate cause will be addressed in the next section.

In requiring proof of actual causation, the law requires the negligence plaintiff to establish that the defendant's breach of duty had something to do with the plaintiff's getting injured—that the happening of breach and injury was not mere coincidence. Suppose a restaurant carelessly serves its customer an undercooked side dish that is tainted with bacteria capable of causing severe diarrhea. Suppose further that, soon after eating at the restaurant, the customer suffers diarrhea. Although it would certainly make sense to suspect that the two events have something to do with one another, if it turns out that the customer never took a bite of the side dish, and that the side dish was the only possible source of bacteria at the restaurant, then the suspicion has proven to be false. Whatever caused the injury, it was not the defendant's carelessness, and therefore the defendant, even though it acted carelessly, cannot be held liable to the plaintiff for negligence. That the plaintiff's injury occurred soon after the defendant's careless act was a mere coincidence.

Subject to certain exceptions discussed in Chapter 6, the test for actual causation in tort cases, including negligence cases, is the *but-for test*, also known as the "necessary condition," "*sine qua non*," or "counterfactual" test. The question posed by the but-for test is easy enough to state, although answering the question in a given case may require inference and even outright speculation on the part of the fact finder. The question is this: "*But for the defendant's carelessness, would the plaintiff have suffered the injury that she suffered?*" If the answer is "No, she would not have suffered the injury," then the but-for test is satisfied and actual causation is established: the defendant's careless conduct has helped to bring about the plaintiff's injury. If the answer is "Yes, she would have suffered the injury anyway, even if the defendant had not been careless," then the test is not satisfied and the plaintiff's claim fails on the issue of actual causation.

The but-for test requires fact finders to reconstruct a hypothetical state of affairs that is in all respects identical to the actual state of affairs that led to the plaintiff's injury except for one: the defendant's carelessness is erased from the picture. Accordingly, the fact finder must engage in a certain amount of surmise in considering what would have happened in a scenario that never actually happened. In many cases, one can be extremely confident about the relevant surmise. If a perfectly healthy person dies from head injuries moments after being run over by a driver who ignores a stop sign, there will be little doubt that the careless driving has caused the death. In many other cases, however, the surmise will be more speculative. Imagine a plaintiff who lives near a chemical plant and who, because of plant managers' carelessness, is exposed for a period of time to unsafe levels of airborne chemicals. Imagine also that some of these chemicals have been shown in laboratory studies to cause cancer in a small percentage of rats exposed to high concentrations of them. If the plaintiff is diagnosed with lung cancer, it might be plausible to infer that the cancer would not have occurred without the managers' carelessness. But given both scientific uncertainty as to the exact conditions under which exposure to the chemicals generates lung cancer and the fact that lung cancer has other causes, some known and some unknown, it may also be plausible to conclude that the cancer would have occurred even if the managers had not been careless. In a case like this, plaintiffs and defendants will enlist scientific and medical experts to attempt to prove or disprove actual causation.

The issue of actual causation is by no means the only one subject to uncertainty. As we saw above, judgments about breach of duty are often contestable, though perhaps more so because of differing normative judgments than uncertainties over facts and counterfactuals. Evidentiary rules that apply to tort litigation (and other forms of civil litigation such as litigation over property rights and contract disputes) are designed in part with these uncertainties in mind. To require a tort plaintiff to establish *to a certainty* that she would not have been injured but for the defendant's carelessness is to ask too much and would guarantee that many deserving claimants would not recover. Instead, the burden of persuasion that usually applies in tort cases is set by the *preponderance-of-the-evidence* standard. It places the onus on a tort plaintiff to gather and present evidence sufficient to permit the fact finder to conclude that the plaintiff's factual allegations are *probably* true—i.e., more likely to be true than false. This burden stands in contrast to the higher burden that criminal prosecutors face, which is to prove facts beyond a reasonable doubt.

Thus, on the issue of actual causation in the case of the lung cancer victim imagined above, it will be incumbent on the plaintiff to offer proof (e.g., medical studies and expert testimony) sufficient to permit a reasonable fact finder to conclude that her assertion of a causal link between her cancer and her exposure to the defendant's chemicals is *probably true*. It follows that, even if jurors entertain some doubts—perhaps even considerable doubts—about whether the plaintiff's exposure is what caused her illness, they may still impose liability for negligence so long as they conclude that it is *more likely than not* that she would not have developed cancer *but for* the exposure.

It is important to emphasize that each of two or more actors' careless acts can function as a necessary condition of a single injury. Suppose Driver *D1*, heading north, and Driver *D2*, heading east, both fail to observe a stop sign at the same four-way intersection. The two cars collide in the center of the intersection, become interlocked, and then veer off and run down *P*, a pedestrian standing lawfully on the sidewalk. The evidence presented at trial shows quite conclusively that if either driver had heeded the relevant stop sign, the collision would not have happened and plaintiff would not have been injured. On these facts, *D1*'s carelessness is *an actual cause* of *P*'s injury. But so too is *D2*'s. Absent either driver's breach of duty, the collision would not have happened. The critical lesson of this example is that the actual-cause inquiry in negligence raises the question of whether a given actor's carelessness functioned as *a* cause of a plaintiff's injury, *not* whether it functioned as *the* cause.

To be sure, in situations in which two careless acts function as causes of a single injury, questions may arise as to whether it is *fair* to hold both actors liable, and, if it is fair, *the extent to which* each should be held liable. These, however, are *not* questions of actual causation. Instead, they are questions of *duty, proximate cause*, and/ or *apportionment*. (These subjects are addressed below, and in Chapters 6 and 12.) Suppose that, on a scorchingly hot day, a babysitter carelessly leaves an infant unattended in her car while she runs into a store in a safe neighborhood to buy a bottle of water for herself. If a vicious prison escapee takes the occasion to snatch and kill the child, the babysitter will likely *not* be held liable for the death. However, if she is spared from liability, it will not be because

her carelessness was not an actual cause of the child's death. Had
she properly minded the child, a jury might conclude, the kidnap-
ping and killing probably would not have happened. Rather, it will
be because her carelessness will not count as a *proximate cause* of
the death of the child.

⁜ 5.6 Aligning the Elements: Proximate Cause and the Relationality of Breach

Sometimes the effort to reduce a whole to its parts loses something
along the way, especially if the parts are referenced in an abbreviated form. To cook a particular dish, more than a list of ingredients
is needed; one also needs to know how to combine them. This sort
of risk is very much present in the otherwise helpful practice of
reducing negligence to a list of elements. To think of the tort only
in terms of "injury," "duty," "breach," and "cause" is to be in
danger of missing something about the tort—indeed, two aspects
of it—that are critical to defining the legal wrong of negligence.

The first of these aspects is the *relationality of breach of
duty*—"relationality of breach" for short. This is a phrase that we
have coined rather than one that is commonly used by judges
and lawyers, although they sometimes (confusingly) refer to the
same idea under the general heading of "duty." The second of
these aspects is *proximate cause*. To return to the list of negligence
elements from the beginning of this chapter, the relationality-
of-breach requirement is expressed in the phrase "by acting
carelessly toward her" that appears in the breach element. The
proximate cause requirement is, of course, expressed by the
qualification that the defendant's carelessness must not only have
been an actual cause of the plaintiff's injury, but also a proximate
cause.

We present these two aspects of negligence together because
each has a similar function, which is to make sure that the
plaintiff's allegations of duty and breach, on the one hand, and of

actual causation and injury, on the other hand, are *properly aligned* with one another. Relationality of breach requires that the carelessness about which the plaintiff is complaining is *carelessness as to persons such as her*, not carelessness as to someone else or to no one in particular. Proximate cause requires that the actual causal connection between breach and injury be the *right sort of connection*, i.e., one that is not merely haphazard.

5.6.1 The Relationality of Breach of Duty

The relationality-of-breach requirement figures centrally in the most famous twentieth-century tort case, *Palsgraf v. Long Island Railroad.*[9] Plaintiff, Mrs. Palsgraf, a paying customer of the railroad, was standing on a crowded platform at defendant's station, waiting for her train. Another train arrived and then began to pull out. As it did, a man carrying a nondescript package attempted to jump aboard one of the train's cars, landing in its open doorway. There, two train conductors attempted to steady him. In doing so, they dislodged the package, which, unbeknownst to them, contained powerful fireworks. When the package fell between the moving train and the tracks, a large explosion occurred. Its concussive force knocked over a large scale used for weighing packages that stood on the platform, perhaps thirty feet from the site where the fireworks were dropped. The scale fell onto Mrs. Palsgraf, who suffered a neurological injury as a result.

Mrs. Palsgraf sued the train company on the theory that the conductors' conduct in attempting to steady the package-carrier—acts attributable to the company through the doctrine of respondeat superior—was careless and that but for this carelessness, she would not have been injured. The jury found for her, a decision affirmed by an intermediate appellate court. However, the New York Court of

---

9. 162 N.E. 99 (N.Y. 1928).

Appeals reversed in a 4–3 decision, with the majority opinion written by Judge Cardozo.

What makes Cardozo's opinion initially puzzling is that it seems to suggest that the defendant *owed no duty of care to Mrs. Palsgraf* because she did not fall within the *Heaven-MacPherson* orbit of persons who might foreseeably be injured were railroad employees to act carelessly. Yet, as a person standing on the platform, Mrs. Palsgraf was surely someone whom the railroad could foresee harming through any number of careless acts by its employees. In any event, as a ticketed passenger, Mrs. Palsgraf quite clearly was owed a duty of care by the railroad. So why would Cardozo, author of *MacPherson*, deny that a duty of care was owed? In fact, closer inspection reveals that he identified a different problem with her negligence claim.

Granting that Mrs. Palsgraf was owed a duty of care, and granting that the jury was entitled to deem the conductors to have acted carelessly, there was still the following problem: the conductors' carelessness at most posed a risk of foreseeable injury to the package carrier and to those standing in his immediate vicinity (e.g., persons who were standing right next to the scene of the pushing and pulling and who might have been struck if the package carrier or his package fell as he was being grabbed by the guards). By contrast, their conduct could not be deemed *careless as to the physical well-being of persons standing well away from the immediate site of their actions*. It is on this point—not the existence or nonexistence of a duty owed to Mrs. Palsgraf—that the absence of foreseeability fits into Cardozo's analysis. Given the nondescript nature of the package, he reasoned, no one could foresee that actions like those taken by the conductors would have *any effect* on persons standing where Mrs. Palsgraf was standing. For this reason, the jury could not reasonably have concluded that their conduct was careless *as to her*. And therefore, even though Mrs. Palsgraf could establish that she was owed a duty of care, and even though the jury could reasonably have found that the conductors' actions were careless *as to certain persons*, she could not establish that the duty and breach elements of her claim were properly aligned up with each other. The sort of breach she needed to prove, but could not prove, was a breach of the duty owed to her, which would require evidence of conduct that was careless with regard to the physical well-being of persons standing where she was standing in relation to the site of the conductors' actions. Her inability to do so meant that her claim failed for not satisfying the relationality-of-breach requirement.

Now that we have a better sense of *Palsgraf's* rationale, it will be helpful to place it in context. One reason the decision has caused confusion is because the relationality requirement is often buried within ordinary duty and breach analysis. To say the same thing, in a wide array of cases, a plaintiff who can establish duty and prove breach will thereby also implicitly establish the relationality of breach. For example, if a careless car driver runs over a nearby pedestrian, neither the lawyers nor the court will dwell on the *Palsgraf* issue because proof of the careless driving will constitute proof of carelessness *as to* a nearby pedestrian (among others). The same is true if a doctor commits malpractice on one of her patients. The gist of a standard malpractice complaint is that the doctor has been careless *in treating the plaintiff.* Cases in which the relationality issue emerges tend to be ones that involve freakish occurrences or claims that are brought by persons injured indirectly by a defendant's careless act. As we will see, the same tends to be true with respect to proximate cause.

A somewhat more recent example a relationality-of-breach of case also comes out of the New York courts. In *Moore v. Shah*,[10] the defendant doctor was alleged to have treated his patient carelessly so as to require the patient to undergo a kidney transplant that he would otherwise not have needed. The suit, however, was brought not by the patient, but by the father of the patient, who had donated one of his kidneys to his son. In denying the father recovery, the court ruled that while the defendant's conduct was a breach of a

---

10. 458 N.Y.S.2d 33 (App. Div. 1982).

duty of care owed to the son, it was not a breach of any duty owed to the father and hence not actionable by the father.

One might be tempted to conclude that, since the relationality of breach is not a focal point of analysis in many negligence cases, it is trivial or unimportant. But this conclusion does not follow. The requirement is at work in every negligence case, just as the requirement of duty is at work even in a situation in which it is obvious that a duty was owed. And part of the reason a wide range of imaginable negligence claims are never brought is because it is quite apparent that they would run afoul of the relationality requirement, a point to which we will return in Chapter 6's discussion of claims for negligent infliction of emotional distress.

At a more theoretical or conceptual level, the relationality-of-breach requirement is part of what makes negligence a genuine tort—i.e., a relational wrong of the sort that justifies the law's giving the victim the power to respond to the wrong through a lawsuit for damages. Cardozo emphasized this point in his *Palsgraf* opinion:

> One who seeks redress at law does not make out a cause of action by showing without more that there has been damage to his person. . . . Affront to personality is still the keynote of the wrong. . . . The victim does not sue derivatively . . . to vindicate an interest invaded in the person of another. Thus to view his cause of action is to ignore the fundamental difference between tort and crime. He sues for breach of a duty owed to himself.[11]

In other words, it is entirely in keeping with the nature of torts as relational, injurious, civil wrongs (*see* Chapter 1) that a negligence plaintiff is required to establish not merely carelessness toward another person, but also carelessness as to persons such as herself. Insofar as it makes sense for there to be a legal response to careless

---

11. 162 N.E. at 101.

conduct in and of itself, irrespective of the persons toward whom the conduct was careless, that response can and often does come in the form of regulatory law.

Unlike many subsequent commentators, Judge William Andrews, the author of the *Palsgraf* dissent, clearly grasped the gist of Cardozo's reasoning. He dissented because he favored a radically different conception of negligence and of tort law. Conduct, on this account, is tortious not because it is wrongful toward a victim whom the law in turn empowers to respond to the wrong. Instead, conduct is tortious insofar as it is a wrong "to the world." In our view, there are profound problems with Andrews' way of thinking about negligence and tort. At the most general level, it has trouble making sense of why the characteristic response to a tort is the arming of the victim with a right of action as opposed to a government prosecution or some other response. At a more immediate doctrinal level, it fails to make sense of various settled aspects of tort doctrine, an issue to which we will return at various points in subsequent chapters.

5.6.2 Proximate Cause

The concept of proximate cause essentially mirrors the idea of relationality of breach, except that it ensures a proper alignment between the breach and injury elements of negligence rather than between the duty and breach elements. In short, it demands that a negligence plaintiff not only prove that the defendant's breach played a role in bringing about her injury (actual causation), but also that the injury 'flowed from' the breach in a natural or expected manner. Proximate cause analysis assumes that the plaintiff can establish under the rules discussed above that the defendant's carelessness functioned as an actual cause of her injury. The question is whether, notwithstanding the existence of actual causation, there is something about the *manner in which causation occurred* that warrants a finding of no liability.

To take an oft-invoked example, suppose a father absentmind-
edly hands his small, loaded handgun to his four-year-old son. The
gun itself is no heavier or more unwieldy than the sort of object one
would normally hand to a child of that age. While playing with the
gun, the child drops it, and it lands on his playmate's foot, breaking
her toe. If a suit were brought on behalf of the injured playmate
against the father, it would not be difficult to identify a breach of a
duty of care by the father as to the playmate. It is readily foreseeable
that if one is so careless as to give a handgun to a young child, that
child and other children playing with him might get hurt. And it is
certainly a failure to act with ordinary care to give a loaded gun to a
young child. Moreover, there is clear proof of actual causation. After
all, if the father had not been careless with his gun, the playmate
would never have been injured.

And yet the victim's claim will nonetheless fail, and it will fail on
proximate cause grounds. The danger associated with the handing
of the gun to the child is the danger of an accidental shooting and
that danger never came to pass. Because the connection between
the defendant's carelessness and the injury that actually occurred is
fortuitous rather than natural or ordinary, the plaintiff's claim fails
because of a lack of a *proximate causal link* between the defendant's
carelessness and the plaintiff's injury.

As with the *Palsgraf* requirement, it is important to keep the issue
of proximate cause in perspective. Even though this feature of negligence law blocks the imposition of liability for certain unexpected
causal sequences, it would be a mistake to suppose that *any* sort of
surprising twist or turn in the path from careless conduct to injury
will suffice to defeat liability on proximate cause grounds. Some
twists will, and some twists will not. Figuring out the line(s) that separate the ones that do from the ones that do not is not a simple task.

Much judicial and academic ink has been spilled over how to
capture the idea of proximate cause in a word or phrase. At one
time, courts were inclined to say that the causal connection between
a defendant's breach and a plaintiff's injury had to be *direct* in
order for the breach to count as a proximate cause. However, the

directness test was rejected in perhaps the most famous modern proximate cause case, an English Privy Council decision that has heavily influenced Anglo-American doctrine and is commonly referred to as *Wagon Mound*.[12] In fact, the Privy Council issued two *Wagon Mound* decisions. Each addressed a different claim arising out of the same incident. The more important of the two, which will focus this discussion, is the first, which is often referred to as *Wagon Mound (No. 1)*.

The ship Wagon Mound was moored at a wharf in Sydney Harbor. Its crew carelessly spilled furnace oil into the harbor. Workers at nearby Morts Dock were repairing another ship (the Corrimal), which called for the use of welding torches. Their supervisor noticed the spill and discussed with the owner of the wharf where the Wagon Mound was moored whether there was a danger that the oil slick might ignite. The supervisor concluded that there was no danger and ordered his men back to work. The next day, sparks from the welding operation at Morts Dock ignited some floating debris, which in turn ignited the oil, resulting in a fire that destroyed Morts Dock and the Corrimal.

Wagon Mound (No. 1) concerned a negligence suit brought by the owners of Morts Dock against the owners of the Wagon Mound. Injury, duty, breach, and actual causation were not at issue. Instead, the difficult question was proximate cause. On the basis of expert testimony, the trial court concluded that the crew of the Wagon Mound could not reasonably have foreseen that an oil slick of furnace oil atop water posed a risk of fire, only that it ran the risk of mucking up others' property and equipment. Nonetheless, applying the directness test, the trial court held for Morts Dock, reasoning that the link between the spilling of the oil and the burning of the dock was "direct" in the sense that the slick had reached the dock without the intervention of some other person or force.

---

12. Overseas Tankship (U.K.), Ltd. v. Morts Dock & Eng'g Co., [1961] 1 All E.R. 404 (P.C.).

On appeal, the Privy Council reversed, rejecting the directness test as arbitrary and artificial. If it is entirely predictable that one's carelessness might cause harm to another indirectly, the opinion asks rhetorically, why should indirectness in and of itself provide a reason to deny liability? Conversely, if harm to a victim is entirely unpredictable, why should the fact that it is caused directly provide a reason to hold the careless actor who causes the harm responsible? Under the heading of proximate cause, the court insisted, the correct question to ask is whether the sequence of events that led from the defendant's carelessness to the plaintiff's injury was a reasonably foreseeable sequence. Since here the trial judge, acting as fact finder, had concluded that the ignition of the floating oil was not foreseeable, the spilling of the oil could not have been a proximate cause of the destruction of the dock by fire, even though it was of course an actual cause.

The use by modern courts of foreseeability instead of directness as the lynch-pin of proximate cause analysis in many respects marks an improvement. Yet it also can create confusion because, as we have seen, foreseeability sometimes figures in the analysis of breach of duty. Indeed, some skeptics have argued that judges' use of foreseeability in applying the concepts of duty, breach *and* proximate cause demonstrates that these supposedly distinct concepts are redundant, except that duty poses a question for the judge, while breach and proximate cause are for the jury. This skeptical view is mistaken, as can be shown by returning to the dropped-gun example. Suppose that a broken toe to the companion from being struck by the dropped gun was *not* a reasonably foreseeable consequence of the father handing the gun to his child—suppose the child was eleven and the companion was wearing shoes. How would the absence of foreseeability figure into the clements of a negligence suit against the father? It would be preposterous to assert that the father owed no duty to act carefully with respect to the physical injuries that persons in his immediate vicinity (including the companion) might suffer as a result of his handing the gun to his child. It would also be preposterous to suppose that the father cannot be found to have acted carelessly toward a person such as the companion by handing a loaded gun to his child in the companion's presence. Insofar as unforeseeability poses a problem for this negligence claim, it can only be a proximate cause problem, not a problem pertaining to breach of duty.

Some readers might bristle at this last contention and argue that in fact the breaking of a playmate's toe by the child was foreseeable or at least that a jury could so find. We have some sympathy with this complaint, though not because we think breach and proximate cause are redundant. Rather, it is because there is probably a better way to express the concerns that the *Wagon Mound* court rightly expressed with regard to the directness test. This 'better way' has been articulated by a number of scholars under different names, including *the risk rule* and the *scope of the risk* test. Regardless of the name, the basic idea is this: in order for a careless act that causes an injury to count as a proximate cause of that injury, the injury must be *the realization of one of the risks that leads the law to deem the conduct careless in the first place*. When the law 'says' to a father, "Don't hand a loaded gun to your child," it is prohibiting and condemning that conduct on certain grounds, with certain scenarios in mind. A careless shooting is the most obvious of these scenarios, and were the child to have accidentally shot his playmate, one would have no trouble concluding that the shooting was the realization of one of the risks—indeed the principal risk—that leads the law to label the father's conduct as careless. By contrast, the risk of injury through the gun being dropped (again assuming it is not particularly heavy or unwieldy) is not one of the risks that rendered the father's conduct careless with respect to his son's playmate, and hence the realization of that risk does not generate liability.

Although we think risk-rule formulations tend to frame the proximate cause requirement more elegantly and sharply, we readily concede that its application, like that of almost any legal test, requires the exercise of judgment about how to describe the risk in question. If one describes the relevant risk in sufficiently generic and abstract terms (e.g., the conduct of handing the gun to a child was careless because it was conduct that risked some sort of physical harm to someone by some means), then the risk rule will be readily satisfied in all but the strangest of cases. If one describes it narrowly (e.g., the conduct was careless insofar as it involved the handing of a .35 caliber pistol with a full clip of bullets to a child under the age of seven who was at the time less than five feet away from his playmate), then many injuries will be deemed to fall outside the scope of the rule. This 'levels of generality' problem is endemic to negligence law and to law generally and requires lawyers, jurors, and judges to exercise judgment about appropriate descriptions. Although the correctness of different descriptions will in some cases be contested, in many they will not be.

It is also probably the case that, however useful, the risk rule does not fully cover the proximate cause terrain, or, if it does, that it does so as a kind of 'umbrella' concept that houses several distinct but related ideas. For example, some proximate cause cases hinge not so much on the type of risk that unfolded into the plaintiff's injury as on the *timing* with which events unfolded. Imagine a truck driver who carelessly runs a car driver off the road. Fortunately, no injuries or damage result, and after a few minutes, the car driver resumes his trip. Five minutes later, the car driver is injured in a collision with another car for which neither car driver was at fault. If the injured car driver were to sue the truck driver, he could plausibly assert that his injury in the subsequent car crash was actually caused by the truck driver's carelessness. After all, but for his being delayed by being run off the road by the careless truck driver, he would not have been at the intersection at the time he collided with the other car driver. Moreover, the car crash arguably amounts to the realization of one of the risks that prompted the law to deem the truck driver's driving careless—namely, the risk of collision with other vehicles. Yet there still would be no liability here because the risk posed by the careless truck driver to the car driver had already *run its course* by the time the car driver was injured in the later collision. The notion at work here is that some risks 'expire.' In the language of one famous opinion, there is no negligence liability for an injury caused by carelessness if the "disturbed waters [created by the carelessness] have become placid and normal again" prior to the occurrence of the injury.[13]

Finally, as with the *Palsgraf* rule of relationality, it is worth taking a step back to consider what is being accomplished by negligence law's proximate cause requirement. The standard answer given by contemporary courts and commentators is that proximate cause prevents the imposition of "excessive" liability. Unfortunately, the phrase "excessive" is ambiguous. Among other things, it might refer to the idea that, without a proximate cause requirement, negligence law will generate (1) more aggregate liability across all negligence cases than society is willing to tolerate; (2) more aggregate liability than can be permitted if certain industries or professions can hope to remain viable; (3) more negligence litigation than the court system can handle; or (4) more liability for particular defendants than is fair to impose on them. For this and other reasons, talk of excessiveness is more unhelpful than helpful. Proximate cause is not a 'floodgate' or filter against "too much" liability, whatever that means. Like the relationality-of-breach requirement, proximate cause is part of what makes negligence a tort. In order for a victim to be entitled to complain that *she has been wronged*, in the tort sense of having been wronged, she must show that what has happened is both that the defendant acted wrongfully toward her and that her injury counts as a realization of the potential for injury that rendered this conduct wrongful.

🎶 5.7 A Word on Defenses

We have been discussing to this point the elements that a plaintiff must prove to establish that she has in fact been the victim of negligence. As noted at the outset of this chapter, however, the tort of

---

13. Marshall v. Nugent, 222 F.2d 604, 611 (1st Cir. 1955).

negligence, like all torts, recognizes certain *affirmative defenses*. Affirmative defenses are legally recognized grounds for defeating liability even when a legal wrong has been committed. To treat these grounds as affirmative defenses is to say that it is the defendant's burden, rather than the plaintiff's, to raise them in court pleadings and to prove them.

Some tort affirmative defenses, such as *statute of limitations* defenses that bar claims simply for being brought too late, are procedural. Others amount to justifications for conduct that would otherwise be tortious. To use an example involving a tort other than negligence, a person who commits the tort of battery by intentionally shooting another can justify the battery, and thereby escape liability, by proving that the shooting was in *self-defense* and was a proportionate response to the threat from the victim. Still others take the form of status-based *immunities*. For example, the law renders certain governmental entities immune from tort liability simply by virtue of their being government entities.

Although, as indicated, several affirmative defenses are potentially available to negligence defendants, the defense most commonly raised in negligence suits is that of *comparative fault*. Recall the case of Pedestrian versus Driver from the beginning of this chapter. Suppose Pedestrian is able to prove her case against Driver. Now suppose that Driver in turn can show that the accident resulted in part because Pedestrian, for no good reason, darted out into the middle of the street without looking and chose not to use a nearby crosswalk marked by flashing lights. Based on this evidence, the fact finder (judge or jury) would be entitled to find that Pedestrian's own fault contributed to her injury.

What is the effect of such a finding? The answer can depend on which of three different versions of comparative fault has been adopted by the law applicable to the case at hand. Under the version of comparative fault known as *contributory negligence*, any fault on the part of the plaintiff, even if only a minor contributing factor to the plaintiff's injury, disqualifies the plaintiff from recovering anything from the defendant, even though the defendant was at fault too—indeed, even if the defendant was *more* at fault than the plaintiff.

Contributory negligence was once the dominant rule, but because of its harshness as applied to modestly at-fault plaintiffs, it was abandoned by most jurisdictions in the mid- to late-twentieth century. In its place arose regimes of *pure comparative fault* and *modified comparative fault*. Under a pure comparative fault regime, the fact finder in Driver versus Pedestrian would be asked to assign percentages of fault to each of the two parties, with the total percentage adding up to 100 percent. Plaintiff would then recover a corresponding percentage of the total damages awarded to her. For example, if the fact finder sets Pedestrian's damages at $100,000 but deems her 25 percent at fault for her injuries, she will recover only $75,000. Alternatively, if the fact finder were to deem Pedestrian to be 65 percent at fault, she would recover $35,000. Modified comparative fault regimes—now in placed in about two-thirds of U.S. jurisdictions—work in the same way but with one important difference. In a modified regime, if the plaintiff is found to be *more at fault than the defendant* (or in some jurisdictions, equally or more at fault), the plaintiff recovers no damages whatsoever. Thus, in a modified comparative fault jurisdiction, the 65 percent at-fault Pedestrian would stand to lose her claim against Driver.

A related set of negligence defenses goes under the heading of *assumption of risk*. Assumption of risk comes in two forms: *express* and *implied*. Express assumption of risk is really a doctrine of waiver. When it applies, it is because a plaintiff has, by means of a contract or other agreement, prospectively waived the right that tort law would otherwise grant to her to sue the defendant for carelessly injuring her. Implied assumption of risk, as its name suggests, consists of *conduct* on the part of the plaintiff that indicates both her actual awareness that the defendant is acting or might act carelessly in a way that obviously does threaten or would threaten injury to the plaintiff, as well as a decision on the part of the plaintiff to proceed nonetheless to encounter that risk. Both forms of assumption of risk and their relationship to comparative fault are discussed in Chapter 6.

SIX

Negligence
Advanced Topics

THIS CHAPTER DELVES MORE DEEPLY into the negligence tort, exploring refinements to the core concepts of injury, duty, breach, and cause, as well as affirmative defenses. It does so primarily by analyzing famous judicial opinions that are often featured in introductory torts courses. It differs from other chapters in providing a detailed picture of one particular tort. Our degree of attention to negligence reflects the comparable degree of attention given to the tort by modern courts. It may also further demonstrate that negligence is an 'umbrella' tort that houses a cluster of related forms of injurious wrongdoing.

✻ 6.1 Limited-Duty Rules

Because of duty-expanding decisions such as *Heaven v. Pender* and *MacPherson v. Buick* (discussed in Chapter 5), negligence law in various settings now requires individuals and firms to take care against causing physical harm to any person who foreseeably might suffer such harm were the individual or firm to act carelessly. Thus, whenever a person operates a motor vehicle or a company markets a product, she or it does so subject to this duty. Yet these same decisions left intact a number of *limited-duty* rules that in other settings define narrower obligations of care. Perhaps the most notable doctrinal trend in negligence law from roughly 1920 to 1980 involved efforts by courts to remove some of these limitations. These efforts have generally resulted not in the abolition of limited-duty rules, but in their relaxation. In the United States, no court played a bigger part in this story than the California Supreme Court, which is why we will consider several of its opinions in this section.

6.1.1 Liability for Dangerous Conditions on Premises

An important set of limited-duty rules has traditionally applied—and in some form continue to apply—to owners and occupiers of property ("possessors"). These rules concern the obligations of possessors to remove, repair, or provide warnings about *dangerous conditions* such as uneven or slick surfaces, unsound structures, or unguarded ditches or bodies of water.

The duty rules in this domain traditionally have been keyed to the terms on which the victim has entered or remains on the property. Under common law, possessors of land owed *invitees*—persons explicitly or implicitly invited onto the premises in furtherance of the possessor's business or institutional purposes—premises that were reasonably safe for ordinary use. Note that, insofar as courts use a phrase like "reasonably safe" to specify *the condition* of the premises, as opposed to using "ordinary care" to describe *the measures* that the possessor must take to make the premises safe, the duty rule for invitees perhaps approached strict liability. That a pocket of strict liability might exist in this corner of negligence law makes a certain amount of sense. One might plausibly argue that persons invited onto premises for the possessor's own purposes have received an implicit promise or warranty from her that they will be safe, such that if they are not, and if an invitee is injured as a result, he will have a cause of action regardless of how careful the possessor has been.

By contrast, common law held that, as to *licensees* (persons permitted on the property, but not for the possessor's purposes), possessors owed a narrower and more specific duty to alert them to *hidden* dangers of which the possessor knew or should have known. Under this rule, if a licensee was injured by a clearly visible but dangerous condition that a reasonable person in the position of the possessor would have fixed, the licensee would have no cause of action because of the limited nature of possessors' duties with respect to licensees.

Finally, persons entering without permission—*trespassers*—were generally said to be owed no duty of care, such that they would be denied recovery even if harmed by a dangerous condition resulting from the possessor's neglect. Notwithstanding the no-duty-to-trespassers rule, possessors remained obligated to refrain from *intentionally harming* trespassers. Thus in the famous case of *Katko v. Briney*,[1] the owners of an abandoned farmhouse who arranged a deadly trap for would-be burglars were held liable for battery to a burglar who was shot in the leg when he fell victim to the trap. (*See* Chapter 7.)

By virtue of courts' reliance on the three duty categories, many persons injured by unsafe property conditions have been and still are denied relief even when injured because of unsafe premises. Reacting to this state of affairs, the California Supreme Court in *Rowland v. Christian* took the aggressive step of abolishing the categories altogether.[2] Plaintiff James Rowland had stopped by the rental apartment of defendant Nancy Christian looking for a mutual friend. While there, he severely lacerated his hand on a cracked sink handle. He sued Christian and the apartment's owner for negligence. Lower courts in California had adopted a defendant-friendly rule specifying that possessors owed social guests (licensees) only a duty to refrain from *willfully* injuring them. The high court took the occasion not only to revise this idiosyncratic feature of California tort law, but also to eliminate the special duty categories for premises liability claims. Henceforth, possessors would be held

---

1. 183 N.W.2d 657 (Iowa 1971).

2. 443 P.2d 561 (Cal. 1968).

to a general duty of ordinary care owed to anyone who might enter the property. In the court's eyes, the common law's limited-duty scheme was archaic, arbitrary, and inegalitarian. A famous passage from the opinion reads: "A man's life or limb does not become less worthy of protection by the law nor a loss less worthy of compensation under the law because he has come upon the land of another without permission or with permission but without a business purpose."[3]

The most immediate practical effect of *Rowland* was to shift decision-making power in premises-liability cases from judge to jury. Applying the traditional duty rules, judges could and often would dismiss claims by licensees and trespassers at an early stage of litigation. Under *Rowland*, these same claims now should go to the jury for the fact-intensive breach inquiry into whether, all things considered, the possessor exercised ordinary prudence with respect to the safety of the premises. In principle, the jury can still take into account the plaintiff's 'status' (e.g., whether he entered with or without permission). However, these circumstances are treated nder *Rowland* as but one factor in the jury's decision on the multifaceted issue of whether the possessor exercised ordinary care.

Rowland is often hailed as a standard-bearer for progressive judicial law reform. Yet its legacy is complex. The court's skepticism about the traditional duty categories was in some respects understandable. Judicial attempts to distinguish invitees from licensees have at times approached farce. (Is someone who enters a store to use its bathroom, but with no intent to shop there, an invitee or a licensee?) More important, courts and commentators have had trouble explaining why this distinction should matter for purposes of determining possessors' duties of care. A decade prior to *Rowland*, England's Parliament enacted a statute abolishing the distinction between invitees and licensees. Since 1968, roughly half the states have adopted the rule that possessors owe reasonable care

---

3. 443 P.2d at 568.

to all those who enter property by permission, regardless of the purpose of the entry.

Yet it is equally noteworthy that fewer than ten states have endorsed *Rowland's* abolition of the distinction between persons who enter by permission and trespassers. (For its part, Parliament in 1984 enacted a law requiring a possessor to provide limited protection to trespassers against dangerous conditions.) Thus, on the issue of the duty owed to trespassers, *Rowland's* progressive impulse arguably ran roughshod over plausible and widely held sentiments about the rights of possessors. Is it really incumbent on them to exercise care for the safety of those forbidden from entering? Does it really offend notions of equality to deny such persons the right to sue possessors for injuries caused by dangers on land on which they had no right to be?

Answers to these questions depend in part on the type of trespasser envisioned. It surely offends ordinary sensibilities to suppose that a felonious trespasser—e.g., burglar *B* who trips on owner *O's* poorly maintained walkway as he (*B*) is breaking into *O's* house— should be able to sue for unsafe premises. *Rowland* seems to envision that juries will throw out a claim of this sort on "no-breach" grounds or on a finding of comparative fault on *B's* part. Yet it is unclear how the plaintiff's being a trespasser should figure in the breach inquiry given that it concerns what the possessor has or hasn't done to make the premises safe. Moreover, comparative fault is today only a partial defense in many jurisdictions, and one must imagine that at least some burglars are injured by dangerous conditions during burglaries notwithstanding their having acted with great care to protect themselves from injury.

On the other hand, it is not difficult to imagine a different kind of trespass that might generate a different intuition about duty and liability. A young child who is drawn onto a neighbor's property because it contains a tree well suited to climbing is, if he proceeds without permission, no less a trespasser than a burglar. Should this child be deprived of a right to sue the homeowner if, on his way to climb the tree, he is badly injured when he falls into an unguarded, deep hole which the homeowner was aware of and which he could easily have roped off? Even under the traditional framework that *Rowland* rejected, courts have long recognized exceptions to the no-duty-to-trespassers rule, including an exception for *attractive nuisances*—conditions on land that could be expected to draw the interest of, and pose a danger to, young children who might not appreciate the danger. The retention by most U.S. courts of the no-duty-to-trespassers rule, subject to exceptions such as the attractive nuisance exception, perhaps attests that *Rowland* was overzealous in supposing that there is no role in modern premises liability law for limited duty or no duty rules as applied to some classes of trespassers.

6.1.2 Affirmative Duties

Another California Supreme Court decision that pertains to a different part of negligence law is today equally emblematic of that court's mid-twentieth-century quest to expand the reach of negligence by expanding the circumstances under which a duty of care is owed to a certain kind of potential victim. This decision is *Tarasoff v. Board of Regents of the University of California*.[4] Instead of focusing on premises liability, *Tarasoff* was concerned with affirmative duties—that is, the application of negligence law to situations in which the defendant's alleged carelessness consists of an *unreasonable failure to take positive steps to protect or rescue the plaintiff from a danger arising from a source other than the defendant.*

To appreciate the significance of *Tarasoff*, one must first understand that negligence law has traditionally been reluctant to recognize affirmative duties. Whereas decisions such as *MacPherson* helped establish a broad duty to take care that one's own conduct does not cause physical injury to others, there is no comparable

---

4. 551 P.2d 334 (Cal. 1976).

tort duty to render assistance to another. Thus, absent special circumstances, there is no tort liability for failures to rescue or protect. Imagine a pedestrian *A* who sees that another pedestrian *B* is about to step unwittingly into the street and in front of a moving car that will surely hit *B*. Now imagine that *A* is so indecent as to say nothing, and that *B* is run down. Although we might readily condemn him as callous or worse, *A* will face no tort liability. *A* owed *B* a legal duty not to push him into the street intentionally, and also owed *B* a duty to take care not to knock him accidentally into the path of moving cars. But *A* owed no duty to take steps to protect or rescue *B* from a peril that was not of his (*A*'s) creation.

The no-duty-to-rescue rule has supporters and critics. Supporters argue that it comports with the idea that tort law should be primarily concerned with preventing harm rather than promoting benevolence, and that a contrary rule would be overly demanding, given that there are many situations in which one person is in a position to benefit another by lending assistance. (If tort law recognized a duty to rescue, would it be tortious for the relatively well-off not to give a portion of their wealth to persons for whom the money could prevent disease or starvation?) Critics claim that the law is entitled to ask of citizens that they make at least modest efforts to help others. They also argue that any concerns about overly demanding duties can be met by crafting a rule specifying a limited duty to take *reasonable steps* to protect or rescue (as opposed to a duty requiring the rescue actually to succeed), and further specifying that it applies only if (a) the potential victim faces *imminent physical peril,* (b) of which the would-be rescuer is actually aware, (c) in a situation in which the rescuer can provide aid *easily and without danger to herself.*

Whatever their merits, the latter arguments have not dislodged the no-duty-to-rescue rule from its place as the default rule in contemporary negligence law. However, there are exceptions to the rule, some widely embraced, others more selectively adopted. The particular exception articulated by the California Supreme Court in the *Tarasoff* decision is of the latter sort, though it also provides an occasion to mention other more entrenched affirmative duties to rescue or protect.

Dr. Moore, a psychotherapist employed by the University of California, was treating a man surnamed Poddar as an outpatient. During a therapy session, Poddar confessed his intention to kill a young woman named Tatiana Tarasoff. Dr. Moore took the threat seriously enough that he asked campus police to confine Poddar. However, the police decided to release Poddar with a warning to stay away from Tatiana. Two months later, Poddar killed Tatiana.

Tatiana's parents sued Dr. Moore and the police. They alleged that both defendants had carelessly failed to confine Poddar and had carelessly failed to warn Tatiana of Poddar's plan. The court rejected the first theory on the basis of a California statute that, out of a concern to protect patients' liberty, immunized therapists and police from liability for decisions *not* to commit psychiatric patients. However, it endorsed the plaintiff's failure-to-warn theory as against Dr. Moore, though not as against the police defendants. Thus *Tarasoff* created the rule, now the law in many U.S. jurisdictions, that requires a *treating therapist* who knows or should know that *her patient* plans to harm an *identifiable potential victim* to make reasonable steps to protect that potential victim. (Among courts that follow *Tarasoff*, it is generally accepted that reasonable steps consist of a reasonable effort to warn the victim of the danger posed to her by the patient.)

While clearly innovative, *Tarasoff* was not without some basis in precedent. As noted above, the no-duty-to-rescue rule has histori-cally admitted of important exceptions. For example, one who *vol-untarily commences a rescue* is obligated not to 'botch' or abandon it. (Could one argue that this exception ought to have applied to Dr. Moore or the police?) Also certain pre-tort *special relationships* will support a duty to protect and rescue. Respectively, a store owner, a school, and a hotel operator must take reasonable steps to assist a customer, a student, and a guest whom it knows (or should know) to be in need of assistance while on its premises. These and other relationships sometimes support the imposition of liability in a situation in which the defendant fails to protect the victim against attack by a third party. For example, employers have been held liable for not doing enough to prevent one employee from attacking another. Likewise, building owners have sometimes been held to owe permitted entrants a duty to take measures to prevent them from being attacked in the building's public spaces. (*See* section 6.6 below.)

Note that in all of the foregoing situations, the plaintiff's claim to be owed protection by the defendant rests on *her* having enjoyed a pre-tort special relationship with the defendant. No such relationship existed between Dr. Moore and Tatiana. In certain situations, however, courts have recognized a different kind of special relationship-based affirmative duty, namely, one in which the defendant is charged with a duty to foreseeable victims to take care to maintain control over a person who has been placed in his custody, as is the case for jailers with respect to prisoners. In addition, as the *Tarasoff* court noted, some prior decisions had held doctors liable to patients' family members for carelessly failing either to diagnose the patient's infectious disease, or for failing to warn the patient of the risk that he might infect others, as a result of which the disease was transmitted to a family member. *Tarasoff* thus fuses the idea of an affirmative duty based on a special relationship between the defendant and a potential wrongdoer (as opposed to the victim) with the idea that doctors owe special duties to alert identifiable persons whom the doctor knows to be at risk of physical harm because of something related to her patient's medical treatment (in *Tarasoff*, a dangerous patient's expression of intent to harm a particular victim).

Tarasoff is also interesting because of the interaction it generated between the legal and medical professions. As we will see below, negligence law contains special rules of breach that apply to physicians (and certain other professionals) that are meant to *discourage* judges and juries from second-guessing how physicians practice medicine. One might therefore have expected the California court to heed legal briefs submitted by psychiatrists and psychologists strenuously resisting the recognition of a duty to warn. To do so, the physicians argued, would undermine physician-patient confidentiality by obligating the physician to make known certain information the patient had confided to her, and thereby to inhibit effective therapy. Somewhat sheepishly, they also insisted that they lack the ability to predict with accuracy when a patient can be expected to act on a professed intent to harm another. Undaunted, the California court insisted that it was not asking too much of therapists to require them to exercise judgment about when it will be necessary to contact the potential victims of their patients.

Still another of *Tarasoff*'s notable features is the way in which it blends normative and social-scientific analysis. Relying on little more than common sense speculation, the court opined with confidence that its ruling, despite mandating the disclosure of certain therapist-patient communications, would not deter patients from seeking treatment. Likewise, it supposed, over physicians' protests, that therapists will be able to distinguish with reasonable accuracy between meaningful and empty threats from their patients. If the court had scant empirical evidence for these suppositions, should it have relied on them as key grounds for its holding?

Or would the court have done better to instead focus on more overtly normative considerations—that it is fair or otherwise appropriate to expect this sort of conduct of physicians? Perhaps it was reluctant to do so because emphasis on normative arguments would invite a different set of questions and criticisms. In particular, the court would have been left to defend its decision to focus on therapists to the exclusion of other classes of persons who might be in a position to warn strangers against dangers posed by third parties. In fact, neither the California court nor other courts have extended *Tarasoff* to cases in which an attacker has made known his plans to harm someone to a religious advisor, a teacher, a close business associate, a friend, or a lawyer. Thus, none of these actors face the prospect of liability for failing to warn an intended victim. Why therapists and only therapists? Perhaps the explanation resides in the court's sense that doctors have special public health responsibilities associated with their professional training and status that these other actors do not.

6.1.3 Pure Economic Loss

Premises liability and affirmative duty cases tend to involve claims arising out of physical injuries. As we noted in Chapter 5, other forms of harm will sometimes suffice to satisfy the injury element of the plaintiff's claim. These include *emotional distress unrelated to physical injury* and *loss of wealth unrelated to the physical destruction of property*. However, claims for these forms of injury are subject to limited-duty rules. Claims for negligent infliction of emotional distress are discussed in the next section. This section discusses the rules for *"pure" economic loss*. The adjective "pure" indicates the absence of any tangible property damage suffered by the plaintiff.

As a rule, Anglo-American negligence law does not recognize a duty to take care against causing another to suffer loss of wealth or prospective wealth. This, of course, is in contrast to the rule that one owes a duty to take care not to cause foreseeable physical damage to the property of others, including land, buildings, and personal possessions. The leading U.S. decision for this rule is *Robins Dry Dock & Repair Co. v. Flint*,[5] a Supreme Court decision penned by legendary jurist Justice Oliver Wendell Holmes, Jr.

Plaintiff Flint chartered (leased) a steamboat from the ship's owner. By the terms of the charter, Flint was required to dock the ship for regular maintenance but was also relieved of the obligation to pay the owner for the use of the ship while it was being repaired. The owner separately contracted with Robins to perform this maintenance. During one service stop, Robins carelessly damaged a propeller that was to be installed on the ship, causing a two-week delay while another propeller was obtained. The ship's owner

---

5. 275 U.S. 303 (1927).

settled with Robins for the loss of two weeks' worth of charter revenues that it would have obtained from Flint had the boat not been damaged. Meanwhile, Flint sued Robins alleging that Robins' negligence caused it to lose two weeks worth of profits it would have earned had the ship been available to it.

Emphasizing that loss of profit to *someone*—whether the owner or a charterer—was an entirely foreseeable consequence of Robins' careless damaging of the ship, the trial court and the lower appellate court held that Flint could recover from Robins. However, the Supreme Court reversed, reasoning that Robins had committed no wrong as to Flint. Said Justice Holmes with characteristic confidence: "[N]o authority need be cited to show that, as a general rule . . . a tort to the person or property of one man does not make the tort-feasor liable to another merely because the injured person was under a contract with that other unknown to the doer of the wrong."[6] In other words, Robins' tort obligation to use care in repairing the ship was an obligation owed exclusively to the owner whose property stood to be physically damaged by Robins' carelessness, not to anyone else, including others who might foreseeably be caused economic loss by Robins' failure to exercise care.

Robins itself concerned a situation in which the defendant's carelessness interfered with the plaintiff's ability to benefit from a contractual arrangement. However, it probably carries even greater significance as a limitation on liability in settings in which there is no contractual relationship between the plaintiff suing for economic loss and the person whose property is damaged. For example, suppose that truck driver T carelessly runs his truck into columns supporting a highway overpass, shutting down the overpass for several weeks. Even if G, the owner of a nearby gas station, can prove that he has lost business because traffic was diverted during the period of closure, G will not be able to recover from T. Neither G nor his property were harmed by T's carelessness, only

---

6. 275 U.S. at 309.

the profitability of his business, and tort law imposes no duty on T to take care against causing such harm, even if it was a perfectly foreseeable consequence of T's misconduct.

Arguably, the intervening years have seen some softening of the hard edges of the *Robins* rule. For example, some courts have allowed fisherman to recover from negligent polluters for lost revenues even though the contaminated but as-yet uncaught fish probably cannot be deemed the 'property' of the fisherman. (At most, the fisherman enjoyed a license to attempt to catch the fish.) More broadly, a now-famous New Jersey Supreme Court decision allowed an airline to recover from a defendant that accidentally ruptured a tanker filled with a combustible chemical. The risk of an explosion induced officials to order the temporary evacuation of the plaintiff's nearby offices, which caused the plaintiff to lose revenues.[7] Such an event, the court reasoned, was not merely foreseeable to the defendant, but highly foreseeable, given the proximity of the plaintiff's place of business and the fact that tankers containing hazardous materials routinely were present on the defendant's property. An alternative, speculative, and not entirely satisfactory explanation for this holding is that the court saw in plaintiff's claim a winning combination of elements drawn from three different torts—negligence, nuisance and strict liability for abnormally dangerous activity—none of which was established in its own right: to wit, careless handling of combustible materials by the defendant (which might have supported a negligence or strict liability claim had there been property damage) causing a nuisance-like but only temporary interference with plaintiff's ability to use its property. (Nuisances and abnormally dangerous activities are discussed, respectively, in Chapters 8 and 9.)

Robins' status as a pillar of tort law is somewhat odd, because it is not technically a tort-law decision. Rather, it involves the

---

7. People Express Airlines, Inc. v. Consolidated Rail Corp., 495 A.2d 107 (N.J. 1985).

application of *admiralty law*, a distinct body of federal judge-made law that governs activities on navigable waters in the United States. Moreover, about a decade after *Robins* was decided, the Supreme Court held in *Erie Railroad Company. v. Tompkins*[8] that U.S. federal courts lack authority to fashion substantive rules of tort law, which is instead the exclusive province of state courts and legislatures. One might have expected that progressive state courts would exercise their power in the domain of tort law to depart from *Robins*, which constitutes only an advisory decision outside the domain of admiralty law. As we will see, other admiralty law decisions rendered by federal judges have been similarly influential in the development of tort law.

What, if anything, justifies the *Robins* no-duty rule? Courts today are prone to emphasize that the rule functions to limit what would otherwise be 'endless' and 'disproportionate' liability, given that every careless act that injures someone's person or property promises to have further economic ripple effects. For example, if a ship's captain carelessly causes an oil spill in a busy harbor, causing the harbor to be closed for months, it could easily have adverse economic consequences for other ship owners, businesses that were planning to transport their goods in and out of the harbor, local fishermen, local merchants such as repair shops and restaurants, their employees, the stores at which those employees purchase food and other supplies, and so forth.

The idea that the law needs a no-duty rule that sets 'floodgates' against liability to these sorts of victims may seem counterintuitive. After all, the actors who will most benefit from this rule are precisely those whose carelessness stands to cause particularly widespread harm. But tort is not a system of punishment on the basis of blameworthiness. It is, as Justice Holmes emphasized in *Robins*, a law for empowering victims of wrongs to respond to them. And, with certain exceptions, the law deems accidental interferences

---

8. 304 U.S. 64 (1938).

with economic expectancies not to be legal wrongs. (By contrast, certain *intentional* interferences with others' business arrangements can be tortious, though courts tend to require proof that the interference was not merely intentional, but also motivated by spite toward the victim, or carried about by fraudulent or otherwise independently unlawful means (*See* Chapter 8.).) One rationale for not treating merely careless interferences with economic opportunities as wrongs is that, in market-based economies, one's interest in the continued profitability of one's business or activities is already subject to the vagaries of economic competition. Given this baseline of fragility, tort law opts to treat the interest in continued business as not warranting protection from careless interference.

Although *Robins* sets the rule, it is subject to important exceptions. As is the case for the rule of no affirmative duty (discussed above), the most important of these exceptions arise when there is a special relationship between the careless actor and the victim. This much is attested to by the opinion for the New York Court of Appeals in *Ultramares Corporation v. Touche*,[9] written by Benjamin Cardozo, the jurist who would replace Holmes on the U.S. Supreme Court. Touche, an accounting firm, was hired by a company called Stern to review its financial records and prepare a balance sheet accurately listing Stern's debts and assets. Touche knew that Stern would be presenting the balance sheet to potential creditors, such as banks, as proof that the company was creditworthy. (Indeed, Touche prepared 32 numbered copies of the balance sheet precisely for this purpose.) Because of its failure to follow standard accounting practices, Touche failed to detect false entries on Stern's books. As a result, the balance sheet it prepared stated that the company was solvent, when in fact it was not. Plaintiff, a company that loaned substantial funds to Stern in reliance on Touche's work, sued Touche for negligently causing it to lose the value of the loan, which was never repaid.

---

9. 174 N.E. 441 (N.Y. 1931).

Cardozo's opinion for the New York court followed *Robins* in holding that Touche owed no duty to take care against causing losses to a party simply because that party might foreseeably rely on its audit. (He allowed that a claimant such as Ultramares could recover upon proof that Touche had not merely been careless but had *intentionally* misstated Stern's financial condition as part of a scheme to defraud creditors.) However, the opinion also affirmed earlier decisions recognizing a duty owed by accountants to third-party creditors when the accountant knows or should know that its audit is being conducted to facilitate a specific transaction between the business being audited and *a specific, identified creditor*. Here we see Cardozo—the judge who earlier had authored the opinion in *MacPherson* that eliminated the privity rule as applied to claims for physical harms caused by carelessly manufactured products—adopting a 'quasi-privity' requirement for claims against accountants alleging negligence causing economic loss. This same quasi-privity rule today applies in most courts to permit a claim for economic loss against a lawyer who, by carelessly preparing her client's will, deprives a potential beneficiary of assets that she would have received had the will been correctly prepared.

6.1.4 Infliction of Emotional Distress

As was explained in Chapter 5, if the victim of a physical harm caused by the carelessness of another prevails on her negligence claim against that other, she is entitled not only to payments that compensate her for medical costs and lost wages, but also to "parasitic damages" for pain and suffering and other forms of emotional distress. The rules are different, however, if the alleged injury consists of emotional harm *not predicated on physical harm*.

The doctrine in this corner of negligence law—often dubbed "NIED" for "negligent infliction of emotional distress"—has evolved in an uneven path. Decisions from the late 1800s ruled that free-standing emotional distress or "nervous shock," though obviously a setback to the victim, would not count as an injury in the eyes of negligence law. Yet even at this time, there were some special-relationship-based exceptions to this no-injury rule. For example, telegraph companies sometimes faced liability for carelessly failing to deliver telegrams informing close relatives of the death of a family member, thereby causing the relatives to miss the funeral and to experience distress over that fact. The rationale seems to have been that telegraph companies, when aware that they were being charged by the sender with delivering a particularly important and emotionally freighted message to a specific recipient, were under a duty to take care not to aggravate the distress the recipient already stood to experience when receiving the message. Today one occasionally finds cases in which courts are likewise prepared to deem one actor under a duty to take care to look out for the emotional well-being of another wholly apart from any concern for the victim's physical well-being.

Christensen v. Superior Court concerned a situation in which the defendant mortuaries had accepted decedents' bodies for cremation, but had then unknowingly delivered the bodies to crematoriums that harvested and sold the decedents' internal organs.[10] Surviving relatives, claiming to be devastated over the mishandling of the corpses, sued the mortuary owners, alleging that the owners were careless in dealing with the corpses. (They also brought separate claims against the crematoriums.) Although the California Supreme Court did not go so far as to impose a duty of care for the benefit of anyone who might foreseeably suffer emotional distress as a result of the mortuaries' alleged carelessness, it held that the relatives were owed such a duty. Quoting an older Colorado opinion, it emphasized that mortuaries are charged with "deal[ing] with the living in their most difficult and delicate moments,'" and that their business is largely that of demonstrating "consideration

---

10. 820 P.2d 181 (Cal. 1991).

for the afflicted.'"[11] Hence it was appropriate to charge them with a duty to be careful not to further upset close relatives in their handling of the decedents' bodies. Another example of a successful contemporary NIED claim is provided by the Court of Appeals for the Seventh Circuit, which held in *Beul v. ASSE International, Inc.* that organizations that run student exchange programs must monitor these placements to help reduce the risk that participants will be traumatized as a result of mistreatment by a host parent, particularly sexual harassment.[12]

In cases such as *Christensen* and *Beul*, courts are comfortable departing from the default no-duty rule for negligence causing only emotional distress because of the special vulnerabilities of a certain class of potential victims and because the defendants are undertaking a kind of activity that, even apart from what tort law demands of them, puts them in a position such that they should already be looking out for the emotional well-being of these potential victims. Apart from these sorts of cases, there are two other well-established lines of decisions that permit claimants to recover for emotional distress. In our view, neither of them recognizes a 'genuine' form of NIED liability, because in neither is the gist of the plaintiff's complaint that the defendant *failed to heed an obligation to look out for the plaintiff's emotional well-being*. Nonetheless, courts tend to categorize them under the NIED heading simply because they involve claims for negligence causing psychological injury not predicated on a physical injury.

The first line of decisions operates at the edges of the rule that holds actors to a general duty to take care not to cause physical harm to foreseeable victims. In these cases, the defendant acts carelessly as to the plaintiff's physical well-being, but fortuitously manages not to cause physical harm, instead only causing the victim

---

11. 820 P.2d at 196 (quoting Fitzsimmons v. Olinger Mortuary Ass'n, 17 P.2d 535, 536–37 (Colo. 1932).

12. 233 F.3d 441, 448 (7th Cir. 2000).

distress over having almost been physically harmed. In these near-miss cases, the courts will hold the careless defendant liable so long as the plaintiff can show that she was actually in the *zone of danger*—i.e., placed by the defendant's carelessness at risk of imminent physical harm—and that her being so situated is what traumatized her. Thus, a pedestrian who suffers lasting upset over having been nearly run down by a careless driver can in most jurisdictions recover from the driver for negligence.

As we will see in a later chapter, the zone of danger rule serves as an analogue to the court's recognition of the distinct intentional tort of assault as a companion to the tort of battery. By making actionable not just intentional harmful touchings (batteries), but also acts that intentionally cause a victim to apprehend such touchings, the assault tort errs on the side of protecting the underlying interest in bodily integrity, much like the zone of danger rule does in the domain of negligence. Recent times have seen occasional, incremental expansions of the zone of danger idea. Suppose a person is carelessly exposed by another to a pathogen such as HIV in a manner known to permit infection (e.g., a needlestick), but is later determined not to have been infected. In some jurisdictions, she can recover damages on an NIED claim for the distress she experiences while uncertain as to whether she might contract a fatal or life-altering disease such as AIDS.

The second line of decisions commonly treated as NIED claims are the so-called "bystander" cases. The leading authority here is *Dillon v Legg*,[13] another California Supreme Court decision. Margery Dillon and her daughter Cheryl suffered severe trauma over witnessing defendant Legg carelessly run down and kill Cheryl's sister Erin. Applying the zone of danger rule, the lower courts permitted Cheryl's claim because she was sufficiently near to Erin at the time to have herself been physically endangered by Legg's careless driving. However, they denied Margery's claim because she was outside

---

13. 441 P.2d 912 (Cal. 1968).

the zone. Decrying this differential treatment as "incongruous and somewhat revolting," the court allowed both plaintiffs to proceed with their claims, holding that anyone who creates a risk of *physical harm* to another under circumstances where it is reasonably foreseeable that the same conduct may also generate *emotional distress* to bystanders will be subject to liability for carelessly causing such distress.

Dillon defended its ruling as merely conforming the law of NIED to standard negligence principles. (In this respect, *Dillon* resembles *Rowland*, discussed above, which purported to be merely conforming premises liability law to standard negligence principles.) In doing so, the court identified but rejected two possible policy rationales for adopting a limited-duty rule for bystander claims. First is the worry that NIED claimants, more so than claimants alleging physical harms, might get away with faking their injuries. Judges and jurors, the court reasoned, can be relied upon to weed out fraudulent claims.

Second is the worry that negligence so frequently generates emotional distress as to threaten to flood the courts with litigation. After all, it is not difficult to imagine a range of persons becoming distraught over a negligently caused death, including not just relatives who actually observe a family member being hurt or killed, but friends and associates of the victim, or even strangers. (In addition, some who are not present but only observe the event through media or learn of the event after the fact might likewise be expected to be traumatized.) According to *Dillon*, the standard foreseeability requirement for duty would suffice to bar claims by these sorts of 'remote' victims. However, in a subsequent decision,[14] the California Supreme Court partially backtracked on this aspect of *Dillon*, concluding that the foreseeability constraint on the duty to take care to avoid causing distress to bystanders was too vague and had generated conflicting results in the lower courts. Accordingly, it specified

---

14. *Thing v. La Chusa*, 771 P.2d 814 (Cal. 1989).

categorically that bystander claims would be available only to close relatives of the victim who can demonstrate that they were distressed by virtue of contemporaneously witnessing firsthand the careless injuring of the victim.

Although many courts have followed suit in recognizing bystander emotional distress claims brought by close relatives of the victim who observe her being injured by the defendant's carelessness, the rationale for doing so is in some ways mysterious. Like other torts, negligence is a relational wrong. To prevail, a negligence plaintiff must identify conduct by the defendant that was not merely careless in the abstract, but careless *as to* her or persons such as her. (*See* Chapter 5's discussion of *Palsgraf*.) Conduct like that of the car driver in *Dillon*, though obviously careless with respect to the physical well-being of the person whom he runs down, is *not* careless as to the bystander's *physical well-being*. (A bystander, after all, is someone who, by definition, is outside the orbit of physical danger.) And we have already noted that negligence law does *not* recognize a duty to take care against causing emotional distress to others merely because they might foreseeably be distressed by one's conduct. For this reason, the driver's careless driving cannot possibly constitute a breach of that sort of duty. (If there is no duty to conduct oneself so as to avoid causing foreseeable emotional distress to another, then by definition, conduct that is careless only insofar as it risks causing emotional distress to another cannot be a breach of that sort of duty.) Finally, it makes little sense to see *Dillon* as a general rejection of the restrictive duty rules for emotional harm, because the bystander witness rule is really still quite narrow.

One way to understand the modern law of bystander emotional distress claims is to concede that bystanders are not actually wronged by careless defendants whose physical harming of another has caused their distress. Instead, one might argue that certain bystanders—namely, those who observe the physical harming of a close relative—enjoy a power not ordinarily conferred by tort law to sue *derivatively*, as the "vicarious beneficiary" of the defendant's breach of a duty owed to the relative. Such a theory would be in keeping with the fact that, under Wrongful Death Acts (*see* Chapter 2), family members alone are authorized to sue derivatively for the tortious killing of their decedents. It may also gain some support from the common law's recognition of "loss of consortium" claims, whereby a tortious physical injuring of a victim gives rise to a claim by the victim's spouse for the loss of the victim's companionship.

Dillon's exclusive focus on fraud and floodgates—hardly idiosyncratic among courts faced with NIED claims—suggests that, in the California court's view, there are at most practical rather than principled reasons for negligence law to apply special duty rules to emotional distress claims. At first glance, this view seems powerful. Emotional harm can be at least as devastating as physical harm, and it is therefore difficult to see why the law ought to make recovery more difficult for emotional distress victims. And *Dillon's* progressive instincts on this issue seem particularly commendable given the historical factors that seem to have contributed to the lesser protection in tort law of psychic well-being, including ignorance about the workings of the brain, as well as outright sexism. (On the latter point, it seems that in the period from 1870 to 1950, many members of the male-only judiciary seemed inclined to regard susceptibility to 'nervous shock' as a special vulnerability of the 'weaker' sex.)

And yet, as it arguably was in its eagerness to dismiss the idea that trespassers should be barred from suing for injuries incurred during trespasses (*see* the discussion of *Rowland* above), the California Court in *Dillon* may have overlooked possible principled reasons to circumscribe the reach of NIED doctrine. As we have emphasized, torts are violations of relational norms as to how one is obligated to act toward certain others. Even granted that emotional distress should be deemed no less serious than other forms of harm, there might still be a reason to worry about *demanding of actors that they be equally vigilant* against causing both kinds of harm.

For one thing, a wider range of everyday conduct generates distress as a predictable side effect. Office managers are generally thought to be entitled to demand a great deal of their employees in terms of meeting deadlines, sales targets, billable-hour minimums, and so forth, even though their doing so predictably generates serious distress in some employees. (The same is true for teachers who set high expectations for their students!) For another, emotional distress is a response that is necessarily mediated by the mind of the victim in a way that standard physical injuries—e.g., a broken leg or the contraction of illness from exposure to a toxin— seem not to be. Thus when the law sets standards for determining the obligations one owes to be vigilant of another's emotional well-being, it is necessarily also setting norms as to how victims are expected to handle certain kinds of stressful events. And the law may be reasonable in asking of citizens that they develop a certain resiliency that will permit them to weather even very difficult situations without falling apart. Seen in this light, the courts' invocations of concepts like "zone of danger" or categories such as "close relatives who contemporaneously observe the injuring of their family member" arguably emerge as less arbitrary. It is precisely in these sorts of instances, the courts seem to suppose, that the law should not expect the victim to 'keep it together.' Hence these kinds of situations are ones that actors are obligated to take care against generating.

6.2 Injury and Duty

Tort law recognizes different kinds of setbacks as injuries, including physical harms, property destruction, emotional distress, and economic loss. Two strands of modern negligence litigation pose the question whether the concept of injury can be extended to cover situations in which one person's carelessness *decreases another's chances of surviving an illness* or *increases the risk that she will suffer a future illness*. Intertwined with these questions are duty issues. For, as we have already seen, courts are circumspect about recognizing duties to take care against causing nonphysical injuries.

6.2.1 Loss of a Chance

In *Falcon v. Memorial Hospital*,[15] Nena Falcon was admitted to defendant's hospital to deliver her baby. The child was born healthy but, tragically, Nena died during delivery from a rare biological occurrence known as an amniotic fluid embolism. The plaintiff, Nena's grandmother, brought a wrongful death action (*see* Chapter 2) against the hospital. Her expert conceded in his deposition that the hospital could not have prevented the embolism from occurring. Nonetheless, he maintained that it should have taken the precaution of inserting an intravenous line into Nena, which would have permitted rapid infusion of fluids and medication once the embolism occurred. According to the expert, doing so would have increased Nena's chance of surviving the embolism from zero to 37.5 percent.

Based on this testimony, the hospital asked the trial judge to dismiss the case on the ground that the plaintiff could not possibly meet her burden of proof on the causation element of her negligence claim. After all, her own evidence established that, at best, Nena had a roughly one-in-three chance of surviving if the defendant had taken the relevant precaution. By definition, then, plaintiff could *not* establish that but for the defendant's failure, Nena *probably* would have lived. (*See* Chapter 5's discussion of proof of causation.)

A divided Michigan Supreme Court ruled that the claim on behalf of Nena should go to a jury. Under certain circumstances, it reasoned, even the loss of a less-than-50-percent chance of survival counts as an injury that will support a negligence claim. Hence the rule of liability recognized in *Falcon* is often referred to as *loss of a chance* doctrine. Although the suit was *not* viable on the theory that the hospital's carelessness caused Nena's death (it probably did

---

15. 462 N.W.2d 44 (Mich. 1990), overruled by statute as stated in Weymers v. Khera, 563 N.W.2d 647 (Mich. 1997).

not), the court held that it *was* viable on the alternative theory that the hospital's carelessness had deprived her of better odds of surviving. Although the Michigan legislature later overturned *Falcon*, about half the jurisdictions in the United States now recognize loss of a chance claims. However, this theory of liability is usually applicable only in medical malpractice actions, and even then only for wrongful death claims (as opposed to claims for bodily injuries by patients who survive).

Having ruled for Nena's representative in the foregoing respects, the Michigan Court nonetheless tempered her victory by introducing a special rule of damages for loss of a chance claims. Specifically, it held that the jury should assess the amount of damages that it would have assessed had the plaintiff been able to prove that the defendant's carelessness caused Nena's death, but then multiply that number by the percentage figure representing the chance for survival of which Nena had been deprived. (For example, if the jury would have awarded $100,000 to Nena's estate had it been able to prove that the hospital's failure to insert the intravenous line probably caused her death, and if it found, based on the plaintiff's expert's testimony, that that failure reduced Nena's odds of survival from 37.5 percent to zero, then her estate would receive $37,500 in damages.) The court reasoned that this damages rule naturally fits the loss of a chance theory of recovery. Does it? Note that in a plain-vanilla negligence case, a plaintiff who succeeds in proving that he was, say, 67 percent likely to have avoided physical injury had the defendant not acted carelessly, stands to recover 100 percent of his damages. Why not limit that plaintiff's recovery to 67 percent?

Falcon raises a variety of interesting philosophical and legal questions. Does it really make sense to treat a reduction in already low odds for recovery as an injury? Suppose that, miraculously, Nena had survived. That she did so would not negate the fact that, statistically at least, the hospital's malpractice had reduced her odds for survival. Rather, it would seem only to demonstrate that she was exceptionally lucky in being able to beat even her reduced odds of survival. Should she therefore be entitled to loss of chance damages? The intuitive answer would seem to be "no," although its explanation is perhaps less clear.

Suppose we grant that it makes sense, in the context of medical malpractice actions, to treat a reduction in the odds of survival as an injury. Does the same rationale apply in other contexts? Legal malpractice occurs when a lawyer carelessly mishandles the matter for which she was retained by her client and thereby causes harm to her client. Suppose lawyer *L* is representing business-person *B* in *B*'s breach-of-contract suit against defendant *D*. *L* mishandles *B*'s claim against *D*, as a result of which *B*'s claim is dismissed. *B* then turns around and sues *L* for legal malpractice, but can establish only that *L*'s incompetence reduced his chances of prevailing on his claim against *D* from 40% to zero. Should a court that follows *Falcon* recognize this sort of a lost chance as an injury? Or are there differences between the delivery of legal services and medical services that warrant a different rule? Generally speaking, courts have been reluctant to apply loss of a chance doctrine outside of medical malpractice, and many have been reluctant to recognize the doctrine at all, in part out of concern that this theory of negligence liability invites sheer speculation as to percentages.

Note that, although there are several reasons that might counsel against applying *Falcon* to legal malpractice claims—including worries over the reliability of estimates pertaining to the odds of prevailing in litigation versus statistically based estimates of the odds of surviving a medical condition—one reason for thinking that the loss of a chance doctrine should apply is that lawyers, like doctors, owe their clients special sorts of duties—duties that are in some ways more demanding than a purely negative duty to refrain from causing harm to another. A client expects her lawyer to look out for her interests in connection with the matter for which the lawyer has been retained. Likewise, patients rely on their doctors to give them their best chances for health. Whether in the end it makes sense to apply the loss of a chance doctrine to claims against lawyers or other professionals, appreciating why there is *some plausibility* to such extensions helps us to see why courts have been most receptive to the loss of a chance theory in the medical context. The notion that the loss of a relatively small chance to be healthy is an injury seems to go hand-in-hand with the idea that doctors owe a special sort of duty to their patients: a duty to take care to provide them with their best odds for health.

6.2.2   Risk of Future Injury and Medical Monitoring

In *Metro-North Commuter Railroad Co. v. Buckley*,[16] the U.S. Supreme Court was confronted with a relatively rare opportunity to rule on a substantive tort law issue. The opportunity was rare because, as noted above in connection with *Robins Dry Dock*, the Court's own precedents establish that the fashioning of substantive tort law is exclusively the province of state courts and legislatures, subject to review by federal courts only for possible conflicts between state tort law (on the one hand) and federal common law and statutes or the U.S. Constitution (on the other). Occasionally, however, the Court finds itself faced with the task of interpreting a federal statute that contains provisions that create causes of action for victims of certain injuries. One such statute—at issue in *Buckley*—is the Federal Employers Liability Act (FELA), which was enacted by Congress in 1908. FELA is essentially a federal tort statute. It provides employees of railroads operating in interstate commerce with the right to sue their employers for injuries attributable to employer negligence. (Prior to FELA's enactment, railroad employees could bring state law negligence claims against railroads, but state courts had often made it difficult for workers to prevail, and Congress was anxious to create a federal law remedy to lower some of these hurdles.)

Plaintiff Michael Buckley was a Metro-North employee who worked in the presence of airborne asbestos without the benefit of

---

16.   521 U.S. 424 (1997).

any protective equipment. Asbestos—a natural fiber at one time commonly used as insulation—is well known to be capable of causing serious lung ailments through inhalation, including fatal forms of cancer. Metro North's failure to provide protective gear to Buckley was therefore clearly unreasonable. However, there was a wrinkle to what otherwise might have been a very straightforward FELA claim: when Buckley sued, he had *not* developed cancer and indeed had *no physical symptoms*. Instead, his suit alleged that Metro-North's carelessness had caused him two other kinds of injury. First, it left him emotionally distressed over the fact that he was now statistically slightly more likely to contract lung disease than a person not exposed to asbestos. Second, increasing the odds that he would suffer a lung disease such as cancer had caused him to suffer economic losses in the form of expenditures on medical monitoring for early signs of disease.

The Court rejected Buckley's claim for negligent infliction of emotional distress. Specifically, it held that FELA imposes on railroads only the limited zone of danger duty to take care against causing their employees distress *over the prospect of imminent bodily harm*. (*See* the discussion of *Christensen* and *Dillon* above.) Given that Buckley was not at risk of this sort of harm, his claim failed for lack of a duty. To say the same thing, the Court was unwilling to treat being exposed to a toxin that slightly increases one's statistical risk of contracting a fatal disease as being "endangered" in the requisite sense.

The majority next concluded that medical monitoring expenses associated with increased odds of contracting cancer could *in principle* count as an economic injury of a sort that would support a FELA claim. (Compare *Robins* and *Ultramares* above.) However, it then somewhat bafflingly ruled that, insofar as a FELA claimant can recover for this sort of cost, the remedy to which he is entitled *cannot* take the standard tort form of a lump-sum damages payment from the defendant. Instead, a plaintiff suing for this sort of injury can only ask the court to order the defendant to set aside funds from which the plaintiff can obtain reimbursement for monitoring-related expenses on an ongoing basis.

Like *Falcon, Buckley* raises a host of issues. We will note only two here. First, it is important to point out that loss of a chance nowhere figures in FELA cases like *Buckley*. That is, there is no suggestion from the Supreme Court—and in fact an implicit disavowal of the idea—that a plaintiff like Buckley ought to be able to pursue a claim for having been deprived by his employer's negligence of better odds for health, even though the evidence showed that Buckley's asbestos exposure probably did reduce those odds. Why is loss of a chance a nonstarter in this context? As we suggested above, it probably has something to do with the refusal of the courts to treat employers as owing to employees a duty to take steps to improve their chances for good health of a sort that doctors owe to their patients.

Second, the Court's seemingly odd linkage of Buckley's right of recovery to the form in which he would receive compensation perhaps becomes more intelligible if one considers what it really means for a court to order an employer to pay for a regime of medical monitoring for employees whom it has negligently exposed to a pathogen. The form of the remedy—an ongoing obligation to cover expenses—indicates that it is not after all an award of damages for a completed tort. Rather, it is *injunctive relief* awarded to a plaintiff who cannot (yet) establish that he has been injured, but instead can only establish that he is now at a heightened risk of future injury. In a case like *Buckley*, the employment relationship places a duty on employers to take reasonable care to provide employees with a physically safe workplace. When that duty is breached (as it was by Metro-North with respect to *Buckley*) but causes only a heightened risk of future injury, a court may order the employer to fulfill a 'secondary' duty to assist its employees in their efforts to prevent that risk from ripening into an actual injury.

On this reading, *Buckley* (despite what the majority opinion seems to say) is not a case in which the injury that supports recovery is economic loss in the form of medical monitoring expenses. Rather, it is a case in which there is *no injury* at all. However, the plaintiff is nonetheless entitled to a form of pre-injury injunctive relief against the employer—that is, an order from the court directing the employer to give a particular form of assistance to the employee—because the employer, by carelessly exposing its employee to a risk of a future illness thereby incurred a new, ongoing affirmative duty to assist the employee by shouldering the cost of tests designed to detect and prevent or treat the illness.

6.3 Custom, Cost-Benefit Analysis, and Ordinary Care

We now turn from the duty and injury elements of a negligence claim to the breach element. As explained in Chapter 5, the duty recognized by negligence law is a duty to take ordinary care, which is further defined as care that a reasonably prudent person would take under the circumstances. The question of whether a given actor has met this standard is normally for the jury to decide, based on its consideration of all the relevant circumstances. Thus, both in definition and practice, the standard is relatively open-ended, which is both a strength (in allowing behavior to be judged contextually, and in keeping with changes in information, technology, and norms) and a weakness (in sometimes failing to provide clear guidance).

In this section, we consider two ways in which courts have refined and clarified the ordinary care concept. One focuses on the relationship of ordinary care to the precautions generally regarded as required by persons in the position of the actor whose conduct is being judged. The other suggests that a particular way of thinking about ordinary care—one that frames it in terms of the costs and benefits of precaution-taking—helps to render it more precise.

6.3.1 Ordinary v. Customary Care

The adjective "ordinary" in the phrase "ordinary care" naturally invites consideration of what is typically expected of people as they go about their business. Indeed, defendants anxious to avoid onerous applications of the breach standard consistently have argued to courts that it ought to be interpreted so as to immunize from liability anyone who conforms to accepted safety practices when engaged in the same activity. On this argument, if it is generally acceptable under prevailing social norms for adult drivers to permit young minor passengers to ride without seatbelts, then a defendant's failure to belt a child who is injured because of that failure cannot be deemed careless. Simply by virtue of conforming to convention, the defendant would satisfy the ordinary care requirement.

Although one can find occasional nineteenth-century decisions endorsing the view that extra-legal norms of care set the breach standard, it has steadily been rejected in modern times. The leading authority for this proposition is another admiralty decision. (*See* the discussion of *Robins Dry Dock* above.) Titled *The T.J. Hooper*[17] for the name of a tugboat involved in the underlying incident, the decision was authored by legendary federal court of appeals judge Learned Hand.

The T.J. Hooper and another tug were caught in a storm just off the coast of New Jersey. Because of the storm, barges being towed by each tug sank, as did coal aboard the barges. The owners of the lost barges and coal sued the operator of the tugs, arguing that the losses were caused by the tugs' being "unseaworthy"—an admiralty concept treated like the tort idea of ordinary care—because they were not equipped with working radios. Radios would have permitted the tug captains to receive a broadcasted weather forecast that gave advance warning of the storm, which would have induced the captains to avoid the storm by pulling into a safe harbor before the storm arose.

In response, the tugs' owner argued that it was not standard practice at this time for such boats to be equipped with radios: some had them and some did not. Given that its tugs were outfitted like

---

17. The T.J. Hooper., 60 F.2d 737 (2d Cir.), *cert. denied*, 287 U.S. 662 (1932).

many other tugs, the owner argued, it could not be found to have deviated from the standard of ordinary care. Note the aggressiveness of the owner's position. It is one thing for a defendant to argue that negligence law should not demand the taking of a precaution that, by uniform practice, has *never before* been taken. It is quite another to argue that negligence law should not demand the taking of a precaution that some take and others do not. The latter argument, if accepted, would require near unanimity in the acceptance of a precaution before a failure to adopt it could be deemed legal carelessness, which is surely a standard that is too defendant-friendly.

In any event, Judge Hand rejected both the more aggressive and the less aggressive versions of the argument that compliance with prevailing industry norms is ordinary care. Conceding that "in most cases reasonable prudence is in fact common prudence," he nonetheless insisted that "strictly it is never its measure. . . ." He added, "a whole calling may have unduly lagged in the adoption of new and available devices. It never may set its own tests, however persuasive be its usages. Courts must in the end say what is required; there are precautions so imperative that even their universal disregard will not excuse their omission."[18]

The T.J. Hooper now sets the rule for the greater part of negligence law: evidence that the defendant complied with customary understandings of what ordinary care requires is *highly relevant* to the breach issue, but *not* dispositive. It is always open to a victim injured in a car crash, a slip-and-fall accident, and most other standard negligence scenarios to argue that the defendant acted with insufficient prudence even if she behaved in a way that is widely regarded as acceptable. It does not follow, of course, that the decision maker—the judge and/or jury—must embrace this argument. Rather, it may do so, although it will also be entitled to reject the

---

18. 60 F.2d at 740.

plaintiff's argument and conclude that common prudence was sufficient to constitute ordinary care.

T.J. Hooper notwithstanding, courts have crafted an exception for a particular class of negligence claims. These are claims for professional negligence—i.e., malpractice—and particularly medical malpractice. Thus, an equally well-settled rule of law (alluded to above in the discussion of *Tarasoff*), holds that in medical malpractice actions, physicians are entitled to prevail as a matter of law on the breach issue unless the plaintiff offers expert testimony establishing that the defendant failed to live up to what her professional peer group regards as the standard of care. In other words, for most suits alleging professional negligence against doctors (and probably for suits alleging malpractice by lawyers, architects, and other professionals), prevailing conceptions of appropriate conduct among physicians *do* set the standard of care, such that it is not open to the plaintiff to establish breach by showing that "a whole calling" has "unduly lagged" in the adoption of available precautions.

The contrast between how the standard of care is defined for nonprofessional and professional negligence raises various questions and also calls for certain qualifications. The most obvious questions are: What, if anything, explains or justifies the adoption of the two opposing rules? It seems *un*likely that the more defendant-friendly standard for professionals is simply a reflection of their political clout. Members of manufacturing, transportation, and financial industries probably have more clout and have not secured this 'benefit' for themselves. Perhaps judges, being themselves members of a professional guild, are particularly attuned to worries about the degree to which the *T.J. Hooper* rule would invite uninitiated jurors to second-guess the professional judgments of highly trained specialists. This concern might be amplified because the second-guessing takes place in situations in which physicians are being judged in hindsight, after the occurrence of an injury.

Even if these sorts of consideration help to explain the emergence of the *anti-T.J. Hooper* rule, they do not necessarily justify it. In negligence cases not involving professionals, fact finders are asked to review and second-guess complex judgments made, for example, by highly trained engineers. Is not deference also owed to these expert judgments? Another possible rationale for the *anti-T.J. Hooper* rule is that professions can be relied on to train and police their members sufficiently, such that courts won't accomplish much by further reviewing their actions. Is there any empirical basis for this sort of supposition? Might one worry that members of professional organizations will 'circle the wagons' to protect their own against complaints by 'outsiders'?

Finally, it is worth noting some qualifications that arguably lower the stakes by softening the edges of the sharp dichotomy we have thus far drawn between the rules for standard negligence claims and the rules for malpractice. First, it is important to keep in mind Hand's observation that, even outside the domain of malpractice, common prudence often will be deemed ordinary prudence. Second, the deference shown by courts to professional practice is not abject: there is room for plaintiffs' lawyers legitimately to second-guess practice. For example, in the mid-twentieth century, many courts began to redefine the relevant body of professionals to whom the conduct of a medical malpractice defendant was to be compared. In particular, they shifted from an inquiry into whether the professional acted as would another competent practitioner in the same community to an inquiry into whether he acted in conformity with a regionally or nationally observed standard of care. This in turn created a wedge that permitted plaintiffs to establish fault on the basis of lagging localities. (However, in the last 25 years, tort reform advocates have sometimes successfully lobbied for legislation mandating a return to the use of local standards in medical malpractice cases.)

Third, there is at least one important category of medical malpractice cases in which many courts have explicitly rejected the normal malpractice rule for determining breach. These are *informed consent* cases. In such a case, the patient's allegation is *not* that the defendant doctor missed a diagnosis or mishandled a procedure. In fact, the treatment is conceded to have been performed properly and to have resulted in injury to the patient only because of a risk of injury that is present even when the procedure is done correctly. Instead, the basis of the complaint is that the doctor failed to provide the patient with sufficient information about this risk, with the idea being that had the physician provided it, the patient would have chosen a different course of treatment and thus would have avoided the injury.

At one time, the rule for determining when a physician is at fault for failing to provide information about risks of procedures was the usual malpractice rule: If nondisclosure of the sort of information withheld from the plaintiff was standard practice, no breach could be found. However, starting with the 1972 decision of *Canterbury v. Spence*,[19] courts have increasingly switched to a standard that asks jurors to inquire whether the relevant information is the sort of information that a *reasonable person in the position of the patient* would want to have, regardless of whether doctors regard it as appropriate to provide it. Thus, insofar as medical malpractice takes the form of a doctor failing to enable her patient to make an informed decision about her treatment options, jurors and judges are invited by negligence law to second-guess norms among medical practitioners.

6.3.2 Ordinary Care v. Cost-Efficient Precautions

The openness of the ordinary care standard has attracted another, very different effort to render it more determinate and predictable. This effort is not focused on limiting the extent to which the fault standard can demand nonstandard precautions. Instead, it is part of a larger academic effort to rethink negligence law, tort law, and law more generally—an effort that often goes under the heading of

---

19. 464 F.2d 772 (D.C. Cir.), *cert. denied*, 409 U.S. 1064 (1972).

"Law and Economics." Leaders of this movement, particularly prominent jurist and judge Richard Posner, maintain that the concept of ordinary care is best understood in terms of a trade-off between the cost of taking precautions against injuries and the cost of allowing injuries to happen. In turn, Posner has held out as an emblem of this economic conception of fault the opinion in *United States v. Carroll Towing Co.*,[20] another admiralty law decision written by Learned Hand, the judge who authored *T.J. Hooper.*

The incident that gave rise to *Carroll Towing* took place in January 1944. A barge named the "Anna C"—which was owned by Conners Marine Co. and carrying flour owned by the U.S. government—was moored at a pier on the Hudson River jutting out from Manhattan. During working hours, the pier and the river were quite busy, in part because of supply operations being conducted in connection with the war effort. Employees of another company called Grace Lines operated a tugboat named the "Carroll," which was used to move barges around the river. Grace's employees inadequately secured the lines that were holding the Anna C to its pier. As a result, the Anna C drifted downriver, where it struck a tanker, took on water, and sank, causing damage to the barge and the loss of the flour.

Conners brought a claim against Grace Lines (as well as Carroll Towing, the company that owned the Carroll), alleging that the carelessness of the tug's crew caused Conners to suffer damage to its barge and to incur liability to the United States for the lost flour. Although Conners' suit raised a number of issues, the one for which it is now famous did *not* concern the fault standard that was applied to defendants Grace Lines and Carroll Towing. Rather, it concerned an effort by Grace and Carroll to respond to Conners' suit by asserting that Conners had only itself to blame for the Anna C's sinking. In other words, the key issue concerned the *comparative fault* of plaintiff Conners. According to Grace and Carroll, Conners was at

---

20. 159 F.2d 169 (2d Cir. 1947).

fault because its bargee—an employee paid to be on the barge to make sure it is not damaged or plundered—was absent from the barge when the Anna C was accidentally set loose. Had the bargee been on board, they argued, he could have summoned help after the collision of the Anna C with the tanker, which would have prevented its sinking.

On the issue of Conners' fault, the trial court ruled for Conners, concluding that the bargee's absence did not constitute carelessness. Writing for the court of appeals, Judge Hand reversed. Whether the bargee's absence constituted carelessness, he reasoned, necessarily turned on the circumstances of the accident. In particular, that judgment hinged on three basic considerations: the *burden* (B) incurred by the barge owner and bargee in ensuring that the bargee would be on board; the *probability* (P) that the bargee's absence might cause others to suffer losses; and the value of those expected *losses* (L). Hand further suggested that one could arrange these factors so as to resemble an algebraic formula: $B < P \times L$. By this 'formula,' an actor will be deemed at fault if he fails to take a precaution that imposes on him a burden of lesser magnitude than the losses expected to flow from that failure, multiplied by the probability that the losses will occur. Carelessness, on this conception, consists of a failure to take a precaution that is less costly than the losses one can expect the failure to generate. Applying this formula to the facts of the case, Hand concluded that the burden of having a bargee on board, at least during daylight hours, was smaller than the injury risks associated with not having one, especially given the busy conditions. Hence Conners was also at fault for the sinking of its barge.

Hand himself never supposed that his formula could be calculated or applied with any sort of precision. Rather, he claimed it had value primarily in focusing attention on the sorts of considerations that arguably matter most to the determination of fault. Undaunted by Hand's own circumspection, Judge Posner, then a professor at the University of Chicago Law School, insisted in a famous 1972 article that Hand's opinion laid the groundwork for a rigorous approach to fault, one that assigns dollar values to the costs and benefits of precaution-taking and injuries.[21] In doing so, Posner converted an offhand suggestion into an entire theory of negligence and of tort law. The very point of tort, Posner argues, is to use the threat of lawsuits and liability to induce actors to take all cost-efficient precautions—but only cost-efficient precautions—against causing injuries to others. Tort law, on this view, is nothing other than a scheme for promoting the efficient use of resources by using the prospect of liability to get actors to spend money on safety only when the cost of safety is lower than the expected losses from not acting safely.

Posner's Hand Formula has been highly influential in legal academic circles. However, it is critical to see it for what it is—an abstract model driven by Posner's faith that economic analysis offers greater rigor and predictability than standard legal analysis, and by his strong normative commitment to the idea that common law's primary goal should be to maximize a society's wealth (irrespective of how the wealth is distributed). In fact, the economic conception of fault rather obviously fails to capture what "ordinary care" in American negligence law actually *means*. The standard applied by juries and judges—other than judges committed to Posnerian law and economics—makes no mention of economic analysis. This is not to suggest that factors such as cost are irrelevant to assessments of ordinary care: it is surely the case that a precaution's being expensive can counsel against finding fault in the failure to take it. Rather, the point is that judges and jurors are not asked to perform cost-benefit analysis and rarely, if ever, have before them the sort of information that would be needed to undertake it.

Moreover, even if such information were made available to them, they certainly would not be required to accept, and often in fact reject, an effort to invoke an economic conception of fault.

----

21. Richard A. Posner, *A Theory of Negligence*, 1 J. LEGAL STUD. 29 (1972).

Suppose, for example, the corporate owner of a restaurant chain that serves boiling hot coffee at drive-through windows convincingly demonstrates that the value to consumers of having coffee that remains pleasantly warm for a longer period of time significantly outweighs the costs associated with rare instances in which spills of the coffee cause serious burns. A judge and jury would probably be entitled to deem the corporation careless nonetheless. To say the same thing, there is no reason to suppose that tort law or ordinary morality conceives of fault strictly in terms of a narrow cost-benefit calculation. Judgments about fault, like many other moral and legal judgments, often involve weighing various considerations that, for convenience, could be labeled "costs" or "benefits." But, as Hand observed, in this context the idea of 'weighing' is metaphoric rather than genuinely quantitative. Moreover, it is perfectly commonplace and defensible for decision makers to conclude that, as a matter of ordinary care, an actor ought to have taken certain precautions even though doing so would have required the expenditure of greater resources than could be expected to be saved by not doing so. There are some things more important than maximizing societal wealth, or at least judges and juries can so find in applying the concept of ordinary care.

6.4 Presuming Breach

We continue to refine our understanding of the breach element by considering two doctrines, each of which concerns the sort of evidence that will suffice to permit a decision maker to conclude that an actor has failed to act with ordinary care. The first of these, which goes under the Latin name of *res ipsa loquitur*, sets a *permissive* rule that allows but does not require fact finders to infer a breach from minimal evidence. Where applicable, the second doctrine, known as *negligence per se*, states that judicial and juror assessments of fault must give way to applicable legislative or agency determinations of what constitutes careless conduct.

6.4.1 *Res Ipsa Loquitur*

The phrase *res ipsa loquitur* means "the thing speaks for itself." The idea behind the doctrine is that the mere happening of certain events evidences carelessness on someone's part, even though there is no additional evidence of fault beyond their happening. The leading authority for the doctrine is *Byrne v. Boadle.*[22] In *Byrne*, a pedestrian was struck on the shoulder by a falling barrel of flour as he stood under the window of defendant's shop. No additional evidence about what happened was available. Affirming a jury verdict for the plaintiff, the English Exchequer Court reasoned that certain events are, as a matter of common experience, so likely to be the product of an actor's carelessness that a plaintiff injured by such an event is relieved of the usual burden of production—namely, the requirement that he produce testimonial, physical, or other evidence that will permit the decision maker to conclude that a tort was committed. In a nutshell, because barrels of flour do not tend to fall out of a shop's second-story window unless someone at the shop has been careless, the jury was entitled to presume fault on the part of Boadle.

Res ipsa permits but does not mandate a finding of fault. The jury in *Byrne* was not required to conclude that Byrne's injury was caused by carelessness on the part of Boadle, and indeed the court invited Boadle and other defendants subject to the doctrine to provide evidence undermining the inference of fault created by the circumstances of the accident. For example, if Boadle presented credible evidence that a trespasser had broken into the shop and intentionally tossed the barrel onto Byrne, it presumably would not have been found at fault.

The critical issue raised by *res ipsa* is the appropriate circumstances for its application, for implicit in the doctrine's basic rationale is that only certain special situations suffice to warrant an

---

22. (1863) 159 Eng. Rep. 299 (Exch.).

inference of fault without proof of what the allegedly careless actor did wrong. Decisions subsequent to *Byrne* have spelled out these circumstances in terms of three requirements: (1) the event that injured the plaintiff must be the kind of event that does not tend to occur without carelessness; (2) the instrumentality of injury (e.g., the barrel in *Byrne*) must have been in the exclusive control of the defendant at the time of the event; and (3) the injury must have resulted without the active participation or fault of the plaintiff (i.e., the plaintiff must have been a relatively passive victim).

The first requirement is designed to prevent *res ipsa* from being applied in the myriad cases in which things can easily go wrong without anyone being at fault. Car accidents, slips and falls, and bad medical outcomes typically occur in circumstances that do not support an inference of carelessness on the defendant's part; in these situations injuries often happen even when everyone acts with ordinary care. Second, even if an injury occurs in circumstances that seem to suggest carelessness, if persons acting independently of the defendant also had access to the instrumentality of harm, the doctrine will not apply. If, for example, the evidence in *Byrne* showed that hours before the incident occurred, an independent contractor had been at Boadle's shop moving equipment in an area near the window out of which the barrel fell, then Byrne would not have been able to meet the exclusive control requirement. Third and finally, because situations in which victims are active participants are ones in which victim fault might just as well have played a role in the victim being injured, these are situations to which *res ipsa* does not apply.

Instances of falling objects remain the heartland of *res ipsa* doctrine, as do plane crashes, which are generally presumed to be a result of human error absent evidence to the contrary. The rule is also sometimes applied to certain kinds of malpractice, most notably cases in which medical instruments such as clamps and sponges are discovered in a patient's body after surgery. Modern cases have sometimes shown a willingness to relax the "exclusive control" requirement. A famous example of this is provided by

Ybarra v. Spangard,[23] in which a surgical patient suffered nerve damage because he was placed incorrectly on the surgical table. The problem he faced in seeking to invoke *res ipsa* is that his placement on the table was under the control of several nurses and doctors who, in the eyes of the law, were acting independently of one another. Hence none of them could be said to have had exclusive control. In its interesting and aggressive *Ybarra* opinion, the California Supreme Court nonetheless treated the doctors and nurses as a single unit for purposes of the plaintiff's negligence claim, thereby enabling him to meet the exclusive control requirement. The court emphasized that doing so was necessary in part to overcome what might otherwise be a conspiracy of silence on the part of the defendants, who were the only persons who could have known what happened to the plaintiff during surgery.

6.4.2 Negligence Per Se and Regulatory Compliance

Where applicable, another negligence doctrine provides greater specificity to the ordinary care standard by linking it to rules of conduct set out in statutes or administrative agency regulations. Known as "negligence per se," this doctrine was famously articulated by Cardozo in the case of *Martin v. Herzog*.[24] Like *Carroll Towing*, *Martin* is a case in which the fault at issue was *the plaintiff's* rather than the defendant's, though its treatment of breach applies equally to defendants.

Shortly after sunset, Martin's vehicle was involved in a crash with Herzog's, which resulted in Martin's death. When Martin's widow sued Herzog for negligence, Herzog argued that Martin's failure to use headlights as required by New York statute was fault that

---

23. 154 P.2d 687 (Cal. 1944).

24. 126 N.E. 814 (N.Y. 1920).

contributed to his own death. (Under the rules in force at the time of the decision, a victim found even partially at fault for his own injuries was barred from recovering from even an at-fault defendant.) The trial judge instructed the jury that it should regard Martin's statutory violation as *evidence* that he was at fault, but that it could nonetheless find under the circumstances that he acted with ordinary care even though he was driving at night without his lights on. So instructed, the jury returned a verdict for Herzog's widow.

The New York Court of Appeals reversed and dismissed Martin's claim on the ground that the jury was *required* to find him at fault. Judge Cardozo explained: "[T]he unexcused omission of the statutory [requirement of headlights] is more than some evidence of negligence. It *is* negligence in itself. . . . Jurors have no dispensing power by which they may relax the duty that one traveler on the highway owes under the statute to another."[25] In other words, where legislation sets a specific standard of care, juries have no authority to alter the standard, and hence the legislative rule supersedes the ordinary care standard. Generally, courts have held that the same rationale applies when the rule or standard in question is the creature of regulations promulgated by agencies. Themselves created by statutes, agencies are said to enjoy, at least for these purposes, the democratic legitimacy of the legislatures that created them.

This thumbnail account of negligence per se requires four qualifications. First, not all statutory violations suffice to trigger the doctrine. A defendant who has permitted his driver's license to expire a few weeks before an accident, rather than sending in a form to the Department of Motor Vehicles, has broken the law. But this kind of lawbreaking will not entail a finding of fault, because the law being broken is administrative rather than conduct-oriented. The duty to keep one's driver's license current is a duty owed to the state and

---

25. 126 N.E. at 815 (emphasis in original).

primarily serves the state's interest in record keeping, not a duty to conduct oneself in a safe manner toward others.

Second, even the violation of a conduct-guiding statute will not serve as the basis for a negligence per se argument unless (1) the victim seeking to invoke the statute is among those whom the statute was designed to protect and (2) the harm suffered by the victim was of a sort that the statute was designed to prevent. For example, children can suffer serious injuries if they ride unrestrained in a vehicle that stops suddenly. Statutes and regulations requiring that children under a certain age be strapped into a special car seat are intended to protect children against such injuries. A minivan driver employed by a day care center who is sued in negligence for injuries suffered by an unrestrained child who flies into the vehicle's windshield after a sudden stop will likely be subject to a negligence per se argument in a jurisdiction that has enacted this sort of statute. The court will instruct the jury that if it finds the driver failed to place the child in a car seat as required by statute, it can only conclude that the driver breached the duty of ordinary care owed to the child.

On the other hand, if, while the car is stopped, an unrestrained child in the back seat crawls onto the car floor and suffers a serious hand injury as a result of getting it stuck under the car's front seat, the child's parents will not be able to invoke the statute to establish breach on the part of the driver. This is because car seat statutes are meant to protect children against being injured because of sudden deceleration, not to protect children against exploring parts of the car that they otherwise could not reach if buckled into their seats. The harm realized in this instance was not one against which the statute was meant to protect. In principle, it will still be open to the parents of this child to bring a standard negligence claim against the driver, with the issue of breach being adjudicated under the ordinary care standard rather than determined by the statutory requirement of child seat use. However, as we saw in Chapter 5, the doctrine of proximate cause may prevent the parents from prevailing on this claim. (Some readers will perhaps have noticed correctly that this pair of negligence per se requirements—that the plaintiff be among those protected by the statute, and that the harm-producing incident be among those the statute was meant to prevent—parallels the *relationality of breach* and *proximate cause* requirements of a common law negligence claim, discussed in Chapter 5.)

Third, even if a court is dealing with a violation of the right sort of statute, as well as the right sort of victim and the right kind of injuring, the victim still must prove that the violation *actually caused* her injury. In *Martin*, proof that the plaintiff had been driving with his headlights off and was killed in a vehicular crash sufficed to entitle the defendant to invoke the negligence per se doctrine to establish plaintiff's comparative fault. But the defendant was also required to prove that the plaintiff's statutory violation was a cause of the crash. If instead the evidence showed that the accident would have happened even if Martin had been using lights—for example, if, just before the accident, Herzog was looking for something in the back seat of his car as he drove, and hence would not have seen Martin's vehicle even if its lights had been lit—then the violation, being causally irrelevant, would not give rise to a finding of contributory negligence. The same applies when negligence per se is invoked to establish a defendant's fault.

Fourth and finally, it is sometimes open to an actor subject to an otherwise valid negligence per se argument to establish that the statutory violation was *excused* as conduct that, under the circumstances, was safer than conduct in compliance with the statute. *Tedla v. Ellman*,[26] another New York decision that turned on the issue of plaintiff's contributory negligence, provides an example of an excused violation. Plaintiff, a pedestrian, was struck by defendant car driver. The driver argued that plaintiff was contributorily negligent per se because she was walking along the right shoulder of the road—with traffic, rather than against it, as required by statute. The court deemed the plaintiff's violation excused on the ground that

---

26. 19 N.E.2d 987 (N.Y. 1939).

the road and traffic conditions were such that the plaintiff chose a clearly safer course by walking on the 'wrong' side of the road.

In a case in which the doctrine of negligence per se is applicable, a litigant's *violation* of a statutory provision specifying how an actor must conduct herself is used as a 'sword' by a party seeking to establish that the opposing party must be found at fault. What about the reverse argument that proof of a litigant's *compliance* with such a provision definitively establishes her *lack of fault*? Historically courts have rejected this argument, instead treating statutes as minimum 'floors' rather than maximum 'ceilings.' Thus, a driver who can prove that he was driving below a posted speed limit at the time she collided with and injured the plaintiff might still be deemed by a jury to have acted carelessly if, for example, she should have been driving more carefully because of icy roads or poor visibility. The same tends to be true for a manufacturer who sells an ordinary consumer product that is in compliance with applicable safety standards set by agency regulations, but nonetheless hurts a consumer using it in an ordinary manner.

Although the idea of a "regulatory compliance defense" is *not* part of the common law of negligence, it is one to which modern legislatures and a few courts have been drawn. (*See* Chapter 13's discussion of federal law preemption of state tort law.) Certainly, there are policy arguments in favor of recognizing such a defense. The experts who set regulatory standards arguably know more than jurors about the costs and benefits of taking various precautions against preventing harms, and the costs and uncertainties of the tort system sometimes will not be worth the second level of protection that it provides atop these regulations and the regulatory apparatus (prosecutions and fines) available to enforce them. However, the defense still rarely applies, in part because it is quite alien to the normative and remedial spirit of the common law of negligence. As Learned Hand noted in *T. J. Hooper* (discussed above), courts wish to reserve for themselves and for juries the authority to conclude that a whole industry has fallen behind what ordinary prudence requires. They perhaps feel the same way about agencies. After all, these entities are often under pressure from powerful political figures and private actors to minimize costly regulations or water down the content of controlling standards of conduct. In this way, the common law power of judges and juries to declare conduct imprudent can operate as a check against the tendency of the political branches to at times be 'captured' by regulated entities or special interests.

6.5 Causation Conundrums

In this and the next section, we consider in greater depth the causation element of negligence, and particularly the actual causation component of that element. It will be helpful to recall from Chapter 5 that the causation element has two components: *actual* and *proximate* cause.

6.5.1 Overdetermined Causes and Doomed Plaintiffs

Chapter 5 explained that the test for determining whether a careless act counts as an actual cause of an injury is whether the injury would have happened had the carelessness not occurred. (If there would have been no injury without the carelessness, the carelessness is a cause of the injury.) Given the "preponderance of the evidence" standard, the plaintiff's usual burden in a negligence case is to present enough evidence such that a jury can conclude that, but for the defendant's carelessness, the plaintiff *probably* would not have been injured. We also saw from the example of a crash caused by two careless drivers that jurors often will have grounds on which to find that each of two or more careless acts has operated as an actual cause of a single injury under the but-for test.

There is, however, one special set of circumstances in which each of two careless acts seems intuitively to function as a cause of a single injury, yet *neither* functions as a necessary condition of the injury, and hence neither satisfies the but-for test. This is the problem of *overdetermined* or *multiple sufficient causes*. In *Andersen v. Minneapolis St. Paul & Saul Ste. Marie Railway Co.*,[27] the defendant carelessly started a fire that later merged with another fire of unknown origin. (Let us assume that it too was carelessly started by an independent actor who was acting carelessly.) The merged fire(s) caused damage to the plaintiff's property. The jury concluded from the evidence presented that each fire by itself would have been sufficient to cause the damage. Given this finding, plaintiff could not establish that the defendant's breach was an actual cause of his property damage: the damage would have occurred even without his fire. Nonetheless, the court concluded that the plaintiff was entitled to prevail. So long as the fire started by the defendant was a "material factor" in the destruction of the property, the court reasoned, that fire could count as a cause of the damage. By the phrase "material factor"—frequently referred to by other courts as "*substantial factor*"—the court seems to have intended to exclude from its holding a case in which an actor makes an arguably trivial contribution to an independent force that would have sufficed of itself to generate the plaintiff's injury, an example being that of a person who carelessly tosses a lit match into a raging forest fire that proceeds to burn down plaintiff's house.

It is critical to appreciate that the circumstances that require resort to the substantial factor test are extremely narrow. The standard but-for test is perfectly capable of handling the vast bulk of cases in which two or more independent forces play a role in bringing about a single injury. What makes the joining fires scenario special is that the two forces are operating *simultaneously* in a situation

---

27. 179 N.W. 45 (Minn. 1920), *rev'd on other grounds*, Borsheim v. Great N. Ry. Co., 183 N.W. 519 (1921).

in which *each would of itself have brought* about the injury at issue. By contrast, in Chapter 5's intersection-collision illustration, neither driver's act of careless driving was of itself sufficient to cause the resulting injury—both needed to happen to generate the plaintiff's injury.

Resort to the substantial factor test will also be unnecessary in a case in which the two sufficient causes do *not* operate simultaneously. Suppose the evidence in *Andersen* showed that the fire of unknown origin reached the plaintiff's property first, with the defendant's careless fire reaching the property only after it was burned down by the other fire. In this sort of "preemptive cause" case there is no basis, even under the substantial factor test, for imposing liability on the defendant. That the fire would have been sufficient to burn down the house *had it not already burned down* does not render it a cause of the house being burned down. Likewise, suppose defendant *F* carelessly causes a fire that burns down a house. Later, victim *V*'s body is discovered in the house. However, an autopsy reveals that *V* suffered and died from a heart attack at least a day before the fire occurred. Though *F* will be liable for the property damage, he will not be liable for negligently injuring or killing *V* because his careless setting of the fire cannot be said to have caused the already-dead *V* to be injured or killed.

Before leaving the topic of overdetermined causes, it is worth pausing to consider the logic of a decision like *Andersen*. Couldn't it be said on behalf of the defendant in *Andersen* that there is something odd about holding it liable to the plaintiff when the evidence shows that the plaintiff was going to suffer the same injury anyway because of the operation of an independent force? Is the answer to this challenge that a defendant who has been proven to have acted carelessly (regardless of whether that carelessness caused injury) has no entitlement to benefit from this sort of luck? Does it change the analysis to imagine a case in which each of two joining fires were independently set by careless actors, as opposed to one being set by carelessness and one by natural origin?

Yet another variation on the unusual scenarios we have been considering is provided by *Dillon v. Twin State Gas and Electric Co.*[28] A young boy playing on the frame of a bridge lost his balance and was about to fall a great distance onto rocks below. However, before doing so, he grabbed a nearby high voltage wire placed next to the bridge by the defendant utility company. As a result, he was killed by electrocution. The court found that a jury was entitled to conclude that the defendant was careless for maintaining uninsulated wires in a location where someone might come into contact with them, and that this carelessness was a cause of the boy's death. Nonetheless, the court also held that if the jury were to determine that the boy faced certain death moments later on the rocks below, the defendant could be held liable *only* for any added increment of suffering he may have experienced as a result of dying by electrocution, as opposed to dying by falling.

The *Dillon* court treated the scenario before it as raising an issue of damages, not actual causation. The court's thinking seems to have been that the actual causation inquiry should be framed in terms of the particular moment in time at which the plaintiff's injury occurs: i.e., *whether, but for the defendant's carelessness, the plaintiff would have died more or less at the moment at which he died.* (This is as opposed to framing the question in terms of whether, but for the defendant's carelessness, the plaintiff would have died in the same sequence of events that led to his grabbing of the wires.) Difficult in its own right, the *Dillon* holding raises some tough follow-on questions. Suppose that because of *D*'s carelessness, plaintiff *P* suffers a broken leg that leaves her with an incurable limp. A year later, by which time *P* is about to go to trial against *D*, *P* loses the same leg as a result of an unrelated incident. Should that subsequent event be taken into account at trial in assessing *P*'s damages? If not, is *Dillon* any different?

---

28. 163 A. 11 (N.H. 1932).

6.5.2 Tortfeasor Identification: Alternate and Market Share Liability

A special kind of problem related to the proof of actual causation concerns instances in which it is clear that *someone's* tortious conduct has injured a victim, yet the victim cannot identify who that person is. Another famous California Supreme Court decision, *Summers v. Tice*,[29] illustrates one iteration of this problem. Summers was quail hunting with two other men, Simonson and Tice. Although they had planned to stay in a line while hunting, Summers got ahead of the other two, such that the three men were standing in a triangular formation. When a bird flew out of the brush near Summers, Simonson and Tice both shot at it. A shotgun pellet struck Summers in the eye, partially blinding him. (Another pellet struck him in the lip, but generated incidental harm and was effectively ignored by the court.) Unfortunately, there was no way for Summers to trace the pellet that struck him in the eye to the gun of either Simonson or Tice. He thus confronted the following problem when he brought negligence claims against each of the shooters: the careless shooting by each was *equally likely* to have caused and not to have caused his injury. For this reason, Summers' claim against each defendant fell just shy of the required proof that the defendant's carelessness *was more probably than not* the source of Summers' injury. And so Summers stood to lose both claims, even though one of the defendants surely committed the tort of negligence against him.

It is important to see why *Summers* presents a situation that is distinct from standard cases in which a single injury results from multiple careless acts, as when two careless drivers collide with each other in an intersection and run down a pedestrian. In the collision situation, the victim faces no special difficulty on the issue of actual causation; she will just have to show in the usual way that,

---

29. 199 P.2d 1 (Cal. 1948).

but for the carelessness of each driver, there probably would have been no crash and she would not have been injured. *Summers* is also different from cases of overdetermined causation, such as the joining fires case discussed above. Only one of the shooters actually succeeded in shooting Summers, so it would be false to say that careless shooting by each was sufficient of itself to cause his injury. In *Summers* we know that, but for a careless act of discharging a gun, the plaintiff would not have been partially blinded. What we don't know is which of two identically situated shooters committed the careless act that actually injured the victim.

One way to approach the problem in *Summers* is to ponder whether, as in the *Ybarra* case (discussed above under the heading of *res ipsa loquitur*), the causation problem can be finessed by treating the two shooters as a single actor. Certain rules of tort law do allow the acts of one person to be attributed to another. For example, if Simonson and Tice had secretly formed a plan to shoot Summers, then they would be treated as having conspired with each other to commit battery against Summers and held jointly liable to him. Even absent the level of coordination required for conspiracy, each of two actors who are consciously engaged in a joint activity—for example, an illegal drag race—can be held liable even if only one of them injures someone during the course of the activity. If it were applicable, this "concert of action" doctrine would also hold each shooter responsible, regardless of who actually succeeded in blinding Summers. Unfortunately, the doctrine was unavailable to Summers, both because his lawyers failed to proffer it as a theory of liability and because it requires a degree of coordination between the relevant actors that was absent in this instance.

And yet the court still concluded that Summers had viable negligence claims against both defendants. It reasoned as follows. Whereas in an ordinary negligence suit, the plaintiff bears the burden of proving a *probable* connection between a defendant's carelessness and the plaintiff's injury, in this special situation, the *burden of proof ought to be shifted to the defendants*, such that it was incumbent on Simonson and Tice to establish which of the two was the one who actually shot Summers. If unable to do so, then they would each fail to meet the burden of disproving causation that the court had shifted onto them. In turn, they would be held *jointly and severally liable*, which means that Summers would be entitled to collect up to 100 percent of his damages from each, so long as the total damages collected did not exceed that amount. (*See* Chapter 12.)

The scheme of liability created by *Summers'* burden-shifting rule has come to be known as *alternate liability*. Alternate liability is open to a narrow and a broad interpretation. The narrow interpretation holds that it is an appropriate solution only to the exact situation presented by *Summers*, namely: (a) two actors independently engage in identical careless acts toward the victim; (b) it is clear that only one of them actually caused the victim to suffer an injury; (c) both actors are brought before the court by the plaintiff; and (d) the plaintiff through no fault of his own has no way of proving which of the two actors caused his injury. In this situation, the notion that the court is shifting a burden of persuasion has real traction. Essentially it is changing the applicable evidentiary rule from "tie goes to the defendant" to "tie goes to the plaintiff." And it is doing so on the equitable ground that, as between an innocent victim and each of two actors who committed identical acts of carelessness toward the plaintiff, one of which hurt the plaintiff, it is fair to impose the burden of proof on the issue of causation on the defendants.

The broader interpretation of *Summers* moves past a notion of burden-shifting to the idea that a plaintiff should be able to benefit from a presumption of actual causation even if *more than two careless* actors are involved. So, for example, if there were four shooters, each of whom carelessly shot in the direction of Summers, but only one of whom shot him, the burden of disproving causation would shift to each defendant, and if none could meet it, then all would be subject to liability. On this broader reading, *Summers* cannot be understood as changing a rule for breaking evidentiary 'ties.'

After all, when the number of defendants is greater than two, and there is no evidence indicating that any one of them is more likely the one who shot the plaintiff, the odds of any of them having been the actual shooter is by definition less than 50 percent. (In the case of four shooters, it is 25 percent.) In these situations, there is no 'tie' to break, because, as to each defendant, it is more likely than not that that defendant was *not* the shooter. Hence the justification for invoking alternate liability on these broader terms must reside in some other rationale. And yet the rationale cannot be that, as between an innocent victim and any persons who have acted carelessly toward her, it is equitable to shift the burden of proof on causation. For that rationale would presumably justify shifting the burden of proof on causation in *any case* in which there is evidence of defendant fault and no evidence of plaintiff fault.

Regardless of whether *Summers* is given a narrow or broad reading, its application presupposes that all of the persons who acted carelessly, and one of whom injured the plaintiff, have been haled into court by the plaintiff. This feature of the *Summers* rule helps distinguish it from a notable extension of it, which now goes under the name of *market share liability*. The font of this doctrine is yet another California Supreme Court decision—one that in fact marks the end of the line of innovative decisions it issued during the period from roughly 1945 to 1980.

Sindell v. Abbott Laboratories involved claims arising out of the use of a drug known as DES, which from the mid-1940s to the late 1960s was prescribed to pregnant women to help prevent miscarriages.[30] Disastrously, the drug proved to be not only inefficacious but to cause a rare form of cancers—adenocarcinoma—and other diseases in a certain percentage of woman who had been exposed to it *in utero*. Plaintiff Sindell, who developed a tumor in her bladder while a young woman, sued several DES manufacturers. However, there were no medical records or other bases for determining which

---

30. 607 P.2d 924 (Cal.), *cert denied*, 449 U.S. 912 (1980).

of the scores of manufacturers that made and sold DES produced the pills that her mother had ingested.

As in *Summers*, the courts were faced with a person who had a powerful claim to have been the victim of a tort, yet could not identify who among several actors that had engaged in identical tortious conduct (marketing the same defective drug) was the actor that injured her. However, unlike in *Summers*, the plaintiff in *Sindell* had not sued—and for jurisdictional and other reasons could not sue—each of the many DES manufacturers. Thus the court could not be sure that the firm that actually manufactured the drug that was ingested by plaintiff's mother was one of the defendants in the litigation. Therefore even on a broad rendering, *Summers'* alternate liability doctrine was unavailable to Sindell.

Rather than leave Sindell and hundreds of other victims of DES remediless, the court instead fashioned the doctrine of market share liability. It works as follows. First, the situation must be one in which a number of actors have produced identical, fungible products. Second, the plaintiff must bring into court a group that is big enough to be "substantially likely" to contain the actor who actually hurt the plaintiff. Third, the plaintiff, through no fault of her own, must be unable to prove which of the defendants caused her injury. Fourth, the plaintiff must be prepared to meet the normal burden of proving that the defendant had acted carelessly (or, under the doctrine of products liability, had sold a defective product), that she suffered an injury, and that the misconduct in question is generally capable of causing the type of injury she suffered. With these conditions met, the burden shifts to each defendant to *disprove* that its misconduct caused the plaintiff's injury. (In a DES case, a manufacturer might do this by producing records indicating that its products were never distributed to the geographic area in which plaintiff's mother resided at the time at which she took the DES that injured the plaintiff.) Defendants who can meet this burden are spared from liability. Those who cannot are subject to liability, *but only for a percentage of the plaintiff's total damages corresponding to the defendant's share of the California DES market* during the period in which the plaintiff's mother ingested it. It is this last feature of *Sindell's* holding that earned its rule the title of market share liability.

For example, suppose a plaintiff such as Sindell were to sue five DES manufacturers responsible for 75 percent of the total California market for DES at the time her mother ingested the drug. Suppose also that none could exonerate itself, and that their respective shares of that 75 percent overall market share were 10 percent, 15 percent, 20 percent, 25 percent, and 30 percent. Finally, suppose that the plaintiff can show that she has suffered $1 million in damages. Each defendant would then be liable to the plaintiff, but only in an amount corresponding to its percentage of the aggregate market share controlled by the defendants: here, $75,000, $112,500, $150,000, $187,500 and $225,000. Because the non-exonerated defendants controlled only 75% of the relevant DES market, the plaintiff is denied recovery of 25% for her damages.

The *Sindell* court acknowledged that its liability scheme can only hope to deliver rough justice. Yet it professed hope that in the run of cases, manufactures would by this scheme end up paying amounts corresponding to the aggregate amount of harm their actions caused. It also emphasized that an equal or greater injustice would be done by not adjusting standard tort doctrine and thereby permitting an entire universe of known tortfeasors—the firms that sold DES and thereby injured someone—completely off the hook. Note that unlike in *Summers*, where the defendant who actually shot the plaintiff was a tortfeasor while the other was not, the *Sindell* court could be reasonably certain that each of the defendants had, by manufacturing and selling DES, committed an identical tort against *someone*.

Market share liability has attracted a great deal of academic attention, both from admirers and critics. This attention is at one level disproportionate, for the doctrine has by and large failed to make further headway in the courts. While a few state high courts have recognized the doctrine in DES litigation, many have declined to adopt it. And despite the efforts of plaintiffs' lawyers to extend it to litigation over injuries arising out of the sale of handguns or tobacco products, as well as the use of asbestos or lead-based paint, one can still today count on one hand the number of high court decisions that authorize the use of the doctrine in these other settings. In part, this pattern reflects the fact that the DES context has proven to be almost unique in that the defendants' tortious conduct was in all relevant respects identical, and because the plaintiffs—having been *in utero* at the time of injury—were completely passive, utterly blameless victims. Even in the DES context, courts are reluctant in part because it is not even clear that there is evidence from which to form reliable judgments about market shares.

Yet if market share liability has not made much of an impact doctrinally, it is still deserving of careful attention. Some see it as a model for how tort law ought to operate in modern conditions of mass manufacture and marketing. Others decry it as marking the point at which tort law clearly ceases to be about empowering victims to hold responsible those who have wrongfully injured them and instead becomes a shadow regulatory system for spreading losses or deterring socially undesirable conduct. Still others see it as a principled extension of the idea in *Summers* that courts can, under special conditions, shift the burden of proof on actual causation from a plaintiff alleging having been wronged to the defendant(s) accused of doing wrong.

6.6 Intervening Wrongdoing

We have previously addressed the concepts of affirmative duty (this chapter) and proximate cause (Chapter 5). In this section, we confront a class of cases that invites us to consider how these two concepts interact. The common feature in this class is that the carelessness of one actor (the "remote actor") causes harm to a victim only because of the subsequent intervention of another wrongdoer (the "immediate injurer").

Suppose the owner of an apartment building neglects to repair broken locks on the building's lobby doors and that a tenant is attacked by an assailant who has taken advantage of the absence of locks to lie in wait for her. The assailant is the immediate injurer and the owner is the remote actor. In cases like the one just described, the immediate injurer usually will be subject to liability. The question is whether his intervention should cut off the responsibility of the remote actor *even though the remote actor's carelessness functioned as an actual cause of the victim's injury.* When courts conclude that responsibility should be cut off, they often express that conclusion by describing the intervening wrongdoing as a *superseding cause* of the plaintiff's injury.

As a threshold matter, one might fairly wonder why, if the immediate injurer is likely to be subject to liability, a victim would bother to bring an additional negligence claim against a background actor? In fact, she will often have principled and practical reasons to pursue such a claim. She may justifiably believe that the remote actor bears some responsibility for what happened to her. She may also believe that she will have a better chance to collect on a judgment against the remote actor than the immediate assailant.

It is also worth emphasizing at the outset that our present concern is not with intervening conduct per se, but with intervening *wrongful* conduct. Recall *MacPherson v. Buick* from Chapter 5. There, a car manufacturer sold a badly made car to the victim through a local dealer. That the dealer's actions intervened between the defendant's carelessness and the plaintiff's injury did not, and would not today, give rise to an inquiry into whether the dealer's act of selling the car might relieve the manufacturer of responsibility. No wrong by the dealer was alleged; the dealer was a mere intervening actor, not an intervening wrongdoer.

In cases involving intervening wrongdoing, the situations that raise the most difficult questions are ones in which the remote actor and the intervening wrongdoer are acting *independently* of one another. By contrast, if there is a recognized basis for attributing the immediate injurer's wrong to the remote actor, liability will attach for both actors. Where applicable, doctrines such as civil conspiracy, accomplice liability, and especially concert of action—the latter being exemplified by the case of two participants in a drag race, only one of whom runs into the victim—allow a negligence plaintiff to hold liable a person other than the immediate injurer on the ground that the injurer was 'doing the bidding' of that other.

Unfortunately for plaintiffs, there is a vast domain of instances, like the lobby attack example, in which the intervening wrongful acts of the immediate injurer are not attributable to the remote wrongdoer. Is the rule for these cases that the intervening wrongful infliction of injury will always block the imposition of liability on the remote actor? Clearly not. Indeed, there are at least three recognized grounds for holding remote actors responsible notwithstanding the independent intervening wrongful conduct of another.

The first of these grounds is one that we encountered in Chapter 5's discussion of actual causation. The relevant example is that of the two careless drivers who collide with one another and thereby injure a pedestrian. Now imagine that the careless acts of the two drivers operate *successively* rather than contemporaneously. Thus suppose driver *D* carelessly drives into a lamppost, knocking it over. Five minutes later, taxi driver *T*, because he is not paying attention to where he is going, strikes the lamppost as it is lying in the road. As a result, *T*'s passenger *P* is injured. *D* will not be able point to *T*'s intervening careless failure to avoid the fallen lamppost as a ground for relieving him of responsibility for the injuring of *P*. *D* and *T* both acted carelessly so as to cause harm to *P*, and both will be on the hook. (To what extent each will be held liable is discussed below and in Chapter 12.)

To isolate the grounds of liability in a case like the one just described, it will be helpful to contrast it with a very different kind of scenario, one well illustrated by *Port Authority of New York and New Jersey v. Arcadian Corp.*[31] This litigation arose out of the first

---

31. 189 F.3d 305 (3d Cir. 1999).

terrorist attack on New York's World Trade Center (WTC), which took place in 1993 and involved a successful plot to detonate a van filled with explosives as it sat in a parking garage underneath one of the WTC's towers. One lawsuit growing out of this incident involved claims by the Port Authority, the owner of the building, for property damage caused by the explosion. The claim was not against the bombers, but instead against the manufacturer of the chemical fertilizer that provided the main ingredient for their bomb. The theory of the suit was that the manufacturer was aware, or should have been aware, of the amenability of its product to being used as a powerful explosive, and that it could and should have altered the product's chemical composition or controlled its distribution to reduce the chances that it would be so misused.

The federal trial and appellate courts that heard this claim rejected it, reasoning that even if the manufacturer had been careless, it could not be held liable for injuries arising out of the bombing. Why not? Isn't this case just like the case of the successively careless car drivers D and T? One obvious difference between them is the nature of the wrongful intervention—the terrorists' intentional effort to murder and destroy, as opposed to T's careless failure to attend to the safety of his passenger. However, as we will see, there are instances in which remote actors will be held liable notwithstanding that another's intentional wrong also functioned as a cause of the victim's injury. So some other consideration must also be at work here.

As it turns out, the key difference has to do less with the nature of the respective intervening wrongdoers' wrongs, and more with *the nature of the remote wrongdoer's wrong*. On the face of things, there seems to be no difference. After all, we are supposing that the wrongfulness that inheres in the conduct of initial driver D and of the fertilizer manufacturer consists of carelessness. And yet the kinds of carelessness each committed are quite distinct. A driver who drives carelessly is already creating a risk of collision-related injuries to persons that include passengers in other cars; it is the creation of this sort of risk to this sort of person that renders the conduct careless. The fact that in a particular instance, the careless driver only happens to injure a passenger because of the intervention of another careless driver, while an essential part of the causal account of how the victim came to be injured, is *normatively irrelevant.* In other words: the taxi passenger's complaint against the first careless car driver *D* will identify the wrongfulness of his behavior as driving carelessly so as to pose a danger of injuring another user of the road in a crash.

Now contrast the fertilizer case. One cannot give a description of what renders the manufacturer's conduct careless without reference to the intervention of the terrorists: the gist of the charge of wrongdoing is that the manufacturer was careless *with respect to the risk of someone misusing its product for nefarious purposes.* In the car accident case, the remote defendant creates a freestanding risk of harm that could just as easily result in injury to the plaintiff with or without the intervention of another wrongdoer. In the fertilizer case, the remote defendant's conduct can only be careless by virtue of making it too easy for an intervening actor to commit an independent wrong. The lesson of this contrast is as follows: the intervening wrongdoing in the case of the successive careless drivers does not defeat the imposition of liability on the more remote actor because the latter's conduct *was wrongful toward the plaintiff irrespective of the contribution of another wrongdoer,* and hence such intervention is normatively irrelevant even though it functioned as a necessary condition of a particular person being injured.

We are almost to the point of having an adequate handle on the problem of intervening, independent wrongdoing. However, one more step is required to complete the analysis. The fertilizer manufacturer case has helped us to see why there is no problem imposing liability on the remote defendant in cases of successive wrongful acts where the second act essentially runs parallel to the first and just happens to function as a second cause of a single injury. Still, we don't yet have an account of why the nature of the wrongfulness of the fertilizer manufacturer's conduct—i.e., that it is wrongful only because it provides another with a means of wrongfully inflicting injury—provides a reason to defeat claims against remote defendants. We can get at that account by contrasting the fertilizer suit to another claim by a different plaintiff arising out of the same terrorist incident.

In *Nash v. Port Authority of New York and New Jersey*,[32] the plaintiff, who worked in an office in the WTC, was parking her car in the underground garage when the terrorists' bomb exploded. Having suffered devastating physical injuries, she sued the Port Authority claiming that it was careless in failing to take steps to reduce the risk that the WTC would be subject to a terrorist attack. (Evidence of the Authority's imprudence included its failure to act on internal documents and warnings from outside security agencies that the WTC was at considerable risk of exactly the sort of attack that was perpetrated.) The Port Authority argued that even if it had been careless, the intervening acts of the terrorists provided grounds for excusing it from liability—the very same argument that Arcadian, the fertilizer manufacturer, invoked successfully to defeat Port Authority's claim that the manufacturer was responsible in part for the bombing damage to the WTC buildings.

In a 2008 decision, an intermediate New York appellate court affirmed a jury verdict in *Nash* in favor of the plaintiff. In rejecting the defendant's superseding cause argument, it relied on a rule of New York tort law stating that landlords owe occupants of their buildings a duty to take reasonable measures to protect them from foreseeable criminal activity taking place on the premises. On this score, New York law is hardly unusual—most U.S. jurisdictions recognize this duty in one form or another. (A leading authority is *Kline v. 1500 Massachusetts Avenue Apartment Corporation*,[33] a decision that held the owner of a Washington, D.C., apartment building liable to a tenant who was attacked in the building's lobby.

---

32. 856 N.Y.S.2d 583 (N.Y. App. Div. 2008).

33. 439 F.2d 477 (D.C. Cir. 1970).

Kline reasoned that the owner was obligated to take certain basic security measures to protect occupants against foreseeable criminal acts, such as installing a 'buzzer' system for gaining entrance to the building.) In *Nash*, the appellate court upheld liability on the grounds that the Port Authority not only could have foreseen, but actually did foresee, that the WTC was a target of special significance for terrorists, as well as one that was highly vulnerable to attack, and that certain security measures (including the elimination of open-to-the-public parking spaces and inspection of entering vehicles) could and should have been taken that probably would have prevented the bombing.

What, then, is missing from *Arcadian* yet present in *Nash*, such that it would make sense to bar a negligence claim for property damage arising out the WTC bombing against the fertilizer manufacturer, but permit a negligence claim for personal injuries against the Port Authority? The answer is *duty* and, more specifically, affirmative duty. It is precisely because the Port Authority owed users of its building an affirmative duty to take reasonable measures against criminal attacks in (or on) the building that the Port Authority—the remote actor—was appropriately held liable along with the terrorists for injuries caused most immediately by the terrorists' attack to users of the building. (Recall in this regard a case of intervening wrongdoing we encountered above: *Tarasoff.* The lynchpin of that decision is its holding that therapists owe identifiable potential victims of their patients an affirmative duty to take steps to warn them of the risk of attack.) By the same token, it is the *absence* of any affirmative duty on the part of the fertilizer manufacturer to take steps to protect persons or structures from foreseeable criminal misuse of its product that explains why the terrorists' bombing is deemed a superseding cause that blocks the attribution of any liability to the manufacturer. The law, following ordinary notions of responsibility, does not charge makers and sellers of standard commercial products with an obligation to protect the public from their being criminally misused. As such, the manufacturer could not be charged with any responsibility for what the terrorists did with its product, even though its carelessness was (or was presumed to be) a necessary condition of the terrorists' actions.

Although there are plenty of instances in which actors owe an affirmative duty to protect certain persons against the injurious wrongful acts of others, the set is nonetheless finite, which is why in many instances (such as *Arcadian*) no liability will attach even to an actor whose carelessness has contributed to the injuring of a victim by another wrongdoer. A particularly important, if somewhat unusual, category of affirmative duty cases concerns duties that attend the possession of dangerous instrumentalities, especially firearms and motorized vehicles. Simply by virtue of maintaining lawful control over such an instrumentality, the possessor incurs a duty to protect against its being misused by a third-party wrongdoer. Thus, one who carelessly entrusts one's loaded weapon to a drunken adult who cannot be expected to use it safely will be subject to liability to someone who is carelessly (or perhaps even intentionally) shot by that person. The critical difference between these *negligent entrustment* cases and *Arcadian* is that the latter involved the outright sale of a product. If one is prepared fully to alienate one's property, such that any right to control it is abandoned, one is generally not obligated to make sure that it will not be misused once alienated.

To summarize, in cases of intervening wrongdoing, the remote actor can be held liable if (1) there is a basis for attributing the immediate injurer's misconduct to the remote actor (e.g., a conspiracy between them); (2) the remote actor's conduct was already tortious as to the victim irrespective of the prospect of wrongful conduct by anyone else (the case of the two successive careless drivers); and/or (3) the remote actor's conduct was only wrongful in creating a risk of intervening wrongdoing by another, but the actor owed persons such as the victim an affirmative duty to take steps to protect her against criminal misconduct by third parties (*Nash, Kline*). If none of these conditions are present, as was the case in *Arcadian*, the remote wrongdoer is spared from liability on the ground that only the immediate injurer can be deemed responsible for having injured the plaintiff.

Having laid out this framework, we should stress that these categories, like all legal categories, will admit of clear applications and borderline cases. Consider in this regard two noteworthy lines of contemporary negligence litigation. In the 1990s, some plaintiffs' lawyers began pressing negligent marketing claims against gun manufacturers. These complaints, brought on behalf of persons who had been shot with illegally possessed handguns, alleged that the manufacturers had failed adequately to supervise the downstream distribution of their products so as to facilitate illegal gun purchases and thereby help cause the shootings. The few state courts to entertain these claims rejected them, essentially for the reasons discussed in connection with the claim in *Arcadian*. Such claims are now explicitly barred by a federal law enacted in 2005 known as the "Protection of Lawful Commerce in Arms Act."

Another theory of liability that arguably presents a closer question on the issue of affirmative duty, yet has also met mostly with a chilly reception from the courts, is so-called "social host" liability. In this sort of case, the host of a party makes available alcohol for consumption by her adult guests (but does not ply the guests with alcohol or otherwise encourage them to drink). A guest drinks to excess, drives away drunk, and injures a user of the road because of her drunkenness. In *Childs v. Desormeaux*,[34] the Canadian Supreme Court, following the majority approach, rejected social host liability, and did so on facts that were particularly favorable to the victim. (The host knew the guest to be prone to excessive drinking.) And yet in many U.S. jurisdictions, *commercial* sellers of alcohol (bars and restaurants) are by statute subject to liability if they knowingly or carelessly over-serve a customer who later injures a third party because of his drunkenness.

One final note on the imposition of liability on remote wrongdoers for injuries caused in part by the intervening wrongful acts

---

34. [2006] 1 S.C.R. 643 (Can.).

of others: To conclude that, on one ground or another, a remote actor can be held liable along with the more immediate injurer is not yet to determine the *extent* to which each should be held liable. That question is determined by rules of apportionment, which are discussed in Chapter 12. Typically, however, if there is a basis for holding both immediate injurer and remote tortfeasor liable, the fact finder will be asked to assign a percentage of fault to each, with the total adding up to 100 percent, assuming no fault is attributable to the plaintiff. One of the most striking and controversial features of the outcome in *Nash*, upheld on appeal, was the jury's decision to allocate 68 percent (!) of the fault for the 1993 the terrorist bombing of the WTC to the Port Authority.

6.7 Immunities and Exemptions

In tort, an immunity is a defense that blocks the imposition of liability on an actor because of the actor's status or identity. Historically, the most important tort immunity has been *sovereign immunity*. At common law, this doctrine prevented a person wrongfully injured by a federal or state employee acting in the scope of his employment from obtaining compensation from government coffers, though not necessarily from the individual official. In the middle years of the twentieth century, both the federal government and the states enacted statutes that partially relinquished the blanket immunity provided by common law. The Federal Tort Claims Act (FTCA) is a statute that now permits persons injured by acts of federal government employees to recover from the government under a modified version of standard principles of *respondeat superior*. (*See* Chapter 4.) For example, if, while on the job, a health inspector employed by the federal Food and Drug Administration carelessly crashes his government vehicle into the victim's vehicle, the victim can recover from the federal government, just as she could recover from a private employer for an employee's careless act within the scope of employment.

However, the FTCA's waiver of immunity contains a number of important exceptions that narrow the scope of liability faced by the federal government. These include the *discretionary function* exception, which is meant to discourage courts from using the occasion of private litigation to second-guess legislative and executive branch policy decisions. An agency decision to pursue a particular economic policy, or to subsidize a particular industry, or to decline to mandate the use of a particular safety device (such as air bags for new-model cars) often will have adverse consequences for someone (e.g., the victim of a car crash who would have been spared injury had air bags been mandated). Yet if this sort of victim were to sue the relevant agency on the theory that the agency's decision was unreasonable, the suit will be dismissed without any inquiry into the merits of that decision. The fact that it was a decision calling for a policy judgment as to the costs and benefits of pursuing a particular regulatory course is sufficient to render the government immune from liability under the discretionary function exemption. In recent years, out of a concern to err on the side of protecting government from tort suits, federal courts have tended to expand the scope of this exception to the FTCA's waiver of sovereign immunity, applying it even to low-level officials' implementation of standing policies.

As its name indicates, sovereign immunity applies to political entities that have the status of sovereigns—in the U.S. system, the federal government and the individual states. Yet local governments have argued that they ought to benefit from comparable restrictions on liability when acting in a governmental capacity. Because they are not literally entitled to sovereign immunity, these local entities have instead asked courts to grant them an equivalent protection through the recognition of special no-duty rules—i.e., rules that make it difficult or impossible for a claimant to establish the duty element of her negligence claim. And courts have in some instances accepted these arguments. Although judges and litigants frame these limitations on liability as no-duty or limited-duty rules, we believe that their contours and justifications reveal them to be immunities by another name.

The most notable of the no-duty rules that benefit local governments goes under the name of the *public duty rule*, which is an odd
label for a rule that in fact frees governmental actors from tort liability for carelessly failing to provide certain services. A notorious
application of the public duty rule is found in *Riss v. City of
New York*.[35] A married man named Pugach became obsessed with
plaintiff Linda Riss. When Pugach refused to leave his wife for Riss,
Riss became engaged to another man. Enraged, Pugach repeatedly
told Riss that he would harm her if she did not break off the engage-
ment. Riss contacted New York City police asking them to protect
her, but they did nothing. Pugach eventually hired a thug who
attacked and seriously injured Riss.

Riss sued the police department, arguing that their indifference
to her pleas for protection constituted a dereliction of their duty to
protect members of the public from harm. The New York Court of
Appeals ruled that the department owed no duty to take steps to
protect Riss and other citizens from injury at the hands of others.
Acknowledging that it is quite literally the job of police to enforce
laws designed for the safety of the public, the court nevertheless
insisted that this duty is owed to the public at large, not to any particular individual. The breach of this sort of duty, even though a
wrong in some sense, was a wrong to no one in particular and
therefore not civilly actionable, even by a person who clearly stood
to benefit from its performance. (Recall that a similar result was
reached in *Tarasoff*, discussed above, in which the California
Supreme Court refused to hold the police defendants liable for failing to warn an identifiable victim of her murderer's intention to
harm her.) Where recognized, the public duty rule is equally protective of other local government actors who carelessly fail to provide
essential services that they are charged with providing, thus blocking claims, for example, against firefighters for inexcusably failing

---

35. 240 N.E.2d 860 (N.Y. 1968).

to respond to an alarm and thereby permitting a victim's house to burn down.

As the lone *Riss* dissenter pointed out, there is something counterintuitive about the terms on which the New York court denied liability. How can a governmental entity that quite clearly bears a duty to serve and protect the public be deemed under "no duty" to serve and protect members of the public? It is for this reason that we do not take at face value the idea that the public duty rule is a genuine duty rule. (If a decision like *Riss* is to be defended, it cannot be on the ground that the police owe no obligation to individual members of the public to do the jobs that they are paid to do. Rather, it must be because there is a reason to grant them an exemption from the normal operation of the principles of tort law, which would otherwise call for liability.) Here, it is noteworthy that among the court's principal reasons for rejecting Riss's claim was a worry that permitting suits such as hers would interfere with police department decisions about how to allocate limited funds and personnel. The worry is that the prospect of liability for failing to protect individuals subject to serious threats of violence will induce police departments to shift resources away from other tasks, such as placing more police on the streets or employing more detectives to investigate crimes. This sort of concern to not have the judicial branch second-guess or interfere with executive branch policy decisions, we would suggest, is closely akin to the animating idea behind the FTCA's discretionary function exemption—hence our inclination to treat the public duty rule as a de facto judicial grant of immunity from conduct that is tortious and would otherwise be actionable.

Another set of actors that benefits from these sorts of 'no-duty immunities' are utility companies that provide essential services to the public, such as water, sewage, gas, and electricity. These companies operate in a special business environment. Often they function as local monopolies. The rates they charge tend to be set by regulatory bodies, and they are required to serve every member of the general public, as opposed to serving only those communities or areas where it is profitable to do so. Out of recognition of these special circumstances, courts have fashioned doctrines that protect utilities against liability that might threaten to undermine their ability to provide services at reasonable rates. For example, in *Strauss v. Belle Realty Co.*,[36] another New York Court of Appeals decision, the plaintiff tripped and fell in common area of a darkened New York City apartment building during a citywide blackout attributable to the defendant Con Edison's carelessness. Noting the vast potential for physical harm and property damage in crowded urban conditions during a blackout, the court denied the plaintiff's claim and limited recovery only to persons injured during the blackout who enjoyed contractual privity with Con Edison.[37] The *Strauss* court conceded that it was drawing an arbitrary line so as to limit the aggregate liability a utility would face for harm caused by its careless failure to provide essential services.

Decisions like *Riss* and *Strauss* do not confer complete immunity on local governments and utilities. *Strauss*, of course, permits negligence claims by persons in privity with the utility. And the privity rule itself, because it is a true floodgates rule, will not apply to situations in which there is no threat of 'excessive' liability. In *Goldberg v. Florida Light and Power Co.*,[38] an employee of the defendant electric company, working near a busy intersection, accidentally cut power to traffic signals at the intersection. An accident resulted in which plaintiff's decedent was killed. The court declined to invoke *Strauss*'s privity rule, reasoning that the class of potential victims of the defendant's carelessness was sufficiently self-contained to permit the ordinary operation of negligence law.

---

36. 482 N.E.2d 34 (N.Y. 1985).

37. In fact, Strauss was in privity with Con Edison, but only with respect to the electricity provided to his apartment. Because he fell while in a common area, electricity for which was purchased by the landlord, the court deemed Strauss ineligible to recover.

38. 899 So.2d 1105 (Fla. 2005).

Local governments are subject to liability under standard principles of respondeat superior for garden-variety employee misfeasance. For example, careless driving by a police officer on patrol or a utility worker on the job, is actionable under standard negligence principles. In addition, where local police or firefighters go so far as to make assurances to a particular victim that they will protect her, only to carelessly fail to do so, they may also face liability. The notion in a case like this is that the specific undertaking to protect, at least when coupled with the victim's reliance on that undertaking to her detriment, generates a special relationship that supports the imposition of liability notwithstanding the public duty rule.

6.8 Assumption of Risk

We learned in Chapter 5 that courts and legislatures have created *affirmative defenses* for every tort, including negligence. Affirmative defenses must be pleaded and proved by the defendant. Where applicable, they defeat the plaintiff's claim even though the defendant acted tortiously toward the plaintiff. Recognized defenses rest on various grounds: that the defendant's conduct was justified (or excused), that the plaintiff is ineligible to complain about it, or because of a concern to ensure that the legal system functions fairly. Self-defense is an example of an affirmative defense that applies to torts such as battery. A person who intentionally strikes another to protect himself from attack is immunized from liability if his response is proportionate to the attack. Likewise, one who freely and knowingly consents to being locked in a room for a certain period of time cannot recover on a claim of false imprisonment for being so confined. Statutes of limitations, which bar the filing of even valid claims after a specified time period, are policy-based rules designed to preserve the integrity of legal proceedings and to permit closure of the period during which a potential defendant might be vulnerable to suit.

In negligence law, it is rare to see a defendant invoke an affirmative defense that rests on the justifiability of an actor's careless act. This is because the factors that might provide a justification for the actor's conduct will tend to have already been considered in the analysis of the breach element of the plaintiff's prima facie case: in gauging whether an actor exercised ordinary prudence, the fact finder will naturally take into account the sorts of considerations that might figure in the establishment of a justification-based defense for other torts. We encountered one defense applicable to negligence in Chapter 5, namely, *comparative fault.* When invoked, it either reduces the plaintiff's recovery or bars her claim altogether on the ground that the plaintiff's own carelessness contributed to her being injured. In this section we consider three related eligibility defenses to negligence claims. Unfortunately for the cause of clarity, all of them are referred to by lawyers and judges under the single heading of "assumption of risk." Because this usage is well settled, we will invoke it even as we attempt to clarify this murky area of law.

6.8.1 Express Assumption of Risk

The duties of care generated by negligence law are mandatory—they are imposed by tort law rather than assumed voluntarily. (Of course they are also in a sense conditional—one does not incur the mandatory duties associated with driving a car until one elects to drive.) Yet individuals can sometimes formally agree to forego or waive the rights that are normally derived from these mandatory duties. When they do so, they may be barred from recovering for negligence by the doctrine of *express assumption of risk.* An express assumption of risk is almost always embodied in a writing signed by the eventual victim or her representative, by which she agrees in advance of the occasion of her injury to waive the right she would otherwise enjoy to sue the defendant for negligence should the defendant carelessly injure her. If the victim brings suit for such an injury, the defendant will invoke this writing as a basis for dismissing it at the outset, irrespective of the merits of the victim's negligence claim.

As a rule, courts are reluctant to enforce agreements of this sort. They will examine closely both the context in which the agreement was made and its content to ensure that it was formed under the right conditions—i.e., by a victim who was competent to sign away her rights, and who did so knowingly and voluntarily. Many waivers are voided for lack of genuine, knowing consent on the part of the victim, especially boilerplate waiver provisions preprinted on the back of entry passes and tickets.

From a libertarian perspective, the law presumptively ought to respect freely chosen private arrangements without concern for the fairness of those arrangements or for anyone else's interest in whether they are enforced. In principle, then, a true libertarian would want courts only to engage in the sort of scrutiny of waivers just described—i.e., to ensure that they are not the product of coercion or ignorance. Yet courts often decline to enforce even knowing and voluntary waivers on grounds that enforcement would be against public policy.

For example, in *Tunkl v. Regents of the University of California*,[39] a negligence suit was brought on behalf of an alleged victim of medical malpractice against the not-for-profit hospital in which he had been treated. The hospital sought dismissal of the suit on the basis of a signed form purporting to waive the victim's right to sue for any negligence on the part of hospital employees. The court voided the agreement, holding that, *even when they are knowing and voluntary*, waivers of liability will not be enforced with respect to any activity "affected with the public interest." In turn, it offered what has become an influential list of factors relevant to the determination of whether a genre of activity is affected with the public interest. They are: (1) whether the defendant's activity is a service

---

39. 383 P.2d 441 (Cal. 1963).

of great importance to the public, on which some members of the public tend to rely; (2) whether the defendant generally holds himself out as willing to perform this service to any member of the public; (3) whether the defendant is in a position to demand the waiver on a take-it-or-leave-it basis; and (4) whether the transaction, once completed, puts the victim largely under the control of the defendant.

Adopting *Tunkl*'s analysis, courts have struck down agreements by passengers to waive liability for injuries arising out the negligent operation of buses, trains, and other forms of public transportation. Some courts, including most notably the Vermont Supreme Court, have likewise cited *Tunkl* in refusing to enable ski resorts to obtain waivers of negligence liability from skiers. The Vermont decision,[40] like *Tunkl* itself, was motivated by the court's sense that there are certain activities that are so important or widespread that the public has an interest in denying actors who undertake them the ability to escape the mandatory obligations of tort law. In essence, courts that refuse to uphold these waivers in the name of public policy are denying regulated entities the ability to 'deregulate' themselves by inducing thousands of individual patrons to sign standard-form waiver provisions.

To keep *Tunkl* and like cases in perspective, it is useful to observe, first, that some courts will enforce waivers, particularly when issued in connection with more exotic recreational activities, such as skydiving. Where enforceable, these agreements do effectively bar persons who would otherwise have valid negligence claims from pursuing them. Second, it is probably the case that even courts suspicious of waivers will be more willing to enforce them as applied to claims for negligence causing property damage or economic loss, as opposed to personal injury. Insofar as this is the case, it reflects a notion that the public's interest in not permitting entities to deregulate themselves is less pressing when the rights being

---

40. Dalury v. S-K-I, Ltd., 670 A.2d 795 (Vt. 1995).

waived do not concern the protection of one's interest in bodily integrity.

Third, there are other special rules that will sometimes limit the negligence liability faced by certain actors who have been prevented from availing themselves of waivers, including ski resort operators. For example, many state legislatures have enacted *inherent risk statutes* that prevent participants in certain recreational activities such as skiing from suing for risks "inherent" in such activities. Thus, even in a state like Vermont that refuses to enforce contractual waivers of negligence liability by skiers, those skiers might still lose what would otherwise be valid negligence claims if, for example, they are suing the resort owner on the theory that it did not do enough to train novice skiers how to avoid colliding with other skiers. The resort's failure to address such a risk might be a failure to exercise ordinary care, but it is also probably a risk inherent in skiing and hence not one that, when realized in the form of an injury, will give rise to negligence liability. By contrast, if a skier were injured because the resort incorrectly marked an expert run as a beginner's slope, the claim would probably be permitted to proceed on the ground that such a risk is not inherent in skiing.

6.8.2 Implied Assumption of Risk

Suppose that two novice skiers, *N1* and *N2*, follow an incorrectly labeled trail and soon find themselves at the top of a slope quite obviously meant for experts. Luckily, *N2* spots a safe path to a beginners' slope and takes it to safety. *N1* declines to follow her, however. Declaring himself glad that the resort's careless mislabeling of the trail has given him an unexpected opportunity to "test his true inner strength," *N1* proceeds down the trail and predictably falls, breaking his leg.

Were *N1* to sue the resort for negligence in marking the trail, and were the suit governed by traditional common law rules, it would fail on the ground that *N1* had *implicitly* assumed the risk of suffering just this sort of injury on the trail. At its core, the implied assumption of risk doctrine denies relief to a plaintiff who, while voluntarily engaged in a recreational activity involving physical exertion, and while fully appreciating the dangers posed to him by another actor's negligence in connection with that activity, chooses to expose himself to those dangers.

Although its application in the preceding hypothetical case is straightforward, the implied assumption of risk doctrine is regarded with a jaundiced eye by modern tort scholars for two reasons. First, the doctrine was frequently deployed against laborers by turn-of-the-twentieth-century judges with such a heavy hand as to render it a poster-child of law doing the bidding of laissez-faire capitalism. Seemingly captive to an unrealistic or unsympathetic conception of the position of workers, or of their entitlement to safe working conditions, judges during this period often treated an employee's 'decision' to stay at his job in the face of evident dangers as sufficient to establish that he had implicitly assumed the risk of injury from such dangers. It is no surprise, then, to learn that the removal or circumvention of this obstacle to recovery was a major spur behind the adoption of FELA (*see* section 6.2) and of workers' compensation laws.

Second, on a less political and more conceptual level, the concept of implied assumption of risk turns out to overlap uncomfortably with distinct yet related concepts of duty, breach, and comparative fault. The proneness of implied assumption of risk analysis to bleed into analysis of other aspects of a negligence claim is evidenced in Judge Cardozo's opinion for the New York Court of Appeals in *Murphy v. Steeplechase Amusement Co.*[41] Plaintiff, "a vigorous young man," boarded an amusement park ride called "The Flopper," which consisted of a fast-moving treadmill surrounded by some padding. The challenge for participants was to keep their balance as they stepped on the moving belt. After observing others

---

41. 166 N.E. 173 (N.Y. 1929).

try their luck, including some who fell, plaintiff hopped on the ride, fell, and injured his knee. He sued the ride's operator alleging, among other things, that the machine had malfunctioned while he was on it, causing it to jerk forward rather than moving smoothly, as he had expected it would. Cardozo's opinion held that the claim should be dismissed because the plaintiff had assumed the risk of injury associated with falls. In support of this outcome, Cardozo invoked the Latin aphorism *volenti non fit injuria*: no wrong is done to one who chooses to engage in a dangerous activity and is injured because the danger is realized.

At first glance, *Murphy* seems to present a clean example of implied assumption of risk. The plaintiff chose to participate in a frivolous activity that presented a completely obvious risk of falling and, with it, injuries associated with falling. Those who wanted no part of this sort of activity needed only to choose to refrain from partaking of it. "The timorous," Cardozo emphasized, "may stay at home."[42] And yet closer inspection reveals a weakness in this analysis.

Here, it is critical to observe that Murphy pressed his claim on the theory that "The Flopper" had caught him off guard. According to his complaint, he expected that it would move smoothly but it instead jerked forward. To be sure, Murphy would have faced serious difficulties in prevailing on this theory—he would have had to prove that the jerking motion actually occurred (a fact about which Cardozo's opinion expresses skepticism), and that its doing so made a difference, in that he would not have fallen had the motion been smooth. But these obstacles have nothing to do with the issue of implied assumption of risk. Simply put, there is no reason to suppose that Murphy realized and accepted that he might be injured by the *jerky motion* of what had allegedly been a smooth running belt. In this respect, Cardozo's assumption of risk analysis seems nonresponsive to the facts actually alleged

---

42. 166 N.E. at 174.

in Murphy's complaint—a testament to the difficulties that even a master of the common law might encounter in applying the doctrine.

Perhaps Cardozo found the "jerking" theory so implausible as to entail that the plaintiffs' complaint had to be understood as alleging that his fall was caused by the ordinary (smooth) movement of the treadmill. Taking this to be the gist of the complaint, an implied assumption of risk argument would indeed be quite powerful. At the same time, it is not clear that, on this theory of liability, there would be any occasion for such an argument. For if the complaint is merely that the plaintiff fell because of the smoothly running conveyer belt, there would seem to be no basis for concluding that the plaintiff could satisfy the breach element of his prima facie case. The argument for breach would have to be that the mere act of operating an amusement ride of this sort is unreasonable, which seems highly implausible. And if there was no evidence of breach, there was no reason for Cardozo to reach the issue of whether Murphy had assumed the risk.

Some courts—including the California Supreme Court in its influential decision in *Knight v. Jewett*[43]—have seized on the continuity between assumption of risk and no-breach arguments as a ground for recognizing a distinct version of the implied assumption of risk doctrine known as "primary assumption of risk." What marks "primary" assumption of risk as distinctive is its focus on the *nature of the activity* in which the plaintiff is participating when injured, as opposed to the particular victim's knowing and voluntary acceptance of a risk of injury. In the typical case in which the doctrine is invoked, one participant alleges having been injured in an informal recreational activity (e.g., a pick-up basketball game) by the careless actions (e.g., overly aggressive play) of another participant. Because the focus of this inquiry is on the nature of the activity—as opposed to the plaintiff's actual awareness of and accession to risks

---

43. 834 P.2d 696 (Cal. 1992).

associated with careless acts undertaken as part of the activity—even a novice participant who has little or no appreciation of the risks of bodily harm associated with the activity can find her claims defeated by the invocation of primary implied assumption of risk. This is because the doctrine ultimately rests on judicial judgments that certain acts that might well meet the legal definition of carelessness should not be second-guessed by judges and jurors because they take place within activities that: (1) already tend to generate physical injuries to participants even when all are careful; (2) are common and widely accepted; (3) tend to take place among friends or acquaintances who perhaps ought to be able to settle their disputes without resort to the courts; and (4) operate with an informality that arguably militates against the idea that they should generate litigation and potentially large damage awards.

As indicated, the doctrine of "primary" assumption of risk, despite its name, does not treat assumption of risk as the sort of affirmative defense to a claim of negligence that it has been traditionally understood to be. (No wonder there is confusion about the meaning of the phrase "assumption of risk!") Worse still, confusion arises even when the doctrine is understood in its traditional sense as grounded in the plaintiff's implicit choice to face a particular hazard. The problem here resides in the difficulty of distinguishing implied assumption of risk from comparative fault.

Consider the case of P, who, while in full possession of his faculties, voluntarily and for his own amusement takes a ride in a car being driven by D, whom P knows at the time to be heavily intoxicated. Because of his intoxication, D crashes, injuring P. One might plausibly assert that P should lose his negligence suit against D for having implicitly assumed the risk of D's drunk driving. Yet one could perhaps just as easily say that P acted unreasonably—i.e., *was comparatively at fault*—by exposing himself to the risks associated with D's impaired driving. Note that the former characterization entails that P's claim will fail. Yet, at least in a "pure" comparative fault jurisdiction, P's claim might succeed, although his damages will be reduced. So which is the correct description?

With examples of the foregoing sort in mind, some commentators have argued that traditional implied assumption of risk must be understood as just a special case of comparative fault—one in which the plaintiff *adverts to the risk* rather than confronting it unawares. They further reason that, in an era in which the all-or-nothing rule of contributory negligence has been replaced in almost every jurisdiction by comparative fault, it would be anomalous to retain implied assumption of risk as a complete defense. Instead, there should be only comparative fault, with the fact finder exercising discretion as to how much fault to attribute to the plaintiff's choice to face the risk of being injured by the defendant.

There is a certain tidiness to the foregoing argument. And yet there are grounds for resisting it. First, even in the age of comparative fault, legislatures and courts have not simply abandoned the idea of all-or-nothing defenses. Most states have adopted *modified* comparative fault schemes that entirely bar claims by plaintiffs who are deemed more at fault (or as much or more at fault) for their own injuries than defendants. In this environment, it hardly seems inconsistent to continue to recognize the implied assumption of risk defense. Moreover, insofar as they are anxious to reduce uncertainty and err on the side of keeping flimsy claims out of the courts, judges might be entitled to treat instances of advertent comparative fault as leaving fact finders with no discretion partially to compensate plaintiffs. Indeed, a number of courts have accepted exactly this line of argument.

As a conceptual matter, it is also too hasty simply to equate implied assumption of risk with comparative fault. The easiest way to see the gap between the two is to think of a case in which a plaintiff acts *perfectly reasonably* in knowingly exposing himself to a risk of harm at the hands of a careless defendant. Imagine a highly accomplished ice skater who chooses to skate recreationally at a rink that, because of the operator's carelessness, lacks the normal perimeter railing that prevents skaters from falling from the ice surface to the carpeted floor several inches below. While skating, the skater is unexpectedly cut off by another, loses his balance, and, because of the missing railing, falls off the skating surface, injuring his wrist. Given his competency, the skater's decision to encounter the danger associated with the defendant's carelessness may have been perfectly reasonable (i.e., not comparatively at fault). And yet it seems plausible to suppose that he assumed the risk of skating without the railing. In this sort of case, at least, courts might well decide that as between the two available descriptions of the plaintiff's conduct, the right one to adopt is the one that focuses on his knowing and voluntary decision to proceed notwithstanding his knowledge of a particular danger posed by the carelessness of the defendant.

SEVEN

Battery, False Imprisonment, Assault, and Related Torts

TODAY, NEGLIGENCE MAY BE the tort that is most frequently the subject of litigation and most frequently elaborated in judicial opinions. Yet it would be a mistake simply to equate tort law with negligence law. In terms of modern litigation practice, claims for products liability and fraud are very common in high-stakes personal injury and business litigation. Gender discrimination and copyright or trademark infringement are statutorily defined forms of wrongdoing for which victims often seek and obtain recourse at law.

The distortions that result from an exclusive focus on negligence become even more obvious when we turn from court dockets to everyday conduct. Individuals and firms adjust how they act in part because they are cognizant of the various ways in which one might wrongfully injure another. It does not take a law school education to know that it would be wrong, and would expose one to liability, to beat someone viciously or to kidnap someone. That these sorts of wrongs are so basic, and for most people, so clearly out of bounds, attests not to their irrelevance but to the degree to which the norms they contain have been internalized. Many Torts courses commence with a discussion of some of the torts covered in this chapter precisely because they provide particularly clear and gripping examples of tortious conduct.

This chapter begins by introducing readers to three torts—battery, false imprisonment and assault—that have for centuries been recognized as actionable wrongs. Although of ancient pedigree, and although admitting of many clear instances, these torts, no less than negligence, sometimes raise thorny interpretive and normative questions. The chapter concludes with an analysis of two other legal wrongs—intentional infliction of emotional distress and workplace sexual harassment—that have emerged relatively recently as offshoots of battery and other long-standing torts.

7.1 Battery

On August 1, 1943, Franklin Cecarelli, aged 25, was attacked by George Maher, John Heinz, and an unknown third assailant. Cecarelli had attended a dance, at the conclusion of which three female attendees asked him to drive them home. The judge who presided over the trial of the suit against Maher—Cecarelli had already settled with Heinz—described the ensuing events as follows:

[Cecarelli's] willingness to meet [the women's] request appears to have provoked the anger and wrath of the defendant and his two companions, who, at a secluded and lonely spot adjacent to the dance hall, set upon him to administer a severe, and painful beating. Fists and dangerous instruments constituted the implements of aggressive warfare.

In consequence, the plaintiff's upper right central and upper right lateral teeth and roots were severed from their sockets; his upper left central, lower right central, and lower right lateral teeth were so destroyed as to necessitate ultimate removal; his upper lip was severely lacerated, requiring sutures and resulting in an involvement of the nasal septum; his nose and left eye were abrased and contused; and his right arm, right shoulder, and right side became exceedingly sore and tender as a result of a vicious kicking process. Thereafter, the plaintiff required emergency hospital treatment and a complete restoration of the dental structures with the replacement of five teeth. In addition, the plaintiff was forced to absent himself from his employment for a complete week, experiencing acute pain for an extended period after his return to work.[1]

Recognizing in the foregoing an obvious tort, the court entered a judgment against Maher for $2,315, representing $315 for lost wages and medical expenses, and $2,000 for general damages.

It seems difficult to imagine a clearer instance of a wrongful injuring—of a tort. Or is it? Isn't what happened here even more obviously *criminal*? The answer, of course, is that it is both. Some wrongs are sufficiently egregious, or threatening to the public interest, or in need of deterrence, or unreliably privately handled, that we classify them as crimes, and our legal system empowers a prosecutor, representing the interests of the public, to seek punishments such as imprisonment. But this does not mean that they are not torts. In our system, a vicious beating is not only treated as an offense against the public—a *criminal assault*—it is an offense against the victim—the tort of *battery*—for which the victim is given recourse against the perpetrator.[2] As we will now see, while the paradigm case of this paradigmatic tort is a brutal physical attack, the tort has long been understood to extend well beyond that case to other wrongful touchings.

7.1.1 Act, Intent, Touching

A battery by D upon P has occurred if (1) D performs act a; (2) D does a intending to cause bodily contact with P of a type that tends

---

1. Cecarelli v. Maher, 12 Conn. Supp. 240 (Conn. C.P. 1943).

2. A terminological oddity of Anglo-American law is that the word "assault," when used in criminal law, usually refers to an intentional physical attack, whereas the name of the tort that covers such attacks is "battery." In tort usage, "assault" refers to the act of intentionally causing another to *apprehend* that she is about to be harmfully or offensively touched. Adding to the confusion, judicial opinions sometimes mix and match criminal law and tort law usage.

to be harmful or offensive; and (3) *D*'s doing of *a* to *P* causes harmful or offensive contact. Examples of conduct that fit this definition are not difficult to conjure up. Each of the following is a prima facie battery, meaning that it will count as a battery unless the defendant can establish an affirmative defense, such as consent or self-defense. Most are drawn from now-famous battery cases that tend to show up in law school classes.

D punches *P* in the nose.

D spits in *P*'s face.

D, a stranger to *P*, fondles *P*'s genitals.

D pulls out a chair from underneath where *P* was intending to sit, and *P* falls to the ground.

D sets up a "spring gun" so that if a person opens a certain door, a switch will be tripped that will cause the gun to shoot that person; *P* opens that door and is shot.

D poisons *P* by secretly placing an undetectable toxin in a drink that *P* consumes.

D grabs the yarmulke off *P*'s head.

From this list one can glean that a battery can occur without the causation of physical harm to the victim and without the perpetrator directly striking the victim. An offensive contact can suffice, as demonstrated by the spitting and fondling examples. Moreover, as the pulling-of-the-chair and spring gun examples indicate, the touching need not take the form of a striking or shooting of the victim by the batterer. Finally, there need not be a literal touching of the other's person: a battery can occur when something very closely connected with one's person is touched, such as clothing or a hat one is wearing, or a cane one is holding.

So what, really, is the wrong of battery? The core idea that gives shape to the tort is that one's person is inviolable in the specific sense that one has a right against all others to be free from their intentional touches. The tort of battery sets a 'line' that is not to be crossed. It is built around the admonition: "Hands Off; Do Not Touch!"

Of course, physical contact is a part of daily life. For example, people bump into one another all the time, whether on a bus, at school, or in a store. Insofar as these contacts are *unintentional*, they will not give rise to a claim for battery (though, if harmful, they might support a claim for negligence). To bump into someone accidentally is not to flout the "Do Not Touch" directive, because the concept of a touch, as it is used here, incorporates a notion of a purposeful or intentional contact. In turn, having the right sort of intention is necessary but not sufficient to generate a battery. A defendant who purposefully passes up the opportunity to pull the plaintiff away from an approaching bus, wishing the plaintiff the worst, has not committed a battery because he has not *acted*. Likewise, a defendant who intends a touch and acts on that intent, but fails to succeed in touching the plaintiff—a missed punch, for example—has not committed a battery, though he may have committed another tort such as assault.

Even if accidental contact falls outside the ambit of battery, what about all the intentional touching that is part of the fabric of everyday life? People shake hands, hug, and sometimes wrestle playfully. Masseurs, chiropractors, surgeons, and athletes have jobs that require them to touch others in sometimes painful or invasive ways. It is not the least bit uncommon for a person to force his way through a crowd to get to a train or to gently but firmly push a nosy coworker out of an office doorway. Police and private security guards regularly grab hold of suspects. Tort law would be completely out of step with reality if all of these intentional touches amounted to actionable batteries. But they do not.

Much of this conduct is rendered nontortious by the fact of *consent*. When an intentional touching is properly consented to by the person being touched, the latter has no ground to complain. (Proper consent, as is discussed below, is a *defense* to a claim of battery.) Various other refinements contained in the elements and defenses of battery further ensure that the tort more or less tracks social norms as to acceptable forms of touching.

7.1.2 Norms of Acceptable Touching

Acts that are undertaken for the purpose of causing, and that succeed in causing, bodily harm to another are the most straightforward batteries. But an intentional act of touching that does not physically harm can also be a battery. Indeed, as we have already seen, spitting upon another person in a way that causes no bodily harm is plainly a battery. Courts typically capture this type of battery by invoking the concept of *offensive contact.*

What will count as an offensive touching? Today, at least, it is easy enough to grasp the sense in which repeated shoulder caresses from a predatory coworker amount to a violation of one's interest in controlling access to one's body. It is equally clear that gently tapping the shoulder of someone standing in front of you on a movie line to get his attention is *not* offensive contact. What about an intended, but unintentionally obnoxious, stroking of the fuzzy sweater one is wearing, or a slap on the rear end by one's disliked and victorious soccer opponent, done to rub in the defeat? Are these offensive touchings? To answer this question, must a judge become an expert in etiquette or political correctness?

Some instances of potential offensive contact battery are difficult because there is a mismatch between the intended outcome and the actual outcome. As in the sweater example, one can intentionally touch another without intending offense, yet nonetheless succeed in causing a contact that offends the person being touched, and that may be offensive in a more objective sense. The rules for resolving this sort of mismatch are discussed in the next section. But even apart from intent issues, there is the threshold question of whether the kind of touching experienced by the plaintiff can qualify as offensive. Clearly the standard here is not purely subjective—the issue is *not* simply whether the plaintiff in fact took offense at being touched. Some people are no doubt offended at being gently tapped on the shoulder by a stranger, but being so tapped will not give them grounds for a battery claim.

Battery law approaches this problem by asking the fact finder—usually jurors in the American system—to determine whether a reasonable person would have found the sort of touching experienced by the plaintiff to be offensive under the circumstances. Here, as in many other areas of tort law, the courts have not aimed to provide a detailed code of conduct, but rather to frame a question that is sensibly delegated to a fact finder that can rely to some extent on common sense, with oversight by appellate courts. At the cost of some uncertainty, this approach has the advantage of permitting the law to track changing mores regarding the propriety of different kinds of touching.

To say that the standard for determining offensiveness is largely in the hands of the fact finder is not to suppose that there are thousands of battery cases working their way through the courts in which juries are sorting out which touchings are offensive and which are not. Litigation is not a business to get into lightly, and potential plaintiffs and their lawyers must consider whether the intentional touching at issue is one that a jury is likely to think a reasonable person would find offensive. They will also have to factor into that decision what a jury is likely to identify as appropriate compensation for a physically harmless but offensive touching. The figure might be quite small. At an even earlier pre-litigation stage, it is not uncommon to find companies, schools, and other entities, through training exercises and manuals and other means, taking an important role in helping to define the permissibility of different sorts of touching.

7.1.3 Nuances of Intent

A fundamental difference between battery and negligence is that battery requires the tortfeasor intentionally to cross a line—i.e., intentionally to cause a harmful or offensive touching of the plaintiff. While fundamental, the intentionality requirement contains important ambiguities. A cyclist who is trying to avoid a nearby pedestrian but accidentally runs into him has not intentionally touched the victim and cannot be held liable for *battery* (though there may be liability for negligence). By contrast, a college student who sneaks up on another student with whom he is barely acquainted, and who delivers a modestly forceful kick to the other's rear end that breaks his tailbone, may have committed a battery. In any event, the mere fact that he intended no lasting or serious harm to come of the kick will not save him from liability.

Two lawsuits occasioned by the acts of mischievous boys provide American law's most famous battery decisions. Both raise issues of intent; one easy, the other more subtle. In *Garratt v. Dailey*,[3] the five-year-old (!) defendant, Brian Dailey, pulled a chair out from under his elderly relative as she was about to sit on it. She fell to the ground and was seriously injured. Assuming the boy's harnessing of gravity to generate a harmful contact of the plaintiff with the ground constituted a "touching", Brian's lawyer argued that Brian should nonetheless not be held liable because he did not intend a fall that would cause harm. The appellate court concluded (consistently with the clear majority rule) that Brian's conduct would constitute a battery so long as a jury could infer from the circumstances of the event that Brian pulled the chair *either* for the *purpose* of causing the plaintiff to fall to the ground, or with *knowledge* that pulling the chair was almost certain to result in her falling. That he did not mean the plaintiff any harm, or did not fully appreciate the potential for harm in his actions, was deemed irrelevant.

Note that, whatever its precise definition, the concept of "intent" refers to what was actually going on in the mind of an actor at the time of acting—what purposes he had in mind when acting, or what he knew would happen as a result of acting. Mental states are, of course, not directly observable the way that, say, movements associated with a kick are observable. Thus, absent confessional

---

3. 279 P.2d 1091 (Wash. 1955).

testimony from a battery defendant as to his state of mind at the time of acting, the fact finder will have to reconstruct the actor's mental state by considering the act and the circumstances in which it took place.

Garratt clearly stands for the negative proposition that the absence of a preconceived plan to hurt the victim does not rule out liability for battery. More affirmatively, it supports the idea that an intentional act that one knows is certain (or all but certain) to bring about contact of a sort that tends to be harmful or offensive will support a claim for battery. Here, it is vital to appreciate that when courts, following *Garratt*, talk of a defendant being held liable for battery on the ground that the requisite contact was substantially certain to result, they are referring to what the individual defendant *actually knew* about the consequences of his actions at the time of acting, *not* what a reasonable person in his position could or should have known. Moreover, courts require not merely that the defendant knew of a *risk* or *chance* that the plaintiff would suffer the requisite contact, but instead that the defendant knew the plaintiff *would in fact* suffer the contact. The relative stringency of these requirements is part of what distinguishes battery from negligence. As we have seen, an actor who *should have been aware* that his conduct posed a *risk* of physical harm to another, and proceeds without making efforts to guard against that risk, might be subject to liability for negligence if the risk is realized.

Equally central to the Anglo-American canon is *Vosburg v. Putney*,[4] a decision that is embraced by torts professors as much for its enduring perplexities as for the clear messages contained within it. The parties to the lawsuit were schoolmates. After they returned from the school's playground and class had been called to order, Putney lightly kicked Vosburg in the leg. Unexpectedly, the plaintiff later became lame in that leg.

---

4. 50 N.W. 403 (Wis. 1891).

After a jury verdict for Vosburg, Putney appealed, arguing that he should be entirely spared from liability on three grounds: (1) that he did not intend to harm Vosburg; (2) that there were defects in the trial evidence presented by Vosburg to establish that the kick actually caused the lameness; and (3) that Vosburg had implicitly consented to the sort of physical contact associated with ordinary childish behavior. (Putney also argued that even if he should be held liable for *some* damages, he should not be made to pay damages for the unforeseeable development of Vosburg's becoming lame. The court rejected this last argument and, by doing so, became a leading authority for the 'eggshell skull rule.' *See* Chapter 12.)

We can consider Putney's no-liability arguments in reverse order. As to the third, the court allowed that school children perhaps do implicitly consent to kicks and other contacts that occur in the more physical environment of the playground, but not to physical contact in the classroom. As to the second, the court accepted Putney's argument and remanded the case for a new trial on the causation. (When the case was re-tried, Vosburg again prevailed.) On the first issue—the issue of intent—the court reasoned that because Putney's kicking of Vosburg was an "unlawful" act, a battery could be found.

The hard question in *Vosburg* is what the court meant by describing the defendant's kick as "unlawful." The conduct was not a violation of criminal law. And the court could not have meant that it was unlawful in the sense of being tortious, for that would beg the question. Instead, the court seems to have had in mind a looser notion of unlawfulness—unlawful in the sense of violating norms of permissible behavior in the setting in which it took place. In short, according to *Vosburg*, the intent that matters for purposes of battery liability is the intent to undertake a touching of a sort that is not allowed under norms that govern the propriety of touching. If one intentionally performs this sort of act, and if it ends up causing harm or offense, then there is a battery. At least in a setting in which roughhousing is not permitted, a kicking of another is among the sort of touchings that fits this description. To kick someone intentionally, in the midst of a standard social interaction, is intentionally to perpetrate an impermissible, frowned-upon touching.

Vosburg's approach to intent sensibly forges a middle path between two extreme alternatives. One would deem the intent element satisfied so long as the defendant intended *any sort of contact* with the plaintiff. In principle, this approach would allow for absurd results, though perhaps those results could be avoided by the liberal invocation of defenses such as implied consent. For example, on this approach, if *D*, while standing next to *P* on a street corner, were gently to tap *P* on the shoulder and thereby unexpectedly cause permanent nerve damage to *P*, *P* in principle could recover for battery (*D* acted, intentionally touched *P*, and caused *P* harm). The other extreme would be to require intent to cause the precise type of harm or offense that the victim ended up suffering. One problem with this approach is that it would spare from liability actors who deliberately touch others thoughtlessly. ("I only meant to push him! It never occurred to me that doing so would be offensive or harmful.") In lieu of these alternatives, *Vosburg* sets as a condition of battery liability proof that the plaintiff suffered a harmful or offensive contact because the defendant acted with *the intent to cause a kind or type of contact that is typically harmful or deemed offensive under prevailing social norms*, such as a kick or a grope.

Another wrinkle on intent sometimes goes under the heading "transferred intent." Suppose *S*, walking down a residential street, intentionally aims and fires his gun at *T*, but misses and instead strikes and wounds *U*, whom *S* had no intention of shooting. Can *U* sue *S* for battery notwithstanding that he was never *S*'s target? Yes. Courts will sometimes defend this intuitive conclusion by asserting that *S*'s intention to shoot *T* "transfers" to his shooting of *U*. A less metaphorical way of making the same point is to say that *S*'s unjustified act of shooting at *T* is also a reckless or careless act toward anyone who was in the vicinity of *T*, such that if any of them are injured, it is actionable by them on that basis. (Alternatively, some might say that the act of shooting a gun, or at least the act of using a gun in a criminal manner, is a special type of wrongful activity, for which the shooter may be held strictly liable to any person shot, regardless of whether the shooter intended to harm the person, and even if the shooter was not in fact careless as to the risk of others being shot.)

Note that if, in the situation just described, *T* is blissfully unaware that *S* shot at him, but learns about the incident a week later, he will have no claim for battery against *S*, because battery requires an actual touching, and there is no tort of attempted battery. We will see shortly that the tort of assault allows recovery by certain persons who are not touched, but who *apprehend* that they are *about to be harmfully or offensively touched* by another. But given *T*'s lack of awareness at the time of the shooting, this cause of action will also be of no assistance to him.

Intent can also sometimes "transfer" from one kind of intentional tort to another. For example, suppose *A* points a loaded gun at *B*, intending only to scare *B*, but the gun accidentally goes off, and as a result, *C* is shot. *C* will be able to recover against *A*. Some courts will say that the *A*'s intent to assault *B* 'transfers' to the harmful touching of *C* so as to generate a battery of *C* by *A*. Again, however, a less metaphorical way to handle this kind of case is just to say that *A*'s pointing of a loaded gun at *B* was reckless or careless as to *C*'s physical well-being, which misconduct toward *C* became actionable by *C* when it resulted in *C*'s being shot.

7.1.4 Defenses

The most important defense to battery is consent. A professional hockey player who, during a game, breaks his opponent's collarbone with a hard check; a physician who cuts into her patient's abdomen; a lover who is accused of sexual assault—each of these actors will assert in response to a suit for battery that he or she did no wrong because the recipient of the contact actually consented to the touching that occurred. The unconsented-to nature of the defendant's touching of the plaintiff is indeed so central to the wrong of battery that some courts treat "lack of consent" as an element of the plaintiff's prima facie case, rather than treating consent as an affirmative defense. While it is probably not quite right to go that far, the wrong of battery clearly goes hand in glove with lack of consent.

There are several aspects of consent that require scrutiny. Was the consent given by the plaintiff *express*—that is, given overtly by spoken or written word—or was it *implied* (i.e., fairly inferred from the plaintiff's acts or gestures)? If it was inferred, was the defendant's inference correct, or was it mistaken? If the inference was mistaken, was the defendant's mistake a reasonable one to have made? If so, who should bear the risk of that reasonable mistake? On this last question, the position staked out by the Restatement (Second) of Torts[5] is that the defendant's reasonable misperception of implicit consent will *not* count as consent that undermines the plaintiff's battery claim *unless* the defendant's misperception owes to something that the plaintiff himself did (e.g., if the plaintiff's ambiguous gestures were reasonably interpreted by the defendant as conveying consent).[6]

Even assuming plaintiff has consented to being touched by the defendant, additional questions remain. To count as a defense, the consent must have been uncoerced and knowing, and cannot have

---

5. The Restatement of Torts is a particularly influential treatise published by the American Law Institute ("ALI"), a private organization of judges, lawyers, and legal scholars. It aims to clarify and provide greater uniformity to tort law by "restating" it in a series of numbered provisions accompanied by commentary and case citations. (Other Restatements address topics such as agency and contracts.) The Second Restatement of Torts, a revision of an earlier First Restatement, was published in the period 1965–1977 and was authored primarily by legendary torts scholar William Prosser. The ALI has been publishing the Third Restatement of Torts on a topic-by-topic basis since 1998, which saw the publication of its products liability provisions. Publication of its central Negligence provisions is expected in 2010.

6. Restatement (Second) of Torts § 51, Illus. 1 (1965).

been induced by trickery on the part of the defendant. Moreover, there are instances in which the law does not credit even a competent victim's properly given consent. For example, a participant injured in an illegal 'street fight' will be permitted by some courts to sue the other participant notwithstanding that the fight was perfectly consensual. (The plaintiff's consent is deemed unenforceable, in part to protect participants from their own choices.) Finally, consent is effective only when the defendant's conduct falls within the scope of the consent given. To implicitly consent to hard tackles in a football game is not to consent to being beaten by an opposing player on the sidelines after the game is over.

These complexities notwithstanding, the basic theme remains the same: battery has to do with an invasion of the person of the plaintiff by a wrongful touching. The inviolability of the person is the core idea. Thus, if consent is to negate the battery, it must be because the autonomy-based right not to be touched has genuinely been waived. Judicial assessments of the shape, form, and circumstances of consent are all in service of ensuring that a genuine waiver has actually occurred. Out of concern to vindicate this right, courts have tended to scrutinize consent very closely, most notably in the famous decision of *Mohr v. Williams*.[7] The defendant physician was authorized by the plaintiff, his patient, to repair surgically the hearing in one of her ears. Once she was anaesthetized, he decided that her other ear was in greater need of treatment and operated on it. Even though the procedure did not harm Mohr, her battery action succeeded because Williams' conduct fell outside of the scope of the consent she had given—he had touched her in a way that she had not authorized. While today a court might not be so exacting on the scope question—and while medical defendants are now usually careful to obtain from surgical patients broader forms of consent than the circumscribed consent given in *Mohr*— courts remain cautious about too easily giving defendants the

---

7. 104 N.W. 12 (Minn. 1905).

benefit of this defense. (The application of the reasonable patient standard to 'informed consent' claims, discussed in Chapter 6, shows a similar concern for patient autonomy.)

Another ground for defeating a claim of battery—perhaps as intuitive as consent—is *self-defense*. One who pushes another in order to defend herself against imminent physical harm at the hands of that other person is within her rights to do so. In these circumstances, she has a right to defend herself with force, albeit only so long as that force is proportionate to the reasonably appre-hended harm. In addition, one may touch another in a harmful or offensive manner if one reasonably believes that doing so will pro-tect a third party from being caused imminent physical harm by that other. Indeed, one may even do so to protect one's property, but again, only so long as the force one uses is proportionate to the property damage against which one is protecting.

A failed claim of privilege underlies the famous decision of *Katko v. Briney*.[8] Katko, a petty thief, suffered serious injuries when he was shot in the midst of burglarizing an uninhabited, rundown farmhouse owned by Edward and Bertha Briney. The farmhouse had been a frequent target of intruders, although it contained noth-ing of great value. Katko was apparently planning to take some old glass jars when he broke in. Once inside the house, Katko opened a closed bedroom door. Unbeknownst to him, the Brineys had set up a shotgun attached via a spring mechanism to the door. Aimed at the leg, it went off as Katko opened the door, causing him perma-nent injuries. There was no warning inside or outside the house of the presence of the mechanism.

After pleading guilty to larceny, paying a $50 fine, and serving a suspended sentence on parole, Mr. Katko brought a battery suit against the Brineys, prevailing at trial with a $30,000 verdict. On the battery claim, the defendants asserted a privilege to use force to protect their property. Like the privilege of self-defense, however,

---

8. 183 N.W.2d 657 (Iowa 1971).

the privilege to protect property is calibrated to the magnitude of the interest protected. Potentially lethal force or force sufficient to cause serious bodily injury cannot be used to protect personal property. Of course, the situation of a homeowner wielding potentially deadly force to protect his actual dwelling is quite different than the situation in *Katko*, because an invasion of a home in which one is living usually can reasonably be perceived as presenting an imminent and grave danger to those in the house. Today, spring guns and other mechanical devices are for the most part outlawed, in part because of their inability to distinguish between an adult intent on theft and a child engaged in exploration. Some states, however, have enacted laws that aim to give broader rights to property owners to use deadly force in response to invasions of their homes and to attempted carjackings, even when there is no reason to perceive an imminent risk of death or serious bodily harm.

While the inadequacy of Briney's asserted privilege defense is relatively easy to grasp, Katko's substantial verdict surprisingly included—in addition to his $20,000 compensatory damages award (primarily for pain and suffering)—$10,000 in punitive damages. (*See* Chapter 12.) It is one thing for a criminal wrongdoer to recover compensation from another wrongdoer who injured him by greatly exceeding his privilege to use force. It is perhaps another for the legal system to vindicate the criminal with a supplemental award of punitive damages. A dissenting judge offered the novel argument that the equitable principle of "unclean hands" should disqualify a wrongdoing plaintiff like Katko from obtaining punitive damages. The majority affirmed, however, because Briney's lawyers had not preserved his right to appeal the punitive damages award.

𝕸 7.2 False Imprisonment

The tort of false imprisonment has a pedigree no less distinguished than that of battery. The interest it protects is not the interest in being free from others' touches, but liberty of movement. If battery promises to shield individuals from being wrongfully targeted for contact by others, false imprisonment promises to free them from others' efforts to keep them located in a particular space. In short, to commit false imprisonment is intentionally to confine another against his will. Although false imprisonment can take many forms, it generally fits one of two types: (I) those in which the defendant claims to possess an authority to confine the victim and (II) those in which there is not even a pretense of authority to confine.

The late-eighteenth-century English decision of *Huckle v. Money*,[9] now recognized as among the first tort cases to allow an award of punitive damages, provides a good illustration of a Type I case. The English Secretary of State had issued broad warrants authorizing the arrest of anyone who played a role in publishing a newspaper that allegedly had libeled King George III. On this basis, the defendant, a royal messenger, held the plaintiff, a journeyman printer, in custody for several hours. The goal was to remove him from his residence so that it could be searched for evidence linking him to the newspaper. The printer sued and was awarded £300—an amount the appellate court deemed to be well in excess of what would have sufficed to compensate him for being temporarily held under relatively pleasant conditions. Yet the award was upheld, with Lord Chief Justice Pratt deeming it necessary to rebut the government's claimed authority to confine its citizens indiscriminately for investigative purposes—a "most daring public attack . . . upon the liberty of the subject." Apart from official confinements, one can readily find instances in which private actors confine others on a claim of authority. A store owner who detains a suspected shoplifter in one of the store's back rooms will do so out of a sense, backed to some degree by the law, that he is entitled temporarily to detain customers in order to protect his property.

---

9. (1763) 95 Eng. Rep. 768 (C.P.).

Type II cases, in which the defendant claims no authority to detain, take many forms. The kidnapper who puts his victim in the back of his van and then drives off, the sweatshop owner who barricades his employees in their workplace, the jealous ex-boyfriend who locks his former girlfriend in a closet, the disgruntled employee who lures his supervisor to his house and then ties him up and terrorizes him—all of these are examples of false imprisonments without any pretense to authority.

Although distinct, the two types of false imprisonment cases can both be fit within the same general description. Broken down into elements, the tort can be defined as follows. D is subject to liability to P for false imprisonment if: (1) D performs act a; (2) D does a intending to confine P; (3) D's doing a causes P to be confined; and (4) P is aware of the confinement. Note that on this definition, a failure to release someone whom one is not responsible for imprisoning in the first place is not a false imprisonment. It may be in some sense wrongful for X not to take an easy opportunity to release Y from a confinement imposed by Z. But assuming that X is not somehow complicit in the confining of Y, X has not committed the false imprisonment tort. To be liable for that tort, X must have been the doer or an accomplice to the doer, just as in battery.

To commit false imprisonment, the actor must also have *intended* to confine the victim. An accidental confinement, as when a library at closing time unintentionally locks in a patron who has fallen asleep in his kiosk, will not suffice. It is the intentional exercise of power over the defendant to deprive him of his physical liberty that is of concern to this tort. To be sure, a negligent confinement could cause physical harm, and then there might be a negligence claim, just as a negligent touching could cause actionable damages. But the former would not be false imprisonment, just as the latter would not be a battery. One need not be vigilant of creating confinements; one merely needs to refrain from intentionally (or knowingly) bringing such confinements about.

The requirement of actual confinement is in most cases straightforward, though there are some conceptual subtleties here.

Even a victim whom another has intended to confine will not be deemed confined if it turns out that she has a readily available and safe avenue of escape that she does not take. A gang of teenagers that means to lock a nerdy classmate in the girls' bathroom has not committed false imprisonment if there is another door through which she can safely and easily escape. On the other hand, confinement can occur even if the victim is not physically incapable of leaving the space. For example, one can be confined in an unlocked room if she reasonably believes her captor's false claim that there is a guard at the door who has been instructed to shoot her if she attempts to leave.

As rendered above, false imprisonment's elements include not just confinement, but awareness of confinement. On this description of the tort, a defendant who locks the plaintiff in his office for an entire workday has not falsely imprisoned the plaintiff if the plaintiff spends the entire day at his desk, and if the door is unlocked by a janitor before he first tries to leave. Although the taking away of the plaintiff's liberty is the core of the wrong, that taking is regarded as hollow and nonactionable if the victim remains unaware of her loss of liberty. Some jurisdictions have rejected or criticized the awareness requirement precisely on the ground that the relevant injury takes place as soon as there is confinement, irrespective of the victim's cognizance of her situation.

Because the elements of a prima facie case of false imprisonment are in most applications straightforward, the action in this tort often lies in a defendant's effort to take advantage of an affirmative defense, particularly efforts by defendants in Type I cases to claim authority to confine. To be sure, the defenses of consent (express and implied) and self-defense also apply to this tort. It is permissible for one to lock another in a room if the other freely consents to being confined, or to ward off the other's physical attack. But the most distinctive and practically important efforts to justify confinements that would otherwise be false imprisonments involve claims by officials or private citizens to enjoy a privilege to confine for particular purposes.

Jailers are obviously authorized to keep convicted criminals in prison for the duration of their terms. Likewise, police are often entitled to arrest or briefly detain suspected criminals. For example, a valid, judicially issued warrant that specifically identifies the plaintiff as a crime suspect provides police with a privilege to arrest and confine the plaintiff, at least for a certain period of time. (The problem in *Huckle* was the indiscriminate general warrant, which the court deemed too broad and vague to be valid.) Police are also permitted to engage in warrantless arrests when they have probable cause to believe that the person arrested has committed or is attempting to commit a crime. Tort law recognizes privileges such as these to aid the cause of law enforcement and public safety. Even private citizens enjoy a limited privilege to detain another in aid of law enforcement. Essentially, they may do so only if the other has in fact committed a serious crime, or is about to. However, 'citizen's arrests' of this sort are undertaken at the peril of the actor. If the person confined turns out not to have committed a serious crime or not to have been about to commit such a crime, there will be no privilege—even if the actor's mistaken supposition that a crime had been or was about to be committed was perfectly reasonable.

In practice, the most important privilege to confine enjoyed by private actors is the so-called *shopkeeper's privilege*. By statute in most jurisdictions, a business owner or operator is authorized to detain persons on their premises as long as the owner reasonably believes that the person being detained was stealing or about to steal the owner's property. As compared to the common law rule, in which one confines another at his peril and therefore bears the risk of being mistaken about whether there are actually grounds to confine, the shopkeeper's privilege gives businesses leeway to make reasonable mistakes in confining innocent persons. However, even if based on a reasonable belief as to the guilt of the suspect, the detention will be unprivileged if it is conducted in an unreasonable manner either as to the conditions of confinement or its duration. A storeowner who holds a suspected shoplifter for 12 hours of interrogation, or who subjects him to psychological torture, has abused the privilege and will not benefit from it.

Related to false imprisonment is the distinct wrong of *malicious prosecution*. It permits the imposition of liability in a case in which the defendant, out of malice toward the plaintiff, takes steps to instigate what she knows to be an unfounded criminal investigation of the plaintiff. Confinement is not an element of malicious prosecution. Rather, the commencement of unfounded criminal proceedings against the plaintiff suffices. Note that this cause of action is available as against informants who initiate unfounded prosecutions, as opposed to prosecutors themselves, who are by and large immune from liability for decisions to prosecute.

7.3 Constitutional Torts

Confinements imposed by government officials are a special case, in part because governments claim forms of authority over individuals' lives that private actors do not. The same is true for harmful intentional touchings. Police, for example, are authorized to use physical force in the name of law enforcement in ways that civilians are not. As it turns out, the genre of cases in which a citizen is suing a government official for beating her or detaining her is sufficiently distinct that, among lawyers, it carries its own name: *constitutional torts*. Even though they are the subject of separate law school courses, constitutional torts are still torts: they are relational, injurious wrongs for which the law provides victim recourse. In fact, the domain of constitutional torts is probably the most active site of lawsuits that, in substance, are suits for battery or false imprisonment.

Batteries and false imprisonments committed by governmental officials are dubbed constitutional torts for good reason. First, the conduct involved, such as beatings and confinements, is of a sort that fits within some of the most basic paradigms of tortious behavior. Second, the efforts by those who perpetrate these acts to defend them by invoking governmental authority are defeated precisely by virtue of provisions in the U.S. Constitution stating that citizens have a right not to be mistreated by officials in these ways. These provisions include the Fourth Amendment's right against unreasonable searches and seizures, the Eighth Amendment's right against cruel and unusual punishment, and the Fourteenth Amendment's right against being deprived of liberty without due process of law. A battery or false imprisonment perpetrated by a government official is an invasion of a set of rights guaranteed by the Constitution, and hence is a constitutional tort.

Federal, state, and local officials, such as FBI agents and police officers, are perhaps the most common defendants in constitutional tort actions, though these wrongs can be committed even by private actors if the latter are acting in a governmental capacity "under color of law." To ensure the availability of victim recourse against persons acting under color of *state* law, Congress long ago enacted a statute—42 U.S.C. § 1983—that specifically authorizes suits for damages by victims of abuses perpetrated by persons acting in such a capacity. When brought against *federal* governmental officials, constitutional tort claims are not statutory, but arise directly from the Constitution's rights-guarantees, some of which have been interpreted by the U.S. Supreme Court as implicitly authorizing private rights of action for such violations.

A notorious example of a constitutional tort taking the form of a battery was the 1997 beating of Abner Louima. A Haitian immigrant, Louima was taken into custody by New York City police, beaten while being transported to a Brooklyn police station, then, when at the station, held down by one white police officer and brutalized by another. The latter officer was sentenced to a long prison term, and others were either criminally punished or were fired or demoted. In addition Louima brought a constitutional tort action against New York City, as well as the police officers' union (which, according to Louima, had attempted to cover up the officers' misconduct). The case eventually settled, with Louima obtaining more than $7 million from the City and another $1 million from the Union.

Although often less scandalous than the Louima case, instances of false imprisonment actionable by persons confined by officials are not difficult to find. For example, *Earles v. Perkins* involved allegations that a local police officer had arrested and detained the plaintiff only because the plaintiff had complained to the officer about his (the officer's) reckless driving.[10] Such allegations, if proven, would make out a Section 1983 claim for a violation of the plaintiff's right to be free from unreasonable seizure and to not be deprived of liberty without due process of law.

In adjudicating constitutional tort claims, courts are charged not only with interpreting the content of the rights-bearing provisions of the Constitution, but also with identifying and defining the scope of various privileges from which officials benefit, and that permit them in various circumstances to touch, hold, hit, shoot, arrest, and imprison. As noted above, an officer who arrests someone on the basis of a valid warrant or probable cause to believe the person has committed or is committing a crime is privileged and cannot be held liable even if the officer turns out to have been mistaken. Likewise, in the interest of law enforcement, officers may use reasonable force against others (e.g., by tackling fleeing suspects). These sorts of privileges are qualified, which means they are lost when abused. A police officer who shoots a robbery suspect solely to prevent him from escaping (as opposed to defending himself or others from physical attack) will be deemed to have used excessive force and to have exceeded any privilege to harm the victim physically. Even apart from the foregoing privileges, officials also benefit from special *immunities*. Specifically, a federal, state, or local official cannot be held liable for a constitutional tort unless the conduct in question involves the violation of a constitutional right clearly established by U.S. Supreme Court case law.

---

10. 788 N.E.2d 1260 (Ind. Ct. App. 2003).

Although constitutional tort law is in the foregoing ways very protective of officials, it also offers certain potential benefits to plaintiffs, including federal court jurisdiction, fee-shifting provisions that allow successful claimants to recover attorneys' fees on top of their compensatory awards, and the symbolic advantage of being able to claim not only that they have been injured, but also that their constitutional rights were violated.

⁂ 7.4 Assault

In legal and popular usage, one encounters the couplet "assault and battery" so often that it is natural to suppose that it is the name of a single wrong, just like "macaroni and cheese" is the name of a single dish. (Alternatively, one might suppose that it is a hyperbolic redundancy, as is the phrase "cease and desist.") Both of these suppositions turn out to be mistaken. Assault renders conduct wrongful even if it does not involve a touching of the plaintiff by the defendant. An assault occurs when, because of the right kind of intentional act by the defendant, the plaintiff *reasonably apprehends that she is about to be touched in a harmful or offensive manner.* In short, while batteries are about certain kinds of touchings, assaults are about *threats* of such touchings.

The linkage of assault to battery is hardly unmotivated. Both causes of action are of ancient pedigree, as evidenced by the famous old case of the innkeeper's wife. She (through her husband) successfully sued a guest who, angered at her unwillingness to serve him, swung his ax at her, missing his target.[11] Each is also a form of wrongdoing that involves intentional mistreatment. Assaults often take the form of 'near batteries.' Finally, many attacks include both harmful touchings and apprehensions of such touchings. Still, there are many assaults that involve only the

---

11. I de S et ux. v. W de S (1348).

creation of a perception in the victim and not of contact. Thus, even if an actor induces his victim to perceive a nonexistent threat of contact by pointing an unloaded gun at her, there can still be an assault. Conversely, there can be batteries that do not involve assaults, as in the case of an attack on an unconscious victim or a surreptitious poisoning.

Assault and battery both give expression to a notion of personal inviolability. Both acknowledge and protect one's 'personal space.' A credible threat of bodily harm undermines the sense of physical security even if no touching occurs or was going to occur. For these reasons, assault could almost as easily be coupled with false imprisonment as with battery. Just as false imprisonment protects one's interest in physical freedom of movement, assault protects one against being burdened in the exercise of one's liberty by others' threats. Although many assault plaintiffs will experience distress and will be able to obtain compensation for that distress as one component of their damages award, the core of an assault claim is *not* the emotional distress caused by being threatened; it is the fact of having been intentionally placed by the defendant in what is, or is reasonably perceived to be, a certain kind of menacing situation.

Like battery and false imprisonment, the duties associated with the tort of assault are *not* duties of prudence or vigilance. This part of tort law does not direct us to *take care* to avoid bringing about threats of harmful or offensive contact. Instead, we are told simply to refrain from setting out to create such threats. Note also that the threats at issue must be of a certain kind: they must put the plaintiff in apprehension of imminent harmful or offensive bodily contact. Even if P's enemy D menacingly says to P, "someday, you'll get what's coming to you," and even if D clearly means by this that he is planning to attack P at some indefinite future time, P will not be able to prevail on a claim of assault against D. Likewise were D to threaten P with imminent disclosure of embarrassing private information, P would not have a valid claim for assault. In circumscribing the reach of assault in this way, the courts seem to have supposed (accurately or not) that the *P*s of the world will have available to them other ways of dealing with indefinite threats, or that it is not practical for courts to take cognizance of vague threats, most of which are probably never acted upon. We will see below that the tort of intentional infliction of emotional distress was developed in part to relax the imminence limitation in certain special cases.

As with offensive-contact battery claims, which sometimes raise the question of whether certain kinds of contacts, even if offensive to the plaintiff, can be deemed to count as offensive, so too there is an inquiry into whether the objective features of the situation in which the defendant placed the plaintiff were such that the law will credit the plaintiff's sense of having been threatened. An especially timid soul who regularly sees threats of imminent harmful contact in the ordinary gestures of those around him will not prevail in his assault suits, no matter how genuine his feelings. The threat must really be there—that is, unless the defendant happens to know that the plaintiff is particularly fearful of contact, and deliberately plays on that vulnerability. (The same is true in battery for an actor who touches someone in a way that would not be offensive to a reasonable person, but, to the actor's knowledge, will be offensive to the plaintiff.)

A special subset of cases addressing the issue of when to credit the plaintiff's sense of threat falls under the heading of the "words alone" doctrine. The gist of this doctrine is that a mere verbal threat to attack someone will not usually give rise to a valid claim for assault, even if it was intended to create apprehension of an attack. Some of these cases are perhaps just particular instantiations of the more general requirement that the plaintiff's perception of imminent harmful or offensive contact be *reasonable*. At least in some contexts, verbal threats provide no basis for feeling threatened. In other cases, however, the doctrine seems to apply even in circumstances were the words in question create a reasonable basis for perceiving a threat of contact. Here, perhaps, assault doctrine gives expression to the idea that violent talk should not generate litigation, in part because it is desirable for the law to give people the outlet of using angry and threatening words as an alternative to carrying out violent acts. The law may also be taking the position that the mere utterance of words, no matter how impassioned and suggestive of violence, does not amount to an interference with another's liberty in the way that more physical forms of threatening do.

7.5 Intentional Infliction of Emotional Distress

False imprisonment and assault are notable because they are intentional torts that do not require the plaintiff to plead or prove physical harm or even physical contact. Nor do they require proof of property damage, economic loss, or reputational harm. Although both might therefore seem to be "emotional distress torts," we have suggested that this characterization is not right either. Instead, they identify categories of acts that are invasive of basic liberty interests: the right to remain free to move, unconfined by others, and the right to remain free of the menace of physically threatening acts by others.

On its face, the tort that goes by the ungainly name of *intentional infliction of emotional distress*—often abbreviated as "IIED" and also known as the tort of "outrage"—would seem to be designed exactly to protect emotional tranquility. Its name notwithstanding, this tort, too, identifies and vindicates in the first instance an individual's right to be from having a certain kind of pall cast over him by another. As such, it is a member of the same family as assault and false imprisonment.

Relative to torts such as battery, IIED is an upstart, tracing its origins to English and American judicial decisions from the late 1800s that began to permit damage awards in cases involving clear instances of morally wrongful conduct that did not quite seem to fit any of the well established torts. One recurring type of case was that of the defendant who carries out a vicious practical joke on the plaintiff, leaving her profoundly traumatized or humiliated. Another type of case involved overbearing creditors or organized crime members whose threats against and harassment of the plaintiff, while falling short of battery, false imprisonment, or assault, nonetheless justifiably left the plaintiff fundamentally shaken. By the early 1960s, Prosser and other scholars had collected these and other lines of cases and molded them into a new, general purpose emotional distress tort—the tort of IIED.

The canonical formulation of this wrong is provided in Section 46(1) of the Restatement (Second) of Torts, which subjects to liability one who, "by extreme and outrageous conduct intentionally or recklessly causes severe emotional distress to another." On its face, this sparsely defined tort might seem to provide broad protection for emotional tranquility as such. And indeed courts defined the wrong loosely precisely so as to catch miscellaneous instances of gross and injurious misconduct. Yet in doing so, they simultaneously (and somewhat contradictorily) built in substantial constraints on the tort's reach, both to prevent a flood of lawsuits and to reinforce the sense that we are all expected to endure everyday meanness with a certain amount of resilience. As to this latter concern, note that the plaintiff's prima facie case requires proof of "severe" emotional distress. Few other torts contain an injury element that is defined in terms of the *degree of impact* on the victim, and the rarity of this feature probably encourages judges to be relatively aggressive in dismissing certain IIED claims, including those brought by plaintiffs who seem 'only' to have suffered intense but transitory distress.

More significantly, the "extreme and outrageous" element sets a very high bar that few plaintiffs are able to meet. For IIED liability to attach, the defendant's conduct must not merely be intended to cause severe distress in the victim, and must not merely succeed in generating such distress, it must do so by means of conduct that is abominable or atrocious. This is why the reports of state court decisions are littered with IIED claims thrown out prior to trial on the ground that the defendant's conduct could not be deemed extreme and outrageous. The seduction of a victim's spouse by the victim's trusted advisor, the hurling by a store clerk of vile racist epithets at a customer, the endless, bad faith stonewalling of an insurance company on an insured's obviously valid claim—each of these are serious wrongs. Probably none rise to the level of being "extreme and outrageous."

Although the cases in which IIED claims succeed do not reduce to a single pattern, some features tend to show up frequently. Often there are premeditated and persistent efforts to harass and unsettle the victim, threats that fall outside the ambit of assaults (because they are conditional or indefinite), and a significant power imbalance between the person issuing the threat and the person being threatened, which imbalance the defendant know-ingly exploits. Also, the sheer gratuitous nastiness of the defendant's conduct—its having no social value or remotely plausible justifica-tion—matters. An overtly racist landlord who stalks and terrorizes a minority applicant for an apartment can be found to have acted outrageously; so too can a bitter ex-husband who posts sexually explicit photographs of his ex-wife in the neighborhood in which she now lives; as can a person who holds himself out as an animal lover keen to care for beloved pets, only to butcher them once they are in his care.

Whatever the precise contours of its particular incarnations, the gist of the wrong of IIED, no less than the gist of assault or false imprisonment, lies in the defendant's imposition on the plaintiff of a certain kind of oppressive circumstance—in this case, an environ-ment of such stress as to be unbearable even for persons of ordinary fortitude. There are common and unavoidable situations in which a person faces extreme stress and is thereby rendered distraught or inconsolable. But it will not be enough for liability that the defen-dant's conduct was a cause of this stress—after all, the conduct of an innocent bearer of bad news will often fit this description. In addition, the defendant must have targeted the plaintiff as a person on whom to impose an extreme degree of stress and must have generated that stress through conduct that amounts to such a gross deviation from norms of acceptable conduct as to be abominable or vile.

Conduct that may qualify as outrageous will often be actionable as some other tort. One person's torturing of another is surely outrageous, but it will give rise to straightforward claims of battery, assault, and/or false imprisonment. Generally speaking, courts prefer to address conduct of this sort by reference to the more traditional, narrowly defined torts, some so much so that if the conduct in question fits the definition of a tort such as battery, and if the plaintiff files her claims after the running of the statute of limitations for battery but before the running of the statute applicable to IIED, the latter claim will be disallowed on the ground that it should have been brought earlier as a battery. In this sense, IIED tends to serve as a kind of 'backstop' or 'gap-filling' tort.

It is significant that in Section 46's formulation of the IIED tort, the plaintiff can prevail on a showing of *recklessness* as to the risk of causing her extreme emotional distress. This is a distinctive feature of IIED as compared to other "intentional" torts, and was probably included to capture the case of the cruel jokester who professes with some plausibility not to have even considered whether his conduct might cause his vulnerable target to be devastated, even though the risk of such devastation was enormous and blatantly obvious.

Finally, it is worth noting that in contrast to the other tort causes of action discussed in this chapter, IIED has a less developed law of affirmative defenses. This is in part because many of the considerations that factor into affirmative defenses such as consent and self-defense will already have been accounted for in the analysis of the pivotal issue of outrageousness. Conduct that would be abominable if not consented-to becomes less wrongful, and perhaps not wrongful at all, when proper consent is given. Thus, one who maintains active membership in a church that employs certain ceremonies for the purpose of publicly humiliating members found to have acted contrary to church teachings, and who is himself subject to such a ceremony, will be hard-pressed to show that the church's conduct was as to him outrageous.

※ 7.6 Workplace Sexual Harassment

We have suggested that IIED can be seen as a broadening of the torts of false imprisonment and assault. Confinements and physical threats of imminent bodily harm are particular kinds of interference with liberty that one is entitled to be free from; others have a duty to respect this liberty interest, subject to various privileges. In turn, IIED gestures toward a domain of egregious, invasive actions, done for the purpose of causing upset, against which we are protected. The emergence of another distinctively modern wrong—the wrong of *employment discrimination*—perhaps also fits this description. Under a federal statute commonly known as "Title VII," it is a privately actionable wrong for firms of a certain size to discriminate against employees on the basis of race, color, religion, ethnicity, or gender.

The law of employment discrimination is sufficiently rich and complex to merit a book of its own. In this context, we aim to touch on only one aspect of it—gender discrimination in the form of sexual harassment—and only to note that this aspect has characteristics that suggest a connection to the other wrongs canvassed in this chapter. One type of workplace gender discrimination takes place when an employer conditions an employee's employment, or the terms of her employment, on the granting of sexual favors— so-called "quid pro quo" harassment. It is also actionable for an employer to foster or maintain a "hostile work environment," i.e., one in which sexist and demeaning comments, lewd remarks and gestures, and/or the display of pornographic materials unreasonably interfere with an employee's right to non-oppressive working conditions. The wrong here—particularly the wrong of creating a hostile work environment—rather evidently takes the form of acts that are intended to create, and do create, an environment in which the victim is deprived of freedom. In this case it is the freedom to do one's job without certain forms of interference by others.

As was the case with IIED, conduct that amounts to sexual harassment often amounts to other torts as well. For example, a reptilian supervisor who regularly presses himself against a subordinate employee and whose conduct generates in the employee a reasonable fear that he is about to molest her, will probably be subject to liability for battery and assault. In its more extreme forms, sexually harassing conduct may also give rise to a separate claim for IIED. The wrong of harassment remains distinct from these other wrongs, for the interest it protects is not the interest in freedom from being touched, threatened, or subjected to unbearable stress. Rather, the interest protected is the freedom to go about one's work in a setting unpolluted and uncluttered by sexism.

Today, harassment of someone on the basis of gender in an employment setting is a legal, relational, and injurious wrong, the commission of which generates in the victim a private right of action for damages (and injunctive relief) against the wrongdoer. As such, it is plausibly characterized as a tort, even though its source is statutory rather than common law. If this characterization is correct, then the law of workplace sexual harassment stands out as another particularly lively, and practically significant body of tort law. Like the law of constitutional torts, it gives further lie to the notion that tort law today is concerned exclusively with accidents. And also like constitutional tort law, it suggests that one can best appreciate the works in some of the newest rooms in tort law's gallery of wrongs by attending to some of the oldest, especially those in which hang portraits of the hoary actions for battery, false imprisonment, and assault.

EIGHT

Property Torts, with Notes on Fraud and other "Transactional Torts"

"FORGIVE US OUR TRESPASSES, as we forgive those who trespass against us," reads a passage from the Lord's Prayer. For centuries, English lawyers used the word "trespass" in this way to refer to the idea of a wrong or transgression. (*See* Chapter 2.) And yet even when trespass was invoked in this broad sense, it was exemplified by trespasses in the narrower sense of *unpermitted touchings*, whether a touching of the person (battery) or of real property (trespass to land).

Today the word "trespass" refers almost exclusively to the particular wrong of physically invading or occupying another's land. This is the same reference one encounters in everyday life in the form of "No Trespassing!" signs, which convey to passersby that entrance on property is forbidden without permission. They also serve to assert a right that, when unjustifiably invaded, generates in the victim an entitlement to recourse against the invader.

Trespass to land is but one of several torts concerned with protecting a person's interest in possessing and using her property. Indeed, the gallery of wrongs has a whole wing devoted to property torts. Other rooms house the torts of *nuisance, trespass to chattel,* and *conversion.* Interferences with *intellectual property* rights can also generate actions for recourse by victims. Thus, if one were to include in the ambit of tort law statutory regimes for creating and protecting intellectual property, then *copyright, patent,* and *trademark infringements* should also be considered property torts. Likewise, to exploit for commercial purposes the persona or likeness of a celebrity—a modern common law wrong known as the violation of one's *right to publicity*—is in some respects a property tort.

Another set of wrongs belongs in a separate but adjoining room in tort law's gallery. This room houses what might be dubbed "transactional wrongs," in that each involves interference with a person's interest in freely transacting with others. Because the transactions in question typically are business transactions, loss of intangible property—wealth—is usually the harm alleged. The most familiar of these transactional wrongs is *fraud* or deceit. Others include *tortious interference with contract* and its close cousin, *tortious interference with business expectancy*.

8.1 The Structure of Property Torts

Trespass to land is as old and as basic a tort as there is. Other, newer property torts such as copyright infringement figure prominently in contemporary litigation. Related torts such as fraud are also of great practical significance. Yet these wrongs tend to get little attention in first-year torts classes. Why? Partly the answer is found in academic categories. Copyright, trademark, and patent law, as well as fraud in connection with the sale of stocks and other securities, are addressed in separate upper-level courses. But what explains the relative inattention to long-standing common law torts such as trespass, nuisance, and conversion?

Here is one conjecture. The common law property torts do not fit comfortably within the standard framework by which academics usually arrange the different torts. By and large, casebooks and treatises tend to divide torts into three categories: intentional torts, negligence, and strict liability. In doing so, their aim is to organize the field along a culpability scale similar to the scale used to gauge the relative seriousness of criminal offenses (albeit with the recognition that tort law more regularly allows legal sanctions to attach to less culpable or even innocent conduct).

It is a weakness of this tripartite framework that wrongs such as trespass and nuisance defy its categories. A trespass is a genuine wrong: liability for trespass is not "strict" in the sense of attaching even though the defendant's conduct was entirely appropriate. Yet the wrong of trespass has nothing to do with failing to take care against causing injury. Nor does it require an intent to undertake the sort of act that ordinarily will cause harm or offense. Instead, the wrongfulness of the tort of trespass resides in the fact that the defendant has set out to make contact with or occupy a particular piece of land and, in so doing, has succeeded in crossing the boundary of the plaintiff's property.

For example, it is quite clearly a trespass to land to park one's car in another's driveway without permission. And this is so regardless of whether the driver acts with ordinary care with respect to the 'risk' of parking on another's property. Suppose that the driveway to P's house is situated between P's house and the house of N, his next-door neighbor. N's driveway is in turn located on the other (far) side of N's house. D asks N for permission to leave some old appliances in N's driveway for a week, until he (D) can arrange to dispose of them. N agrees. However, N accidentally describes his driveway as being located on the south side of his house, when in fact it is on the north side. This mistake induces D—who, when he arrives, sees nothing to suggest that the driveway is not N's—to unload his appliances in P's driveway, where they remain for a week, much to P's consternation. D has trespassed on P's property. And this is so even if D was perfectly reasonable in believing that he had permission to place the appliances where he did.[1]

This example shows that trespass is not a wrong that involves a failure of care or vigilance. But it is a wrong nonetheless. As we will see in Chapter 9, tort law in rare instances imposes genuine strict

---

1. *See* Burns Philp Food, Inc. v. Cavalea Continental Freight, Inc., 135 F.3d 526 (7th Cir. 1998) (applying Illinois law) (the builder of a fence on another's property is liable for trespass notwithstanding that he reasonably relied on an inaccurate survey).

liability for injuries stemming from certain kinds of activities, including the use of high explosives. In these cases, the plaintiff can recover from the defendant even though the defendant was behaving exactly as he ought to have behaved. By contrast, a trespass defendant is held liable because he has infringed a right of the plaintiff's. The infringement resides in the defendant's intentional act of treading upon or occupying land that is someone else's. This is why there is no trespass if a driver carelessly loses control of his car while driving on a public road, and as a result ends up stuck in a ditch on the plaintiff's property. The defendant must set out to make contact with the land in question, although the defendant need not know or have any reason to believe that he is not permitted on that land.

Because trespass to land requires an intentional entrance onto (or occupancy of) land, torts scholars tend to classify trespass as an intentional tort. But there is a problem with doing so. The appeal of the liability spectrum is its promise to organize the different torts on the dimension of culpability. On this spectrum, negligence lies in the middle, with intentional torts at the high-culpability end and strict liability at the no-culpability end. Yet insofar as the intentionality of intentional torts is meant to connote a higher level of culpability, trespass to land does not fit. *Some* trespasses are highly culpable. But the legal definition of trespass requires intent only in the sense of intending to touch the land in question, which means that many trespasses are far less culpable than standard instances of battery or false imprisonment. In this regard, trespass seems more on par with negligence. But, as we have seen, trespass is not a carelessness-based wrong.

If the distinctiveness of the wrong of trespass helps explain why academics are prone to downplay or ignore it, the same quality naturally invites the question of whether it (and other property torts) is an anomaly. Our answer comes at two levels. First, we would deny that property torts stand as oddities in need of special defense or explanation. Trespass to land was one of the original common law torts, suggesting that it has at least as strong a claim to authenticity as 'newer' torts such as negligence. Moreover, as Chapters 7 and 11 indicate, many other torts, including battery, assault, slander, and libel, have a structure similar to that of the property torts.

Second, and more substantively, we would suggest that torts such as trespass to land look as they do in part because they reflect values and commitments that are built into the law of property, which determines in the first instance what counts as the sort of possessory interest that will give rise to a tort claim when invaded. Private property has long formed a pillar of our economic, political, and social arrangements. Its importance is attested to by, among other things, the Fifth Amendment's prohibition on the taking of private property by government without just compensation. Although, as history shows, the recognition of private property rights is fully compatible with extensive regulation of its ownership and use, this fundamental commitment has shaped our tort law by generating a law of wrongs to property that is in certain respects more generous to victims than even the law of personal injury. One might suppose that tort law has its priorities backwards, and there are undoubtedly instances in which the relative burden placed on personal injury claimants, as compared to certain classes of property tort claimants, seems misguided. But it should also be noted that the law—including criminal law and tort law—generally permits individuals more room to take self-protective actions in response to threats to their persons than to their properties: the privilege of self-defense is a substantially broader and more robust defense to a claim of battery than is the privilege to defend property. Perhaps then tort law makes life easier for property tort plaintiffs as compensation for the fact that the law more generally is anxious to dissuade property owners from trying to protect their property rights by means of self-help.

⅛ 8.2 Trespass to Land

A defendant has trespassed on land when he has acted so as to interfere tangibly with a possessor's right to the exclusive possession of her real property. This definition can be broken down in several ways, but principally, we must explore. (1) What *sort of action* must the defendant have engaged in and *how* must the defendant have engaged in it? (2) What counts as a tangible *interference* with real property and *how seriously* must it interfere? (3) When is property *real property*, and when does a *plaintiff qualify* as having a right to exclusive possession of it?

8.2.1 Intent to Touch

We have already discussed the basics of what the defendant must do to be eligible for liability for trespass. He must act, he must intend to make physical contact with a particular swath of land, and he must succeed in making such contact. As noted above, a defendant may be liable in trespass even though his conduct was entirely reasonable or diligent. Conversely, unreasonable conduct that foreseeably damages property does not of itself generate a trespass: there must be an intentional act of intrusion or occupation. A city that negligently permits water from its water main to leak into a homeowner's basement is not a trespasser,[2] though if actual damage results, there may be a claim for negligence.

In recent decades, plaintiffs whose properties have been contaminated by tangible pollutants have pushed for a softening of the "intentionality" requirement of the tort of trespass, occasionally with success. In *Scribner v. Summers*,[3] the plaintiff suffered property damage when hazardous waste flowed down a swale from defendant's property whenever defendant washed its furnaces. The Second Circuit Court of Appeals accepted the argument that if defendant knew its method of furnace-washing consistently caused the introduction of hazardous waste fluid to plaintiff's land, this

---

2. Snow v. City of Columbia, 409 S.E.2d 797 (S.C. Ct. App. 1991).

3. 84 F.3d 554 (2d Cir. 1996).

could satisfy the intentionality requirement of trespass, and therefore could state a claim for trespass. *Scribner*, however, lies at the outer limit of what is needed to prove intentional intrusion.

8.2.2 What Counts as a Touching?

To act with the intent to touch land is not sufficient to create trespass liability. The act must succeed in generating a physical invasion of the land. A classic example of a physical invasion of real property consists of a person's physical presence on the land of another—his taking up physical space on the property. By the same token, placing an object or building a structure on the plaintiff's property would also be a prima facie trespass. A defendant who intentionally directs his herd of cattle onto another's land has also invaded it in the requisite sense. Likewise, one in a position of authority who instructs or orders another to occupy land—for example a company that mistakenly orders an independent contractor to excavate on property that is in fact owned by the plaintiff—is subject to trespass liability even though another actor actually made contact with the land.

The interferences that constitute trespasses must consist of *physical invasions*. Odors and sounds that waft onto property are not trespasses. This is true even if the odors and sounds are highly disruptive to the plaintiff's use of her property or significantly impinge on the value of the property.

It may seem that the law is unduly demanding of plaintiffs in requiring a tangible invasion to support a trespass claim, but several important qualifications counterbalance this requirement. First and foremost, as we will see below, non-tangible invasions will frequently generate a claim for the separate tort of nuisance. Second, some jurisdictions today permit intangible invasions (such as electromagnetic waves) to constitute a trespass if those invasions in turn cause tangible physical damage to the property.

Third, although the requirement of a tangible physical invasion is rigid, in most other ways, the criteria for actionable invasion are generous to possessors of property. Any permanent structure, no matter how small and unobtrusive, constitutes an invasion, including, for example, the installation by a cable television company of a small and barely visible box on the roof of an apartment building.[4] And permanence is not required. Quite the opposite, a momentary physical invasion or occupation can constitute a trespass. Note also that courts have long recognized a vertical dimension of property ownership that further expands the possibilities for a trespass action: invasion of subsurface of property (to a certain depth) and invasion of air rights over property (to a certain height) can also constitute a trespass. Conceivably, then, a pilot could be held liable in trespass for flying a plane at too low an altitude over the land of the plaintiff.

As these examples already suggest, a plaintiff can prevail on a trespass claim *without proof that the defendant's invasion caused actual property damage*. In this respect, trespass law is again very charitable to property possessors (more so than negligence, which requires proof of actual damage to permit recovery). Although in some ways similarly plaintiff-protective, even the tort of battery holds actors liable only for certain kinds of touchings, namely, those that are harmful or offensive. Trespass to property does not impose even this modest threshold. If there is harm flowing from a trespass, the plaintiff will be able to obtain damages to compensate for it. Sometimes, however, the plaintiff can successfully sue for an entirely nonharmful trespass and recover nominal damages,

---

4. Although not a case directly involving the application of trespass law, the U.S. Supreme Court's decision *in Loretto v. Teleprompter Manhattan TV Corp.*, 485 U.S. 419 (1985), ruled that a state law requiring building owners to permit cable television companies to install small pieces of equipment on their buildings constituted a government "taking" of private property that required compensation. In doing so, the Court, consistent with the common law of trespass, held that any governmentally imposed permanent installation on another's property, no matter how small and unobtrusive, constitutes a "taking."

yet also benefit from other remedies, including injunctive relief and punitive damages.

A case exemplifying this feature of trespass law is *Jacque v. Steenberg Homes, Inc.*[5] The defendant was in the business of selling and delivering mobile homes. Unable to use a narrow road to make a delivery, it asked en elderly couple, the Jacques, for permission to traverse part of their farm. When the Jacques refused, Steenberg's employees crossed their land anyway, without permission. Because the land was covered with a thick blanket of snow, the property suffered no damage whatsoever. Still, the Jacques sued in trespass. The jury awarded them $1 in nominal damages and $100,000 in punitive damages, a verdict that was affirmed on appeal. The defendant had committed a flagrant trespass by physically invading the plaintiffs' property in willful disregard of their entitlement to exclude others from it.

8.2.3 Who May Complain?

Although an unharmed plaintiff may state a claim for trespass, this is not to say that claims for a given trespass will be available to a wide class of plaintiffs. On the contrary, conduct that is trespassory will not generate a claim except on behalf of the person or persons who has or have a possessory interest in the property: in the typical case, an owner or tenant. If police, through a terrible error, batter down the front door of X's house while X's friend Y happens to be there, only X, not Y, will have a trespass claim. Indeed, if X is physically injured because of the trespass (for example, if he trips and falls in his understandably panicked response to the police intrusion), he may be able to obtain compensation for his physical injuries as damages parasitic on the underlying trespass. By contrast, even if Y were similarly injured, he could not seek compensation for

---

5. 563 N.W.2d 154 (Wis. 1997).

his physical injuries by means of a claim for trespass, and would instead have to make out a claim for negligence as to his physical well-being. Trespass claims are rooted in the infringement of the property right. Where there is no property right, there is no trespass claim. To observe this feature of trespass law is to observe that trespass to land—like negligence and every other tort—is a relational wrong. Every actionable trespass is a trespass *as to* an owner or occupier of property.

8.2.4 Consent, 'Private Necessity,' and other Defenses

Like every other tort, trespass to land recognizes several affirmative defenses. Some are very fundamental and broadly defined; others are more carefully honed to particular scenarios. Consent is plainly the broadest and most important defense to trespass to land. The list of narrower defenses includes private necessity; entry to reclaim goods ("recapture of chattel"); entry to effect an arrest or otherwise prevent crimes; entry incidental to the use of a public highway or navigable stream; and entry to abate a nuisance.

So fundamental is the defense of consent that many jurisdictions deem *lack of consent* to be an element of the tort that must be proved by the plaintiff. Indeed, it is common to define a trespass as an "unpermitted entry"—a definition that indicates how natural it is to conceive the nonconsensual quality as part of the essence of the wrong. Part of the reason for the ambiguity as to consent's role in the tort has to do with ways in which permission to enter land can be built into property rights through the operation of property law. Suppose D drives along O's driveway to reach a public road from D's house. In determining whether D is to be held liable to O for trespass, we would want to know whether O has in this instance consented to D's driving on his driveway. However, the question sometimes goes beyond consent to the question of whether D has an "easement"—a special kind of property right—to use O's driveway.

For example, imagine that *D*'s house sits on land that was originally part of a larger tract owned by *O*. As it turns out, the part of the tract that *O* eventually sold to *D* is located such that *D* can only gain access to the nearest public road by crossing *O*'s property. Thus, when *O* sold the land to *D*, *D* demanded and *O* granted to *D* an easement to use *O*'s driveway for road access. In these circumstances, if *O* were to sue *D* for trespassing on his driveway, *O*'s claim would fail for a very basic reason: *D* has not infringed any property right of *O*'s because *O*'s property rights have been defined in such a way as not to encompass a right to exclude *D* from driving his car on the driveway.

As they do with respect to battery and other intentional torts, courts clearly allow a notion of "implied" or "tacit" consent to shape the potentially broad trespass tort in ways that generally render it consistent with social norms. The driver for a delivery company such as UPS leaves at Homeowner's doorstep a package that the sender has mistakenly labeled with Homeowner's address. Homeowner—who did not actually consent to the delivery of the package, and would have refused delivery if present—will not have a trespass claim against UPS or its delivery person. He will be deemed to have tacitly consented to such 'intrusions.'

Difficult questions as to the conditions under which consent will be deemed to have been given are easy to find. Suppose that the defendant, a process server, knocks on the door of an apartment. The roommate of the plaintiff, who is co-renting the apartment, answers. The process server represents that he is a courier who has a package for the plaintiff, for which the plaintiff must sign. The roommate grants the process server entry, whereupon he delivers a complaint and summons to the plaintiff. Is the roommate's consent to entry valid, or is it vitiated by the process server's ruse? A reporter poses as an applicant for a menial job in the plaintiff's supermarket in order to investigate allegations of unsanitary practices. The reporter obtains the job, does it competently, then quits, having gathered the information for her story, which is later published in a damning exposé. Has the storeowner consented to her presence on its property? (Even if not, the plaintiff's damages probably ought to be limited to compensation for the intrusion itself, and should not include compensation for losses caused by the publication of the exposé, a constitutionally protected activity.)

Although consent is in practice the most important limitation on trespass liability, the defense that has received the most academic attention is the so-called *incomplete privilege of private necessity*. A familiar hypothetical example illustrates the intuition behind it. Jones is in a helicopter crash in the mountains. No one else survives the crash. Facing death from exposure, Jones happens upon an unoccupied log cabin. It belongs to Smith, but Smith does not use it in the winter months. Most would suppose that, to save his own life, Jones has a right to use Smith's cabin until help arrives. This supposition is usually interpreted to mean that where conduct that would amount to a trespass is *necessary* for one's survival, or to avert imminent and grave harm, the use of another's real property is not actionable as a trespass.

Against this backdrop, consider the much-analyzed decision of the Minnesota Supreme Court in *Vincent v. Lake Erie Transportation Co.*[6] The defendant's ship, the Reynolds, was delivering cargo to a dock owned by the plaintiff Vincent. The defendant's crew had permission to use the dock for as long as was necessary to unload its cargo, after which time it was required to depart to make room for other ships. However, after unloading its cargo, the defendant's captain refused to unmoor the ship because of a severe storm that, in his judgment, posed a significant risk to the ship. The storm ensued, and the ship remained unharmed because it was tied to the dock. However, the plaintiff's dock sustained serious damage because the force of the storm smashed the ship against the dock.

Vincent, the dock owner, sued the defendant for trespass. He argued that he should be compensated for the dock damage

---

6. 124 N.W. 221 (Minn. 1910).

because of the defendant's purposeful decision to keep the ship tied to the dock after permission to remain there had expired. The defendant countered that that it should be spared liability because its captain's behavior was entirely reasonable under the circumstances. In making this argument, it pointed to an earlier decision, *Ploof v. Putnam*,[7] in which a dock owner was held liable for cutting loose a boat moored to its dock during a storm, which action caused the boat and its occupants to suffer injury.

In *Vincent*, the court ruled for the dock owner. It accepted that the ship captain's conduct was entirely reasonable under the circumstances. It also agreed with *Ploof* that a landowner has no right to forcibly expel a person if doing so exposes that person to grave risk of death or serious injury. Nevertheless, it required the ship owner to compensate the dock owner. In the view of the court, a person such as the helicopter crash victim hypothesized above, while surely within his rights to enter another's property to save his own life, is also under an obligation to provide compensation to the owner for the invasion.

In the eyes of most torts scholars, *Vincent* stands for the recognition in trespass law of the *incomplete privilege* of private necessity. It is a *privilege* because the necessity faced by the defendant is deemed to override the property owner's right to take reasonable measures to expel an unpermitted entrant onto its property. It is an *incomplete* privilege because the defendant must nonetheless compensate the property owner for damage caused to the property. Although this is the standard reading of *Vincent*, our view is that this reading is more question-begging than helpful. If the defendant really was privileged to remain on the land, then why is he required to compensate the plaintiff?

Our own view of *Vincent* is that it deserves all the attention it has drawn, but not because it identifies a special affirmative defense. Rather, it deserves attention because it vividly demonstrates the

---

7. 71 A. 188 (Vt. 1908).

distinctiveness of the wrong of trespass to land. *Vincent*, we believe, is a plain-vanilla trespass case. The ship owner intentionally occupied the defendant's property (the dock) even after it was no longer permitted to do so. It therefore committed a trespass for which compensation was owed. Of course its decision to trespass was entirely reasonable. However—as we have emphasized all along—the wrong of trespass, at least in the first instance, has nothing to do with whether the defendant behaved reasonably. In this regard, the ship owner in *Vincent* is no different from the hypothetical case, offered above, of the person who unwittingly places his appliances in the driveway of the property owner who has not given him permission to do so. Both trespasses are reasonable trespasses. They are trespasses nonetheless.

Even though the reasonableness of the trespass in *Vincent* does not prevent it from being a trespass, it does have *some* significance for the outcome of the case. First, the reasonableness of the ship captain's decision to stay at the dock entails that the dock owner (unlike the plaintiffs in *Jacque*, discussed above) would have no claim for punitive damages or injunctive relief: there was nothing willful or wanton about the trespass warranting a punitive response, and the equities of the situation would clearly disfavor a court order commanding that the ship set sail in the storm.

Second, the same circumstances that explain why the captain's decision to stay put was entirely reasonable also explain why the dock owner in *Vincent*, like the dock owner in *Ploof*, would have faced liability if it had forcibly ejected the Reynolds from the dock, thereby causing it or its crew to suffer harm. A property owner has a limited privilege to take measures to ward off trespassers; it may even at times use reasonable force to eject trespassers. But as we saw in Chapter 7's discussion of the "spring-gun" case of *Katko v. Briney*, a property possessor cannot do just anything in response to trespasses. *Ploof* tells us that if a property owner expels trespassers under circumstances where the expulsion exposes them to a grave risk of death or bodily harm, the property owner will have abused his privilege to defend his property and therefore will be subject to liability for battery. For this reason, the result in *Ploof* is entirely consistent with our reading of *Vincent*. In awarding damages to the Ploofs, the court did not need to deny that the Ploofs (like the ship owner in *Vincent*) had committed a trespass. Nor did it need to suggest that, had the Ploofs damaged that dock, they would have avoided liability for the damage. It merely needed to say that there are limits on what property owners can do in the face of trespasses, limits that never became an issue in *Vincent* because the dock owner did not attempt to force the defendant's ship off the dock.

The defendant ship owner was held liable in *Vincent* for the very simple reason that it trespassed on the plaintiff's property. No resort to the cumbersome machinery of 'incomplete privilege' is required to explain this result. *Vincent* thus serves as a stark reminder that one who commits the legal wrong of trespass to land has not necessarily committed a moral wrong or acted unreasonably. Of course, as we have seen elsewhere, tort law often gives credence to good reasons for acting in a way that otherwise would be tortious by deeming those reasons to be grounds for treating the act as not tortious after all. When it does so, it recognizes a privilege. (Such is the case, for example, with the privilege of self-defense to claims of assault and battery.) But *Vincent* shows us that, in other instances, even if there is a good reason—practically or morally—to do what is tortious, the law may decline to convert that reason into a legal privilege. The importance of avoiding being on open water in a storm seems to have been just this sort of reason.

⁂ 8.3 Nuisance

Perhaps the most distinctive property tort, and certainly the one that has drawn the greatest attention from contemporary scholars, is the tort of nuisance. A nuisance is an unreasonable interference with another's right to use and enjoy her property. Repeated outdoor rock concerts that generate late-night noise; a waste processing plant or pig farm that frequently generates sickening odors; a shop with machinery whose vibrations can be felt in neighboring homes—these are classic examples of the sort of conduct that can amount to a nuisance. Unlike trespass, nuisance does not involve a *tangible* interference with plaintiff's possession of her property. Conversely, a legal nuisance consists of something more substantial than a mere boundary crossing, although it does not require—and typically does not even include—a boundary crossing at all. The key question is whether the defendant is doing something that interferes *unreasonably* with plaintiff's right to enjoy her own land, and in this sense, there is a threshold of significant interference that must be met for nuisance that is absent from the tort of trespass to land.

Tort law distinguishes between public and private nuisances. An action for a public nuisance is typically brought by a government entity seeking to enjoin an activity that carries harmful consequences for the public at large. For example, a city might sue to enjoin the operation of a nightclub functioning as a brothel and thereby undermining the quality of life in its neighborhood. A state might likewise sue a company for committing a public nuisance by discharging pollutants into a public body of water. When a private citizen is able to show that an actor is responsible for a public nuisance, and that it has caused her to suffer a distinctive injury (relative to others around her), she is entitled to recover on a claim of public nuisance, although government officials are usually permitted to intervene in such suits and to help determine their resolution (e.g., by accepting settlement terms even if the individual plaintiff might not).

Private nuisance litigation is what judges and jurists are usually referring to when they invoke the word "nuisance." Private nuisance suits are almost always brought by one or more neighbors against another and typically allege that the latter's activity is disruptive and out of place. Although nuisance suits commonly reflect the inability of neighbors to work out disputes arising from certain ways in which they annoy one another, nuisance suits also served as an early form of "environmental law." Residents facing a significant setback in the quality of their lives because of the operation of nearby industrial facilities or mines have at times successfully used nuisance suits to prevent deterioration of the quality of their water and air.

One of the appeals of nuisance law to plaintiffs, where available, is that it tends to come with a particular and potentially powerful remedy. Those who establish that the defendant is generating an interference with their use of property that is beyond what a reasonable person should have to tolerate usually receive from the court an *injunction* that orders the cessation of the interfering activity. This means that, if there is no way for the defendant to continue its operation without generating the nuisance, the defendant must shut down. Although damages are also available as a remedy for nuisances, the fact that the injunction is the *characteristic* remedy obtained by a nuisance plaintiff renders the tort unique.

It is no surprise, then, that the most famous American nuisance case—*Boomer v. Atlantic Cement Co.*[8]—is known for its analysis of remedies rather than the underlying elements of the nuisance claim. The plaintiff homeowners sued a cement company in nuisance for generating huge volumes of dust, smoke, and noise that interfered with their ability to live in their homes. The New York Court of Appeals accepted the determination of the courts below that there was a nuisance and directed that a permanent injunction against the operation of the plant be issued. Yet it proceeded to undercut this command by giving the defendant the option of avoiding the injunction by paying "permanent damages" to the plaintiffs (i.e., paying them for the diminution in the value of their homes resulting from the nuisance). In essence, the court allowed the factory owner to buy its way out of the injunction.

Boomer is typically read as embracing a purely utilitarian standard for when injunctions should issue in nuisance cases, one under which a defendant should always be given by the courts the

---

8. 257 N.E.2d 870 (N.Y. 1970).

option to 'pay its way' out of a legal prohibition. Allowing it to do so, some have argued, ensures that scarce resources such as limited physical space are put to their 'highest-value' use. (If it is worth it to the defendant to continue operating its plant even after paying full compensation to neighbors who suffer unreasonable interferences with their property rights because of it, then society is better off in the sense that the land is being used for the activity that generates the highest dollar value.) Perhaps a better reading is that the New York Court of Appeals took seriously the legal standards for determining when permanent injunctions should be issued. These include the principle that, although courts will enjoin activities that are 'worth' more than the damages they cause, they will nonetheless refrain from enjoining conduct when doing so imposes a cost massively disproportionate to the benefit it generates. In *Boomer*, the issuance of an unconditional and permanent injunction would have entailed the shutting down of a $45 million plant that served as the region's main employer, a substantial and widespread hardship that the court deemed disproportionate to the benefit to the plaintiffs. It therefore allowed the defendant wrongdoer the 'benefit' of having the option to pay damages.

Given that nuisance is not a pure line-crossing tort such as trespass, and that determinations of reasonableness figure centrally in determining whether a nuisance has occurred, it is natural to ask whether nuisance is really just a form of negligence. Many theorists have said it is, but their view is not a fair interpretation of the law. Fundamentally, negligence is about a careless *damaging* of the plaintiff in some way. Nuisance is not about doing damage. It is about interfering with a property possessor's affirmative right *to use and enjoy her property*. Moreover, in nuisance law, the word "reasonable" does *not* refer to qualities of the defendant's conduct. It refers instead to what the plaintiff can be expected to endure. The issue is whether the plaintiff has suffered too great an interference in light of what may otherwise be perfectly legitimate activity on the part of the defendant. The harmonization of the plaintiff's and the defendant's rights is the name of the game.

To a significant extent, the idea of harmonizing plaintiffs' property rights with defendants' rights suggests that each is being trimmed, or defined, to fit alongside the other. The enterprise is intrinsically reciprocal in the sense that the right of one to be free of certain interferences by others is analytically equivalent to the denial of the other's right to engage in that activity. In this sense, judicial resolutions of nuisance cases can seem to constitute a piecemeal form of zoning or centralized land-use planning. For just this reason, nuisance law has been at the forefront of economics-based approaches to legal analysis: questions of how to allocate scarce resources among conflicting uses and users naturally invite economic analysis. In fact, two of the three 'founding documents' of the modern law-and-economics movement address nuisance law: Coase's *The Problem of Social Cost* and Calabresi's and Melamed's *Property Rules and Liability Rules: One View of the Cathedral.* (The third is Posner's *A Theory of Negligence.*)[9]

Coase's analysis starts from the (undefended) assumption that in cases of conflicting land use, the goal for government and law is to figure out how to allocate use-rights to ensure that the land ends up being put to its most highly valued use. His insight is that government often can accomplish this goal best not by deciding for itself to what use land should be put, but instead by focusing on how to lower "transactions costs"—i.e., impediments to private, consensual transactions between potential buyers and sellers of land. By doing so, Coase argued, courts would allow private actors to decide for themselves which of them most valued the property, which in turn would (in the absence of transaction costs) lead higher-value users to buy out lower-value users. Calabresi and Melamed's article—building on Calabresi's earlier work on the potential for forms of strict liability to incentivize different classes

---

9. Guido Calabresi & A. Douglas Melamed, *Property Rules, Liability Rules and Inalienability: One View of the Cathedral,* 85 HARV. L. REV. 1089 (1972); Richard A. Posner, *A Theory of Negligence,* 1 J. LEGAL STUD. 29 (1972); Ronald Coase, *The Problem of Social Cost,* 3 J. L. & ECON. 1 (1960).

of actors well positioned to prevent certain accidents to take precautions against those accidents—similarly saw in the tort of nuisance lessons about how tort law might be harnessed to promote efficient use of resources. In particular, they argued that decisions on how to define and distribute entitlements to use property (what constitutes a nuisance or trespass) are entirely separable from decisions about what sort of legal rule and remedy should be used to protect those entitlements.

In the view of these and other economic scholars, the issue before courts in a case like *Boomer* is not whether the nearby homeowners had a 'right' to enjoy their properties free of the levels of dust and noise being generated by the factory, such that the court ought to enjoin the factory from operating so as to protect that right. In the absence of a legal prohibition against operating the factory, its owner had as much of a 'right' to pollute as the property owners had to enjoy their homes. (Their enjoyment, Coase or Calabresi would say, as much 'interfered' with the factory owner's freedom to operate its plant as the plant interfered with their freedom to live in their homes.) In this dispute among rights, the issue boiled down to whether it was worth it to the cement factory owner to operate the plant even after paying all the property owners for their damages. Thus Calabresi and Melamed argued that the *Boomer* court's refusal to issue an unconditional injunction was exactly the right thing to do, for it gave the factory owner the opportunity to buy out his neighbors, which it would presumably do only if the factory generated enough profit to remain viable even after the owner paid this cost.

Notwithstanding the valuable insights these articles have shed on certain dimensions of tort law, they cannot be understood, as some have understood them, to have somehow captured the 'deep structure' of nuisance law, much less tort law taken as a whole. In part, their flaw is that they reflect a top-down, theory-driven picture of what nuisances are like, one that is often incongruent with actual law. For example, many nuisances are not appropriately treated as cases of reciprocal interference, but instead are quite clearly cases of one person wrongfully and unilaterally imposing burdens on his neighbors. In addition, courts continue to issue 'inefficient' injunctions that leave victorious nuisance plaintiffs with no incentive to accept even economically efficient buyouts from nuisance-generating defendants. More fundamentally, the nuisance room in the gallery of wrongs is quite distinct in addressing interferences that, although wrongful, often arise out of nothing more than an unfortunate conflict between two otherwise permitted uses of land. By contrast, most other torts involve interferences that are not 'reciprocal' in this way. Except as an exercise in purposeful misdescription, no one would treat *D*'s punching of *P* as arising from an unfortunate incompatibility between *D*'s preferred activity of hitting and *P*'s preferred activity of being left alone. To treat the economic analysis of nuisance as uncovering the deep structure of tort is akin to supposing that a brilliant approach to understanding the aesthetics of marble sculpture provides the key to understanding all forms of art.

8.4 Trespass to Chattel and Conversion

As land is only one form of property, so trespass to land is only one kind of property tort. Someone who decides to camp inside another person's minivan is a trespasser just as much as someone who decides to squat on another's land. But because an automobile is "chattel"—personal property—rather than real property, the former tort would be classified as a *trespass to chattel*, not a trespass to land. Chattel is a broad category that covers everything from clothing, sculptures, and jewelry to pets, livestock, legal and illegal drugs, business papers, briefcases of cash, automobiles, furniture, groceries, and truckloads of widgets and washing machines. It excludes not only land, structures, fixtures, and water, but also various intangibles: ideas, patents, trademarks, copyrights, goodwill, and reputation.

One might suppose that the tort of trespass to chattel would be defined identically to its sibling trespass to land (apart from the type of property being intruded upon). In many respects, this assumption is correct. The defendant must intend to make physical contact with property, and must succeed in doing so, and can be held liable for trespass to chattel even if the contact was made in the reasonable but mistaken belief that the property was not owned by someone else. By the same token, only a person with the requisite ownership interest in the property has standing to prevail on a trespass-to-chattel claim. And roughly speaking, the same defenses apply, including, most importantly, the defense of consent.

However, in many jurisdictions, the law of trespass to chattel departs from the law of trespass to land in requiring the plaintiff to demonstrate *actual harm*—either physical damage to the chattel or deprivation of use of the chattel for a substantial period of time. The idea is commonsensical enough: there are too many chattels and too many minor interferences with them to permit the litigation system to cover these sorts of interferences on the same terms as physical invasions of land. (Of course this line of reasoning might induce one to wonder why trespass to land does not itself have a harm requirement.)

If the quaint-sounding tort of "trespass to chattel" seems far removed from current reality, that impression is mistaken. Among the most important cyberlaw decisions of recent years is *Intel Corp. v. Hamidi*,[10] which focused on the question of whether trespass to chattel requires the plaintiff to prove harm or damages apart from the intrusion itself. Plaintiff Intel's company intranet was repeatedly bombarded by mass e-mails sent by defendant, a disgruntled former employee. Intel made clear that this mass e-mailing was not welcome, and claimed that the e-mails interfered with its operations and harmed its chattel—i.e., its computer equipment. Hamidi argued that there was no tangible damage to Intel's equipment and

---

10. 71 P.3d 296 (Cal. 2003).

that, in the absence of harm to property, there could not be a trespass to chattel. The Supreme Court of California accepted Hamidi's
argument, reasoning that Intel could not recover without proof that
Hamidi's e-mails either damaged its computer equipment or significantly interfered with the functioning of that equipment.
Other courts, including several lower federal courts, have issued
decisions treating electronic communications that significantly
diminish the functionality of a plaintiff's computing systems as a
trespass to chattel.

The tort of *conversion* is in some ways a special case of trespass
to chattel: it occurs when a defendant intentionally exercises physical dominion over personal property owned by the plaintiff such
that the plaintiff is entirely or almost entirely deprived of its use.
Conversion is thus the tort law equivalent to the crime of theft. (It is
called "conversion" because the defendant is converting the plaintiff's property to his own use.) A standard instance of conversion
would be the international theft and sale of one's car or jewelry, or
the killing of one's pet. The victim can in principle sue the converter
for compensation equal to the value of the property and, depending
on the circumstances, might recover punitive damages as well.

As has been the case with trespass to chattel, contemporary
plaintiffs have pushed courts to apply the tort of conversion to
cases outside of the paradigm of theft of a tangible object. For
example, they have argued with some success that the theft of
assets such as stock shares should count as conversion, in part on
the theory that thefts such as these involve the physical seizure of
the paper certificates that symbolize and record the plaintiff's ownership of these items. Not surprisingly, courts have recently been
pushed to recognize the applicability of conversion to electronic
data. In *Thyroff v. Nationwide Mutual Insurance Company*,[11] the
plaintiff was terminated from a job where he had worked for twelve
years as an insurance agent. The job involved use of a personal

---

11. 864 N.E.2d 1272 (N.Y. 2007).

computer that was owned by the employer, but that the employee was permitted to work on as part of a lease that was executed in conjunction with the employment contract. The employee saved personal information on the hard drive of the computer, but the defendant/employer refused to give him access to the computer after the employment relationship had been terminated so that he could retrieve this personal information. When the case went up to the New York Court of Appeals, the question was whether electronic data, despite being intangible, can support a claim for conversion. The court answered "yes," reasoning that "[a] document stored on a computer hard drive has the same value as a paper document kept in a file cabinet."[12]

Perhaps the most puzzling feature of the tort of conversion is its obscurity. Assault and battery are household words. "Conversion"—at least as a legal term—is barely in the educated person's lexicon. Odd nomenclature aside, everyone knows that it is wrong to steal, and that is what conversion is about. As *Thyroff* demonstrates, the defendant need not believe that the property belongs to another in order for there to be a conversion; like battery and trespass, the tort version of the wrong, generating a private party's right to redress the wrong, is less demanding than the criminal version of the wrong.

🖋 8.5 Intellectual Property Torts

Today it is common for pharmaceutical companies to argue that it should be easier to get patent protections for new drugs and that those protections should be stronger. Celebrities claim that advertisers have, without permission, used their personas to sell products. Songwriters argue that other performers have stolen a

---

12. 864 N.E.2d at 1278.

melody or 'hook' that they created. Competitor businesses are regularly embroiled in disputes about alleged infringements of trademark and trade dress. High-tech companies, software designers, chemical manufacturers, and their investors, offshoots, and executives dispute copyright, patent, and trade secrets. In all of these cases, courts are asked to delineate what are in some sense property rights.

What is not always recognized is that these lawsuits are in effect today's most prevalent form of property tort litigation. A person who claims to have a property right alleges that the right to the exclusive possession of the property has been invaded *and that therefore she is entitled to a court's assistance in responding to that invasion.* These plaintiffs are claiming to be victims of property wrongs of a certain kind. Like trespass to land and trespass to chattel—and indeed battery—the plaintiff is claiming a boundary-crossing has occurred. Unlike negligence, she is not alleging a lack of diligence by the defendant and is not claiming any harm concretely specifiable in a manner independent of the defendant's gain or the interference with the entitlement to control what is done with the property in question. (In a famous case, former Beatle George Harrison was successfully sued for writing a song ("My Sweet Lord") that copied without permission an earlier song recorded by the Chiffons ("He's So Fine").[13] The court held that liability for infringement would attach so long as Harrison in fact wrote an almost-identical song, even if his copying of it was more a matter of subconscious repetition than conscious appropriation.)

For these torts, as for trespass, the defense of consent is fundamental in a number of ways, and the question of designing privileges that are satisfactory from a policy point of view is a very delicate one. To take but one example, does an unauthorized parody of a song that incorporates its melody constitute a noninfringing

---

13. Bright Tunes Music v. Harrisongs Music, 420 F. Supp. 177 (S.D.N.Y. 1976).

"fair use" of the melody? What about a book that purports to re-tell a famous novel from the perspective of one of its minor characters?

Of course, as this chapter has indicated, the common law of torts has no quick or easy answers to these questions about property torts. The recognition that a great deal of today's commercial litigation can be characterized as a descendant of property torts is not going to generate simple resolutions to difficult questions. On the other hand, it should remind us, yet again, that negligence and accident law form only a part of the modern law of torts.

🎞 8.6 Fraud and Other "Transactional Torts"

An utterly familiar form of wrongdoing involves the use by one person of trickery to induce another person to part with something of value. Works of history and literature, not to mention today's newspapers, are filled with stories of hustlers, charlatans, scam artists, and swindlers who use trickery to extract money from both unsuspecting and sophisticated victims. Not surprisingly, such conduct is both criminal and tortious.

The tort of *fraud* (also known as *deceit*) occurs when an actor *A* makes a misrepresentation of fact, knowing that it is false, for the purpose of inducing others to part with something of value or otherwise suffer a detriment, and when *P*, in justifiable reliance on the misrepresentation, suffers such a consequence. Suppose a used car dealer represents to a prospective buyer that a particular car is sound, when in fact the dealer knows that the car has a hidden defect that will require very expensive repairs within a year. If the buyer purchases the car in justifiable reliance on these representations only to have the car fail shortly thereafter because of the defect, he will have a valid action for fraud and can recover compensatory and perhaps punitive damages.

When fraud occurs in connection with the purchase or sale of shares of stock, it is known as *securities fraud*. Though it usually fits the definition of common law fraud, this particular form of misconduct is now typically sued upon under federal statutes and regulations enacted in the wake of the Great Depression that outlaw the making of false statements in connection with the sales or purchases of securities. Given the centrality of publicly traded companies to our economy, and the huge volume of stock transactions that occur daily, it is no surprise that securities fraud suits are regularly brought in courts around the country. Because these claims—like FELA claims and admiralty law claims—are governed by federal law, the U.S. Supreme Court has issued numerous important decisions articulating the elements of and defenses to claims for securities fraud, which decisions in turn have influenced state courts' interpretations of common law fraud.

The law of fraud is as rich and interesting as any branch of tort law, though it is typically addressed only in Advanced Torts and Securities Law courses. With what sort of mental state must the defendant act to be held liable? Must he intend to induce action on the part of the plaintiff, or is it enough that the plaintiff was a person who might foreseeably rely on the defendant's deliberate misrepresentation to others? Why does the wrong of fraud include the element of reliance by the plaintiff, as opposed to the weaker requirement of actual causation? (Suppose the young lover of an aged tycoon tricks him into altering his will to prevent the tycoon's only daughter from receiving anything under his will. Even though the lover has intentionally used deceit to cause foreseeable harm to the daughter, the daughter has not herself been deceived, and thus has no claim for fraud.) When is the law prepared to say that a fraud plaintiff should have "known better," such that her reliance on the defendant's misrepresentation will be deemed unjustified?

In addition to fraud, other torts protect the interest of individuals and firms in making decisions and undertaking transactions free from interference by others. In particular, courts have deemed it a wrong for a third party intentionally to induce one party to a contract to breach that contract, albeit only if the third party does so out of *malice* toward the victim or *by independently wrongful means* (e.g., by using misrepresentations). In the most famous early articulation of this tort, the owner of one opera house knowingly induced a famous opera singer to walk away from a contract to perform at the establishment of the owner's bitter rival.[14] The "malice-or-wrongful means" component of the tort is meant to ensure that it is not used to suppress healthy economic competition. Suppose a gym owner posts an ad on the Internet offering discounts to any new member who currently is under contract with another gym, intending thereby to encourage members of competitor gyms to leave theirs and join his. Even if some gym members breach their contracts to join the new gym, most courts would say that this conduct does not amount to tortious interference with contract absent proof that the owner acted out of spite or used fraudulent or other wrongful means. In some instances, courts have expanded the tortious interference cause of action to include cases in which the defendant by wrongful conduct disrupts not a contractual relationship, but the plaintiff's noncontractual expectancy of future business. However, because the interference-with-expectancy tort is even more threatening to competition than its interference-with-contract counterpart, it is a tort that courts are by and large reluctant to apply.

---

14. (1853) Lumley v. Gye, 18 Eng. Rep. 749 (Q.B.).

NINE

Strict Liability for Abnormally Dangerous Activities

❦ 9.1 Prohibitions, Duties of Care, and Strict Liability: The Case of Blasting

There are some activities that, in part because of their dangerousness, the law flatly forbids. Engaging in these activities is prohibited irrespective of whether they can be done carefully so as to avoid injuries to others. An example is the selling of illegal drugs such as heroin or cocaine. In part because the law bans these activities, persons who engage in them are subject to significant criminal penalties and an array of informal social sanctions.

By contrast, the activities to which negligence law applies are for the most part activities that, despite being somewhat dangerous, are permitted. Take driving for example. Millions of people drive motorized vehicles every day, although driving can be dangerous. To help make driving safer, the law requires drivers to obey traffic rules. It also requires that drivers exercise prudence as they drive. Subject to these and other restrictions, the activity of driving is allowed, with each member of society aware of the perils it entails and most benefiting in various ways from its availability. As we have seen, the common law of tort adopts this same approach toward the overwhelming majority of risky activities. So long as one exercises due care as one goes about these activities, one will not be liable for the injuries that flow from them.

A consequence of this approach to driving and other activities is that persons who are injured by *careful* actors have no basis for seeking redress. They are instead left to bear the costs of any injuries they suffer because of the realization of any risks posed by conduct that remain even when due care is exercised. Implicit in tort law's broad embrace of negligence as the appropriate framework for addressing harms arising out of most accidents is the notion that this residual risk is tolerable, in at least two respects. First, the frequency with which serious personal injuries flow from careful activity is not so great as to indicate that reliance on a negligence framework is gravely unjust or inadequate. Second, the liberty granted to actors by predicating liability on a showing of fault redounds to the benefit of most everyone.

In rare instances, common law courts have identified forms of conduct that fit neither of the foregoing categories. Activities of this kind are deemed socially valuable and hence are permitted rather than prohibited. Yet they also pose a significant risk of serious injury to nonparticipants, even when they are undertaken with great care. As a result, merely to demand care from those who engage in them would allow actors to reap significant benefits associated with these activities without having to incur the substantial losses often imposed on others. And relatively few of these others will be in a position to take advantage of, or benefit directly from, the ability to engage in this sort of activity.

The paradigmatic example of an activity of this sort is the use of explosives for blasting operations. A landowner who wants to get rid of a building on his property so that he can put up a new one will sometimes hire a company to use explosives to demolish the old structure. Blasting is generally regarded as a valuable and, at times, necessary activity. And yet it is (or at least historically has been) a difficult-to-control activity, and hence one that is (or has been) particularly prone to cause damage to nearby persons and property even when done carefully. So there is a dilemma. If it is deemed wrongful to engage in blasting because of its greater dangerousness, then people will not do it, or do it at the cost of suffering a loss of reputation, liability for compensatory and perhaps punitive damages, and susceptibility to injunction and other aspects of prohibition and normative disapproval that go along with doing wrong. On the other hand, it seems inequitable for blasting to be permitted subject only to the usual requirement of ordinary care, for that will entail many instances in which no liability will be imposed even though blasting as a general matter is frequently productive of harm to innocent bystanders.

The courts' solution to this dilemma has been to split the difference between prohibition and the demand for care. They do so by allowing actions for damages based simply on proof that the defendant engaged in the activity of blasting, the inherent risks of which were realized in an injury to a nonparticipant victim. For liability to attach, there need not be any evidence that the defendant went about blasting carelessly, nor that the underlying choice to engage in the activity was itself unreasonable or otherwise wrongful. In other words, blasting that generates foreseeable personal injuries and property damage to nonparticipants is subject to a rule of *strict liability*. (For a sketch of the contrast between strict liability and negligence, *see* Chapter 4's discussion of laws imposing liability on dog owners for dog bites.) Blasting falls under this special rule *not* because it is especially wrongful and therefore deserving of harsh treatment. Quite the opposite, the idea is that those who blast are engaged in a legitimate activity that, just because it generates risks of harm that are in some sense unusual, carries with it an obligation to pay for those harms irrespective of fault.

Before turning to consider what unites the cases in which strict liability is imposed, it is worth clarifying what is and what is not entailed by the doctrine. To hold a blasting operator strictly liable for injuries it causes to bystanders is to say that the plaintiff may recover regardless of whether the operator acted with ordinary prudence or even extraordinary care. And yet not all injuries caused by blasting fall within the ambit of the strict liability rule. In addition to the requirement of actual causation, there is also a proximate-cause-like requirement that the injury must be the realization of the risk(s) that rendered the activity subject to strict liability. For example, in

Foster v. Preston Mill Co.,[1] the defendant's blasting operations unnerved a mother mink that resided on plaintiff's mink farm, located two miles away, inducing her to kill her kittens. Plaintiff sought to recover for his substantial economic loss, but the court denied the claim because the link between the blasting and the injury complained of was too fortuitous. In addition, not every plaintiff will be the right kind of victim to assert a strict liability claim. Active, voluntary participants in the activity in question—as opposed to bystanders and other passive victims—generally do not benefit from the strict liability rule. Thus a person who volunteers to clean the barn where the defendant keeps his wild animals probably will not be able to recover on a strict liability theory if she is attacked by one of the animals, although she may be able to prevail on a negligence claim. Finally, while courts at one time rejected the application of the all-or-nothing rule of contributory negligence to strict liability claims, it is probably now the case that most courts recognize comparative fault as at least a partial defense to such claims.

✺ 9.2 What is an Abnormally Dangerous Activity?

The imposition of strict liability for an activity like blasting on the terms just sketched raises three interrelated issues, two of which will be explored in this section, and the third of which will be discussed in the next. First, we need to gain a sense of the activities to which courts have applied the special rule of strict liability. Second, we will want to know what features, if any, link these to one another, and whether these common features provide a plausible justification for the application of a strict liability rule to them. Finally, it is useful and interesting to ask whether there is reason to extend

---

1. 268 P.2d 645 (Wash. 1954).

common law strict liability to other activities, including even those to which the courts have thus far refused to apply it.

On the first question, the takeaway point is simple and stark. Judges have been extraordinarily stingy in applying strict liability to activities other than blasting. Indeed, there are perhaps only two other scenarios in which courts consistently have applied the rule. (For reasons explained in the next chapter, we do not include products liability law as embodying strict liability of the sort found in blasting cases.) The first involves injuries caused by certain kinds of animals. Specifically, owners of wild animals or of domesticated animals known to have vicious propensities are held strictly liable for personal injuries caused by those animals. The second scenario, which has garnered a more mixed reception in U.S. courts, involves injuries caused by the escape of large volumes of water from reservoirs and other man-made water bodies. Although one can locate occasional judicial decisions applying the strict liability rule to other activities, including the transportation of radioactive materials and the displaying of fireworks, these are but tiny islands in a vast ocean of decisions that overwhelmingly *reject* arguments by plaintiffs asking for the application of the strict liability rule to activities ranging from aviation and driving to the transportation of hazardous material and the production and sale of weapons.

Now to the second question. What is it about blasting operations, the ownership of wild animals, and the keeping of reservoirs that warrants the application to them of a distinct rule of liability? Even today, judges and scholars look for answers to this question in the nineteenth-century decision *Rylands v. Fletcher*.[2] Rylands, the defendant at trial, hired a company to build a large reservoir to supply water to his milling operation. The reservoir gave way, which caused its contents to flood abandoned mine shafts beneath

---

2. (1868) L.R. 3 H.L. 330.

it, which in turn caused the flooding of Fletcher's nearby and still-active underground mining operations. Fletcher sued Rylands on various theories including: negligence (because of the careless-ness of the engineers who constructed the reservoir); trespass to land (because of the physical invasion by Ryland's water of Fletcher's mines); nuisance (because of the interference with Fletcher's use and enjoyment of his land); and a catch-all claim of strict liability. As against Rylands, Fletcher's negligence claim failed because the engineer was an independent contractor whose actions could not be attributed to Rylands through the doctrine of *respondeat superior*. The trespass claim failed because the intrusion was not part of an intentional touching of Fletcher's property by Rylands. And the nuisance claim failed because the flooding was a one-off event rather than a continuing interference. Only strict liability remained.

Although the trial court dismissed Fletcher's suit, the intermedi-ate appellate court reinstated it, with Judge Blackburn opining that Rylands should have to pay for the injuries he caused by keeping such a dangerous thing on his land. He wrote:

[T]he person who, for his own purposes, brings on his land and collects and keeps there anything likely to do mischief if it escapes, must keep it in at his peril; and if he does not do so, is *prima facie* answerable for all the damage which is the natural consequence of its escape.

On appeal, the House of Lords upheld the intermediate court's decision. Lord Cairns added to Judge Blackburn's opinion a concept that has helped to make *Rylands* both famous and notorious: the distinction between "natural" and "non-natural" uses of land. Not any use of property that might cause injury to a neighbor would be actionable in strict liability, he reasoned. Only non-natural uses. Because the housing of a large reservoir of water in a man-made structure was a non-natural use, and because the flooding damages that ensued were foreseeable, liability was appropriate.

Criticisms of Lord Cairns' distinction between natural and non-natural uses are legion. Clearly the term "non-natural" cannot be so broad as to apply to any enterprise that involves the introduction of improvements on land. (On this definition, strict liability ought to apply if runoff from a paved parking lot floods a neighbor's basement.) Perhaps if *Rylands* had been decided as a nuisance case, the distinction would have made more sense, because it is well established that local norms of land use are highly relevant to the determination of whether a defendant's use of his property counts as an unreasonable interference with another landowner's enjoyment of her property. But *Rylands* was not itself decided as a land use case. (However, we should note that several of the British Law Lords have retrospectively deemed *Rylands* to have turned on an application of the principles of nuisance law.[3])

Subsequent commentators, including the authors of each of the three Torts Restatements, have interpreted *Rylands*' notion of a non-natural use of land as making oblique reference to the idea of conduct that is "ultrahazardous" (First Restatement of Torts), "abnormally dangerous" (Second Restatement), or "extremely dangerous" (Third Restatement). Taken as statements about the aggregate amount of harm threatened by activities such as the keeping of reservoirs, these characterizations seem unmotivated. Surely automobile driving causes more mayhem than the keeping of wild animals. But taken in a slightly different way, these reconstructions of *Rylands* perhaps become more intelligible. In particular, the idea of an *abnormally* dangerous activity seems to go some way toward identifying activities and situations that might call for a special rule of liability, a point best articulated by the (aptly named) scholar George Fletcher.

In an influential article,[4] Fletcher argued that the common law distinguishes risky activities in which there is widespread

---

3. Cambridge Water Co., Ltd. v. Eastern Counties Leather, [1994] 2 A.C. 264 (H.L.).

4. *Fairness and Utility in Tort Law*, 85 HARV. L. REV. 537 (1972).

participation—such as driving—from idiosyncratic but highly risky activities, such as the building of a reservoir or the keeping of wild animals. Activities of the former sort generate what he terms "reciprocal risks." The residual risks of *careful* driving, for example, are imposed and borne more or less equally among all drivers, and therefore the law deems each to have implicitly accepted this risk and to have foregone the right to collect damages when injuries are caused by careful driving. On the other hand, none of us can be supposed to have accepted the risks of others' *careless* conduct. Quite the opposite, we are entitled to expect carefulness from others. Likewise, we do not accept that we will be exposed to unusual and unusually grave risks—what Fletcher, building on *Rylands*, terms "non-reciprocal risks." Actors may still be entitled to take these sorts of risks, but they must also stand ready to pay for the injuries they cause, regardless of fault.

A sea of secondary literature has shown that Fletcher's analysis does not quite work on the terms he proposes. For example, suits by pedestrians or cyclists against car drivers are governed by a negligence standard, yet it seems odd to suppose that there is reciprocity of risk between drivers, on the one hand, and pedestrians and cyclists on the other, such that the law can presume that the latter have accepted the risk of being injured by careful driving. Still, his general approach remains promising, at least as an effort to make sense of *Rylands* and the doctrine that it has generated. Our legal system's treatment of strict liability appears to be tied to a notion that certain activities are exceptional in the following respects: (1) they are unusual or not conventional for the locus in which they take place; (2) they quite obviously generate significant risks of physical injury to passive nonparticipant victims such as owners of neighboring properties; and (3) they remain substantially risky even when ordinary care is used.

At a minimum, there seems nothing patently erroneous about the courts' decision to make use of strict liability to address activities of the sort just described. For one thing, the main beneficiaries of this doctrine tend to be fault-free bystanders, and the injuries they suffer can be very serious. (Note here a passing resemblance to *res ipsa loquitur* (Chapter 6), a doctrine that aims in a different way to benefit a special class of passive victims.) Moreover, the activities in question are of a nature that those who undertake them will already be quite aware that they have chosen to embark on an unusual undertaking that poses obvious dangers to others.

⅏ 9.3 Why Confine Strict Liability to its Narrow Domain?

The central normative or policy puzzle that attends the imposition of strict liability on abnormally dangerous activities is not whether it is defensible. Rather, it is why the same rule ought not to apply universally, or at least to many other activities, rather than the very few activities to which judges have thus far applied it. A number of scholars and advocates over the past century have argued that personal injury law regarding accidents should move toward strict liability, either wholly or at least in significant part. And advocates for strict liability obtained one particularly important victory in the early years of the twentieth century, namely, the replacement of negligence law in the domain of workplace accidents with worker's compensation schemes. (*See* Chapter 2.) Indeed, for at least some of the reasons described above, all fifty states have shifted to a system of holding certain employers strictly liable for accidental workplace injuries suffered by employees. (However, this adoption of strict liability went hand in hand with a reduction in the damages available to injured employees.) The adoption of these schemes was an enormous achievement for those favoring prompter compensation for employees injured in workplace accidents. And yet—with some significant caveats regarding products liability, discussed below—the effort to expand strict liability has, as we have seen, made almost no headway in the courts. Moreover, even with respect to workers compensation, it would be misleading to see the change as internal to the common law of torts. After all, it took the form of legislatively mandated replacements of judge-made tort law. The structure of standard first-year Torts classes is indicative of what probably remains the prevailing mindset of most judges and certainly many tort scholars toward tort law's treatment of accidents: strict liability is and should be the exception, negligence the rule.

Still, many have suggested that the logic of decisions like *Rylands* entails or at least permits judges operating on an incremental, common law model to give strict liability a much wider role in modern tort law. In particular, they suggest that *Rylands*, its forbearers, and its progeny are best understood as standing for the general idea that engaging in risky conduct of a certain type, particularly when doing so as part of a profit-making enterprise, should generate liability for foreseeable injuries caused to innocent persons that flow out of that risky conduct. A commonly invoked rationale for such a liability regime is that it is appropriate for one who profits from an activity to bear the costs of the injuries that flow from it. Doing so is arguably fairer than requiring victims to demonstrate fault, and may also better achieve efficient deterrence because profit-makers will see that they are now on the hook for all the costs that their profit-making activity foreseeably imposes on others. It also stands to streamline the process through which claims for injuries are made and settled, since the delicate and fact-intensive issue of fault will no longer figure in the determination of liability, which means trials will probably be cheaper, faster, and more predictable in outcome, which in turn will promote settlement. Finally, if one were to extend strict liability more broadly, one would not need to deal with the issue, discussed above, of how to define "abnormally dangerous" activities and of how to justify the imposition of strict liability only on those activities.

Not surprisingly, there is no short answer to this normative challenge. Some of the most salient responses are as follows. First, if an activity is widely accepted and clearly being conducted on reasonable terms, and if the vast majority of people benefit from it directly or indirectly, it is arguably neither fair nor socially productive to condition the right to engage in that activity on the readiness to pay for *all* injuries (foreseeably) flowing from it. Second, there may well be enormous inefficiencies, the costs of which will be borne by everyone, of a system that invites so much cost-shifting through the awkward and expensive process of litigation. (Even if, with the adoption of strict liability, fault no longer needs to be proved, causation, damages, and other issues still must be.) Third, the recognition at the margins of tort law of instances of strict liability for very risky conduct does not threaten the idea that one is free to do that which is not wrongful to others. By imposing liability for injuries caused even by prudent conduct, widespread strict liability might undermine that sense. Fourth, if victim compensation is the goal, there are probably better means of achieving it than making it easier for injury victims to prevail in tort suits, including the use of first-party insurance, employment benefits, and government programs. In dozens of articles, books, and opinions, Judge Richard Posner has articulated these and other counter-arguments against the broad adoption of strict liability. As he acknowledges, his view owes a large debt to Justice Holmes, who more than a hundred years ago argued that it would be wasteful and inhibiting of productive activity to abandon a regime of negligence for a general regime of strict liability.

While there is no consensus on this normative debate, there may well be consensus on how difficult and unruly it is. We mention this because judges, scholars, and legislators seem to agree today on an institutional point that probably reflects a judgment about how tricky the strict liability/negligence debate is with regard to personal injuries arising from accidents. The institutional point is that shifts to a strict liability system should probably not be made across-the-board, but at most for certain categories of injuries and activities. And they should probably not be made judicially, but rather legislatively, or by other sorts of institutions that are able to make more sensitive judgments comparing institutional advantages and disadvantages of different ways to compensate injuries. So it is that we have moved to strict liability legislatively for workplace accidents. More aggressively, New Zealand has adopted a scheme by which all accident victims are compensated out of a state fund supported by general taxes and without regard to whether anyone else was at fault. Not surprisingly, given the radical nature of this change, it also did so legislatively.

9.4 Does Common Law Strict Liability Belong in the Gallery of Wrongs?

Law professors, who are overwhelmingly lawyers by training and temperament, tend to support their arguments about what principles should guide the development of the law, as a normative matter, by reference to arguments about what principles currently do form the foundation of the law, as a descriptive matter. It is therefore no surprise that those who favor more strict liability as a basis for liability for personal injuries caused by risky activities have tended to offer interpretive theories of tort that contend that strict liability is (despite appearances) widespread, rather than quite limited (as we have argued, and as most suppose to be the case). Conversely, those who argue that liability for personal injury should be covered by a negligence principle have tended to offer interpretive theories that say the negligence principle really is the basis of all tort liability—an overstated view that we have also rejected.

Seen as arguments about how far liability for extremely dangerous activities goes in the actual common law of torts, there is not much to argue about here as a descriptive matter. Genuine strict liability clearly exists in American tort law, and yet it applies only in a few special situations. The interesting interpretive debate about strict liability and negligence has not been about this. It is about whether the vast and overwhelming majority of tort law that *purports* to be about liability for wrongs, rights invasions, and breaches of duty—can be taken seriously on its own terms. As we have made clear, we believe that whether tort law is what it should be as a normative matter or not, it is best interpreted as a law of wrongs. That is the interpretive effort at the heart of this book, evident, among other places, in Chapter 4's discussion of how negligence law's 'objective' standard of care can fit within a conception of negligence as a genuine wrong; Chapter 8's discussion of *Vincent v. Lake Erie* and the wrong of trespass; and the discussion of 'strict' products liability in the next chapter.

We must acknowledge that our insistence that tort law is a law of wrongs puts us in a difficult spot when it comes to explaining the presence of common law strict liability for abnormally dangerous activities. After all, as we noted at the outset of this chapter, the rationale that seems to prevail in this domain is that liability should attach to activities that are not wrongful in and of themselves, and without regard to whether they are undertaken in a wrongful (i.e., careless) manner. How does liability imposed on these terms fit within a law that is supposed to be all about defining wrongs and providing victims of wrongs with recourse?

The short answer is that it does not fit. Although by convention, strict liability for abnormally dangerous activities clearly is part of what lawyers define as "tort law," strictly speaking it does not belong in this department. For the premise of this form of liability is that the defendant can be held liable even though she has done nothing wrong.

Having offered this concession, we nonetheless believe we are entitled to mitigate the damage it does to the interpretive accuracy of our conception of tort along two lines. First, it is important to reemphasize just how small the domain of abnormally dangerous activity liability really is. It essentially is confined to two or three rarified kinds of activity and, as we noted above, courts have steadfastly beat back the relentless efforts of plaintiffs to expand the category. The courts have done so, we would suggest, out of recognition that tort law, as a law of wrongs, can only operate as such if genuine strict liability remains at its margins.

Second, we note that in cases like *Rylands v. Fletcher*, and perhaps many of the blasting cases as well, the plaintiff is often within a hair's breadth of prevailing on a genuine tort cause of action, yet unable to do so. As we saw in *Rylands*, for example, the plaintiff there could almost make out claims for negligence, trespass, and nuisance. This observation in turn suggests that strict liability for abnormally dangerous activities tends to sit right on the borderline between wrongful and nonwrongful injurious conduct. We have seen that, in other contexts, tort law recognizes certain wrongs that effectively 'round out' the protections afforded by other torts. For example, tort law recognizes the wrongs of assault and intentional infliction of emotional distress partly to fill out and shore up the norms set and the recourse provided by the torts of battery and false imprisonment. Likewise, it recognizes certain claims for negligent infliction of emotional distress to increase marginally the reach of the negligence tort (e.g., by permitting liability for 'near misses'). In a similar manner, perhaps, tort law's recognition of strict liability for blasting and the keeping of wild animals and reservoirs fills out the protective regime created by the torts of negligence, trespass, and nuisance. One arguably sees a similar pattern in other common law domains, such as contract. At least certain forms of promissory estoppel, for example, can be understood as generating an enforceable contract even though, strictly speaking, no contract was properly formed.

TEN

Products Liability

CONSTITUTIONAL LAW AND CRIMINAL LAW receive a great deal of public attention. Tort suits usually do not. When they do, they tend to involve injuries caused by defective products. Consider headlines such as these: "Oregon Supreme Court Affirms $79.5 Million in Punitive Damages Against Philip Morris"; "Merck Agrees to Pay $4.85 Billion in Vioxx Suits"; "Ford Ordered to Pay $31 Million in Rollover Case."

Why do these sorts of lawsuits attract attention? The huge numbers involved are notable in and of themselves. And, like a lottery winner, the wildly successful plaintiff engages the public imagination. So too does the chastised household-name defendant. Victorious plaintiffs are happy to spread the news of their vindication. Out of professional pride and concern for business development, plaintiffs' lawyers are equally keen to have their victories noted. Perhaps more surprisingly, many defendants are eager to have the public attend to these events. Drawing the media spotlight on large tort verdicts—such as was rendered in the infamous (and widely misreported) McDonald's coffee-spill case—is a key part of an ongoing and successful effort by corporate America to prompt reform of tort law based on the sense that it is out of control.

Still, to focus on only the most newsworthy aspects of products liability law is to adopt a distorted view of it. Claims resulting in blockbuster awards are but the visible tip of the doctrinal iceberg. Most products liability suits work their way through the litigation system without great fanfare. And, as we will see, the most visible

269

suits tend to be unrepresentative not only in outcome, but also with respect to the theory of liability invoked by the plaintiff. The story of products liability law is a rich and distinctively modern tale that takes place at the intersection of law, commerce, morality, and politics. Still under construction, this area of tort law continues to pose a host of fascinating questions from within a doctrinal framework that is not quite ready to provide the answers.

🕮 10.1 History

By the late 1800s, suits for injuries caused by dangerous products were not unusual. Sometimes victims brought claims alleging negligence by the manufacturer. (As we saw in Chapter 5, the New York Court of Appeals' 1916 *MacPherson* opinion would make negligence actions available not only to direct purchasers but also to consumers more generally.) Other victims, particularly those injured by tainted or impure foods, sued for breach of contract. Typically, these suits alleged that the producer/seller had breached a *warranty*—a guarantee—of the product's fitness for ordinary use.

These historical antecedents notwithstanding, the birth of modern products liability law can be dated to 1963, the year in which the California Supreme Court decided *Greenman v. Yuba Power Products, Inc.*[1] Greenman was using a home wood-working machine manufactured by Yuba when a piece of wood being turned on the machine flew out and struck him, causing serious injury. He sued Yuba for both negligence and breach of warranty. The crux of the claim was that the machine was defective because its frame was held together by screws that could loosen during normal use, thereby permitting objects that were supposed to be secured by the machine to fly off. Writing for a unanimous court, legendary progressive jurist Roger Traynor held that a plaintiff such as Greenman could prevail

---

1. 377 P.2d 897 (Cal. 1963).

even without proof of manufacturer carelessness and *even absent a warranty of safety issued by the manufacturer.* Under *Greenman*, it is enough to hold a product manufacturer liable if a person uses its product in a way in which it was intended to be used and if, because of a defect in the product, the user is physically injured.

Greenman was issued at a time when William Prosser, the principal architect of the Second Restatement of Torts, was in the midst of completing that treatise. Traynor and Prosser were friends and intellectual fellow travelers, which helps explain why, a mere two years after *Greenman* was decided, the Second Restatement was published with a new section—Section 402A—that presented Traynor's innovative opinion as black letter law. In keeping with *Greenman*, the critical language of 402A read as follows:

One who sells any product in a defective condition unreasonably dangerous to the user or consumer or to his property is subject to liability for physical harm thereby caused to the ultimate user or consumer, or to his property. . . .

Within ten years of Section 402A's publication, almost every state had adopted some form of defect-based products liability. Defect-based liability that exists independently of warranty and without a showing of fault came to be known as *strict products liability.*

Because of the (somewhat misleading) label "strict," the logic of *Greenman*, the imprimatur and guidance of Traynor and Prosser, and the theorizing of other prominent jurists including Guido Calabresi, products liability law took off. By the 1970s, products liability claims against manufacturers and retailers were a staple of tort litigation, being raised in suits for injuries caused by foodstuffs, vehicles, appliances, drugs, cosmetics, tobacco, alcohol, weapons, airplanes, boats, asbestos, construction materials, paints, fertilizers, medical devices, tools, and many other products. Distinctive products liability actions in both common law and civil law systems in industrialized nations also arose in the decades following *Greenman* and are now emerging in developing countries.

In America, the emergence and rapid growth of the new doctrine owed something to the sense of affluence that prevailed in the post-World War II period. Dominant American manufacturers such as the big three car makers were assumed to be fully capable of either absorbing the costs of injuries caused by their products or passing through those costs to consumers by means of higher prices. At the same time, the modern consumer protection movement was getting underway, symbolized by Ralph Nader's damning exposé of auto manufacturer's inattention to safety. The tragedy of thalidomide—an anti-nausea drug prescribed to expectant mothers that caused severe birth defects in thousands of European and African children—and revelations about the toxicity of pesticides such as DDT (most famously in Rachel Carson's 1962 book *Silent Spring*) also fed the sense that chemical products and drugs were sources of injury against which the public needed protection.

The idea that these concerns and values might translate into new law that would make it easier for consumers to sue manufacturers was bolstered by the widely hailed success of public-interest litigation. In the 1950s, 1960s and 1970s, lawsuits—including class action lawsuits brought by one or a few plaintiffs on behalf of many victims—played an important role in dismantling laws imposing racial segregation and in forcing governments to improve substandard public housing and mental hospitals. (On class actions, see Chapter 4.) Some of the same activists, lawyers, judges, and academics involved in this sort of litigation believed that lawsuits and courts could play a comparable role in changing business behavior with respect to product safety. The appeal of court-centered approaches to social problems also led to efforts to harness the class action device to enable litigation on behalf of hundreds, thousands, or even millions of persons alleged to have been injured by a certain kind of product. The politically charged class action brought against Dow Chemical and other companies by Vietnam veterans claiming to have been injured by exposure to Agent Orange (a defoliant procured and used in Vietnam by the U.S. military) was perhaps the most prominent example of the fusion of the new public law and tort doctrine.

No less important than these developments have been changes in the plaintiff's bar. As noted in Chapter 2, most plaintiffs' lawyers in the American legal system operate through contingency fees, which typically specify that an amount (usually one third) of a plaintiff's recovery through verdict or settlement will go to her lawyer. A significant revision of substantive tort law that promises to make recovery easier for plaintiffs therefore is a revision that favors plaintiffs' lawyers. This change had special significance in a professional culture, like that of the American bar, in which lawyers tend to work exclusively on one side of litigation. Once caricatured as the 'ambulance chaser' in the ill-fitting suit, the image of the American trial lawyer became that of the smooth-talking, jet-setting millionaire whose telephone call could unnerve a Fortune 500 CEO. Products liability law was not the only area in which plaintiffs' lawyers have fared well, but it has probably been the area of greatest remuneration.

These institutional and professional developments are important in their own right, but they are also critically important in understanding the current controversies in tort doctrine and in the politics of tort law. Just as the rise of pro-plaintiff products liability law in the period 1965–1980 brought significant benefits to plaintiffs and their lawyers, it also brought substantial financial and reputational costs to product manufacturers and sellers. Businesses have not taken these hits lying down. Indeed, since about 1980, there has been an extraordinary backlash against tort, one that has focused primarily on products liability law. Current debates over damages caps, class action reform, federal preemption, joint and several liability, and many other topics are, to a significant extent, debates spurred by the tremendous success of products liability claims in the twenty years after *Greenman*. Yet even now, more than two decades into the backlash, products liability law remains an active and important part of tort law in the United States and common law countries.

🦋 10.2 The Cause of Action

Like negligence law, products liability suits require the plaintiff to prove that she suffered a cognizable harm and that the harm was causally connected in the right way to the defendant's conduct. To this extent, a products liability claim shares with negligence both the "injury" and "cause" elements, the latter encompassing both actual cause and proximate cause. (*See* Chapter 5.) The differences between the two emerge in the remaining elements.

The conduct that matters in products liability law is the selling of a defective product. And the key issue is *the nature and condition of the product that was sold*, not how carefully the defendant acted. Thus in a products liability claim against defendant *D*, the duty and breach elements of the negligence tort are replaced by these three elements:

1. *D* is in the business of selling the product at issue (a "commercial seller");
2. *D* actually sold the product that injured the plaintiff; and
3. The product was dangerously defective when sold.

If the plaintiff can establish these elements, while also proving that the defective product proximately caused her to suffer an injury—and if the defendant fails to mount a successful affirmative defense—the plaintiff is entitled to compensatory damages.

The most discussed and difficult doctrinal question in products liability law is what counts as a *dangerously defective* product. We will devote attention to that question below. But there are other important doctrinal questions. For example, can a *retailer* who played no role in designing a product, and who had no realistic opportunity to check its quality, be held liable on a strict products liability theory as a "seller" of the product? Somewhat surprisingly, the answer today in many jurisdictions is "yes."

Since *Greenman*, manufacturers have been the central target of products liability law. Yet the doctrine was initially formulated so as to reach all *commercial sellers*, including retailers. This has meant that even retailers with no reason to believe they are selling a defective product can be held liable if the product turns out to be defective and causes injury—a happy fact for a plaintiff injured by a product made by a shallow-pocketed manufacturer, but purchased from a major retailer. To varying degrees, retailers have been able to protect themselves against this form of liability by contractual agreements with manufacturers that require the manufacturer to indemnify the retailer for liabilities imposed as a result of the defective product. (On indemnification, *see* Chapter 12.) Today, many U.S. jurisdictions have also adopted statutes that protect innocent retailers from products liability claims.

The converse of the question of retailer liability is the question of whether the manufacturer of a *component part* of a product that is not in itself dangerous can be held liable when the larger product into which it is integrated turns out to be dangerous. Again, there is no single answer. There are also nuanced questions about what sort of defendant can count as a "commercial seller" and what sorts of things count as "products." Used car dealers are commercial sellers of cars, but individuals selling their own used cars are not. Human blood and blood products are not usually considered products, but prosthetic joints and pacemakers are. Unsurprisingly, there are borderline cases for all of these questions.

Courts have also regularly had to wrestle with questions about what sort of plaintiff can invoke products liability law and what sort of circumstances and injuries fall within its ambit. Though early opinions like *Greenman* focused on product *users* as the primary beneficiaries of the new tort, most jurisdictions today also make it available to a bystander, such as a pedestrian struck by a driver because of a defect in the driver's car. In addition, as noted above, Traynor's focus was on injuries that occurred as a result of defective products being put to uses *intended* by the seller. Most courts have since relaxed this restriction to include all *reasonably foreseeable uses*, even ones not specifically envisioned by the seller at the time of sale. Their doing so has raised difficult questions about when, and on what grounds, a plaintiff's *misuse* of a defective product should partially or completely disqualify the plaintiff from recovering. (Imagine, for example, a teenager who, while attempting to steer his bicycle with his feet, is badly injured because a cracked wheel rim gives way as he is riding.) Although some courts recognize a distinct "product misuse" defense, most allow the plaintiff to prevail so long as the misuse was reasonably foreseeable. However, in such a case, the fact finder will also be instructed to apply the same comparative fault and assumption of risk defenses that apply to negligence actions and that can either lessen or bar the plaintiff's recovery. (*See* Chapters 5 and 6.) Finally, as to the issue of cognizable harms, although physical injuries and property damage are the focus of products liability law, some courts have held that victims who suffer *emotional distress* under circumstances that would support a claim for negligent infliction of emotional distress (*see* Chapter 6) can invoke products liability law to recover without a showing of fault. For example, a plaintiff who contemporaneously witnesses a close relative suffer a serious injury because of a defective product may be able to recover from the manufacturer on a products liability theory.

In considering these and other issues pertaining to the scope of products liability law, it is important to keep in mind that even when certain types of actors or forms of conduct are deemed *not* to fall within the ambit of products liability law, an actor may still be subject to liability for other torts. Indeed, plaintiffs injured by products can sometimes recover from sellers under theories of negligence, breach of express or implied warranty, fraud, negligent misrepresentation, and even nuisance.

10.3 Rationales

Before turning to consider the core issue of "defect," it will be worthwhile to pause to consider the rationales most frequently invoked by courts and commentators as justifying the shift from negligence and warranty to defect-based liability. One of the first and most enduring statements of these rationales can be found in *Escola v. Coca Cola Bottling Co.*,[2] a 1944 California Supreme Court negligence decision that presaged *Greenman.*

The plaintiff worked as a waitress in a restaurant. Her hand was badly cut when a glass Coca-Cola bottle that she was holding exploded. She sued Coca-Cola Bottling, arguing that it had either carelessly overcharged the bottle with carbon dioxide (thus creating too much pressure for the glass to contain) or had carelessly failed to notice a defect in the bottle. Having no access to evidence bearing on the bottling process as it applied to the bottle that injured her, or on the condition of the bottle prior to the explosion, her lawyers relied on the doctrine of *res ipsa loquitur,* arguing that bottles do not tend to explode absent fault on the part of the bottler. (*See* Chapter 5.) In response, the defendant emphasized that another firm had manufactured the bottle in the first place. It also argued that its procedure for testing bottles prior to filling them was not merely prudent, but state-of-the-art.

A jury found for Escola, and the California Supreme Court affirmed on the basis of the *res ipsa* argument. Its analysis was strained, however, given that an explosion of this sort could just as easily have been attributed to a problem in the original manufacture of the bottle, or to the handling of the bottle after it left the possession of the defendant (e.g., by plaintiff's coworkers). In a famous lone concurrence that, two decades later, would serve as the template for the court's unanimous *Greenman* decision, Justice Traynor insisted that the court had erred in relying on *res ipsa.* Liability, he argued, should be imposed on product sellers without proof of negligence for injuries caused by defective products being used as intended. "It is needlessly circuitous," he claimed, "to make negligence the basis of recovery and impose what is in reality, liability without negligence."[3]

---

2. 150 P.2d 436 (Cal. 1944).

3. 150 P.2d at 441.

This last assertion is both arresting and puzzling. As we have seen, tort law requires proof of fault from plaintiffs seeking compensation for most accidentally caused injuries, whether they arise out of driving, the practice of medicine, or the ownership of property. And historically, the very same showing had been required of many persons accidentally injured by dangerous products. So on what basis could Traynor conclude that the requirement of proof of fault had suddenly become "needlessly circuitous" with respect to claims such as Escola's?

Like a brief aimed to win over the diverse membership of an appellate court, Justice Traynor's concurrence presents a bevy of possible justifications. Two of them echo *MacPherson* and *Byrne v. Boadle*—the foundational *res ipsa loquitur* decision discussed in Chapter 6—by suggesting that manufacturers are obligated to observe a high standard of care relative to defenseless users and that worries over victims' lack of access to evidence warrants a helping hand in the form of more relaxed evidentiary requirements. But neither of these really pushes beyond the conclusion that courts should apply negligence law to products in a way that is sensitive to the practical difficulties faced by injured consumers.

The most unvarnished sentiment expressed by Traynor is redistributive. Injured individuals, his opinion suggests, are simply less well situated than business defendants to pay for the product-related injuries that they have endured, and hence defendants should pay. But one has to worry that this justification proves too much. As stated, it would seem to apply whenever an injured individual sues a large business. This is why Traynor's opinion elaborates two further considerations. Here is the crucial passage from his concurrence:

> *Even if there is no negligence . . . public policy demands that responsibility be fixed wherever it will most effectively reduce the hazards to life and health inherent in defective products that reach the market. It is evident that the manufacturer can anticipate some hazards and guard against the recurrence of others, as the public cannot.*

<u>Those who suffer injury from defective products are unprepared to meet its consequences. The cost of an injury and the loss of time or health may be an overwhelming misfortune to the person injured, and a needless one, for the risk of injury can be insured by the manufacturer and distributed among the public as a cost of doing business.</u> *It is to the public interest to discourage the marketing of products having defects that are a menace to the public.* If such products nevertheless find their way into the market it is to the public interest to place the responsibility for whatever injury they may cause upon the manufacturer, who, even if he is not negligent in the manufacture of the product, is responsible for its reaching the market. *However intermittently such injuries may occur and however haphazardly they may strike, the risk of their occurrence is a constant risk and a general one. Against such a risk there should be a general and constant protection and the manufacturer is best situated to afford such protection.*[4]

Traynor states his conclusion in the third-to-last sentence (reproduced in regular font): if an injury results from the sale of a defective product, it is in the public interest to place financial responsibility for that injury upon the manufacturer who, even if not negligent, was still responsible for the product's reaching the market. The remainder of the passage embeds this conclusion in a deterrence argument (italicized text) and a compensation argument (underlined text).

The deterrence argument reasons that placing the costs of accidents upon manufacturers will most effectively lead to a reduction in product-related accidents by creating disincentives to the placement of such products on the market and by creating incentives for guarding against the features of such products that can cause injury. The compensation argument reasons that the legal system can provide the equivalent of accident insurance for individuals by

---

4. 150 P.2d at 440–41 (emphasis added).

imposing liability for product-related injuries upon the manufacturer. This is because the scale of modern product manufacturing is so large that businesses like Coca-Cola will be able to treat expected liability as a cost of doing business and spread that cost among consumers in the form of slightly higher product prices. The passage as a whole says that strict products liability for manufacturers of defective products can simultaneously satisfy both deterrence and compensation goals.

Let us call this intertwined argument *the Traynor argument* for strict products liability for manufacturers. Whatever its strengths or weaknesses, whatever its influence on courts, the Traynor argument has had an enormous impact on the way legal scholars have understood products liability and tort law more generally. Among the most significant scholarly books on tort law published in the modern era is Judge Guido Calabresi's *The Costs of Accidents*.[5] While it does not overtly discuss Justice Traynor's *Escola* opinion, Calabresi developed an entire theoretical framework around the idea that tort should impose liability for injuries upon whomever is best situated in the long run to take steps to reduce the costs associated with those injuries, regardless of whether the actor has been negligent. Calabresi supposed that managers of certain large-scale operations (like manufacturers and retailers) are probably best situated to take cost-effective precautions to reduce product-related accidents: this is his version of Traynor's deterrence rationale. He also observed that another way to blunt the impact of accidents on victims' lives (what he deemed "secondary" accident costs) was to make the dislocation associated with them less severe by shifting the victim's concentrated losses to members of the consuming public, each of whom would assume a miniscule fraction of that loss in the form of slightly higher product prices. This was his version of the compensation rationale. In short, Calabresi erected a

---

5. GUIDO CALABRESI, THE COST OF ACCIDENTS: A LEGAL AND ECONOMIC ANALYSIS (Yale University Press 1970).

sophisticated theoretical edifice grounded in economic analysis for which the Traynor argument appears to provide basic guiding tenets. As a normative matter, the best solution to the problem of accidents (both product-related and otherwise) is a regime that imposes strict liability on continuing participants in large-scale, injury-producing enterprises. Apart from becoming an influential federal appellate judge, as an instructor of two generations of torts students coming out of Yale Law School and as the Dean of that school, Calabresi also played a founding role in the application of law and economics to torts and the development of an entire paradigm for thinking about tort law.

Perhaps because the strict liability agenda for a time seemed so intellectually appealing and so unimpeachable from multiple normative viewpoints, numerous mid- and late-twentieth-century torts scholars passionately advocated the greater use of strict liability. Moreover, because lawyers and legal academics are educated in a mode of thinking that puts a premium on linking normative arguments to past and present practice, many depicted strict liability in tort as not simply ideal but also historically and doctrinally grounded. Indeed, historians argued that modern tort law's emphasis on negligence and its fault requirement in the realm of accidents reflects a distinctively modern and politically conservative departure from an earlier, more plaintiff-friendly strict liability regime that was in place under the old English writ system. (*See* Chapter 2.) Doctrinalists meanwhile insisted that judicial decisions speaking the language of negligence and fault often had implicitly sanctioned forms of strict liability by, for example, applying the breach standard very aggressively to conduct that really was not at fault or by developing and applying doctrines such as *res ipsa* that in effect spared plaintiffs from actually having to demonstrate fault.

Interestingly, neither Traynor nor Calabresi endorsed these efforts to cast strict products liability as restoring an 'original' tort principle of strict liability or as giving explicit expression to accepted practice. Instead, they argued that non-fault-based liability for certain kinds of accident-causing enterprises was justifiable, at least in some domains, because it was consistent with what they took to be the animating goals of tort law, and even though it would require substantial doctrinal *revision*. To be sure, Traynor in particular went some way toward capturing the sense in which the changes he favored were organically linked to preexisting negligence and warranty law. Yet neither hid from the fact that tort liability for accidental harm had long been, and was still in their times, primarily fault-based. Thus, both presented themselves as critics of the status quo commitment to fault-based liability for accidents either as it applied specifically to product-related injuries (Traynor) or as it applied to accidental injuries generally (Calabresi).

As the larger arc of this book indicates, we believe that, whatever one might say about Traynor's and Calabresi's normative arguments, their sense that tort law has for the most part *not* been about strict liability is descriptively correct (and, if anything, understated). Even if their prescriptions for a nontraditional allocation of liability in the domain of products are sound, the bulk of tort law is wrongs-based. Indeed, contrary to what they seem to have supposed, and contrary to what is probably prevailing wisdom, we maintain that, notwithstanding the label "strict products liability," tort law as it pertains to defective products—even post-*Greenman* and post-Section 402A—*is wrongs-based*. To say this is *not* to deny that there are important differences between causes of action for "strict" products liability and for negligence. Rather, it is to say that tort law identifies the injuring of a person through the rate selling of a defective product as a distinct form of wrongdoing. It is to the characteristics of this special form of wrongdoing that we now turn.

🎗 10.4 The Three Kinds of Product Defects

Modern products liability law recognizes three distinct kinds of defects that can generate a claim for products liability: *manufacturing defects, design defects*, and *failures to warn*. A *manufacturing defect* exists where the individual item that injures the plaintiff fails to live up to the safety standards set by the manufacturer for this type of product. An overpressured soda bottle, a cupcake sold with a metal fragment in it, a toaster manufactured with a frayed wire that might spark a fire, and a bicycle sold with a cracked wheel rim are examples of products containing manufacturing defects. In these instances, the manufacturing process failed to yield what it was supposed to yield with respect to the particular specimen causing the injury. Critically, even though the plaintiff bears the burden of proving that this type of defect existed when the product left the control of the defendant (and that this sort of defect caused the injury), the plaintiff need not point to some act or omission by the defendant that establishes a failure to use ordinary care in preventing the presence of the defect. It is sufficient that the defendant is a commercial seller that sold the product in a defective condition.

Design defect is a different idea from manufacturing defect because the specimen causing the plaintiff's injury is (or is presumed to be) a perfect instantiation of the manufacturer's specifications for it. The problem is in the design itself. A classic example is the machine in *Greenman*—the household tool that, according to its design, was held together by inadequate screws, such that it was vulnerable to coming apart during ordinary use. A different design using more screws, larger screws, or better-placed screws or welds could have averted this danger. Similarly, the Ford Pinto was defectively designed because the gas tank on each Pinto was located at the rear of the car, level with the rear bumper, such that a modest rear-end collision could puncture the tank and cause an explosion.

Grammatically, *failure to warn* is an awkward label for a defect. (The idea behind it is perhaps better rendered as "warning defect" or "instructional defect.") What makes the product substandard is the absence of information that would render the product safe for ordinary use, notwithstanding the presence in the product of certain dangers. A bottle of pain-relieving pills with a label mistakenly indicating that twelve pills should be taken every two hours rather than that two pills should be taken every twelve hours is dangerous because of this defective instruction. A microwave oven that does not warn that using it to heat objects containing metal may cause fire is likewise defective, at least until such time as this sort of risk is a piece of common knowledge, such that the danger is obvious to all users.

A person injured by a product may allege that the particular product in question suffered from any or all of these kinds of defects; they are not mutually exclusive categories. Note, however, that while some issues (e.g., the running of the statute of limitations) will typically be common to claims for each kind of defect, other issues—such as defining the defect and proving causation—are relative to the type of defect alleged.

10.4.1 Liability for Manufacturing Defect: In What Sense Strict?

The decisions that set the stage for the recognition of the products liability cause of action were overwhelmingly manufacturing defect cases. Indeed, flawed specimens were at the center of each of the three most important forbearers of *Greenman*—*MacPherson*, *Escola*, and *Henningsen v. Bloomfield Motors, Inc.*,[6] a New Jersey decision allowing a breach of warranty claim to a person injured when the steering mechanism of her car failed. Even by the time of *Greenman* in the early 1960s, one could find scores of reported cases of liability for 'lemons' such as these. When plaintiffs prevailed in these cases, they often did so by means of a claim that the seller had breach an *implied warranty of fitness* or *merchantability*. The idea behind an implied warranty claim is that, in placing a product on the market, sellers implicitly guarantee that the products are safe for ordinary use but then fail to deliver on that guarantee. Moreover, because these claims formally sound in contract rather than in tort, there is no inquiry into whether the seller *took care* to prevent the defect or

---

6. 161 A.2d 69 (N.J. 1960).

the injuries that it caused. Unless explicitly qualified, contractual guarantees are just that—*guarantees* of performance. To fulfill them, one must *actually, successfully perform*, not merely take reasonable efforts to perform.

Although warranty claims technically fall within the domain of contract law, it did not require much of a stretch for *Greenman* and other decisions to see in them the basis for a new form of tort liability. The paradigm of contractual liability involves the failure of a party to an agreement to do what he has explicitly agreed to do. However, as just noted, warranty claims for product-related injuries tended to rely on "implied" rather than express guarantees of safety. And, as they sometimes conceded, courts that recognized implied warranty claims were as much constructing the terms on which a product was sold in light of moral and policy considerations as they were interpreting the actual agreed-upon terms of particular sales transactions. Finally, decisions such as *Henningsen* were notable precisely because they modified or eliminated some of the most distinctively contractual features of warranty law. For example, they relaxed the privity requirement—in *Henningsen*, it was the buyer's wife rather than the buyer himself who recovered from the seller for its breach of warranty. They also refused to enforce express contractual provisions that, on their face, disclaimed or significantly limited implicit promises of safety. In short, the assertion in *Greenman*, and later by the American Law Institute in Section 402A of the Restatement (Second) of Torts, that the law had evolved toward strict liability for defective product specimens was reasonably well grounded in evolving doctrine. The warranty sources of products liability law were rooted in considerations as to what consumers could legitimately expect of product sellers by way of product safety, irrespective of agreement.

To the extent that products liability law deserves the adjective 'strict,' it most clearly does so in the domain of manufacturing defects. As Traynor's *Escola* concurrence attests, the idea that a commercial seller is subject to liability for causing injury through the sale of a defective specimen of a product is quite distinct from the idea of a seller's being held responsible for carelessness. With regard to the former, there is no call for an inquiry into what the seller did or failed to do. As a result, even sellers who act prudently—by, for example, adopting entirely reasonable quality control measures—are subject to liability if it turns out that despite these efforts, a defective product slips out into the stream of commerce and injures someone using it in the ordinary course.

And yet, despite this critical difference from fault-based liability, even strict liability for defective specimens of products can fairly be characterized as wrongs-based. One of the lessons to be drawn from the implied warranty decisions is that participants in our legal system—consumers as well as manufacturers, distributors, and retailers—understand there to be a norm that products are to be sold in a condition that is safe for ordinary use. Selling a soda bottle that is overcharged and that explodes or a car that of its own accord suddenly veers sharply violates this norm and in that sense is wrongful. Obviously the norm against selling a defectively manu-factured product is not a norm of careful conduct—that is what distinguishes this body of law from negligence. Instead, it resembles the norm of not invading another's property that is embedded in the tort of trespass to land and in the norm of not intentionally touching another that grounds the tort of battery. (*See* Chapters 7 and 8.) The viability of a plaintiff's claim turns in the first instance on whether a certain type of act has been performed—one that, like all other forms of wrongdoing, carries with it a stigma associated with other conduct that is improper.

The term "strict" in the phrase "strict products liability" is thus both accurate and misleading. It is accurate insofar as it empha-sizes that liability in this domain does not turn on a failure to heed a norm of careful conduct. It is misleading insofar as it suggests that liability for defective products does not involve a violation of a norm of conduct and is instead akin to liability for abnormally dangerous activities (discussed in Chapter 9). The latter, we have seen, really is not wrongs-based. Rather, the animating idea there is that the conduct in question, though permissible and often welcome, is unusual and so dangerous to nonparticipants that it comes with a responsibility to pay for injuries that it proximately causes to them. For an activity such as blasting, liability is *not* built around a norm of conduct stating: "Do not injure others by blasting." Rather, blasting is permissible, but linked to a rule of strict liability for injuries caused. In the products context, by contrast, commercial sellers are subject to a norm that specifies conduct that is to be avoided because wrongful: "Do not injure others by sending into commerce a product that contains a dangerous defect." If that norm is violated, then there is a completed wrong—a tort.

In sum, when a manufacturer is successfully sued for selling a defective product that injures someone, there is a plausible sense of misconduct: one *shouldn't* sell a toaster that, because it is incorrectly wired, bursts into flames during ordinary use. A seller who does so and who injures someone as a result is being held responsible for wrongfully injuring someone. As evidenced by the majority's reliance on a *res ipsa* theory in *Escola*, courts have at times been more comfortable identifying the wrongfulness in the sale of a defective product as a failure of care and thus have treated the presence of a defect as circumstantial evidence of such a failure. Since the 1960s, however, at least in the case of products containing manufacturing defects, courts have been prepared to define the wrong at issue in a different and more consumer-friendly manner—as the wrong of selling a product that, for whatever reasons, does to not live up to the standards that the seller already acknowledges it ought to have measured up to.

Probably the 'strictest' form of strict products liability for manufacturing defects occurs when an individual injured by a mass-produced, defective product sues not the manufacturer but the *retailer*. The retailer, a commercial seller of the product, has sold a defective product that has injured the plaintiff. Thus, if the norm in this domain of tort is the norm of not selling defective products, that norm has been violated. Still, imposing liability on sellers, even for defective products, is entirely distant from fault-based liability when the seller is not a manufacturer, at least if the retailer is selling the goods of a reputable manufacturer. And yet it is important to see retailer and distributor liability within the larger legal and commercial framework. Typically, the retailer will seek and obtain a promise from the manufacturer of indemnification for liability. When retailers are held liable and exercise their rights to indemnification, it is in effect the manufacturer who is paying the plaintiff, with the seller serving as a medium through which liability passes. In its zeal to protect consumers, products liability law was deliberately set up this way so that they might be more quickly and reliably compensated. Retailers were thus given the role of indemnified guarantors of the liability of product manufacturers. (As we noted above, many jurisdictions have decided to protect 'innocent' sellers from liability for the sale of defective products.)

10.4.2 Design Defect, Negligence, and the Third Restatement

Curiously, although manufacturing defect liability is in some ways the most aggressive form of strict products liability, it is probably the least controversial branch of this body of law. Perhaps because quality control measures can go a long way toward eliminating poor product specimens and because there is very little risk of punitive damages being awarded when the claim concerns an isolated 'lemon' that slips through quality control, manufacturing-defect liability has by and large come to be accepted as a cost of doing business. The same cannot be said for claims that attempt to hold manufacturers liable for *design defects*. In terms of the amount of litigation and judicial lawmaking that it has generated, and the amount of academic attention that it has received, the design defect concept has, since the early 1970s, been at the center of the products liability storm.

Like manufacturing defect claims, design defect claims draw in part on warranty law, as *Greenman* attests. The plaintiff there could justifiably claim to have been surprised and disappointed (to say the least) that the defendant's machine was designed in such a way as to allow objects to fly out from it. Similarly, the Ford Pintos that notoriously exploded when rear-ended at low speeds were designed in a way that rendered them all unsafe for their intended use. No less than in the case of a product that is dangerous because it happens to come off the production line ill-formed, a product with a design flaw that renders unduly dangerous each of its instantiations fails to live up to what it is warranted to be. Indeed, an ordinary consumer is likely to be more indignant over a product defect that may be traced to conscious engineering and design decisions than over an assembly-line hiccup.

If design defect liability is like manufacturing defect liability in displaying its warranty heritage, it is quite *unlike* manufacturing defect liability in that it more significantly overlaps with the law of negligence. It is easy to conceive of prudent quality control procedures that nonetheless fail to catch every last nonconforming product, and thereby to grasp the difference between liability based on fault and liability based on manufacturing defect. It is not as easy to explain how one can say that an entire product line has been defectively designed without saying at the same time that the manufacturer has been careless in its design decisions. Other than carelessness, what wrong can be assigned to Yuba, the defendant in *Greenman*, or to Ford with respect to its Pintos?

It turns out that, at least in principle, there is space between the concepts of liability for a design defect and liability for negligent design. But even if we grant the existence of this space, we are left with three difficult questions. The first question, which is normative, is discussed above. It concerns whether there is something special about injuries caused by defective product designs that warrants a liability rule that does not require a showing of fault. Of the remaining pair of questions, one is interpretive and the other process-related. The interpretive question is whether, in design defect cases, courts actually do require a showing of carelessness or instead impose liability on other, stricter terms. The process-related question is whether a test for design defect can be developed that captures the idea in a way that gives the concept content yet does not reduce it in theory or practice to negligence law's ordinary prudence standard. We will address these last two questions in the remainder of this section.

The doctrinal question is at one level easy to answer. Clearly, some courts do impose or have imposed design defect liability on terms distinct from the terms called for by negligence law. Recall that products liability law predicates liability on the defendant's status as a commercial seller. In design defect law, as elsewhere, the standard rule has been that retailers can be held liable for injuries caused by products with design defects. Here, at least, imposing liability looks utterly different than imposing liability under a negligence theory and looks instead like an instantiation of the norm, discussed above, against selling products that are in fact defective.

In addition, although it is probably incoherent to conclude that a defendant can be held liable *in negligence* for failing to guard against an *unforeseeable risk* that was realized in an injury to the plaintiff,[7] courts, with different degrees of aggressiveness, have been willing to impose such liability under the heading of design defect liability. Imagine that a drug manufacturer markets a vaccine that is efficacious against a certain nonfatal illness (e.g., sinus infections) that affects a small percentage of the population. Now imagine that, twenty years later, evidence emerges establishing that as many as a third of the persons who received the vaccine are developing early-onset debilitating arthritis that they would not have developed otherwise. Finally, suppose that at the time of manufacture, there was no reason to believe the vaccine would have this terrible side effect. That the vaccine carries this danger renders its design defective. And it does so even though the manufacturer was not careless in designing it in the way that it did. Insofar as design defect claims

---

7. To act carelessly with respect to a risk of harm presupposes that one has some meaningful opportunity to guard against it.

generate a standard of conduct that takes advantage of hindsight, it yields a form of liability quite different from negligence.

The hypothetical example just offered is often countered with a normative argument that the imposition of liability for failure to guard against unforeseeable risks is unfair. This sort of argument is today often given expression in doctrine in the form of the so-called *state of the art defense* to products liability claims. However, the fact that fairness might counsel against adoption of certain forms of design defect liability does not render the latter concept coextensive with negligence: quite the opposite, it presupposes their distinctiveness. Moreover, there are intermediate versions of design defect that employ a less stringent hindsight test than the one just imagined, and yet still carve out different terrain from negligence. *Greenman's* poorly designed lathe provides a good example. One does not need to ponder the design decisions that a reasonable manufacturer in the position of Yuba would have made in order to ascertain whether the design that it actually employed was defective. One may conclude instead that it was a bad design because, *as we now know*, the risks of the chosen design were unnecessary or too great. Even if these risks were not *readily* foreseen at the time of design, it seems an overstatement to describe them as unknowable.

The question of the extent to which courts have truly accepted hindsight-based design defect liability has been the subject of a long-standing, intense, partisan, and still inconclusive debate among courts and commentators. Perhaps regrettably for the cause of clarity, this debate has been linked to the process-related question we noted above—i.e., the question of how to phrase the doctrinal test for design defect. For better or worse, this latter question has often been cast in term of a binary choice between two candidates. They are known respectively as the *risk/utility test* and the *consumer expectations test.*

At an abstract level, the risk/utility test is easy enough to grasp. Under it, a design is defective if the risks of injury that accompany the design features under scrutiny are not justified by the functionality or value that they add to the product. If, for example, a machine to be used as a lathe will be better held together by welds rather than screws, and if the use of welds does not impede the machine's usefulness and adds only slightly to its cost, then the risks of designing the machine with screws can be found, and probably should be found, to outweigh the utility of using them.

Notably, as it was first developed, the risk/utility test specifically included a hindsight component that expresses a relatively strict conception of design defect. Here is a model jury instruction on the definition of design defect once proposed by Dean John Wade, one of the principal architects of the risk/utility test:

A (product) is not duly safe if it is so likely to be harmful to persons (or property) that a reasonable prudent manufacturer (supplier), *who had actual knowledge of its harmful character* would not place it on the market. It is not necessary to find that this defendant had knowledge of the harmful character of the (product) in order to determine that it was not duly safe.[8]

As we will see in a moment, many contemporary advocates of the risk/utility test are anxious, in a way that Wade and others were not, to eliminate the hindsight component of this test and thereby to equate it with a reasonable care standard.

In contrast to the risk/utility test's focus on the costs and benefits associated with different design choices, the *consumer expectation test* asks a deceptively simple question: is the product that injured the plaintiff more dangerous than an ordinary consumer would expect it to be? In framing this question, the test is not exactly empirical or sociological—its content is not determined by polling data as to what consumers actually expect of different products. Rather, "expectations" are being invoked in a normatively

---

8. John W. Wade, *On the Nature of Strict Tort Liability of Products*, 44 MISS. L.J. 825, 839–40 (1973) (emphasis added).

richer sense, one that incorporates an idea of what consumers are *entitled to expect* by way of product safety. A pregnant woman is entitled to expect that a drug prescribed to combat nausea will be effective and will not cause her child to suffer birth defects, even if she knows that it is not unheard of for drugs to cause birth defects, and even if she worries that something like that might happen to her. As is perhaps apparent, the consumer expectation test derives from warranty law and the notion that product sellers are supposed to stand behind the safety of products that they put on the market. Like Wade's version of the risk/utility test, the consumer expectations test departs from a genuinely fault-based notion of design defect.

Interestingly, advocates for plaintiffs and defendants have over time switched allegiances between the two tests. In the early years of products liability, defendants frequently advocated adoption of the consumer expectation test because it seemed to exclude liability for *patent dangers*. If a product carries its dangers on its face—for example an industrial shredding machine with an automatic feeding mechanism that rather obviously poses the threat of grabbing and maiming the hands of workers feeding materials into the machine—then its users perhaps should be barred from later claiming that their expectations about the safety of the product had been defeated. ("We all knew that someone was going to get hurt some day.") To forestall this envisioned problem, plaintiffs tended to urge the adoption of a risk/utility test. The thought was that even an obvious danger that could easily be avoided by means of an alternative design could still count as a risk that substantially outweighs the design's utility. As it turns out, however, courts have tended not to treat the issue of obvious or patent dangers as a reason to favor one test or another. Indeed, regardless of the test deployed, most have rejected the idea of disallowing recovery on a design defect theory just because the defect at issue is obvious, concluding that there is little merit to the idea that the obviousness of the dangers associated with a bad design somehow excuses the manufacturer's failure to use a safer design.

With the patent danger issue now largely resolved, positions on the issue of the proper test for design defect have flipped. Defense lawyers today tend to favor the risk/utility test because it forces plaintiffs to go through the expense of providing expert testimony as to the design choices faced by the manufacturer and because it forces jurors to think about the plaintiff's allegation of defect in technical engineering and budgetary terms. Moreover, with some important exceptions, most cases that have adopted the risk/utility test have required plaintiffs to bear the burden of proving that the defendant made the wrong design choice, all things considered. Defendants typically have better access to experts and technical information, enjoy superior resources for litigating, and have time on their side in that the longer a judgment for the plaintiff is delayed, the longer the defendant gets to keep and use its money. Therefore, the capacity to turn design defect cases into a 'battle of experts' who will debate the risks and benefits of various design alternatives is thought to generally redound to defendants' advantage. Defendants have also sought to bolster the credentials of the risk/utility test by linking it with the Hand Formula, which, because of its supposed centrality to negligence law, gives judges the comfort of treating design defect cases as more or less akin to negligence cases. (In Chapter 6, we expressed doubts as to the centrality of the Hand Formula to negligence.)

By contrast, the consumer expectation test invites lay persons to opine on whether a product is more dangerous than an ordinary consumer would have expected. Of course, this invitation is extended only after the occurrence of an accident that is allegedly linked to some design feature of defendant's product. In some jurisdictions, like California today, expert testimony is not even permitted in cases governed by this standard on the ground that it will only cloud the minds of jurors on a question that ought to be uniquely within their ken. Even where expert testimony is permitted, it must be funneled into the larger question of whether the dangers of the product exceeded what an ordinary person would expect. Because of its simplicity and its invitation of a relatively unreviewable discretionary decision by fact finders, plaintiffs' lawyers today tend to favor this conceptualization of design defect. And they have supported this view by emphasizing the roots of the idea of disappointed consumer expectations in the warranty law out of which products liability grew.

Most jurisdictions have not settled on one test to the complete exclusion of the other. After issuing a number of seemingly conflicting decisions in the period from 1965 to 1990, the California Supreme Court in *Soule v. General Motors Corp.*[9] held that while trial courts may use a consumer expectations test for injuries allegedly caused by 'simple' products whose design can easily be assessed by lay jurors, they must otherwise use a risk/utility test. *Soule's* clearly expressed expectation is that the vast bulk of design defect claims will be adjudicated under the risk/utility test. Interestingly, although *Soule* is generally and probably rightly regarded as a defendant-friendly decision, it offered plaintiffs one important bit of solace, which is that defendants bear the burden of persuading the fact finder that their chosen design satisfies the risk/utility test. In contrast to California, New York uses a risk/utility test for *all* design defect claims, but it also continues to recognize a separate breach of implied warranty action that essentially calls for application of a consumer expectations test. Connecticut purports to use a consumer expectation test, but requires that risk/utility factors be incorporated into that test for sophisticated products.

Perhaps the most accurate descriptive statement that can be made about the current state of affairs is that most jurisdictions require that risk/utility analysis be performed in cases involving complex products. However, they vary as to whether this analysis is couched within a framework that allows the fact finder to consider consumer expectations, and whether they require a showing of an alternative design. And most jurisdictions will find a way to recognize a cause of action for design defect in egregious cases without

---

9. 882 P.2d 298 (Cal. 1994).

requiring the plaintiff to produce elaborate evidence on the risk/utility issue.

Given the uncertainty surrounding the concept of design defect, the provisions pertaining to products liability in the Restatement (Third) of Torts—which were enacted in 1998 ahead of the rest of the Third Restatement—take what would seem to be an aggressive position on both the doctrinal and process questions under discussion. Section 2(b) of Third Restatement's products liability provisions flatly rejects the consumer expectations test and calls instead for the application of the risk/utility test to determine if a product has been defectively designed. It also insists that the risk/utility test be applied as a foresight-based test rather than as a hindsight-based test of the sort envisioned by the likes of Wade, thus rendering it quite similar to interpretations of negligence law's fault standard that define lack of ordinary care as the failure to take cost-justified precautions. And it not only places the burden of proof on the plaintiff, but further specifies that to satisfy this burden, the plaintiff must provide specific evidence to the fact finder of a "*reasonable alternative design*" that the defendant could and should have adopted in the place of the design actually chosen. Some academic commentators have argued that Section 2(b) advances a conception of design defect that, from both a doctrinal and normative perspective, is inappropriately defendant-friendly, and some state high courts have rejected it on these grounds. Still, even the Third Restatement—in Section 3—permits the fact finder to infer the existence of a design defect from the mere causation of injury by a product if the incident in which the plaintiff is harmed is "of a kind that ordinarily occurs as a result of a product defect."

One final note on design defect: at the beginning of this section, we pointed out that the wrongfulness of defectively designing a product seems in some ways distinct from the wrongfulness of allowing an individual 'lemon' to slip into the stream of commerce. The design process, after all, involves conscious decision-making and, with it, cognizance of and judgments about certain risks and what to do about them. Even though we maintain, along with most courts, that design defect liability, no less than manufacturing defect liability, is product-based rather than fault-based, it is certainly true that in some instances, a product that is defectively designed will have been defectively designed because of wrongdoing on the part of the designer that stands apart from, and in addition to, the selling of the defective product. For example, a manufacturer might consciously make an inexcusable design choice—one that it knows poses a grave risk of serious injury for little corresponding benefit. Alternatively, a manufacturer might knowingly misrepresent a product design as safe when it knows it to be very dangerous. In these special cases, when a plaintiff injured by the product sues and recovers, her entitlement to compensatory damages will require proof only that she was injured by a defectively designed product. Proof tying the existence of the defect to egregious wrongdoing—e.g., the manufacturer knew of but suppressed information about a grave risk of harm posed by the product—may in addition entitle her to seek and obtain *punitive damages*, which enable the victims of egregious wrongs to 'punish' those who have injured them. (*See* Chapter 12.)

10.4.3 Failure to Warn

The third form of "defect" recognized by products liability law is failure to warn (or to instruct). As noted, it is somewhat awkward to fit the roundish peg of a claim predicated on a seller's failure to warn into the squarish hole of "defect." The problem here is partly semantic, but not entirely. The real question is whether a failure-to-warn claim is a claim alleging a deficiency in the seller's conduct—failing to act as one ought to—as opposed to a deficiency in the product itself. And this is an important question because products liability is supposed to be defect-based. Moreover, when it comes to conduct, consumers probably expect different things from different sorts of actors. For example, they may expect manufacturers to incorporate warnings and instructions but not expect distributors or retailers to do so. If the absence of warning is really depicted as an attribute of the product sold, then it may still be tenable to impose liability on the latter sorts of actors on the ground that the defect 'runs with the product.' If, by contrast, the absence of warning is simply viewed as unjustifiably risky conduct, then liability perhaps should be limited to manufacturers.

As with manufacturing and design defects, warnings law has generally adhered to the product-based idea. And so, for example, when retailers are held liable as sellers who failed to warn, they are being held strictly liable in a strong sense of that phrase. However, in light of indemnification agreements and statutes relieving non-manufacturing sellers from at least some forms of liability, this form of liability is probably substantially less onerous in practice than in principle.

A simple example of a failure-to-warn case might involve a household cleaner that is sold without warnings of its toxicity.[10] Even when a product contains warnings, it may still be informationally defective because warnings and instructions must be *adequate* to the injury risks at issue. This means not only that they must be sufficiently prominent (whether displayed on the product itself, or contained in a separate instruction manual), but also that even a prominent warning may be inadequate if it flags only a lesser risk when greater risks are present. Suppose the label affixed to a bottle containing household cleaner warns that it contains substances that can cause a rash if it contacts exposed skin but fails to warn that inhalation may cause lung damage. A person who inhales fumes from the product and suffers lung damage stands to recover on a failure-to-warn theory. When failure-to-warn claims are tried, it is the fact finder (usually a jury) that adjudicates the adequacy issue.

---

10. *See, e.g.,* Advance Chemical Co. v. Harter, 478 So. 2d 444 (Fla. Ct. App. 1985).

Contrary to some current folklore, sellers are not generally subject to liability for selling products that fail to warn of obvious or patent dangers. A kitchen knife, for example, is not defective for not carrying a warning that its sharp blade may cause lacerations. Also, although our focus in this section will be (as it has been throughout this chapter) on the litigation side of products liability law, it is worth mentioning that lawyers often confront warning issues in a counseling rather than a litigation posture. Their job often is to advise clients on how to avoid liability by adequately warning or instructing of dangers that attend their products.

We saw above that the conceptual space between the idea of a product with a design defect and the idea of a manufacturer's failure to exercise ordinary prudence in making design choices is defined in part by the law's willingness to hold sellers responsible for injuries caused by design-related risks that were unforeseeable or at least difficult to foresee at the time of design. Courts have faced a similar issue in trying to gauge whether a seller can be held liable for failing to warn of a risk, knowledge of which only emerges in hindsight. Many courts permit defendants to introduce evidence as to the "state of the art" of scientific and technological knowledge at the time of sale to defeat failure-to-warn claims on the ground that sellers cannot sensibly be obligated to warn of dangers of which they were not and could not have been aware. However, a failure to warn of risks that were unknown yet knowable may subject the defendant to liability. Moreover, because warnings for durable products can sometimes be easily issued after the fact, some courts hold that manufacturers that only learn later, and could not have learned earlier, of a danger posed by their product incur a 'post-sale' duty to take reasonable steps to warn users of the newly discovered danger.

Perhaps the aspect that most distinguishes failure-to-warn claims from manufacturing defect and design defect claims is the issue of actual causation. A suit that complains of a product that is defectively designed or manufactured is usually a suit alleging physical injury or property damage caused by some dangerous feature of a product, such as faulty brakes on a car. Although there are certainly suits of this sort in which there is a difficult-to-resolve dispute between the parties as to whether the defect in the seller's product caused the plaintiff's injury (e.g., would the car have crashed even if the brakes had not been defective?), there is a distinct issue concerning causation in failure-to-warn cases. This is because the theory of liability in every such case rests on the notion that had the seller provided an adequate warning, the plaintiff would in fact have *heeded* it. Everyday experience suggests that consumers frequently do not read, or read but decline to follow, even prominently displayed warnings of serious dangers. (Think of warnings on lighter fluid cans stating the fluid should never be squirted onto a lit fire.) How is a plaintiff to prove that, regardless of what other people tend to do with warnings, she in this instance would have heeded a warning on the defendant's product and thus would have avoided injury?

The first-level answer is that the question of causation posed by failure-to-warn claims, as it is for other tort claims, is left to the fact finder, who is directed to consider the relevant circumstantial evidence and make a judgment as to whether it is more likely than not that the plaintiff would have heeded an adequate warning had one been given. But failure-to-warn law adds two interesting qualifications to the normal approach to actual causation. First, some jurisdictions, based on a reading of comment j to Section 402A of the Restatement (Second) of Torts, have adopted the so-called *heeding presumption*, whereby the fact finder is required to presume that the plaintiff would have heeded an adequate warning, which presumption the defendant is then left to rebut, if possible.

Second, there is a special rule of actual causation that has historically applied to actions based on the absence of adequate instructions and warnings for dangers posed by prescription medications. Known as the *learned intermediary doctrine*, it holds that a commercial seller of a prescription drug fulfills its duty adequately to warn of the drug's dangers by providing adequate information about those dangers *not* to the consumer but to physicians who will prescribe the drug. It follows that, if an injured consumer's physician was adequately warned of the danger associated with a drug, but the physician failed to warn the patient injured by the drug, the patient will have no cause of action against the manufacturer even if she can prove that she would not have taken the drug had she received the warning. And this is so regardless of how easy and efficacious it would have been for the seller also to warn consumers with labels, instructions, or advertisements. (One bit of comfort for this sort of plaintiff is that she may have an "informed consent" claim against the prescribing physician. *See* Chapter 6.)

More troubling still are cases in which neither the physician nor the consumer is warned. In these, the plaintiff, instead of having to prove that she would have heeded an adequate warning, must instead prove that her physician would have heeded a warning and also would have passed the gist of the warning along to her. If the injured patient is unlucky enough to have been treated by a physician who, during pretrial discovery or on the witness stand, conveys to the fact finder the sense that he was too indifferent or unconcerned to have passed along the relevant information to the plaintiff had it been provided to him, the plaintiff's claim will fail on the issue of actual causation. A few courts have held that the learned intermediary doctrine has no application to a manufacturer's failure to warn consumers about risks associated with a prescription drug that is marketed by means of direct-to-consumer advertising.

As is the case with design defect litigation, suits containing allegations of failure to warn often contain additional allegations of related wrongs, such as negligence and fraud. They do so in part because plaintiffs' attorneys want to leave open the possibility that during the course of discovery, they will determine that the absence of a warning or instruction on the defendant's product was a particularly culpable oversight or perhaps even a deliberate withholding of information about serious risks of which the consuming public would surely have a right to know. If this sort of 'smoking-gun' evidence emerges—as it arguably did in the recent litigation over Merck's failure to disclose information from its own studies on the heart attack and stroke risks posed by its drug Vioxx—litigants may be entitled to recover not only compensatory, but also punitive damages in light of the defendant's reckless disregard for consumers' safety. (Punitive damages are discussed in Chapter 12.)

🕮 10.5 Moving to Extremes?

One goal of this chapter is to capture the spirit of the movement that led to the rapid adoption by courts in the 1960s and 1970s of the doctrine of strict products liability. Another is to demonstrate that, while novel, the defective products cause of action can claim for itself doctrinal roots in the law of negligence and warranty—in some sense decisions like *Greenman* simply effected a fusion of the broad conception of duty found in leading negligence cases like *MacPherson* with the particular notion of wrongdoing at work in implied warranty cases. Yet another has been to demonstrate that the use of the label "strict" for this part of tort law is as much misleading as it is helpful. It is helpful because it emphasizes that tort liability for injuries caused by products is defect-based rather than carelessness-based. It is misleading because it suggests that liability for defective products that cause injury attaches without proof of wrongdoing. To injure someone by selling a product with a defect that renders it dangerous is to wrong her.

Finally, we have briefly presented the leading arguments that favor the deployment of this special sense of wrongdoing in the domain of products, as opposed to the many other domains— driving, professional services, etc.—that are governed by a fault-based conception of wrongdoing. In particular, we emphasized the significance for jurists such as Traynor and Calabresi of the idea that the fusion of negligence and warranty into strict products liability held out special promise for effectively (and perhaps efficiently) deterring product-related injuries and for blunting the impact of such injuries on victims by spreading their losses. To say that these goals are being served by products liability law and that they have played an important motivational role in courts' decisions to adopt the doctrine is *not* to say that products liability law (much less tort law in general) is nothing more than a means for achieving these goals. A body of law has a content and a life that stands at least somewhat independently of the reasons that may have justified its adoption. Instead, it is to observe that judges, on the basis of a variety of considerations, decided to cobble together a new legal wrong out of a mix of existing doctrinal materials and policy considerations, one that commercial sellers are directed not to commit and that confers a right on consumers.

As originally articulated, the wrong of selling a defective product was fashioned to be both demanding and forgiving of sellers. To regard the injuring of another through the sale of a dangerously defective product as itself a wrong, irrespective of fault, is to set a demanding norm of conduct, one that can be difficult to meet and that can be harsh in particular applications. Yet Traynor, Prosser, and others seemed to envision this form of wrongdoing as nonetheless relatively less culpable. A commercial seller does wrong to a consumer by selling an overcharged soda bottle that explodes and hurts her, but (assuming sound quality control measures were in place) this is not the sort of red-blooded wrong over which there ought to be widespread outrage. It also mattered enormously to them that the entities who might face significant liability for having committed this special sort of wrong would tend to be businesses who could soften the liability blow through devices such as insurance, indemnification agreements, and small adjustments in the prices of their goods.

Over the course of a half-century of litigation, the doctrine and the institutions spawned by the emergence of products liability law have evolved in ways that arguably have strayed from this original vision. Indeed, as we suggested at the outset of this chapter, this part of tort law, at least in most visible incarnations, has become quite polarized.

We commenced our discussion of products liability law with news headlines about blockbuster awards and settlements. Later we mentioned the emergence of a well-heeled products liability plaintiff's bar. And we noticed that in design defect and failure-to-warn litigation, there is room for plaintiffs to argue that the defendant has not 'merely' committed the wrong of selling a dangerously defective product that injures someone, but also has done so with reckless disregard for the well-being of consumers or with the kind of knowledge and mental state that amounts to full-blown fraud. All of these features have tended to coalesce in the type of products liability case that most frequently—or at least most visibly—makes its way to state high courts and even the U.S. Supreme Court (*see* Chapters 12 and 13) and into media coverage. In this special subset of products liability cases, the wrongdoing alleged tends to be of the red-blooded variety that does provoke, and perhaps should provoke, outrage. The plaintiff is complaining, for example, that a manufacturer suppressed information that its product poses risks of serious injuries to many potential victims. In turn, these are cases in which jurors are prone to render huge awards of compensatory and punitive damages.

To some degree, the entire body of products liability has today come to be associated with these, its most melodramatic examples. (Indeed, this association has been fostered by plaintiffs' lawyers and consumer advocates who, for various reasons, are anxious to cast product sellers in the role of villains.) In turn, the rise to the fore of this sort of case—in contrast to more pedestrian cases like *Escola* and *Greenman*—has put a lot of pressure on the idea that the 'mere' injuring of someone through the sale of a dangerously defective product can count as a wrong. In this area, as it presently tends to be viewed, tort law seems simultaneously to be casting a very wide liability net by recognizing a less culpable form of wrongdoing and yet allowing plaintiffs who allege such wrongdoing to collect massive damages. Seizing on this apparent mismatch, members of the business community and other tort reform advocates have lobbied with great success for changes in the law that have cut back significantly on liability for injuries caused by defective products by excluding retailers from the ambit of products liability law, raising litigation and evidentiary burdens faced by plaintiffs, and capping damages.

What is in danger of being lost in this highly politicized 'war' between those keen to advance the red-blooded, pro-plaintiff conception of products liability on the one hand and those keen to quash it altogether on the other, is the original notion of the products liability action as a means by which the ordinary consumer could legitimately demand recourse for having been wronged because injured by a defective product. Probably the vast run of products liability suits, and certainly almost all those alleging manufacturing defects, fit this more mundane description. If so, the participants in current debates would do well to keep in mind these heartland cases and the particular conception of tortiousness that they instantiate.

ELEVEN

Defamation and Privacy

IN CHAPTERS 7 AND 8 WE SOUGHT to correct the misconception that tort actions for bodily injuries have deeper historical roots than torts that address other forms of injury. For centuries, plaintiffs suing for trespass, false imprisonment, and assault have obtained redress, respectively, for interferences with property rights, liberty of movement, and 'personal space.' We can now identify another interest that has long supported tort claims: the interest in maintaining one's reputation. Two different torts, *slander* and *libel*, identify interference with reputation—defamation—as actionable. Roughly speaking, to slander someone is to speak words about her that are destructive of her reputation. To libel someone is to defame her by means of statements or depictions contained in writings or scripted broadcasts.

Adjacent to the room in tort law's gallery containing the defamation actions is a room of more recent vintage. It contains several distinct torts that go under the heading of *invasion of privacy*. The privacy torts emerged only in the late 1800s and early 1900s. Although they involve a distinctive kind of injury—the injury of having private aspects of one's life exposed to public view—they share with defamation torts the same root. Both identify conduct as being wrongful and injurious *for altering the way in which third parties view the victim and interact with her.*

It is hardly surprising that tort law would attend to interests such as these. Words may not be able to break bones,[1] but they are capable of causing immense harm. In the era of McCarthyism, one could destroy another's career by labeling him a "communist." In this context, to be thought of as a communist was to be thought of as an enemy of the people—a person to be shunned or run out of town. Likewise, in any era, most couples would be horrified to have their neighbors see in a local newspaper a graphic description of their sexual activities. Even apart from the potential embarrassment, there is a worry that public access to this sort of sensitive information would cause friends, coworkers, and others to act differently towards those whose private lives have been exposed.

At the same time, American law has historically demonstrated a consistent albeit uneven commitment to freedom of speech, one most obviously embodied in the First Amendment to the U.S. Constitution. Courts have thus been left to reconcile, on the one hand, the aim of creating a space in which speakers can speak their minds without fear of legal sanction, and, on the other hand, the aim of holding speakers and writers accountable for communications that cause harm.

Until the 1960s, the general approach was to treat common law actions for defamation and privacy as posing no threat to free speech values. The right to speak freely, judges reasoned, goes hand in hand with a responsibility not to abuse it by speaking in ways deemed tortious under state law. Moreover, as we will see, the defamation and privacy torts included elements and defenses designed to accommodate free speech concerns. As a result, courts did not see in the existence and operation of these civil actions any constitutional concerns. By contrast, influential American and

---

1. A variation on this familiar saying states that "sticks and stones may break my bones, but *names* can never hurt me." Defamation law, as we will see, embraces this version of the saying.

British jurists have long worried that *criminal prosecutions* for libelous speech pose an intolerable threat to free speech. For example, Thomas Jefferson and James Madison denounced as unconstitutional the now-notorious Sedition Act of 1798. Passed by a Federalist-dominated Congress, the Act authorized prosecution and imprisonment for speech that criticized the Adams administration and thereby supposedly threatened to bring the federal government into disrepute. All but obsolete today, criminal prosecutions for seditious libel were for centuries an important and much-abused tool of political control used by English and American officials.

Since the Supreme Court's landmark 1964 decision in *New York Times v. Sullivan*,[2] a new balance has been struck between free speech and *civil* liability for speech that injures others. As explained below, *Sullivan* and its progeny have identified First Amendment limitations on defamation law that in many instances defeat claims that would have been viable under common law. Indeed, among the legal systems of western industrialized nations, contemporary American law stands out for the degree to which it protects speech at the cost of denying persons redress for injuries it causes.

※ 11.1 Defamation: What is the Wrong?

Chapter 7 explained that the tort of battery at its core enjoins certain familiar types of acts. In essence, it instructs us not to shoot, stab, punch, kick, fondle, or spit on others. A deliberate, vicious, and successfully delivered physical blow is quintessentially the sort of act that, absent a justification such as self-defense, will count as an actionable battery. At the same time, we noted that battery reaches

---

2. 376 U.S. 254 (1964).

conduct that, at least viewed externally, is not so obviously the same kind of act. If D knowingly serves to P cookies that contain traces of nuts, with the intention of triggering P's nut allergy, and if he succeeds in his plan, D has committed a battery against P. This is so even though one would not ordinarily describe the serving of food to another as a "battering." Battery concerns the intentional doing of a certain kind of act: a harmful or offensive touching of another. And yet calculated invasions of one's interest in being free from a harmful or offensive touching are not immunized by virtue of having been accomplished indirectly.

This same pattern is present in the defamation torts. At their core, the torts of libel and slander enjoin us not to utter statements that attribute to others qualities or actions that ordinarily tend to lower them in the esteem of others. To say of a person that she is a child molester, that she is a prostitute, that she is a lawyer who steals money from her clients, or that she suffers from a highly contagious disease is to utter a defamatory statement about her. Liability can attach to such statements precisely because, as courts are wont to say, they have a natural tendency "to diminish the esteem, respect, goodwill or confidence in which the plaintiff is held, or to excite adverse, derogatory or unpleasant feelings or opinions"[3] about the plaintiff. However, as with battery, the core defamation law duty to refrain from saying and writing awful things about others is supplemented by a broader duty that expands the reach of these torts. For X to tell others that adult Z was at a tavern at 10:00 p.m. on a given night seems innocuous enough: it would be odd for the law to enjoin this sort of statement about another as a categorical matter. Yet X's statement about Z still might be the basis for a defamation claim. This would be true, for example, if X meant to induce and did induce others to believe that Z had lied about his whereabouts on that night so as to evade prosecution for

---

3. W. PAGE KEETON, ET AL., PROSSER AND KEETON ON TORTS § 111, at 773 (5th ed. 1984).

a crime. As we will see, both substantive and procedural features of the common law of defamation reflect the distinction between instances in which the defendant is being sued for facially defamatory statements and ones in which he is sued for statements that are defamatory only in context.

Preliminarily, it will be useful to identify certain forms of speech and certain interests related to the interest in maintaining one's reputation that the defamation torts are *not* meant to address. Most important, the injunction against defaming is *not* a requirement that one refrain from making statements just because they might hurt another's feelings. Nor is it a requirement that speech must be conducted in a civil tone. However hurtful or inappropriate, speech in the form of reprimands, name-calling, and strongly expressed opinions is not actionable as defamation. Slander and libel are concerned with protecting against attacks on reputation, not preventing emotional distress or enforcing etiquette.[4]

In addition, even overtly defamatory remarks are not tortious if they are made by a speaker directly to the victim, with no one else in earshot. Reputation exists in the minds of third parties. Thus, to prevail on a libel or slander claim, a plaintiff must prove that the defendant's statement was "published"—i.e., received and understood by a third party other than the victim herself.

Finally, defamation law has always recognized privileges that shelter speakers and writers from liability, even when they publish remarks about another that are in fact defamatory and even if the publication actually damages the plaintiff's livelihood or standing. To take one example, courts have historically immunized from liability speakers of true statements. If D accurately informs T that P is a convicted arsonist, D has defamed P—he has said something about P that tends to harm and probably will harm P's reputation

---

4. However, a plaintiff who prevails on a claim of slander or libel often can recover emotional distress damages as parasitic on the underlying reputational injury, just as many negligence plaintiffs can recover pain and suffering damages parasitic on an underlying bodily injury.

among those, such as *T*, who did not know this fact about *P*. And yet tort law deems *D* privileged to defame *P* because the defamatory utterance is true.

⁂ 11.2 Common Law Defamation

Although the torts of libel and slander have carried over from medieval and early-modern times to the present day, they have in the last fifty years changed markedly in their scope because of the doctrinal revolution ushered in by *New York Times v. Sullivan*. In this section we describe the main contours of traditional common law doctrine so as to permit an appreciation of *Sullivan's* significance.

11.2.1 Libel

Prior to 1964, an actor *D* would be subject to liability to person *P* for libel if:

1. *D* includes in a *writing* or *scripted broadcast*
2. a *statement* "of and concerning" *P*
3. that is *defamatory* in nature,
4. which writing *D publishes* (i.e., communicates to a third party)

Absent an affirmative defense, a plaintiff who could prove these elements would be entitled to an award of damages that might include *general, special,* or *punitive* damages. General damages would compensate the plaintiff for the fact of having suffered reputational harm; for being worse off solely in the sense of being less well-regarded. Special damages, if proven, would compensate for any pecuniary harm resulting from a libel (for example, income lost by a business owner whose business is shunned after publication of the libel). Upon a showing of malice in the common law sense—i.e., that the defendant acted out of ill will or spitefulness toward the plaintiff, or with wanton disregard for his well-being—a jury could elect to award punitive damages to vindicate the plaintiff and to punish the defendant. (*See* Chapter 12.)

As may be evident from this thumbnail sketch, the prima facie case of libel was not particularly demanding of a plaintiff. He needed to prove only that the defendant had successfully communicated in writing to a person other than the plaintiff a statement about the plaintiff of a sort that would have a tendency to harm reputation. Under these rules, if today D were to send an e-mail to colleague C stating that coworker P had stolen some office supplies, and if C were to receive and understand it, D would have libeled P. Notice that to prevail, P was *not* required to prove that D's statement was *false*, much less that *D knew or had reason to know* it was false. Under the common law of libel, writers who chose to publish statements with a tendency to cause reputational harm did so at their peril.

Notice also that even though a libel plaintiff who offered proof of economic loss could recover special damages for such loss, a libel plaintiff was *not required to offer proof of economic loss, nor indeed proof of any harm* other than the interference with reputation itself. This is because the wrong of libel was conceived of as being completed upon publication—once the defamatory writing had been received and understood by another, the plaintiff had been libeled. (In this respect, libel resembled the tort of trespass to land, which is deemed complete at the moment of physical invasion, irrespective of whether the invasion causes further damage.)

Libel law was also generous to plaintiffs in its conception of what would count as a "publication" of a defamatory writing. Under the doctrine of *republication*, one who published a writing that contained another's defamatory statement was (and today still is) treated as a publisher of the statement. This is so even if the republisher reproduces the defamatory comment with disclaimers. Suppose D were to send a letter to E including the following passage: "C told me today that P is addicted to gambling. Of course, anything C says must be taken with a grain of salt." Under the republication doctrine, D would be deemed as publisher of the statement by C defaming P and on that basis D could be subject to liability for libeling P.

If the entire substance of libel law were contained in the elements of the plaintiff's prima facie case, the tort would surely have stood to interfere unacceptably with many aspects of public and private life in which candor is highly prized or required. Given the republication doctrine, how could a reporter covering a trial recount a witness's damning statements about the plaintiff without running a serious risk of defamation liability? How could an art critic offer her actual and strongly negative views of the plaintiff's abilities as an artist if doing so meant liability for harming the plaintiff's standing in the eyes of the public? Would the political discourse necessary for a mature democracy be possible if news media were afraid to publish stories about candidates' alleged misbehavior? How could past employers or corporate boards of directors or professional examiners ever provide—or be provided with—trustworthy evaluations of candidates, managers, employees or students if evaluations, to be candid, must often be damning?

Just as battery law has long recognized that the police must be able to detain, that doctors must be able to touch their patients, that school teachers must be able to separate quarreling students, and that friends and lovers must be able to touch one another, so defamation law has long recognized many domains in which candid utterance of good faith beliefs about others is necessary. Specifically, the common law of libel (and slander) recognized several affirmative defenses that writers could invoke to defeat liability. Many of these are still valid today, though separate constitutional limitations introduced by the U.S. Supreme Court have partially superseded them by providing still greater protection of speech.

Some common law defenses have consisted of *immunities* that, where applicable, permit writers to defame others with impunity, even out of pure spite. For example, testimony by a trial witness is absolutely privileged against liability for slander (although there is possible criminal liability for perjury). But most of the affirmative defenses to libel have taken the form of *qualified privileges*: even where otherwise applicable, they are forfeited by the defendant if the plaintiff can prove that the defendant acted out of *malice* or spite toward the plaintiff. Among the most important of the conditional privileges are those that have permitted good faith libels (1) that are true; (2) that reiterate or describe statements made by others in a fair report of an official proceeding such as a trial or public hearing; (3) that amount to fair comment on a matter of public interest; or (4) that are justified in light of the recipient's or the publisher's interest in obtaining or releasing certain kinds of information about the plaintiff.

The truth defense has long provided speakers and writers with a justification for libeling another, namely, the benefit to the public of receiving accurate information. A true libel—on this traditional conception—is still a libel, but it is a libel that is warranted by the public's interest in knowing the truth. The fair report privilege has operated to limit the reach of the "republication" doctrine, thereby allowing for candid news coverage of certain governmental activities. It permits writers to publish accurate reports of official proceedings, even ones that include defamatory statements by a person participating in the proceedings. The fair comment privilege can be invoked, for example, by the author of a book review that accurately describes the book's contents, but then criticizes it as derivative, poorly constructed, or insipid. A standard situation in which the so-called "common interest" privilege might be invoked is one in which a previous employer provides a written reference concerning the plaintiff at the request of a prospective employer of the plaintiff. Even if the reference contains defamatory statements about the plaintiff, so long as it is provided in a good faith effort to aid the prospective employer's hiring decision, no liability can attach.

11.2.2 Slander

With an important qualification contained in the fifth element described below, slander plaintiffs were faced with the same

requirements as libel plaintiffs. Thus *D* would be subject to liability
for slander if:

1. *D* includes in a spoken *utterance*
2. a *statement* "of and concerning" *P*
3. that is *defamatory* in nature,
4. which utterance *D publishes*, and
5. which is either slanderous per se *or* causes *P* special damages.

As noted above, slander defendants could avail themselves of the
same affirmative defenses as libel defendants.

That common law demanded more of certain slander plaintiffs
than libel plaintiffs was in part a historical accident. Unlike the law
of slander, which was developed by the common law courts, the law
of libel emerged in part out of sixteenth- and seventeenth-century
proceedings conducted in a special and notorious royal court called
Star Chamber. (In its eagerness to punish publishers of tracts critical of English officials, the Star Chamber judges had adopted rules
that strongly favored the protection of reputation.) But it also seems
to reflect a sense among the common law courts that there are substantive reasons to treat spoken words differently from written
words. Among these are *evidentiary considerations* (spoken defamation is more easily alleged and the content and context of the defendant's statement more subject to dispute); *culpability/liberty
considerations* (on average, slanders are more likely to be uttered
rashly, often as overstated insults, whereas libels require the defendant to decide to commit his thoughts to paper); and *harm-based
considerations* (the effects of spoken words might tend to be less
broad and lasting than those of written words). Even supposing
that these reasons sufficed to justify placing greater burdens on
slander plaintiffs than libel plaintiffs, the framing of those burdens
in the terms stated in what we have presented as the fifth element
of slander requires further explanation.

The first prong of the fifth element of slander indicates that the
common law deemed some slanders to be categorically so serious

as to deserve comparable treatment to libels. These were the so-called "per se" slanders—a category initially comprised of utterances attributing to the plaintiff (1) the commission of a serious crime; (2) a 'loathsome' disease such as leprosy or syphilis; or (3) incompetency of dishonesty in his trade or business. A fourth "per se" category was added by Parliament and many American state legislatures in the nineteenth century, namely (4) statements imputing a lack of chastity to a woman. If a plaintiff was slandered by a published statement falling within one of these four categories, she would be treated identically to a libel plaintiff in that she would not be required to offer any proof of tangible losses because the very fact of others hearing these statements was considered a significant injury. By contrast, all other slander plaintiffs were typically required to prove that the publication by the defendant of the slander had in fact caused them to suffer economic harm in the form of lost business, a missed employment opportunity, or the like. Proof of this sort was (and is) often difficult to come by.

To illustrate these doctrinal distinctions, imagine that defendant Smith publishes a local newspaper with stories asserting that (a) K shot and killed a town councilman; (b) S spent years persuading her sister to divorce her husband and give up custody of her children, because S, envious, wanted to ruin her sister's happy life; and (c) P performed unnecessary hysterectomies with nonsterile equipment, leading some of his patients to develop terrible infections. K, S, and P would have viable prima facie libel actions against Smith. Now imagine instead that Smith were to utter all of these statements in person to some friends at a party. Each plaintiff would now have to bring slander actions rather than libel actions. Both K and P would benefit from the rules for slander per se and thus would be permitted to sue on the same terms as if the statements about them had been contained in a writing. But S would not be able to make out a prima facie case of slander unless she could prove that Smith's statement caused her tangible (usually pecuniary) loss.

One may fairly wonder how it is that the common law courts came to settle on the slander per se categories as deserving of special treatment. At one level, the answer is easy enough: these slanders are all 'core' cases of defamation that fall well within the basic injunction not to say things about a person that are defamatory on their face. Each category represents the sort of statement that can be counted on to undermine the targeted victim's ability to function in her community. Still, the per se categories are in some ways puzzlingly under-inclusive. For example, at least at one time, it was quite obviously damning to label someone as having been born out of wedlock, or to be a devil-worshipper, yet neither of these allegations was deemed to constitute slander per se.

11.2.3 Common Law Defamation in Perspective

Stepping back, it is worthwhile to highlight three aspects of common law libel and slander. The first is *how unlike negligence* these torts are. There is no requirement of proof that the defendant failed to exercise ordinary prudence, nor must physical injury be shown. Indeed, for claims of libel and slander per se there is no requirement that there be any concrete harm: the publication of the defamatory statement is sufficient. In both of these respects, defamation law is more like trespass to land and battery. A certain intentionality on the part of the defendant is required, though not an intention to harm. The defendant must intend to say something defamatory about the plaintiff. And, as with trespass to land, there must be an invasion of a certain kind of interest—exclusive use of land in the one case, reputation in the other. An invasion by the right kind of intentional act—not consequent harm or carelessness as to such harm—generates the right of redress.

A second aspect of the common law of defamation law that is jarring to modern sensibilities is the irrelevance of *truth and falsity* to the definition of these wrongs. As we have seen, defendants have long been able to raise truth as an affirmative defense to defamation claims. Still, falsity was not considered part of the wrong itself, which instead consisted merely of the publication of words about another carrying a potential for reputational harm. Consider in this regard *Burton v. Crowell Publishing Co.*, a famous opinion written by Learned Hand for the Second Circuit Court of Appeals. *Burton* held that a prominent sportsman could prevail in a libel action against an advertising agency.[5] The agency had placed in several magazines a cigarette ad that included a photograph of the plaintiff, even though the agency knew the photo created an optical illusion that would trick viewers into momentarily thinking that the plaintiff had exposed his (seemingly deformed) genitals while posing for the photograph. Hand's opinion accepted the defendant's argument that viewers would instantly recognize that they were being tricked by the camera and hence that the ad conveyed no actual information about the plaintiff, much less false information about him. Nonetheless, the plaintiff was deemed to have a valid libel claim. The gist of common law libel was *not* the publication of a *false* statement about the plaintiff, but rather the publication of a statement—or in this case, a depiction—that tended to expose the plaintiff to hatred or ridicule. While libel defendants could claim truth as a defense, Hand observed that this privilege was of no help to the agency. Because the depiction of the plaintiff contained no statement at all about the plaintiff, the agency could not possibly justify its publication of the photograph on the ground that it was stating the truth about the plaintiff.

The third aspect of pre-1964 defamation law that comes as a surprise to modern eyes is a combination of the first two: the irrelevance to liability of *the reasonableness of the defendant's belief in the truth of the statement about the plaintiff.* Again, the wrongfulness of libel and slander resided in the intentional making of a certain kind of statement about the plaintiff and the interference that the statement caused (or was presumed to cause) with the plaintiff's right to his good name. Notions of lack of vigilance or lack of

---

5. 82 F.2d 154 (2d Cir. 1936).

diligence simply did not figure in the definition of these torts. Simply put, the injunction contained in the common law of defamation was: "If you don't have anything nice to say about someone, don't say it."

⁄⁄ 11.3 Contemporary U.S. Defamation Law

Over the past half century, American defamation law has become less distinctive in each of the three respects just described. Increasingly, defamation plaintiffs have been required to prove not just the publication by the defendant of a defamatory statement about her, but also fault beyond the intentional making of a statement, as well as harm actually suffered by the plaintiff. In addition, almost all defamation plaintiffs are now required to prove the falsity of the defendant's statement and at least carelessness on the part of the defendant as to its falsity. Thus, today, the tort of defamation much more closely resembles the tort of negligence than it did even as late as 1950.

11.3.1 *New York Times v. Sullivan* and the Actual Malice Requirement

Sullivan was first and foremost a child of the struggle over civil rights that took place in the 1960s and that pitted the federal government against officials of the segregated Southern states. The litigation began as a state court libel suit brought by L.B. Sullivan, a city commissioner of Montgomery, Alabama. The suit was brought against the New York Times, though not for an article or editorial it published, but rather for an advertisement that appeared in its pages, the space for which had been purchased by a civil rights advocacy group. The ad sought support for the group in part by describing instances in which police in Southern states—including police in Montgomery—had used excessive force to suppress student protests and to harass Dr. Martin Luther King, Jr. In addition to suing the newspaper in its capacity as "republisher" of the statements contained in the ads, Sullivan also sued four prominent civil rights advocates whose signatures had appeared in the ad, apparently without their permission.

In the Alabama courts, Sullivan argued successfully that even though he was nowhere mentioned in the ad, it was defamatory of him because he was the official responsible for oversight of the Montgomery police department that was accused in the ad of using excessive force to quell student protests. Although he identified some inaccuracies in the ad that arguably overstated the degree of force used by police, Sullivan offered no proof of reputational harm, instead relying on the doctrine of presumed damages. (One has to suspect that, at least among his peers and neighbors, Sullivan would have been praised rather than vilified for the actions he claimed had been implicitly attributed to him.) The jury awarded Sullivan $500,000 in compensatory and punitive damages, which verdict was affirmed on appeal.

Faced with this result, the U.S. Supreme Court agreed to hear the case and for the first time held that the First Amendment sets limits on the common law of libel and slander. Most important, the majority opinion, authored by Justice William Brennan, held that a *government official* cannot recover for defamatory falsehoods published innocently or as a result of mere carelessness, but instead must prove by clear and convincing evidence that the statements were published with *actual malice*, defined as *knowledge of, or reckless disregard for, the statements' falsity*. The Court also held that published statements criticizing governmental units or departments generically cannot be assumed to be statements "of and concerning" particular officials and hence cannot provide the basis for any of them to recover damages for libel or slander. Having announced these rules, the Court reviewed the record and concluded that it saw no evidence that either the signatories to the ad or the newspaper knew that statements in the ads were false or that they were reckless in disregarding evidence of their falsity. In doing so, the Court signaled emphatically to the Alabama courts that it expected them to dismiss the suit on remand, which they did.

In retrospect, *Sullivan* was "the perfect storm"—everything about the case signaled the propriety of Supreme Court intervention. The underlying litigation was brought at the height of regional strife over the civil rights movement. Indeed, the suit was part of a conscious effort by Alabama officials to discourage media coverage of the Southern states and to derail federal efforts to desegregate. The decisions of the state trial judge had stretched common law defamation to its breaking point (for example, by allowing the jury to conclude that the ad was asserting claims about Sullivan), suggesting that he was himself an active participant in this act of political resistance. The jury's damage award, rendered without any evidence of actual reputational damage, was grossly excessive. Taking a step back, one could thus fairly characterize this nominal civil defamation suit filed by Sullivan as a thinly veiled effort by state and local governmental officials to suppress criticism of their policies. In this respect, the lawyers for the New York Times, including influential legal scholar Herbert Wechsler, were quite right to argue that the tort of libel was in this particular instance operating as the equivalent of a *criminal prosecution* for seditious libel and as such should be struck down as the sort of impermissible effort by government to censor political speech that founders like Jefferson and Madison had long ago decried as unconstitutional.

No wonder, then, that the Supreme Court reached out for the case and held, contrary to its own prior statements, that the civil law of defamation can, at least in some instances, unconstitutionally encroach on protected speech. Indeed, three of the Justices—Black, Douglas, and Goldberg—wrote concurring opinions indicating that they would have gone further than the majority opinion by immunizing from liability even those who, in bad faith or out of malice, publish defamatory statements in the course of addressing "public affairs."

11.3.2 From Public Officials to Public Figures

Sullivan raised significant hurdles for public officials pursuing defamation claims. Its actual malice standard purposely set a high bar by requiring officials to prove that the defendant had acted in bad faith—with knowledge that he was publishing falsehoods or with utter disregard for clear signals of falsity. Moreover, by ruling that state defamation law would now be subject to constitutional limitations, the decision naturally led defamation defendants, particularly media companies, to invite the Court to extend its decision. The Justices proved eager to accept these invitations. For example, they quickly ruled that *Sullivan* applies even to statements about low-level officials, as well as to defamatory statements that address not merely their performance in office, but also personal attributes or experiences (such as past indiscretions) that might bear on their fitness for office.

Most important, the Court ruled that *Sullivan's* constitutional limits should apply not only to public officials, but to any *public figure*.[6] A public figure, it explained, is either a household name—a "general purpose public figure"—or a person who alleges being defamed in connection with his involvement in a matter of public concern, on which he had already voluntarily involved himself,—a "limited purpose public figure." Because of the extension of *Sullivan* to public figures, a celebrity who alleges having been defamed by a tabloid must be prepared to prove actual malice. More troublingly, perhaps, the same goes for a suit brought by an ordinary citizen who is defamed in connection with her voluntary participation in a debate or an event that has caught the public's eye. With the extension of the actual malice rule beyond public officials to even limited purpose public figures, the Court rather plainly concluded that its intervention was needed not only to block government actors from

---

6. Curtis Publ'g Co. v. Butts, 388 U.S. 130 (1967).

using civil defamation actions to suppress political speech, but also to provide speakers with a broad degree of freedom to address matters of public interest without being obligated to avoid causing harm to reputation. According to the court, for speakers and writers to have adequate 'breathing room,' state tort law cannot provide recourse to a defamed public figure, even if she can prove that the speaker or writer was altogether careless as to the truth or falsity of the defamatory statement.

To take one notable example, during the 1996 Olympic Games held in Atlanta, a fatal bombing occurred. In the immediate aftermath of the bombing, a security guard named Richard Jewell was praised for his heroism in helping to evacuate the area. During this time, Jewell agreed to several requests for media interviews. Soon thereafter, the *Atlanta Journal Constitution* and other media outlets ran stories suggesting that Jewell might well have been the bomber. Jewell was exonerated by the FBI, and he sued for libel. However, because he had agreed to interviews when first identified by the media as a hero, Jewell was deemed by the Georgia courts to be a limited purpose public figure whose claim to have been defamed by being falsely identified as the bomber was subject to *Sullivan's* actual malice requirement. Thus, even if members of the media had been careless in insinuating that Jewell was the bomber, as a public figure he could not prevail on a claim of libel.

11.3.3 Emphasizing Fault and Falsity

Even after the Supreme Court extended *Sullivan's* actual malice rule to defamation claims brought by public figures, there was continued pressure from the media and continued interest among some of the Justices to further cabin liability in the name of protecting speech. For example, Justice Brennan, the author of *Sullivan*, wrote an influential plurality opinion in a case called *Rosenbloom* advocating that the actual malice rule be extended to any suit alleging that the plaintiff had been defamed by speech or writings addressing a matter of public interest, regardless of whether the plaintiff met the definition of a public figure.[7] However, by this time, other Justices were beginning to express qualms about the extent to which the Court was involving itself in reshaping state defamation law and limiting the right of victims of defamatory publications to obtain redress.

These countervailing tendencies ultimately produced a doctrinally tangled middle position articulated by the Court in its 1974 decision in *Gertz v. Robert Welch*.[8] In that case, Gertz, a Chicago lawyer, had been described by a far-right newspaper as having aided a communist plot to discredit local police forces. (In fact, Gertz had merely represented the family of a victim of police brutality in a civil suit.) Gertz successfully sued the newspaper for libel. On review, a majority of the justices refused to deem the plaintiff a limited purpose public figure, noting that he had not sought out attention on the issue of police brutality nor attempted to influence public debates about the topic. Having thus concluded that *Sullivan's* actual malice requirement did *not* apply, the Court nonetheless proceeded to impose a different set of constitutional constraints on defamation suits brought by *private figures* with respect to statements bearing on a matter of public interest: here, a newspaper story on an alleged communist conspiracy.

Under *Gertz*, a private figure suing for defamatory speech on a matter of public concern must prove that the defendant acted *at least carelessly* with respect to the truth or falsity of his statement. Thus, in this class of cases, a defendant cannot be subjected to liability if he actually and reasonably believes his statement about the plaintiff to be true. Furthermore, *Gertz* held that any defamation plaintiff attempting to take advantage of the common law

---

7. Rosenbloom v. Metromedia, Inc. 403 U.S. 29 (1971).

8. 418 U.S. 323 (1974).

rule of presumed damages, or to recover punitive damages, must prove not simply negligence, but actual malice.[9]

An example will help clarify *Gertz's* complicated holding. Suppose a local newspaper publishes a story accusing a private school teacher of molesting a student. If the teacher sues for libel, he cannot prevail without proving that the newspaper failed to act with reasonable prudence in determining the truth of the story. If he can prove carelessness, but cannot prove actual malice, he must be prepared to come to court with proof that the defamatory story caused him some form of harm, such as the loss of his job or emotional distress. Finally, if he can prove actual malice, he need not offer any proof of harm to prevail (i.e., he can benefit from the common law rule of presumed damages). Upon proof of actual malice, he will also be eligible to obtain punitive damages, though he must still meet state law requirements for their imposition (i.e., that the conduct was wanton or willful).

In part because of its complexity, the majority opinion in *Gertz* earned a long and impassioned dissent from Justice White, who argued that the Court had strayed far from its original mission in *Sullivan* to prevent defamation law from operating to suppress political speech. Although it took another decade, a majority of the Court seemed to signal that it had reached the end of its efforts to refashion defamation law when it issued *Dun & Bradstreet, Inc. v. Greenmoss Builders, Inc.*[10] There, it refused to extend *Gertz's* requirement of proof of actual malice to recover presumed and punitive damages to a suit brought by a private figure with respect to speech

---

9. As clarified by subsequent decisions, *Gertz* did not hold that private figure-public interest defamation claimants who can only prove negligence—and who are thus constitutionally barred from taking advantage of the common law rule of presumed damages that would otherwise apply to claims for libel and for slander per se—are required to meet the daunting challenge of proving special damages (i.e., tangible economic loss). Instead, they can obtain relief so long as they have proof of some harm beyond harm to reputation caused by the defamation, including emotional distress.

10. 472 U.S. 749 (1985).

addressing a matter of *private concern.* The Court thus let stand a jury verdict awarding both forms of damages without proof of actual malice to the plaintiff company, which had been defamed by a report in a newsletter sent only to a small number of subscribers.

Although *Dun & Bradstreet* might have been thought to herald the end of the *Sullivan* line, the Court continued to fashion new constitutional rules, rules that arguably apply not only to suits governed by *Sullivan* or *Gertz*, but to all defamation claims. Specifically, the Court issued three subsequent decisions—*Hepps, Falwell,* and *Milkovich*—that, in different ways, make *proof of falsity* central to defamation litigation.[11] These decisions, taken together, arguably require all slander and libel plaintiffs to show that the defendant has made a statement about the plaintiff that is *in principle falsifiable* (as opposed to being a statement of pure opinion) and is *in fact false.* Thus under current law, it seems likely that the sportsman who prevailed in *Burton* (mentioned above) would not prevail today. More generally, the spreading of true information seems to be no longer regarded as a *justification* for defaming someone. Rather the wrong of defamation seems now to be defined as the publication by the defendant of a statement about the plaintiff that is both defamatory in nature and false. In this regard, modern defamation law seems nearly as much concerned to protect listeners from false information as it is to protect individuals from reputational attacks.

11.3.4 The *Sullivan* Revolution in Perspective

The Supreme Court has since *Sullivan* continually insisted that the Court's reshaping of defamation law is justified by the need to

---

11. Philadelphia Newspapers, Inc. v. Hepps, 475 U.S. 767 (1986); Hustler Magazine, Inc. v. Falwell, 485 U.S. 46 (1988); Milkovich v. Lorain Journal Co., 497 U.S. 1 (1990).

protect freedom of speech. Absent the imposition of additional impediments to recovery by libel and slander plaintiffs, they have argued, the threat of liability will cause speakers to censor themselves and thus impoverish discourse and the flow of important information.

The Court's interventions on behalf of speakers and writers at the expense of those who have suffered reputational hits has many explanations. As we noted above, *Sullivan* itself cried out for attention, though as much or more because of issues of race and federalism as because of the attributes of defamation law. Once the Court got itself into the business of limiting the reach of libel and slander, it developed a sense of mission with respect to law reform in this area. In part, its continued attention to defamation also has reflected an asymmetry between the diffuse populations of persons potentially subject to being defamed and a collection of well-organized, well-represented, and wealthy repeat-player defamation defendants, especially media companies. One also cannot discount the magnetic force of appeals to the First Amendment, which many regard as embodying the most basic rights enjoyed by members of an open, democratic society.

Interestingly, to the extent the Court's defamation jurisprudence rests on empirical claims about the presumed effects of common law libel and slander on speech, it is potentially subject to testing by means of comparative analysis. For it turns out that no other Western industrial democracy has adopted rules that are as hard on defamation plaintiffs as those of the United States. At least on the surface, it would seem to be that hard-hitting media and a culture of free speech are alive and well in nations like Australia, Canada, and Great Britain, none of which have cut back on defamation law to the extent the United States has. Does this fact call into question *Sullivan's* rationale? The answer to this question is by no means simple. Any serious comparative analysis would be required to assess how different in substance the laws of each country really are, and to discount for possible differences in procedural rules, in the size of typical damage awards, in cultural norms pertaining to the filing of law suits, and so forth. Still, the evidence from jurisdictions such as Great Britain seems to suggest that the legal systems of modern democracies may be able to make greater demands on speakers and writers to refrain from slandering and libeling others without thereby undermining free speech.[12]

⚜ 11.4 From Reputation to Privacy

We have seen that the common law of defamation conceived of the wrongs of libel and slander as hinging on an intentional statement about the plaintiff of a sort that would tend to damage her reputation, with truth conceived as forming the basis for a privilege to defame. Implicit in this categorization of truth is the idea that the wrong is not to be understood, in the first instance, in terms of a misrepresentation by the defendant (as it might be in the tort of fraud), but in his interference with a special sort of individual interest or good: the good of having an unsullied reputation. One can puzzle over exactly what sort of good a reputation is; whether there is something odd about the idea of there being a good for individuals that exists only in the minds of third persons. But even a small child is aware that it matters what others think of her, and, for better or worse, few of us are unconcerned with how we look in the eyes of others.

---

12. The differing protection afforded to defamatory speech in different legal systems, combined with the worldwide transmission of speech via the Internet, has made it possible for persons who believe they have been defamed by an American speaker or writer to sue that speaker or writer in the courts, and under the laws, of another country. Those who worry that American authors and speakers will be sued overseas and thereby inappropriately subject to less speech-protective defamation laws of other countries, decry this phenomenon as "libel tourism." Some state legislatures have enacted laws that purport to give residents who anticipate that they might be held liable under foreign laws the right to seek and obtain in the courts of that state a preemptive "declaratory judgment" stating that any foreign-court judgment of liability based on foreign law that is less speech-protective than U.S. law will not be enforced.

It is hardly surprising, then, that tort law identifies other wrongs beyond libel and slander that protect individuals against intentional interferences with the way third parties view them. In the nineteenth century, the most important of these was entitled "breach of confidentiality." If one person entrusted sensitive personal information to another that he did not wish other persons to know about, then the revelation of that information by the person in whom trust was confided was considered actionable as a breach of confidentiality. The injury caused to a plaintiff by such a breach is similar to, yet distinct from, the injury of defamation. The disclosure of private information affects the way third parties think about the plaintiff and their ways of dealing with her. However, the duty not to reveal the information depends not on its harmfulness to reputation, but on the fact that it was communicated with an understanding of a promise of confidentiality. The existence of the tort reflects an individual entitlement to control whether others have certain information about them.

American law today recognizes rights of action by plaintiffs for breach of the duty of confidentiality in many different arenas, although it is rarely described as such. Today much of this law is statutory. These include HIPAA—a federal statute governing the privacy of medical records—as well as credit-reporting statutes, insurance statutes, academic confidentiality statutes, and so on. Together, they obligate large categories of actors who receive information on condition of confidentiality to respect that confidentiality, and some of them (but not all) empower individuals to sue for damages if the confidentiality is not preserved. In addition, professionals including lawyers, accountants, and physicians are subject to liability for malpractice if they divulge confidential information without their clients' or patients' consent.

As noted in chapter 3, Samuel Warren and Louis Brandeis forcefully argued for more general right to privacy in a 1897 article published in the Harvard Law Review. It planted a seed in the minds of lawyers and judges that would blossom in the mid-twentieth century. The "right of privacy" initiative was no doubt helped along by the illustrious career of its progenitor. Louis Brandeis became an influential Justice of the United States Supreme Court and one of the most highly regarded legal minds of the twentieth century.

While Warren and Brandeis claimed broadly that "the right to be let alone" was fundamental and merited general legal recognition, that has never been the approach of American courts and legislatures to the development of privacy rights. Rather, development has been incremental focusing on areas where some or all of the following features exist: (a) the privacy interest is especially powerful (as in information about one's HIV status); or (b) the invasion of privacy was especially flagrant (as in the broad dissemination of something highly personal to the plaintiff); or (c) the social value or value to the defendant of the privacy invasion was minimal (e.g., the information was not newsworthy and/or was false).

⅜ 11.5 The Privacy Torts

The shape of modern privacy law owes as much to Dean William Prosser as to Warren and Brandeis, for it was Prosser who, in a 1960 article titled "Privacy," teased out of judicial decisions four distinct variations on tort claims alleging privacy invasions. As lead reporter for the American Law Institute's Second Restatement of Torts, he incorporated his article's framework into the new Restatement. In this section we briefly review the four privacy torts. In the interest of concision, we will not dwell on affirmative defenses, though we would note that the defense of *consent* has particular importance in this domain. If, under appropriate circumstances, one consents to having private facts about oneself made public, one will have no cause of action for their being made public. In doing so, we will also have occasion to note ways in which the Supreme Court has intervened in this body of law in the name of protecting free speech against the chilling effect of prospective tort liability. Indeed, one can plausibly argue that the Court has been even more aggressive in restricting the scope of the privacy torts than it has been in crafting limits to liability for libel and slander.

11.5.1 Publication of Private Fact

Among Prosser's four privacy torts, the closest to the confidentiality tort is *public disclosure of private fact*. Indeed, the interest protected is nearly the same: the interest in others not having certain information about oneself. Recall that in the confidentiality tort, the wrong lies in the defendant's having breached the trust in which such information was given by disclosing the information beyond the domain to which plaintiff consented. The classic "public disclosure of private fact" case is different, because the defendant did not obtain the information via a confidential communication from the plaintiff, and so there is no promise-like basis for a duty not to disclose it. However, the defendant injures the plaintiff in essentially the same way. By disclosing private information about her, he alters the way third persons see her, understand her, feel about her, and (potentially) interact with her. The puzzle is why a person in defendant's shoes is supposedly obligated to refrain from this communication if the information was not obtained via a promise of confidentiality? The answer has two parts: (1) the communication by the defendant is not simply conveying information to a third party, but disseminating the information widely into the public realm by means of a newspaper story, a radio or television broadcast, or a posting on a readily accessed Web site; (2) the information in question is of a special, sensitive sort, such that a reasonable person would find it highly embarrassing or offensive if such information about her were publicly disseminated.

In sum, the private facts tort contemplates that there are facts about a person that are sufficiently intimate or personal that it is a wrong to that person for another to lay them out for public consumption and that a person can be genuinely wronged and injured by having this aspect of herself *exposed*. The wrong occurs notwithstanding that the information being disseminated is true. Indeed, it is because the information is true that its revelation is so potentially devastating. It is easy to think of examples of information that nearly everyone would regard as private in this sense. Even if it were not statutorily prohibited, the disclosure to the public that a person is HIV-positive would be considered a disclosure of sensitive private information. So too would dissemination of information as to the nature and extent of a person's physical deformities, his need for psychotherapy, or his sexual activities.

Of course, information of this sort often ends up being publicly disseminated, and often without resulting liability. The affirmative defense of consent sometimes accounts for the non-actionability of public disclosures of private facts. More important still is the defense of *newsworthiness*. Politicians and celebrities have no basis in tort law for arguing that information about their marital infidelities should not be published. The information is private in some sense, but the media's privilege to publish what is newsworthy will protect them from liability for releasing it.

One could spend hours pondering the doctrinal place of "newsworthiness" as a counterweight to the private facts tort. Does the newsworthiness of the putatively private fact show that it is really not a "private" fact at all? Does newsworthiness negate the wrongfulness of the disclosure and therefore show that there is not a prima facie case, even if there is a private fact? Is the news-worthiness defense ultimately grounded not in state tort law, but in the First Amendment? As it turns out, the United States Supreme Court has been so receptive to free speech arguments in private facts cases that some justices and scholars have opined that the entire tort has been rendered unconstitutional—that a state may never allow for liability based on the public release of private infor-mation (unless that release constitutes a breach of a promise of confidentiality).[13] Whether this view will prevail is unclear. What is clear is that many jurisdictions (including, for example, Louisiana) continue to recognize liability for giving publicity to private facts, that many others (including New York) do not, and that some

---

13. This is Judge Posner's contention in *Haynes v. Alfred A. Knopf, Inc.*, 8 F.3d 122 (7th Cir. 1993).

(including California) appear to be scaling back the scope of the tort considerably, largely by adopting a very broad conception of what counts as "newsworthy" information.

11.5.2 False Light

The tort of *false light invasion of privacy* in some ways resembles the defamation torts. Like most defamation claims, a false light claim involves a false statement about the plaintiff that affects the way third parties view her, and thereby harms the plaintiff, albeit in a manner that is often hard to pin down. The difficulty in identifying precisely the nature of the false light injury, as distinct from reputational injury, has in fact induced several state high courts to refuse to recognize this cause of action on the ground that it only sows confusion by rendering conduct tortious that is already covered by defamation law.

However, there are distinctions between the two kinds of wrong. To defame someone, as we have seen, is to publish a statement about him that tends to harm reputation. To expose someone by means of false light is to attribute to him, inaccurately, a quality or act that one would be embarrassed or offended to have attributed to oneself. In a sense, then, the false light tort is really a variation on the public disclosure tort, one for which the defendant presumably has less of a justification, given that the publicization of *false* private information is not likely to be considered newsworthy.

Suppose, for example, that a local newspaper, in the course of reporting on a physician accused of malpractice, falsely states that malpractice by the doctor caused the plaintiff (his patient) to lose the ability to control his bowels, such that the plaintiff must now carry with him at all times a colostomy bag. In fact, the plaintiff suffered no injury at the hands of the doctor. The plaintiff would have a strong false light claim against the defendant, given that this is the sort of fact that, if publicized, would be offensive to a reasonable person. A defamation claim might not prevail, because having this disability may not be a matter of disrepute or contemptibility. On the other hand, a private facts claim will not fly because the allegedly factual statement is false: there is no fact being disclosed. Surely, however, the embarrassing nature of the unwanted exposure does not become defensible simply in light of the falsity of the story told.

11.5.3 Appropriation of Likeness

Some of the earliest decisions recognizing a cause of action for invasion of privacy involved claims by plaintiffs that their names or likenesses had been appropriated for commercial use by the defendant without their permission. In one early leading case, for example, the defendant insurance company used a photograph of the plaintiff in a newspaper ad that purported to present the plaintiff as a satisfied customer.[14] The plaintiff argued to the Georgia Supreme Court that his dignity and autonomy were interfered with and that the insurance company should not be able to expose his image to the public for commercial purposes. For a person to be presented as an emblem of a particular enterprise is to invite the public to alter its view of that person. Whether to be so presented to the public surely is one's own prerogative.

To prevail on a claim for this form of privacy invasion, the plaintiff must show that the defendant, for commercial purposes, used his name, voice, or likeness without permission. Thus a defendant can be subject to liability for using a recognizable image of the plaintiff even without specifically identifying him by name. Even a depiction of the plaintiff from behind, without showing his face, can suffice if it renders the plaintiff identifiable. However, courts have made clear that a newspaper's use of a person's name or image in the course of presenting an otherwise unobjectionable piece of reportage is not actionable.

---

14. Pavesich v. New England Life Ins. Co., 50 S.E. 68 (Ga. 1904).

The appropriation of likeness tort actually protects three interests: a privacy interest in protecting a person against unwanted public exposure (i.e., the right to remain anonymous); an autonomy interest in controlling how one's image is presented to others; and an economic interest in the value of one's image for marketing and trade. The relative contributions of these interests can change dramatically when the name or likeness used without consent is not that of a private individual but of a celebrity. The celebrity's interest in anonymity is small to nothing; her interest in control is great, although already somewhat compromised, and her economic interest is typically much greater. In light of the absence of the first interest, misappropriation of a celebrity's name or likeness does not seem to qualify as an interference with a privacy right; but in light of the other two, it has still struck courts as worthy of protection. For these reasons, judges, lawyers, and legislators have used the phrase *right of publicity* to denote the basis of misappropriation claims brought by celebrities.

11.5.4 Intrusion Upon Seclusion

Perhaps the most viscerally wrongful privacy tort occurs when a person reasonably believes she is in her own protected and private space, but another person (or the government) penetrates that private space to watch her, listen to her conversations, or otherwise intrude upon her personal sphere. This is the wrong of *intrusion upon seclusion*. Targets of surreptitious surveillance can sometimes bring claims for invasion of privacy of this form. Similarly, a person who is viewed in her bedroom or bathroom by a Peeping Tom can sue for the invasion. Although this sort of behavior is often literally trespassory in that it involves the defendant entering onto the plaintiff's property to conduct his surveillance, the intrusion tort stands apart from the action for trespass. Just as a tort (assault) can occur even if there is actually no touching of the person, so intrusion upon a secluded space can occur even if there is actually no touching of real property. One who uses a telescope or listening device to observe another's private interactions from the safety of his home is subject to liability for intrusion upon seclusion even absent a trespass. Note that in order for the plaintiff to succeed on a claim for this tort, she must have a reasonable expectation of privacy with respect to the areas or activities in which she is observed. A person who engages in nude sunbathing in her backyard cannot complain of being observed naked if she knows that neighbors ordinarily have an unobstructed view into the yard, just as one who takes the New York City subway cannot claim an offensive touching against those who, predictably, cram into the subway next to her.

The right against electronic eavesdropping, such as wiretapping of telephone conversations, is now protected by a federal statute commonly known as "Title III,"[15] as well as state statutes that mimic it. Partly enacted in order to clarify government officials' Fourth Amendment obligations to seek warrants for wiretaps used in police investigations, Title III also recognizes a private right of actions for individuals who are eavesdropped upon by government actors or private individuals without at least one-sided consent. Prosser's "intrusion upon seclusion" tort, integrated into the common law, is the original home of this right. Indeed, as in many areas of constitutional law and civil rights law, many current controversies regarding limitations on government officials' right to intercept electronic conversations have a conceptual home in rights-concepts first hashed out in the law of torts.

11.5.5 Doctrinal Overlaps and Legislative Initiatives

As the discussion above indicates, some of the privacy torts bear a strong resemblance to defamation claims and are often brought in

---

15. 18 U.S.C. § 2520.

conjunction with them. This is especially true of the public disclosure and false light torts. Claims for misappropriation of likeness and seclusion upon intrusion are somewhat less likely to be reconceived as defamation claims, but nevertheless have important overlaps with other areas of the law, specifically, property law. Hence it is common to find misappropriation claims brought alongside claims under a federal law known as the Lanham Act[16] for false advertising or under the federal Copyright Act[17], and indeed rights of publicity are frequently conceived of as a form of intellectual property. Similarly, intrusion on seclusion cases are frequently pleaded, and sometimes succeed, as claims for trespass to land, even though the injury put before the jury is principally the interference with privacy.

Some courts and legislatures have viewed the overlap between privacy and other sorts of law as a reason not to fashion new domains of privacy law; in New York, for example, courts and the legislature have chosen not to recognize intrusion against seclusion, in part because the law of trespass provides significant protection to the interest in not being observed when in private. On the other hand, celebrities and artists have succeeded in obtaining recognition for personal rights of control against publicity and against misuse of their creative work by pitching this in terms of an extension of their intellectual property rights.

Perhaps most important, advocates for privacy rights have frequently used a two-tier strategy: on one level, recognizing that the common law already acknowledges the importance of privacy rights and individuals' entitlement to protection of such rights, but at the same time conceding that the vagueness of the common law presents potential defendants and courts with difficulties in determining how they are required to conduct themselves. As noted above, in the area of rights against eavesdropping, rights against

---

16. 15 U.S.C. § 1125(a).

17. 17 U.S.C. § 501(b).

disclosure of medical records, rights against disclosure of HIV status, rights against disclosure of financial information, and rights against misappropriation, advocates have chosen to present lawmakers with fairly detailed legislative schemes as a means of providing protection without generating excessive uncertainty.

11.5.6 The Supreme Court Intervenes Again

Just as it has done in the area of defamation, the Supreme Court has deemed the privacy torts at times to pose a sufficient threat to free speech as to require them to be scaled back. Indeed, as noted above, at least in the view of some lower courts and commentators, the Court has not merely scaled back, but has entirely killed off the tort of public disclosure of private facts.

The Court's first effort at setting constitutional limits on privacy actions came in *Time, Inc. v. Hill*.[18] There, it extended *New York Times v. Sullivan's* "actual malice" standard to cover false light invasion of privacy claims, even false light claims brought by private figures. The plaintiffs, a family, were described in a magazine article as having been the victims of a "desperate" hostage situation in which their captors physically abused and terrorized them. Although the plaintiffs had briefly been held hostage in their home by escaped convicts, they had been treated courteously and had not been subjected to abuse. The Court held that in order to recover, the plaintiffs would have to establish that the defendant magazine's false characterization of the conditions of their confinement was made by the magazine with knowledge of or reckless disregard as to its falsity.

Unfortunately for the law's clarity, *Hill* was decided before the court's decision in *Gertz*, thus raising the question of whether *Gertz* in effect modified *Hill*, such that false light claims by private figures

---

18. 385 U.S. 374 (1967).

on a matter of public concern should now be subjected in the first instance to a negligence standard. Although the Court had an opportunity to answer this question in its 1974 *Cantrell* decision,[19] it declined to do so, leaving lower courts to guess as to whether different and more speech-protective constitutional rules apply to false light claims brought by private citizens as compared to defamation claims.

With respect to the public disclosure tort, the Court has issued two decisions, both concerning suits for newspaper stories that identified crime victims by name. In *Cox Broadcasting Corp. v. Cohn*,[20] the plaintiff's teenage daughter was the victim of a fatal sexual assault. Although there was substantial news coverage of the attack and her death, her name was not disclosed, in part because Georgia statutory law forbade the disclosure of the names of rape victims. However, during legal proceedings in connection with the prosecution of the attackers, a reporter for the defendant's television station saw the name of the victim on court documents. The reporter later identified the victim by name in a news broadcast. The Court held that, insofar as Georgia law granted to the victim a cause of action for invasion of privacy, it generated an unconstitutional burden on speech, noting in support of this conclusion that the court documents from which the reporter learned the victim's name were by state law accessible to the general public, and also that the common law of defamation had long privileged fair reports of judicial proceedings.

Fourteen years later, in *Florida Star v. B.J.F.*,[21] the Court was confronted with facts nearly identical to those in *Cohn*, except that the reporter for the defendant newspaper had received the plaintiff crime-victim's name only because a local police department had broken state statutory law by including the victim's full name in its

19. Cantrell v. Forest City Publ'g Co., 419 U.S. 245 (1974).

20. 420 U.S. 469 (1975).

21. 491 U.S. 524 (1989).

report of the incident. (Although the police department's printing of the plaintiff's name was illegal under the statute, the reporter's obtaining of the information was not itself a violation of the statute.) According to the Court, this difference was not sufficient to change the outcome of its constitutional analysis. Reasoning that any restriction on the publication of true information must survive "strict scrutiny"—i.e., must be the only practicable means available by which a state might achieve a very important governmental purpose—the Court concluded that the states have available to them less speech restrictive means by which to protect victims' privacy.

𝕸 11.6 Conclusion

Justice White, in dissent in *Florida Star*, predicted an end to the development of the right of privacy, and some leading scholars in subsequent years sounded concordant notes (sometimes in celebratory tones). The Supreme Court's aggressive development of free speech restrictions on defamation has drawn similar responses from jurists. From our vantage point, these reactions seem understandable but overstated. The climate in which defamation and privacy law operate has been changing in subtle and unsubtle ways. The coding as electronic data of private information—whether financial or genetic—exposes all of us to greater risks of privacy invasions. Information is now transmitted by a mode of communication—the Internet—that has none of the checks associated with traditional journalism. And traditional journalism increasingly takes the form of 'infotainment' that purposely blurs the line between reporting and titillation. Although prognostication in this area is risky, it would not be shocking to see the defamation and privacy torts begin to reclaim some of the ground that has been lost in the *Sullivan* revolution and its aftermath.

TWELVE

Damages and Apportionment

A SUCCESSFUL TORT PLAINTIFF is entitled to obtain a judicially enforced remedy against the tortfeasor(s) who injured her. Although this remedy can take different forms, by far the most common is a judgment ordering the defendant(s) to pay money damages to the plaintiff. The damages payment is perhaps the most visible characteristic of modern tort law. This is particularly so in the United States, where courts be counted on to produce occasional eye-popping judgments. A skeptic might even say that tort law really is nothing more than a system of 'transfer payments'—i.e., one by which the government randomly reaches out and reallocates wealth from one person to another.

This last description is a caricature. The tort system in its ordinary operation does not involve the government "taking from A and giving to B." As we have seen, the law puts the onus on tort claimants, many of whom face formidable legal and practical obstacles to prevailing on their claims, which is why many persons with valid complaints don't sue. No less than any other real-world institution, the tort system sometimes misfires, which means that claimants sometimes recover damages to which they are not entitled. By the same token, deserving claimants are sometimes denied relief. In the vast run of cases, though, the tort system predicates the defendant's payment to the plaintiff on proof that the defendant has wrongfully injured the plaintiff. The damages payment is thus a 'transfer' only in the particular sense of being recourse that the plaintiff is entitled to have against the defendant by virtue of what the defendant has done to the plaintiff. Despite their being among the most visible and tangible features of the tort system in action, damages are the 'tail' not the 'dog'—the remedy that flows from the commission of a wrong.

This chapter describes the legal standards that govern the terms on which a successful plaintiff is entitled to recover damages. It also briefly discusses other tort remedies, including self-help, nominal damages, and injunctive relief, and it sketches the rules governing *apportionment of damages*—i.e., the rules for determining how much of a given award is to be paid by each of the parties to a lawsuit. Along the way, we mention some important modern reform measures that have been proposed or adopted in an effort to combat what is perceived to be patterns of excessive or otherwise unjustified tort liability.

🕮 12.1 Compensatory Damages

There are two general categories of tort damages that tend to be recognized by American courts: compensatory damages (including nominal damages) and punitive damages. As their names suggest, compensatory damages are provided to compensate a tort victim for having been the victim of defendant's tort, whereas punitive damages in some sense involve punishment of the defendant. We consider the law of compensatory damages in this section, and punitive damages in the next.

12.1.1 Make-Whole Compensation

Black-letter law holds that a successful tort plaintiff is entitled to damages in an amount that will *make her whole* or *fully compensate* her for the injury she suffered at the hands of the defendant. Another phrase used to express this same idea is that the plaintiff's compensatory damages should in principle be enough to return the plaintiff to the *status quo ante*—the condition she was in prior to the happening of the tort. At least in cases of personal injury (as opposed to claims for damage to fungible property), the law cannot hope literally to restore the pre-tort condition. When it comes to scarred bodies or damaged psyches, what has been done cannot be undone. The idea instead is to provide the plaintiff with an amount of money that will in some sense make up for what she has been through and what she has lost.

Although 'make-whole' has come to be the standard way of expressing the measure of tort damages, it is slightly misleading as a matter of both practice and principle. Practically speaking, it is simply not true that jurors assess damages only by accounting for the costs associated with a plaintiff's injuries. They also take into account how the defendant acted toward the plaintiff. Imagine two plaintiffs who incur identical injuries and costs because of another's commission of a tort. Now imagine that the tort against the first plaintiff consisted of an unprovoked attack and the second an inadvertent running down. Even apart from the issue of punitive damages (discussed below), one would expect jurors to come up with a higher compensatory damage award in the former case than in the latter. Such a disparity might be decried as arbitrary. But it should instead be defended as reflecting a holistic judgment as to the amount of compensation to which the plaintiff is entitled in light of what has happened to the plaintiff *and* what the defendant has done to the plaintiff. On this understanding, make-whole is not, strictly speaking, the measure of damages, although it is not irrelevant to that measure. Perhaps the concept of making whole is best understood as a *target* that the law asks jurors to keep in mind as they attempt to provide compensation that is *fair* and *reasonable* under the circumstances of the case. (Jury instructions tend to invoke terms such as "fair" and "reasonable" in specifying how jurors are to set compensatory damages awards.)

In certain unusual situations—namely ones in which the defendant has in fact committed a tort against the plaintiff, but in which the plaintiff happens to have suffered no meaningful loss or setback—the plaintiff will receive only a *nominal damage* award. For example, suppose there is an actor who learns of an emergency at home and decides to take a shortcut on his way home, which entails scampering quietly across the yard of plaintiff's home; and neither the plaintiff nor the yard is the least bit damaged. The defendant has committed a trespass against the plaintiff, but because of the absence of any harm and the good-faith basis for the trespass, plaintiff should only recover a token or nominal damage award of $1. (Note that, in some jurisdictions, a plaintiff who suffers no real harm, and is thus entitled only to a nominal damage award, might still be able to recover sizeable *punitive damages* if, unlike in this hypothetical, the defendant's misconduct is egregious. Punitive damages are discussed below.)

Compensatory damages are divided into different categories or 'heads.' The most common division is between "economic" and "non-economic" damages. Economic damages include expenses charged to the victim because of the tort (including especially medical expenses, lost income during a period of hospitalization or invalidity, and repair costs), as well as losses in wealth that the victim can be expected to incur in the future because of the tort (including costs for ongoing medical care and lost income caused by injuries that prevent one from returning to one's job or require the plaintiff to take a new, less-well-paying job). Non-economic damages compensate the victim for any pain and suffering experienced as a result of the commission of the tort and, in some jurisdictions, for the loss of the ability to enjoy certain aspects of her life. For example, a devoted amateur runner who is left unable to run as a result of a tort may be able to recover for the diminished quality of a life without running.

It would be a mistake to think of non-economic damages as exclusively meant to compensate the plaintiff for her pain and her loss of pleasure. The category is much broader, covering damages that compensate for the underlying injury itself. For example, a person whose hand must be amputated because of medical malpractice is entitled to compensation for the disfigurement itself, apart from the distress it causes him. A plaintiff falsely identified by the defendant as a child molester can likewise recover damages to compensate him for the sheer fact of having taken a reputational hit.

12.1.2 The Eggshell Skull Rule

A notable corollary to the concept of full compensation is the so-called *eggshell skull* rule, which is sometimes expressed through the saying that "a tortfeasor takes the plaintiff as she finds him." The point is that a tortfeasor is in principle on the hook for damages equal to the value of the plaintiff's entire losses, even if, *because of a hidden vulnerability in the plaintiff,* the extent of harm caused to the plaintiff, and therefore the amount of damages she stands to recover, is much larger than anyone could have expected. For example, in the famous battery case of *Vosburg v. Putney*[1] (discussed in Chapter 7), one adolescent schoolboy kicked another in the leg. Unexpectedly, the kick exacerbated an underlying condition such that the victim was crippled. The defendant argued that he should be held liable only for an amount of damage that might have been expected to flow from a modest kick. The court, however, rejected this position, stating the black-letter rule that the tortfeasor is obligated to make good even on losses of a magnitude that could not have been foreseen.

On its face, the eggshell skull rule might seem to run contrary to the requirement of proximate cause that the plaintiff's injury, to be actionable, must have flowed from the defendant's conduct in a natural or foreseeable manner (*see* Chapter 5). Yet there is no conflict. The idea behind that principle of proximate cause is that no wrong is committed by a careless actor if the victim's having suffered *any injury* of the relevant type is only because of a freakish or haphazard sequence of events. It hardly follows that a careless actor

---

1. 50 N.W. 403 (Wis. 1891).

whose carelessness can fully be expected to cause injury to another, and does in fact cause injury, should be spared having to pay an extra increment of damages if the injury turns out to be more extensive than might have been expected. In the first instance, the unexpectedness of any injury to the victim entails that no wrong has been done to the victim by the careless actor. In the second, where the actor *has* wronged the victim, it is just that the wrong causes more harm to the victim than would have been predicted.

To point out that there is no inconsistency between negligence law's insistence on proximate causation and its embrace of the eggshell skull rule is *not* to say that the eggshell skull rule is invulnerable to criticism. Indeed, critics have attacked it on various grounds, including that it sometimes permits the imposition of liability out of proportion to the gravity of the tortfeasor's wrong. However, the eggshell skull rule is not the only tort rule that permits 'disproportionate' liability. Suppose a driver momentarily takes her eyes off the road and thereby runs into a pedestrian, and a result, the pedestrian suffers injuries of an utterly predictable sort. Despite having committed what, in the scheme of things, amounts to a minor delict, the driver may end up having to pay the victim thousands or even millions of dollars. Were it imposed as a fine for her traffic offense, a figure of this magnitude would be unconscionable. But as we have stressed, tort is not a system by which the government fines citizens for antisocial conduct. It is a system that empowers victims to respond to wrongdoers. As such, Anglo-American tort law has made the reasonable albeit controversial judgment that victim satisfaction may require the payment of damages out of proportion to the gravity of the defendant's wrong, whether because of a victim's hidden vulnerability or for various other reasons.

Some supporters of the eggshell skull rule offer a pragmatic defense of the rule as it operates in the American tort system. Recall from Chapter 2 that, unlike in the English "loser pays" system, a victorious tort plaintiff in the United States must pay her own legal fees. It follows that even a recovery of 'full' compensation means that, under a standard contingent fee arrangement, the plaintiff will receive only two-thirds of her award, with her lawyer getting the other third. The eggshell skull rule has been defended by some as a means of overcompensating the plaintiff and thereby effectively implementing a crude version of the "loser pays" rule. This sort of justification, however, suffers from being unprincipled. After all, there is no reason to suppose that the extra increment of unforeseeable damages recovered by the plaintiff will correlate to the amount of the award payable to her attorney. And why should the law only give the benefit of a *de facto* rule of loser pays to the class of victims who suffer unforeseeably large losses because of a hidden vulnerability?

The eggshell skull rule has its natural home in physical injury cases. Consider by contrast a situation in which a careless defendant drives his car at a very low rate of speed into the corner of plaintiff's detached garage, negligently failing to apply the brakes fully before gently bumping into the garage. Because of a previously concealed weakness, the structure unexpectedly collapses. Is the defendant on the hook for the entire value of the garage? The law is not clear, but the correct answer is probably "yes and no." The defendant will have to pay for the 'garage,' but nonetheless can argue with some force that the restoration of the status quo ante calls for damages equal to the worth of a *structurally unsound* garage, rather than a typically sturdy garage. A weaker version of the same argument may in principle be available to certain defendants who face eggshell skull liability for causing personal injuries. For example, a latter-day Putney could perhaps argue that he should not be made to pay for any loss of enjoyment of life experienced by Vosburg as a result of the lameness that unexpectedly resulted from Vosburg's being kicked, because the underlying vulnerability in his leg entailed that sooner or later he would have become lame as a result of some other common occurrence (e.g., a fall).

The application of the eggshell skull rule to claims for negligent infliction of emotional distress (NIED) is also somewhat tricky. As we saw in Chapter 6, the limited duty rules that apply to NIED claims require the plaintiff to establish that she was exposed by the defendant's carelessness to a situation that an ordinary person could not be expected to endure without experiencing distress (e.g., a near-miss that imposed on plaintiff the risk of imminent and serious bodily harm). Thus, a careless actor who seriously traumatizes a hypersensitive plaintiff will not be subject to liability if an ordinarily constituted person would not be traumatized by the same experience. This rule is evidenced in a Canadian decision, *Mustapha v. Culligan of Canada Ltd.*,[2] in which the defendant carelessly supplied plaintiff with a container of water for a home water cooler that contained a dead fly in it. Upon discovering the fly, the plaintiff (who in retrospect clearly was emotionally fragile) completely unraveled and required extensive psychiatric care to overcome the fear, disgust, and severe depression he experienced by virtue of becoming obsessed with the thought of having previously been exposed to impure water. The court denied recovery on the ground that psychiatric distress to a hypersensitive victim by means of conduct that would not cause an ordinary person to suffer severe distress was unforeseeable, and therefore was too remote. The foregoing rule notwithstanding, a plaintiff who is exposed by the defendant's carelessness to the right sort of stressful circumstance (e.g., who is placed by the defendant's carelessness in the zone of danger), such that some serious emotional distress is actionable, can in principle recover full compensation even if some serious distress is substantially more severe than the distress that would have been experienced by an ordinarily constituted person.

12.1.3 Compensatory Damages and Contemporary Tort Reform

Some types of compensatory damages are more capable of numeric valuation than others. If a tortfeasor causes the plaintiff to incur

---

2. 2008 SCC 27 (2008).

certain itemized expenses, the fact finder should be able to value those expenses quite accurately. Other damages resist precise calculation, including especially non-economic damages, as well as damages for future economic losses, which require an educated guess as to what the victim would have earned had the tort not occurred, how long she would have lived, and so forth.

One of the primary concerns of the modern American tort reform movement is centered on the broad discretion that has historically been afforded to jurors to assign a value to nonquantifiable harms such as pain and suffering and lost enjoyment of life. This concern has some justification. Studies suggest that, on average, American jurors have in the last several decades become more generous to plaintiffs in making these awards, even adjusting for inflation. Moreover, awards by U.S. juries for pain and suffering often seem to be an order of magnitude larger than awards provided by European decision-makers in what would seem to be comparable cases. In an effort to control large jury awards of non-economic damages, commentators have proposed, and legislatures have sometimes adopted, several types of measures.

One type of reform empowers trial and appellate judges more closely to scrutinize amounts awarded by juries. Under traditional common law rules, judges are instructed not to second-guess a jury's award of compensatory damages unless they find the award so shockingly excessive as to demonstrate prejudice or bias against the defendant. In many courts today, however, the rules have been changed to empower trial and appellate judges to strike or reduce awards based on the judges' perceptions of what a reasonable award would be.

More aggressively, many states have adopted for some or all tort claims flat monetary caps on non-economic damages. For example, California has enacted a much-copied law that permits successful medical malpractice claimants to recover their entire economic losses, but only up to $250,000 for pain and suffering. Supporters argue that caps such as these are necessary to control 'runaway' juries. Critics argue that caps are unnecessary because huge damage awards occur only rarely. They also argue that caps operate harshly with respect to classes of tort victims who cannot prove substantial economic damages, such as retirees who cannot claim lost future earnings. (Given the expense of litigating even a modestly complex malpractice case, lawyers who know that the maximum they stand to recover under a contingent fee arrangement with this sort of claimant is one-third of $250,000 may reasonably conclude that the cost of bringing even a clearly meritorious suit will out-weigh the recovery.) At least one state (Virginia) has adopted an across-the-board flat cap on the compensatory damages (economic and non-economic) that a medical malpractice plaintiff may recover. In this jurisdiction, a patient rendered paraplegic by mal-practice and in need of $25 million to cover the cost of future health care is, by virtue of the cap, entitled to recover only a very small fraction of his damages from the tortfeasor. Is there any way to jus-tify a 'regressive' rule, like this one, that operates most harshly only with respect to those with the most devastating injuries?

⚡ 12.2 Punitive Damages

Punitive damages—also known as "exemplary" or "vindictive" dam-ages—are at the center of contemporary battles over tort law and tort reform. Although they have been a feature of Anglo-American tort law at least since the late 1700s, they only emerged as a front-page political issue in the last decades of the twentieth century. Prompted by the occasional issuance by juries of blockbuster awards on allegations that a business has defrauded clients and customers, or has recklessly distributed a dangerously defective product, many judges, legislators, and academics have called for their abolition or curtailment.

As their name suggests, punitive damages are *not* awarded simply to meet the plaintiff's entitlement to compensation for her tort-related losses. Instead, when available, they provide an extra increment of damages by which the plaintiff punishes the defendant for the wrong done to her. However, only certain forms of tortious wrongdoing are eligible for punishment of this sort. A prerequisite to an award of punitive damages is proof that the defendant acted not merely tortiously, but also "willfully or wantonly"—with specific intent to injure the victim, out of malice or spite toward the victim, or with reckless disregard for the well-being of persons such as the victim (in many jurisdictions, even recklessness will not suffice). Because this rule excludes recovery by plaintiffs who allege mere carelessness, punitive damages are for the most part *unavailable* to victims of medical malpractice, slip-and-falls, and car accidents. However, a special subset of plaintiffs suing on negligence claims or products liability claims can seek punitive damages, namely, those who can establish that the defendant was, at the time of acting, fully aware that its conduct posed a very serious risk of harm to others yet proceeded without doing anything to mitigate that risk. The fact finder will be permitted to conclude (but need not conclude) that an actor who adverts to this sort of risk and then proceeds to generate it has acted with the reckless disregard that justifies a request from the plaintiff for a punitive award.

Whereas any successful tort plaintiff who presents proof of losses *is entitled to* at least some compensatory damages, *no* tort plaintiff is necessarily entitled to receive punitive damages. Thus, even if the plaintiff proves that the defendant's conduct meets the legal standard for being subjected to punitive damages, the jury (or the judge in a bench trial) is not required to award them; they are disretionary.

At first blush, it may seem odd that there is a part of tort law that metes out *punishment.* And indeed a debate raged among nineteenth-century jurists as to whether punitive damages are an anomalous criminal law interloper that ought to be expunged from tort law. Yet, as noted, punitive damages were already a well-established part of tort law when that debate occurred, and, in any event, the debate ended resoundingly in favor of retaining punitive damages (at least in the United States), with only a few states abolishing punitive damages except when specifically authorized by statute. Still, concerns about the inappropriateness of using tort to punish continue to resonate and to affect judicial and legislative attitudes toward punitive damages.

To get a handle on how punitive damages may or may not fit within tort law, it will be helpful to distinguish two different senses in which punitive damages might operate as punishment. The first sense can be illuminated by contrasting the situation of two tort plaintiffs. One is injured by a momentarily distracted driver. The other is the victim of an unprovoked, intentional physical attack. As a matter of everyday psychology and morality, most would suppose that each of these two victims is entitled to react negatively toward the person who injured him and to demand some form of satisfaction from that person. And yet the attack victim would presumably be justified in being qualitatively more aggravated—outraged, for example—over the way in which he has been mistreated, and accordingly justified in demanding more from his wrongdoer by way of recompense or satisfaction. Indeed, we might suppose that it would be acceptable for this victim to feel vindictive toward, and perhaps even act *vindictively* toward, the assailant or to demand that the state make an example of the defendant.

Here one arrives at the first sense in which punitive damages operate as a mechanism of punishment from within tort law: they provide victims of particularly egregious wrongs with a power to ask the court to enable them to respond punitively or vindictively to those who have wronged them. When awarded, this extra quantum of damages provides the victim with a means of asserting himself against the wrongdoer in a particular way—to be the one who (with the help of the court) expresses concretely to the wrongdoer that he had no right to do what he did to the victim or anyone else.

Insofar as punitive damages provide this special form of victim empowerment, they quite clearly belong in tort law. Tort is a law for the redress of wrongs. Punitive damages, on this understanding, provide a special form of redress to a special kind of victim—they create opportunities for victims of grave wrongs to obtain symbolic vindication against who have wronged them. (To emphasize that punitive damages awarded on this rationale belong to tort, some jurisdictions use the phrase "aggravated damages.") The notion of punitive damages as a special form of redress for victims of egregious wrongs not only fits with the law's threshold for awarding them (intent, malice, or wanton disregard), but also fits with the kinds of cases in which juries tended to award punitive damages, particularly in the nineteenth and early-twentieth centuries. These include cases of intentional defamation and fraud, the gross mistreatment by railroads and other common carriers of vulnerable passengers, and flagrant intrusions on, and willful destructions of, personal property.

Now let us turn to a second sense in which punitive damages might "punish." Suppose a manufacturer consciously employs shoddy manufacturing practices, thereby exposing thousands of consumers to a serious risk of bodily harm, some of whom are injured when the risk is realized. Now suppose a consumer who has been caused serious injury by the product brings suit and presents to judge and jury 'smoking-gun' evidence that high-level employees of the defendant were aware of the risk but inexcusably downplayed or ignored it. Because of the manufacturer's cognizance of its misconduct, we might again think that this is an instance in which the victim should be permitted to take a vindictive stance toward the manufacturer. But in addition, we might suppose that the victim's suit provides an appropriate occasion on which to send a different kind of message to the manufacturer and others like it—namely, that it must not be so cavalier about posing dangers to the consuming public. On this rationale, an award of punitive damages is not so much a special kind of victim redress as it is a means for punishing and deterring misconduct on behalf of public safety.

Precisely because it relies on a public policy rationale rather than a victim-redress rationale, the public punishment/deterrence concept of punitive damages sits more awkwardly within tort law and is more open to challenge as illegitimate or at least ill-advised. Indeed, insofar as this concept goes hand-in-hand with the idea that a single tort plaintiff ought to be deputized to punish a defendant on behalf of all of us—and for that reason ought to be able to collect millions of dollars as a bounty for doing the public's bidding—it raises serious procedural and substantive worries.

To appreciate some of the relevant procedural concerns, let us return to the injured consumer's lawsuit contemplated just above. Until recently, at least, it would not have been unusual for the plaintiff's lawyer to make remarks roughly along the following lines in her closing arguments to the jury.

> *Ladies and gentlemen. We have proved that the defendant's defective product seriously injured my client, for which injuries you must fully and fairly compensate her. We have also shown you that the defendant sold this same defective product to thousands of consumers, and thus knowingly exposed them to exactly the same risk of injury. Now some of these consumers were lucky enough to escape injury, but you have heard evidence that a number of them—as many as twenty in this state alone—were unlucky and were injured. In addition to fully compensating my client for her injuries, you need to send a message to the defendant that you will not stand for this kind of corporate irresponsibility. As the judge will tell you, the law allows you to do this by awarding not only compensatory damages but also punitive damages. On behalf of my client and everyone else who has been put in jeopardy by this defendant, I urge you to award punitive damages in an amount that will make sure big businesses won't behave this way anymore. It is your job to set that amount. But keep in mind that huge corporations like the defendant pay absolutely no attention to numbers in the thousands— that's just pocket change for them. One thing that might help guide you in setting this amount is to keep in mind the social harm that the defendant's misconduct probably has caused. For example, you could take your award of compensatory damages to my client, then multiply it by 20. Then at least you'll be speaking*

*for all the other people around here whom the defendant so
shamelessly victimized.*

Now suppose that the jury returns a verdict that awards the plaintiff $1 million in compensatory damages and $20 million in punitive damages.

One procedural worry associated with this imagined proceeding is that the jurors may be in effect finding that the defendant should be held liable not just to the plaintiff whose case they have heard, but to twenty other persons who may or may not be pursuing their own claims against the defendant, and whose claims may or may not stand a chance of success. (Whether these others have valid claims will depend not only on whether they can prove wrongdoing as to them and injury, but also on the presence or absence of affirmative defenses such as comparative fault.) In fact, the U.S. Supreme Court in *Philip Morris USA v. Williams*[3] ruled that a defendant's procedural due process rights are violated when they are subjected to a punitive award issued as punishment for harms caused to persons other than the plaintiff. Because of *Williams*, it is today probably impermissible for a plaintiff's attorney to present to a jury the argument made in the last two sentences of the fictional closing argument provided above.

Apart from process issues, there are substantive concerns that large punitive awards amount to disproportionate punishment. And if we conceive of such awards as regulatory fines, there does seem to be a problem. Like a $200,000 ticket for a simple parking violation, a $20 million punitive award for the injuring of a single person might seem to constitute an "excessive fine" of the sort forbidden by the Eighth Amendment to the U.S. Constitution. Interestingly, the Supreme Court has rejected this precise argument, ruling that punitive damages are not "fines" within the

---

3. 549 U.S. 346 (2007).

meaning of the Eighth Amendment.[4] However, in its subsequent 5–4 decision in *BMW of North America, Inc. v. Gore*,[5] the Court held that a punitive award can be so large relative to the nature of the defendant's misconduct and the harm suffered by the plaintiff as to amount to a deprivation of the defendant's property (its wealth) without due process of law. In *Gore*, the purchaser of a luxury car claimed that the manufacturer and seller concealed from him cosmetic damage to the car that the jury valued at $4,000. Based on an argument from the plaintiff's attorney emphasizing that many other consumers had probably been deceived in the same way, the jury provided the plaintiff with a punitive award of $4 million, which was later reduced on appeal to $2 million. In striking down the $2 million award as grossly excessive, the *Gore* majority emphasized the "breathtaking" 500 to 1 ratio of punitive to compensatory damages in the jury's award and that the defendant's nondisclosure, even if actionable, was a relatively minor wrongdoing. In *Gore* and later decisions, the Court has suggested that guarantees to defendants of due process ordinarily will forbid judges and juries from awarding punitive damages in amounts that exceed a single-digit ratio with compensatory damages (i.e., 9 to 1).

Decisions like *Gore* and *Williams* have been controversial among the Justices themselves and in the legal community more broadly. Critics argue that the guidelines set out by these decisions leave lower court judges, jurors, and lawyers with little sense of what sorts of arguments and punitive awards are permissible. Others argue that it is simply a mistake to suppose that the U.S. Constitution has anything to say about the size of punitive awards, which have for most of U.S. history been exclusively a matter for state courts and legislatures.

That a court comprised of a majority of justices who at least profess concern for states' rights would in *Williams, Gore,* and other

---

4. Browning-Ferris Indus. of Vt., Inc. v. Kelco Disposal Inc., 492 U.S 257 (1989).

5. 517 U.S. 559 (1996).

decisions invoke both procedural and substantive due process principles to limit the ability of state courts to impose punitive damages is a striking testament to the degree to which punitive damages have (deservedly or undeservedly) come to symbolize concerns about the modern tort system being out of control. In fact, empirical studies show that punitive damages are awarded in a miniscule percentage (roughly five percent) of the already tiny number of tort cases that go to trial. Of itself, this fact does not tell us whether punitive damages are a problem—they may still be unwarranted in particular cases, and the threat that they will be issued when they shouldn't be may inappropriately influence negotiations in cases that settle rather than go to trial. Still, it is clearly incorrect to suppose that large punitive damage awards are a problem in the sense of being a routine occurrence.

🏛 12.3 Apportionment of Liability

For instances in which a single defendant tortiously injures an innocent victim, the defendant will be ordered by the court to pay the entirety of whatever damages have been awarded. By contrast, when two or more defendants are deemed to have injured a single victim, or when a negligence plaintiff and the defendant are each found to have been at fault, the issue of "apportionment"—of how to divide up the plaintiff's losses—arises. We have already discussed in Chapter 5 the basic rule for apportioning liability as between a single at-fault plaintiff and a single at-fault defendant. Under modern comparative fault regimes, the defendant is ordered to pay the full amount of damages minus a percentage that corresponds to the percentage of fault attributed to the plaintiff. (However, in modified comparative fault regimes, if the plaintiff is found more at fault than the defendant, the defendant pays nothing.) In this section, we consider rules for *apportioning damages as among two or more defendants whose tortious conduct toward the plaintiff has each contributed to the events or conditions that injured the plaintiff.*

On this issue, there are two lines of inquiry: (1) how much of her damages may a plaintiff recover from each of two or more tortfeasors; and (2) how can multiple tortfeasors settle accounts between or among themselves?

12.3.1 Joint and Several Liability

Recall from earlier chapters that there are various settings in which two or more defendants can be held liable for tortiously contributing to the happening of a single injurious episode. For example, if two careless drivers collide with each other, then run down the plaintiff, she will be able to bring claims against each of them. Likewise, suppose an adult carelessly entrusts a power lawnmower to his friend's young child, and the child gets her foot stuck under the mower, where it is mangled. The child's parents, suing on the child's behalf, may be able to bring a claim of negligence against the adult who lent the child the mower and a claim sounding in products liability against the mower's manufacturer for not designing it in a way to prevent child-sized feet from getting caught in it. Insofar as plaintiffs such as these are successful in establishing the liability of each of two or more defendants, the question arises as to *what portion* of the damages a plaintiff can collect from each.

The first step—but only the first step—is provided by the principles of comparative fault just mentioned. Thus, if a jury determines that two or more actors have tortiously caused injury to the victim, it must assign a percentage of responsibility to each (as well as to the plaintiff if there are grounds for determining the plaintiff was also at fault for her own injury). For example, in the lawnmower hypothetical, if a jury were to determine that the plaintiff was not at fault, and that the adult who lent it and the manufacturer each were at fault, it would have to assign a percentage of responsibility to each of the two defendants that adds up to 100 percent—e.g., 75 percent to the lender of the mower and 25 percent to the manufacturer. (Prior to the adoption of comparative fault, a defendant's proportionate share was determined on a *pro rata* basis—i.e., by the number of defendants held liable. Under this approach, each of two tortfeasors would in the first instance be assigned 50 percent responsibility, whereas each of three tortfeasors would initially bear one-third responsibility.)

The assignment of these initial percentages of fault is anything but a scientific exercise: the fact finder is asked simply to make an all-things-considered judgment about relative responsibility. Probably that judgment will turn primarily on the fact finder's sense of which of the two defendants is more to blame. Note also that in this context, the phrase comparative *fault* can be slightly misleading because the fact finder will be asked to assign responsibility between or among tortfeasors even if the characteristics that render their conduct is not "fault" in the particular sense of carelessness. For example, if the victim of an intentional attack in the lobby of a poorly secured public building successfully sues the assailant for battery and the building's owner for negligence, the fact finder will be asked to assign a percentage liability to each of these two actors.

As we have noted, the fact finder's percentage allocation of responsibility between or among multiple tortfeasors is only the first step. To understand the next step requires us to distinguish between two rules of apportionment: (1) *joint and several* liability and (2) *several-only* liability. The rule of joint and several liability specifies that, irrespective of the fact finder's assignment of comparative fault percentages, the plaintiff is entitled to collect anywhere from 0 to 100 percent of her damages from each liable defendant, so long as the total collected from all the defendants does not exceed 100 percent. Applied to the lawnmower scenario, joint and several liability permits the innocent victim to recover all of her damages from the lender, all from the manufacturer, or some percentage from each. By contrast, where liability is several-only, the plaintiff may only recover from each defendant a percentage of damages corresponding to the percentage of liability assigned to the defendant by the fact finder.

When does joint and several liability apply? Until recently, this issue was determined by common law rules that deemed it to apply to any situation in which (1) multiple tortfeasors acted in concert rather than independently (e.g., one tortfeasor attacked the plaintiff while another aided and abetted the attack), or (2) the plaintiff's injury is *indivisible*. Because the latter category covers a much wider range of multiple tortfeasor scenarios, it is the more important one. An injury is deemed "indivisible" if there is no basis for the fact finder to assign particular losses associated with a single injurious episode to one of two or more tortfeasors. Suppose a baby is born with brain damage that would not have occurred if either the mother's regular obstetrician or the emergency room physician who delivered the baby had exercised due care. Under common law rules, the two doctors would be held jointly and severally liable, at least assuming that the child's brain damage could not be separated into discrete aspects that could be attributed to one or the other's malpractice. By contrast, if a patient were to undergo a surgical procedure that required one surgeon to work on her eye while another worked on her hand, and if she were to suffer eye and hand injuries attributable to the malpractice of each, then liability will be several only, and each doctor will be liable only for the damages associated with the injury he or she respectively caused. In all likelihood, the two-careless-driver scenario, the lawnmower scenario, and the lobby-attack scenario provided above would each be an occasion that, because of the indivisible injury rule, would call for the application of joint and several liability under common law principles.

To avoid confusion, it is worth emphasizing that joint and several liability is a rule of apportionment, *not* a rule for determining whether a given defendant has committed a tort. (In other words, "joint and several liability" is not the name of a tort cause of action; it is the name of a rule for determining how much a successful tort plaintiff may recover from each of two or more actors already determined to have committed torts such as negligence, battery, trespass, etc.) Its practical effect is to permit a plaintiff to simplify the process by which she obtains her damages and perhaps improve her ability to enforce her judgment and collect on her award. In the lawnmower and lobby-attack scenarios, for example, there is probably a better prospect of recovering the full amount of one's damages from a large manufacturer or a landlord than from a neighbor or an assailant. And so the plaintiffs in these cases will want to take advantage of joint and several liability by collecting all of their damages from the 'deeper pocket' defendant. That this defendant was found by the fact finder to be less than 100 percent responsible for the plaintiff's having been injured is for these purposes irrelevant. The effect of the joint and several liability rule is to give the plaintiff the option to choose how to collect on her award, even if it means choosing to make one of two or more liable defendants pay the full amount of her damages.

12.3.2 Contribution

Before feeling too sorry for one of two or more tortfeasors who is held jointly and severally liable for all of a plaintiff's damages, we must now consider the third and last step by which damages are allocated—namely their allocation between or among multiple tortfeasors. As it turns out, an unlucky defendant who is required by the plaintiff to pay an amount that is excessive relative to the percentage fault that is assigned to it by the fact finder often can ameliorate this bit of bad luck. Specifically, under common law principles, the overpaying defendant can in many instances bring an action for *contribution* against its underpaying co-defendant(s). The action for contribution is not a tort action—the allegation by the overpaying defendant is not that it has been wrongfully injured by the underpaying defendant(s). Instead, it is an action that sounds in *restitution*, i.e., a claim that, as between or among two or more tortfeasors responsible for an injury, one who is made to pay all of the damages has *unjustly enriched* the other(s) who has (have) paid nothing.

Consider again the lawnmower example. If the jury deems the lender of the mower 75 percent at fault, and the manufacturer 25 percent at fault, yet the plaintiff takes advantage of joint and several liability and opts to collect 100 percent of the damages from the latter, then the manufacturer will have "overpaid" by 75 percent. Of course, as between the plaintiff and the manufacturer, this is precisely what joint and several liability permits. But it will now be open to the manufacturer to bring a claim for contribution against the lender to obtain reimbursement for the overpaid 75 percent. (Under modern rules of procedure, this claim can often be brought in the same court proceeding as the one in which the plaintiff asserts her claims against the defendants.) If the manufacturer makes this claim for contribution and it is paid by the lender, then, notwithstanding the manufacturer's initial overpayment, each defendant will end up paying a percentage of the plaintiff's damages that corresponds to the jury's initial fault allocation.

Notice that in the scenario just described, there is no difference in the allocation of liability under a regime of joint and several liability with contribution, on the one hand, and a regime of several-only liability on the other. Under the latter, the defendants respectively pay 75 percent and 25 percent of the plaintiff's damages. Under the former, the defendants initially pay 0 percent and 100 percent of the plaintiff's damages respectively, but then the action for contribution resets those amounts at 75 percent and 25 percent.

If joint and several liability with contribution and several-only liability end up being two routes to the same destination, why worry about choosing between them? The answer is twofold. First, there is a basic difference between the two regimes with respect to *who bears the risk of one or more defendants being insolvent, unreachable, or otherwise judgment-proof.* Under the rule of joint and several liability, the defendant who is made by the plaintiff to overpay bears this risk because it is that defendant who will be left holding the bag if he cannot obtain contribution from an insolvent or unavailable co-defendant. By contrast, under a regime of several-only liability, it is the plaintiff who bears the risk of a defendant's insolvency or unavailability. (Note that despite their differences, each of the two basic apportionment rules is an all-or-nothing rule—either the plaintiff or the overpaying defendant bears the *entire* risk of not being able to collect from an insolvent defendant(s). Some commentators have suggested that it would be more sensible to have a rule that calls for the plaintiff and the overpaying defendant to *share* this risk. Such a rule might state that if one of two tortfeasors is insolvent, the plaintiff and the solvent defendant shall each be assigned one-half of the insolvent defendant's percentage-share of liability.)

A second important difference between regimes of several-only liability and joint and several liability is that the rules of contribution are somewhat more complicated than we have so far suggested. For example, it is typically the case that an *intentional* tortfeasor forfeits the right to contribution from a co-defendant. Thus, in the lobby-assault hypothetical mentioned above, if for some reason the plaintiff obtained 100 percent of her damages from her assailant—even if the jury assigned 25 percent of the fault to the building owner—the assailant, as an intentional tortfeasor, would not be eligible to obtain reimbursement from the building owner for the 25 percent overpayment.

12.3.3 The Demise of Joint and Several Liability?

The apportionment rule of joint and several liability has been a primary target of the modern tort reform movement. Opponents have offered several arguments for its limitation or abolition, some of which are not particularly impressive. A few courts have concluded that the very idea of an indivisible injury—which is the predicate for joint and several liability in a wide array of cases—has been abandoned with the adoption of comparative fault rules. If a jury can assign percentage fault, the argument goes, then the injury must by definition be divisible: division is precisely what the jury does in allocating fault. This line of reasoning contains a basic fallacy. To say that a jury can make a judgment as to the relative degree of fault or responsibility among two or more tortfeasors is hardly to say that one can break down a victim's injury into discrete components traceable to the respective tortious acts of two or more tortfeasors.

Other courts, as well as commentators and legislators, have been impressed by arguments that reject joint and several liability on fairness grounds. In a case like the lawnmower example, they suggest, it is simply unfair to make the 25 percent-responsible manufacturer pay 100 percent of the plaintiff's damages. But we have already seen that this kind of argument is too hasty. Recall that a defendant such as this manufacturer may have available to it an action for contribution, which, if successful, will eliminate any unfairness by allowing it to obtain reimbursement for its overpayment. Of course it is true that joint and several liability will work an unfairness to this sort of defendant if its underpaying co-defendant is unreachable or insolvent. But the opposite rule of several-only liability merely transfers that hardship to the plaintiff, and it is not clear why fairness entails that an actor already determined to be a tortfeasor must be freed of the risk of not being able to collect from a judgment-proof co-defendant when it is the plaintiff who will end up bearing that loss.

A perhaps stronger rendition of the injustice argument against joint and several liability might be stated as follows.

There may be no injustice in making a defendant pay an amount of damages greater than it ought to pay if damages were determined strictly by reference to percentage fault. However, in the real world, the rule of joint and several liability invites plaintiffs to 'stretch' to find additional deeper-pocket defendants (such as building owners) beyond a primarily responsible wrongdoer (such as assailants who perpetrate attacks in buildings) in the hope of collecting from the deeper pocket. Moreover, the system of comparative fault stacks the deck against 'background' or 'secondary' defendants, because it makes it possible for a plaintiff's attorney to argue disingenuously to the jury that it need not worry about whether it is stretching too far in holding the secondary defendant liable. After all, the attorney will tell the jury that it can ease any of its qualms about holding the secondary defendant liable by assigning to that defendant only a very small percentage of comparative fault. Under the rule of joint and several liability, however, the 'compromise' being presented by the plaintiff's attorney to the jury is not a compromise at all since even a defendant found by a jury to be one percent at fault for a plaintiff's injury can be made in the first instance to pay the full amount of the plaintiff's damages.

Whether they are meritorious, arguments such as these now tend to prevail. As a result, most states have by statute or judicial decision scaled back or eliminated the common law rule of joint and several liability for indivisible injuries. Some states have simply adopted several-only liability for all indivisible injury cases. Others have instead held that a defendant can only be subject to joint and several liability if the percentage of fault assigned to it by the fact finder meets or exceeds a certain numeric threshold (e.g., 60 percent). Still others eliminate joint and several liability for particular torts (e.g., medical malpractice) or with respect to certain forms of damages (e.g., pain and suffering damages).

12.3.4 A Note on Indemnification and Liability Insurance

We encountered above the concept of contribution—the notion that a defendant made to pay more than its fair share of liability can obtain reimbursement from an underpaying co-defendant. A related but distinct form of reimbursement consists of *indemnification*. One who indemnifies another for a certain kind of loss takes on the obligation to pay for that loss. In the tort context, the indemnifications with which one is concerned are obligations to pay for tort liabilities incurred by another.

Although there are instances in which restitutionary principles call for one tortfeasor to fully indemnify a co-tortfeasor, the most important forms of indemnification today take place through contractual arrangements. By far the most significant of these comes in the form of liability insurance policies. A liability insurance policy is simply a contract between an insurance company and a person or entity that might eventually face tort liability (the "insured"). Under the terms of the typical policy, the insurer agrees to cover some or all of the costs of certain kinds of liability—usually liability arising out of an *accident* caused by the insured—in exchange for premiums paid by the insured. (As noted in Chapter 2, insurers generally do not provide insurance for liabilities arising out of knowing or intentional wrongdoing by the insured, which is one reason tort plaintiffs sometimes work hard to frame their claims as sounding in 'mere' negligence, even when doing so is a stretch.) In the event the insured is successfully sued in tort for an accidentally caused injury for which the insured is responsible, and which is covered by the terms of the insurance policy, the insurer will pay the cost of the liability up to the limits of the coverage promised in the policy.

As noted in Chapter 4, it is often the case that insurance companies that issue liability policies will agree not only to indemnify the insured for certain tort liabilities, but also will agree to pay for and conduct the defense of the insured. (Typically, it is in the interest of the insurer to take control of the litigation since the insurer will have to pay out if the plaintiff's claim against the insured is successful.) This does not mean that the insurer is now the defendant in the tort suit—the underlying tort cause of action is still against the insured person or company. However, the insurance company will usually provide its own legal counsel who will largely control the management and resolution of the underlying suit.

⅏ 12.4 Self-Help and Injunctive Relief

Although compensatory damages are the standard tort remedy, tort law recognizes other remedies as appropriate to particular situations. One alternative consists of *self-help remedies*, whereby the victim of a completed tort is permitted by the law to respond directly to the defendant rather than by filing a lawsuit. However, precisely because tort law was set up to channel and civilize vengeful responses through the legal system, it generally frowns upon victims taking matters into their own hands. Thus, the victim of a battery is not permitted to respond by later attacking the batterer, or even by defaming him. Nor is the victim of a negligent driver or doctor allowed to respond by subsequently destroying property owned by the tortfeasor. In both instances, the victim who engages in these forms of retaliation might find himself subject to tort liability or criminal prosecution. (Note that the right to *after-the-fact self-help* is distinct from rights to protect oneself against the commission of tort, such as the right of self-defense. In this context, we are assuming that the tort has already occurred and that the victim is now contemplating how to respond to the tortfeasor.)

One circumstance in which a certain degree of self-help is permitted is that of landowner faced with a transitory trespasser (as opposed to, say, a tenant on the land whose lease has expired) who refuses to vacate the premises. The landowner is privileged to take reasonable steps to remove this sort of trespasser. However, in doing so, the landowner runs the risk that his efforts will go beyond what reasonableness permits, at which point he himself may face criminal or tort liability for using excessive force to eject the trespasser. Likewise, the owner of personal property that has been unlawfully taken by another may take reasonable steps to retrieve it. Again, however, there are risks in doing so: the owner might be held liable for using excessive force. In addition, if the owner in good faith thinks the property is his but turns out to be mistaken, he may be subject to liability for taking someone else's property.

The predominant alternative to compensatory damages is *injunctive relief*. An injunction is an order issued by a court that directs an actor to refrain from engaging in certain activity. Failure to comply with this sort of order can result in a contempt-of-court finding, which in turn might generate a fine or even imprisonment.

Precisely because they happen unexpectedly and then are done with, standard accident scenarios are not amenable to injunctive relief. The victim of a car crash caused by a negligent driver has no occasion to seek an order from a court enjoining the driver to drive with ordinary care. Instead injunctions are suited for addressing ongoing tortious activity, particularly nuisances and continuing trespasses. For example, if a defendant operates a sewage treatment plant that regularly produces nauseating odors that make it impossible for the owners of neighboring houses to use and enjoy their properties, the owners may be able to obtain an injunction against the continued operation of the plant. This simple example attests to the potentially onerous nature of injunctive relief. If in this scenario the operator has no technological means of solving the odor problem, the issuance of the injunction will entail either that the plant must shut down and/or relocate, or that the operator must buy off all of the affected neighboring residents.

One can imagine some negligence scenarios that are amenable to injunctive relief. Recall from Chapter 5 the famous old English case of *Vaughan v. Menlove*,[6] in which the defendant stacked hay on his property in a way that created an unreasonable risk of fire, which risk later came to fruition, causing damage to his neighbor's property. In principle, Vaughan may have had the opportunity to seek a court order enjoining Menlove to disassemble the haystacks. However, the issuance of an injunction in this sort of situation seems to be very rare, in part because the person seeking it will have available to him after-the-fact relief in the form of a suit for damages should the danger be realized.

---

6. (1837) 132 Eng. Rep. 490 (C.P.).

THIRTEEN

Tort Trends

TORT HAS ALWAYS BEEN LAW for the redress of wrongs. In some respects, it has remained remarkably constant, while in others has changed substantially. Intentional physical attacks, confinements, and invasions of land have been recognized wrongs since the initial fashioning of the trespass writ in thirteenth century England. Certain instances of what we could today call negligence and perhaps strict liability were also actionable under the writ of trespass and its companion, trespass on the case. Other forms of negligence, as well as the wrongs of libel and slander, gained judicial recognition in the period 1500 to 1700. In the mid-1800s, courts for the first time identified "negligence" as a generic accident tort. Early in the twentieth century, they began to treat inflictions of emotional distress and invasions of privacy as in some instances tortious. The middle years of the twentieth century gave birth to the doctrine of strict products liability. With the gradual realization of robust norms of racial and gender equality, statutory tort claims for civil rights violations and workplace discrimination likewise emerged.

Courts and legislatures have also eliminated or narrowed previously recognized wrongs. The Supreme Court's substantial trimming of the defamation and privacy torts provides but one important recent example. And there have been vitally important developments in related bodies of substantive, remedial, and procedural law. These include, to name but a few: the development and abandonment of the writ system; the legalization of contingency fees; the rise and fall of mass tort class actions; and the emergence of regulatory legislation addressing forms of conduct previously addressed exclusively through tort law.

Sometimes doctrinal change is achieved not by law reform, but by altered perceptions as to the spheres of life that ought or ought not to be governed by the legal system—alterations that can be self-consciously promoted by entrepreneurial plaintiffs and lawyers. A notable recent example of this sort of development has been the imposition of liability on religious organizations for failing to detect or respond adequately to sexual abuse by church employees. For decades, this particular form of misconduct was either ignored or regarded as a matter internal to religious organizations. Now it is quite evidently conduct that is governed by rules of responsibility set by the law of battery and negligence.

In this final chapter, we consider—simply by way of a few illustrations—new forms of conduct and some recent judicial and legislative alterations of tort and related bodies of law that may shed light on tort law's future direction.

⅏ 13.1 Wrongs and Rights in a Digitized, Globalized World

As we noted at the outset of this chapter, judges have at various times been called on to apply existing tort law in novel circumstances. Confronted with new situations, judges and legislatures have also had occasion to reshape the law of wrongs. In this section we briefly address issues of law application and law revision that have arisen with the emergence of a world reshaped by the digital revolution and the increasing interdependency of economic, political, and legal systems.

13.1.1 Internet Wrongs and Privacy Rights

In developed Western nations, service and information industries now drive economic growth. Intellectual property is at least as vital to these economies as are natural resources and chattels. What are the implications for tort law of the emergence of post-industrial economies?

Technological, economic, and sociological changes have already induced and will no doubt continue to induce changes in tort law. But one can also expect a great deal of continuity. The cars of the future will be 'greener,' but presumably they will also continue to generate collisions and tort litigation against their drivers and owners, as well as manufacturers and sellers. The same may be said for slip-and-falls and instances of professional malpractice. That consumer products are increasingly manufactured overseas does not of itself preclude the imposition of liability on manufacturers under domestic tort law for injuries that they cause. However, it may raise questions as to the ability of prevailing plaintiffs to collect on their judgments. Foreign courts have sometimes been unwilling to enforce U.S. court judgments against their citizens, particularly judgments that include a punitive damages award.

Even when they enable new modes of social interaction, transformative technologies allow behavior that, unfortunately, fits the definition of familiar wrongs. One example that earned considerable media attention in 2008 is that of a middle-aged woman who posed on a 'social networking' site as a teenage boy to flirt with, but then cruelly 'dump,' a 13-year-old girl whom the defendant apparently knew to be emotionally vulnerable. Soon thereafter, the girl committed suicide. While the propriety of the defendant's conviction under a statute criminalizing computer fraud has been debated, it seems that a civil jury could conclude that this instance of 'cyber-bullying' amounted to the intentional infliction of emotional distress.

In some instances, legislatures have anticipatorily blocked the emergence of new forms of tort liability that would have corresponded to new forms of activity. For example, the 1980s and 1990s saw occasional lawsuits filed against medical care organizations (MCOs) that administer health insurance plans provided by employers to employees as a benefit of employment. A typical claim would allege that an MCO had carelessly and erroneously denied coverage for the cost of a medication or procedure, thereby depriving an employee of medical care to which he was entitled under her health plan, causing a worsening of his health. In its 2004 *Davila* decision, the U.S. Supreme Court interpreted a federal statute regulating employee benefit plans—the Employment Retirement Income Security Act (ERISA)—as in some instances blocking the operation of state tort law with respect to injuries caused by wrongful coverage denials.[1] Persons with coverage through the sorts of plans addressed in *Davila* can only invoke the less fulsome remedies provided by ERISA itself, such as a refund to the employee of any premiums she paid for the plan. In other contexts, however, states continue to recognize claims by policyholders for insurers' bad faith denials of insurance coverage.

The significance for tort law of the emergence of the Internet as a haven for publications that are defamatory, harassing, or invasive of privacy has likewise been limited by a provision in a federal statute known as the Communications Decency Act (CDA).[2] A number of courts have faced the question of whether a telecommunications company or the host of a particular Web site can be held liable for failing to remove a posting that it knows, or has strong reason to believe, is false and defamatory or invasive of another's privacy. While the extent to which common law tort principles would authorize 'failure to remove' liability of this sort is unclear, the issue has thus far been resolved decisively in favor of the defendants by lower federal court decisions interpreting a particular Section of the CDA—Section 230—as intended to immunize service providers and Web site hosts for any liability that might arise by virtue of a posting that they did not author.

In the leading case, *Zeran v. America Online Inc.*, an unknown person posted an advertisement on an Internet bulletin board made available by America Online (AOL) to its subscribers.[3] The ad

---

1. Aetna Health Inc. v. Davila, 542 U.S. 200 (2004).

2. 47 U.S.C. § 230 (1996).

3. 129 F.3d 327 (4th Cir. 1997), *cert. denied*, 524 U.S. 937 (1998).

invited readers to purchase from the plaintiff T-shirts 'celebrating' the 1995 bombing of a federal government building in Oklahoma City, which killed 168 people. After the plaintiff was subject to intense harassment, including death threats, and after AOL refused his requests to remove the posting, plaintiff sued. The federal Court of Appeals for the Fourth Circuit deemed the suit blocked by Section 230. Section 230 immunity does not extend to "content providers"— the authors of defamatory and other forms of tortious internet speech. However, it is often difficult or impossible for victims to locate the author of anonymously posted comments.

The gathering, storage, and ready portability of sensitive personal information in electronic databases has prompted new forms of regulation to protect informational privacy. With some exceptions, the law's response has *not* been built around the recognition of rights of action by which injured victims of wrongs can respond. The federal Health Insurance Portability and Accountability Act (HIPAA) creates rules that protect against and penalize disclosure of patients' medical information. HIPAA itself does not provide a private right of action to victims of inappropriate disclosures. However, some state courts have invoked HIPAA as a ground for recognizing in state tort law expanded physician duties of confidentiality, or for setting the standard of care in a malpractice action based on disclosure of information. The federal Fair Credit Reporting Act (FCRA) regulates the reporting of personal credit information to credit bureaus by banks and other entities. Like HIPAA, FCRA primarily works by mandating consumers' access to their credit information, which mandates are backed by fines.

13.1.2 Tort Law and Human Rights

In the aftermath of the atrocities of the World War II period, activists, politicians, and others sought to find ways to enforce human rights through the promulgation of international law recognizing, deterring, and punishing rights violations. That campaign has come to fruition in a burgeoning body of domestic and international law. Given that human rights violations are quintessential wrongs and that the law of torts aims to provide redress for wrongs, it is hardly surprising to find efforts by litigants to harness tort to serve the cause of human rights.

A now reemergent recognition in American law of a human rights dimension to tort law involves the application of an odd and long-dormant federal statute known as the Alien Tort Statute (ATS). The ATS was enacted as part of the Judiciary Act of 1789. Awkwardly worded, it permits courts to hear suits in which "an alien sues for a tort only in violation of the law of nations or a treaty of the United States." According to one expert,[4] the ATS's original aim was to empower citizens of foreign countries to obtain redress in U.S. state and federal courts for wrongs done to them by U.S. citizens while lawfully present in this country. On this reading, the "law of nations or a treaty of the United States" is treated by the Act *not* as the law that defines what sort of conduct will count as wrongful and actionable—that was to be determined by the application of ordinary state tort law. Rather, the reference indicates that the Act was meant to empower aliens to bring ordinary tort suits in U.S. courts only when they were properly present in the country—i.e., only when their presence was authorized by international law or a treaty.

For most of U.S. history the ATS sat idle. However, starting with a lower federal court decision issued in 1980 and culminating with the Supreme Court's 2004 decision in *Sosa v. Alvarez-Machain*,[5] the Act has come to be understood to authorize suits by foreign citizens *against other foreign citizens* for the commission *outside the jurisdiction of the United States* of a limited set of wrongs that amount to violations of widely recognized prohibitions contained

---

4. Thomas H. Lee, *The Safe-Conduct Theory of the Alien Tort Statute*, 106 COLUM. L. REV. 830 (2006).

5. 542 U.S. 692 (2004).

within the unwritten 'law of nations.' (In contrast to the reading offered above, *Sosa* reads the Act's reference to "the law of nations or a treaty of the United States" as identifing the body of substantive law that defines the wrongs that are actionable under the statute.)

In setting out its interpretation of the ATS, *Sosa* seems to endorse earlier lower court decisions that have permitted suits in U.S. courts by survivors of non-U.S. citizens who are killed in their home countries in the course of ethnic cleansings or genocides, as well as suits by non-citizens who have been tortured or enslaved by officials of their home governments. As foreign sovereigns are immune from liability, these suits seek redress instead against the individual(s) charged with committing the wrong, not against the governments themselves. Moreover, because it is very difficult to enforce ATS judgments against defendants located in other nations, suits under the statute primarily serve therapeutic, political, and/or information-gathering goals.

Some claimants have sought to impose ATS liability on multinational corporations for 'aiding and abetting' human rights violations committed in the first instance by foreign officials with whom those corporations have done business. This, at least, was the argument in *Doe v. Unocal*, in which alleged victims of atrocities by Myanmar soldiers sued Unocal on the theory that the soldiers were acting as Unocal's agents in providing security for a gas pipeline project being funded and implemented by a joint venture that included Unocal. A three-judge panel of the federal Court of Appeals for the Ninth Circuit deemed the plaintiffs to have stated a viable theory of liability under the ATS. However, that decision was vacated when the Court of Appeals voted to rehear the case before all of the judges of the Ninth Circuit.[6] The case settled and was dismissed shortly thereafter. It is unclear whether this theory of

---

6. Doe I v. Unocal, 395 F.3d 932 (9th Cir. 2002), *vacated & reh'g granted*, 395 F.3d 978 (9th Cir. 2003), *dismissed*, 403 F.3d 708 (9th Cir. 2005) (en banc).

liability will prove viable under the Supreme Court's subsequent *Sosa* decision.

Interpreting a different federal statute, Judge Posner for the Seventh Circuit has recently suggested that American law supports the imposition of liability on domestic actors who support terrorist attacks that occur on foreign soil. In *Boim v. Holy Land Foundation for Relief and Development*, the survivors of an American teenager killed by a Hamas attack in Israel sued individuals and organizations in the United States alleged to have provided financial support to Hamas.[7] The suit was brought under a federal statute authorizing any U.S. citizen who suffers personal injury, property damage, or economic loss "by reason of an act of international terrorism" to sue the perpetrators of that act for treble damages. The trial resulted in a $156 million jury verdict against the defendants, each of which was deemed jointly and severally liable for the amount of the judgment.

While granting that the statute does not authorize the imposition of liability on 'accessory' theories such as aiding and abetting, the *Boim* Court nonetheless concluded that one who intentionally provides funds to an organization while knowing (or recklessly disregarding) that it engages in terrorist acts has himself committed "an act of international terrorism" within the meaning of the statute. It further reasoned that the funding of a known terrorist organization can be deemed an actual cause of *any* injurious act of terror committed by a member of the organization. In straining to expand the "act" and "causation" components of the statute, Posner's opinion for the court is quite upfront about emphasizing the potential value of funding-based liability as a means of deterring terrorism, given that terrorists themselves cannot be expected to respond to threats of legal sanctions.

A final form of civil litigation related to human rights concerns not single occurrences of wrongful injurings, but systematic injustices.

---

7. 549 F.3d 685 (7th Cir. 2008).

In particular, the 1980s and 1990s saw an aggressive effort by some American lawyers to use litigation to respond to some of modern history's greatest atrocities, including Nazi genocide and American slavery. As it turns out, these suits generally tended not to involve true tort claims. Nonetheless, these efforts to use lawsuits to respond to and remedy past injustices were clearly modeled on American tort litigation practice, particularly mass tort practice, and have sufficiently resembled tort claims in their substance to be worthy of mention here.

Lawyers representing Holocaust survivors sued Swiss banks seeking to recover, among other things, funds that had been deposited by Jews for safekeeping against seizure by the Nazi government, but then were not returned to their descendants after World War II. Similar claims were filed against German insurance companies for failing to pay out on property and life insurance policies that had been issued to German Jews. Other plaintiffs sued German, Austrian, and French banks, alleging that they had wrongly profited from racist Nazi policies by being able to buy the assets of non-Aryans at fire-sale prices. Former slave laborers sued primarily German manufacturing companies alleging that the latter had illicitly profited from this heinous practice.

As noted, none of these claims were framed as tort suits. Instead, they were brought as claims for *restitution*, which is a separate branch of the civil side of Anglo-American law. A suit seeking restitution is premised on the notion that the defendant has been unjustly enriched at the expense of the plaintiff and is therefore bound to disgorge its unjust holdings and deliver or pay them over to the plaintiff. In these cases, the plaintiffs alleged that the defendants were in possession of property or wealth that they were not entitled to own and that they were required as a matter of equity to hand over to the plaintiffs as rightful owners.

Of course, the plaintiffs' arguments as to why the defendants were not entitled to possession hinged on the commission of abominable wrongs, many of which included acts that, under other circumstances, would count as torts. But the complaints were not brought on behalf of victims of Nazi atrocities to provide redress to them in their capacity as victims of, say, battery or conversion. For example, as against the Swiss Banks, the claim was not that the banks had unlawfully seized the possessions of victims of Nazi persecution. Rather, the suits asserted that the banks had failed to return assets that they had initially held lawfully on behalf of depositors but now, by the terms of the deposits, were required to release. As against the manufacturers that profited from slave labor, the plaintiffs' claims were for unpaid wages, as well as for a share of the profits that the companies earned from having the benefit of unpaid labor. In each case, the viability of the claims was hotly contested. The cases ultimately settled, in some cases with assets provided by the German government.

In 2002, several lawsuits were filed demanding compensation from corporations that had played a role in the U.S. system of slavery. For example, some insurance companies had issued policies to slaveholders that would compensate them for the loss of the use of a slave from death or injury. Of course, the institution of slavery itself was rife with conduct that, absent antebellum law's denial of basic human rights to African Americans, would have constituted torts such as battery and false imprisonment. However, any suit purporting to seek redress for torts committed by individual slaveholders would seem to face insurmountable hurdles under current law, including the long-ago passing of the limitations period for bringing such claims. Hence the 2002 suits rested primarily on claims for restitution, not tort. At their core, the suits claimed that the defendant companies, having profited from the immoral practice of slavery, were unjustly enriched by it, such that slave descendants could claim a right to these wrongful gains. The suits were eventually dropped voluntarily, but succeeded in generating a substantial amount of public and academic debate over the propriety of reparation payments being made by private entities or government to slave descendants.

One other prominent type of restitution litigation, albeit not one meant to respond to an atrocity, deserves mention in this context. Beginning in the mid-1990s, several state attorneys general commenced civil lawsuits against cigarette manufacturers. Unlike suits brought by individual smokers, which typically sought injury or wrongful death damages based on theories of negligence or products liability, these suits sought "reimbursement" for out-of-pocket expenses incurred by state governments. Specifically, the suits alleged that certain of the states' medical care costs—namely, the portion of their mandatory contributions to the federal Medicare program that supported the treatment of persons suffering from smoking-related diseases such as emphysema and lung cancer— should be borne by the tobacco companies. Again, the merits of the underlying claims were hotly contested, and again settlements were reached, including a global settlement with 46 states by which tobacco companies agreed to pay over $206 billion.

The states' reliance on these restitutionary actions was rather plainly part of an effort to sidestep various problems that had tended to bedevil individual smokers' tort claims against tobacco companies. These included the reluctance of judges to deem ordinary cigarettes defectively designed, as well as the inclination of juries to conclude that, notwithstanding tobacco's addictive properties, smokers had assumed the risk of cigarette-related illnesses. Ironically, the states' aggressive pursuit of their unjust enrichment claims proved to be a boon to some tort plaintiffs. For it was in the course of the states' litigating their restitution claims that certain critical documents were discovered that clearly demonstrated a knowing and active effort on the part of tobacco companies to conceal from the public, or substantially downplay, the health risks of smoking. As a result, a new generation of tort plaintiffs has had some success suing tobacco companies not for negligence or for the selling of defective products, but for fraud. In such cases, juries, incensed by the revealed record of corporate malfeasance, have shown themselves quite willing to impose large compensatory and punitive damage awards.

13.2 Global Integration, Domestic Contraction

Business, communications, and entertainment have gone global. For some areas of law—including trade and the protection of intellectual property—there has been a pressing need to implement through treaties and others means new legal standards to manage and foster globalization. While the need for revisions to the domestic law of torts has been less acute, certain of its aspects have been fashioned in light of, or are now developing because of, activities that reach beyond the boundaries of a single nation. In this sense, globalization is generating pressures that have led or may lead to the revision of tort doctrine. And although twentieth-century tort law included important international treaties and conventions governing, for example, aviation law, intellectual property rights, and enforcement of civil judgments more generally, tomorrow's tort lawyer will undoubtedly confront a far more complex regime reaching out to an array of legal topics affecting tort law that range from banking law and terrorism to environmentalism and labor law. Moreover, many developed and developing nations appear to be fashioning for their own legal systems rules and standards that in some ways incorporate Anglo-American tort doctrine.

Ironically, even as lawmakers around the world are looking to Anglo-American tort law in shaping their own legal systems, the mood and the movement in the United States has for nearly three decades been decidedly anti-tort. Tort law is today blamed for numerous ills. It is said to be harming the competiveness of U.S. industry, and to be a system that nakedly redistributes wealth from corporations and political outsiders to citizens of the locality in which suit is brought. It is deemed responsible for delaying or preventing the release of life-saving drugs, and for inducing doctors to leave their profession, to move their practices out of plaintiff-friendly jurisdictions, or to practice defensive medicine. The threat of tort liability is alleged to have forced municipalities and motels to remove playground equipment from their parks and diving boards from their swimming pools. Tort law is also charged with inviting excessive litigation—much of which is frivolous—and corroding notions of self-reliance and individual responsibility. In no small part because of these sorts of claims, courts and legislatures have imposed various limits on liability, both at the state and federal level.

Has tort law really caused these sorts of problems? In the last two decades in particular, scholars have sought to study and answer these empirical questions. Not surprisingly, given the complexity of isolating the causal contribution of tort law as distinct from other factors, robust conclusions have proved difficult to come by. But some findings seem at this point to be reasonably well established. And many, though not all, cut against the most aggressive claims of those in favor of tort reform. The incidence of new tort suits being filed decreased in the period from 1990 to 2001. As a percentage of the gross domestic product (GDP), the 'cost' of tort liability, in terms of damages assessed, premiums paid for liability insurance, attorneys' fees, etc., seems not to have increased in recent years. There is little evidence to suggest that the threat of liability for injuries—as opposed to the risk of the injuries themselves—brought about the removal of diving boards at motels and public pools. On average, juries decide as frequently for tort defendants as they do for tort plaintiffs, though in medical malpractice cases they rule for the defendant physician nearly three times out of four. Also, juries rarely award punitive damages; probably they do so in less than 5 percent of all cases that go to verdict. Increases in medical malpractice liability do not tend to have a significant effect on malpractice premiums. A vastly more important determinant of premium amounts is whether insurance companies can secure a high enough return on their investments of premium dollars.[8]

---

8. The National Center for State Courts provides statistics on tort litigation. www.NCSC.org/Web Document Library/IR_BrowseByTopic.aspx. On diving boards, see Carl T. Bogus, *Fear-Mongering Torts and the Exaggerated Death*

Although findings such as these suggest that some of the more extreme and broad condemnations of the tort system are probably unfounded, because they are framed very broadly, they do not preclude the possibility that there are particular pockets of socially valuable activity that are being unduly hampered by the threat of tort liability. For example, obstetricians run a special risk of facing large tort damages for acts of malpractice. This is because when things go wrong during a birth, they can generate injuries that negatively affect the child throughout her life, a sort of injury that can in turn translate into enormous costs and enormous damages. It may thus be the case that the tort system, even though on the whole it operates appropriately with respect to the practice of other forms of medicine, too greatly discourages doctors from becoming obstetricians or too readily drives practicing obstetricians into other fields.

But notice that conclusions of the latter sort require interpretation. Suppose, for example, there is evidence that the threat of tort liability has induced a nontrivial percentage of obstetricians to leave the field. Or suppose that products liability law has contributed to the disappearance of a particular kind of product or to its experiencing a substantial price increase. Of themselves, these facts do not tell us whether tort law is working properly or poorly. If the tort system is channeling the job of delivering babies to a smaller number of doctors who, by virtue of the greater volume of business, become more experienced and skilled at delivery, then tort law is serving rather than hindering the cause of good medical practices. Likewise, even if malpractice liability is encouraging doctors to run tests on patients that they would otherwise not run, it does not follow that tort law is making a negative contribution. That may be the right conclusion, but first one needs to know whether reasonable prudence requires the additional testing. As a law of wrongs, tort's job is to set standards of conduct and thereby induce those

---

of Diving, 28 HARV. J. L. & PUB. POLICY 17 (2004). On malpractice insurance, see TOM BAKER, THE MEDICAL MALPRACTICE MYTH (2005).

not living up to those standards to change their way of doing things so as to meet those standards.

Regardless of the resolution of these debates, tort reform has been proceeding apace. Indeed, we have emphasized throughout this book the degree to which, since 1980, American tort law has been dominated by the efforts of "tort reformers" to cut back on tort law. In this concluding section, we focus on the extent to which *federal* law, rather than state law, is now leading the way when it comes to tort reform. We also consider how certain developments in the practice of tort law arguably threaten to undermine its continued operation as a law of wrongs and recourse. Finally we briefly consider whether aggressive efforts at tort reform run the risk of being struck down by state or federal courts under one or more of several state and federal constitutional provisions.

13.2.1 Federalization

Since 1980, many state legislatures have enacted statutes that protect potential defendants by, for example, shortening limitations periods, eliminating joint and several liability, and imposing damage caps. More recently—and in some ways more strikingly, given that tort law has long been exclusively the concern of state governments—federal courts and Congress have engaged in their own versions of tort reform. To be sure, federal involvement with tort law is not unprecedented. Congress's Safety Appliance Acts of 1893 and 1910, followed by the Federal Employers Liability Act (FELA) of 1908, implicitly and explicitly authorized damages actions by railroad employees against their employers on terms more favorable to plaintiffs than the terms set by many states' negligence law. The 1946 Federal Tort Claims Act (FTCA) partially abolished federal sovereign immunity, paving the way for states to adopt comparable legislation. Title VII of the Civil Rights Act of 1964 created a tort-like cause of action for victims of workplace discrimination on the basis of race, color, gender, religion, and national origin.

The recent trend in federal legislation, however, has been to limit tort liability. We have already discussed the provisions of the Communications Decency Act, which has been interpreted to immunize Internet providers for failing to remove defamatory postings. Another federal statute, enacted in 2005, protects gun manufacturers against various potential forms of liability. Starting in the 1990s, shooting victims brought suits alleging that gun manufacturers too readily allowed their products to find their way to persons without permits to carry them, in turn making possible acts of gun violence that would otherwise not have occurred. Framed in terms of "negligent enabling" and "public nuisance," these claims were rejected by state high courts in New York and Illinois on no-duty and superseding cause grounds, among others. Yet notwithstanding the unwillingness on the part of courts to recognize these claims, Congress enacted the Protection of Lawful Commerce in Arms Act. Among other things, it prohibits states from imposing liability on gun manufacturers as to victims of criminal attacks.

In the same year, Congress also enacted the so-called Graves Amendment, which precludes rental car companies from being held *vicariously* liable for injuries caused by negligent driving on the part of renters. (The immunity does not apply if the company itself was careless in renting to a particular driver—e.g., because the driver was obviously intoxicated at the time of rental.) Lower courts to date have split over how broadly to read the law, and whether it is unconstitutional for exceeding the scope of Congress's power to regulate interstate commerce.

It is natural, and partly accurate, to see each of these Congressional interventions as catering to organized special interests with political clout (i.e., large Internet companies, the National Rifle Association, and the rental car industry). But there is perhaps more to these episodes than realpolitik. Rightly or wrongly, all three statutes are born of a certain discomfort with extensions of liability to *background actors* beyond traditional common law categories such as aiding and abetting, concert-of-action, or affirmative duty to protect. In the case of gun manufacturer liability, courts and Congress both expressed concern that "negligent enabling" is too broad a conception of responsibility for tort—that one should not be subjected to an action for compensatory damages simply because one's otherwise lawful actions unreasonably created a risk that a subsequent, independent actor would act wrongfully. (*See* Chapter 6's discussion of intervening wrongdoing.) Likewise, with regard to the Graves Amendment, Congress seems to have been moved in part by concern for the onerousness of the particular form of vicarious liability that, under common law principles, attaches to the ownership of a vehicle. By then, the owner is subject to liability merely by virtue of owning a car that another person drives badly, without regard to fault (or lack of fault) on the part of the owner.

Another recent federal law—one that on its face is quite generous to victims of a particular egregious wrong—arguably fits within the general category of statutes designed to limit the operation of tort law and, more particularly, to ward off attempts by victims to impose liability on remote actors for injuries immediately inflicted by someone else. In 2001, Congress established a fund to compensate surviving family members of victims of the 9/11 terrorist attacks in New York and Washington, D.C., as well as persons injured in the attacks or in responding to them.[9] Although the statute did *not* bar outright tort claims arising out of those horrific events, it imposed substantial procedural and remedial limitations on them. In particular, it aimed to deter negligence claims on behalf of airplane passengers and ground victims against the airlines that operated the hijacked planes, the owners of the World Trade Center, and other actors.

As a result, the alternative provided by the statute—no-fault compensation paid out of general tax revenues in amounts determined by a 'special master'—was eventually chosen by more than 95 percent of those eligible. In total, the fund paid out about

---

9. Air Transportation Safety and System Stabilization Act, 49 U.S.C. § 40101 (Supp. 2003).

$7 billion to more than 5000 persons, with the average award being about $2 million per surviving family and $400,000 per injury victim. In part to encourage eligible beneficiaries to forego tort litigation, Congress mandated that awards from the fund be made on an individualized basis, based on factors including the estimated lost future earnings of the person killed or harmed in the attacks, as offset by the availability to survivors and victims of alternative sources of benefits, including life insurance policies. Final payouts to surviving family members ranged from $250,000 to $7 million, while payouts to injury victims ranged from $500 to $8.5 million. Notably, Special Master Kenneth Feinberg recommended in his final report to Congress that for reasons of both efficiency and fairness, any future scheme modeled on the fund ought to be set up to provide equal compensation to all beneficiaries.

The federal statute that created the 9/11 fund was not without precedent. Congress has in the past established special schemes to compensate children who, as a result of legally mandatory vaccinations, suffer serious side effects, as well as coal miners suffering from black lung disease. Still, doing so was clearly the product of unique events in modern American history. Moreover, such schemes tackle problems that, notwithstanding their political significance, are relatively self-contained. By contrast, Congress has repeatedly failed in its efforts to fashion legislation to address what has been by far the most widespread and significant tort disaster of modern times—the exposure of thousands of workers to cancer-causing, airborne asbestos. In the same vein, there seems little evidence that American politicians and voters are keen to follow the striking example of New Zealand, which, starting in 1974, replaced tort law as it applies to accidents with no-fault compensation provided to accident victims through general tax revenues. Under the New Zealand scheme, any accident victim is entitled to complete coverage of her medical and rehabilitation costs, the bulk of her lost wages, and fixed lump-sum payments for permanent injuries.

Were the federal government in the United States to institute a system of nationalized health care comparable to those that have been adopted in other Western industrialized nations, the implications for tort law could be significant, depending on how the plan is designed. For example, damages awards in personal injury cases might be expected to shrink substantially insofar as patients' medical costs will be borne by the general public. Moreover, with a reasonably functioning social insurance scheme in place, many injury victims might feel less pressured to invoke the tort system to obtain compensation. Certainly many experts believe that the presence of universal health insurance in other industrialized nations helps to account for their populaces being, on average, substantially less litigious than that of the United States.

There is an entirely different aspect to the modern "federalization" of American tort law than those mentioned thus far. It does not involve the enactment of statutes with provisions that explicitly bar or limit forms of tort liability. Rather it concerns the effects on state tort law of statutes that impose *safety standards* on a particular industry or activity. These sorts of statutes pose a potential obstacle to the application of state tort law because of the operation of the Supremacy Clause of Article VI of the U.S. Constitution. The Supremacy Clause states that when federal and state law conflict, federal law prevails. Prior to the mid-twentieth century, the federal government paid relatively little attention to consumer safety issues, which were regarded as the province of the states. However, since the New Deal and especially since the 1960s, Congress—along with federal agencies it has created, including the Consumer Products Safety Commission (CPSC), the Food and Drug Administration (FDA), and the Department of Transportation (DOT)—has developed sometimes elaborate regulatory schemes designed to promote safety in various domains of conduct. The growth of these schemes has increased the chances of a clash between federal risk regulation, on the one hand, and the states' provision of civil recourse law, on the other.

The U.S. Department of Transportation, for example, sets certain design standards that aim to improve the safety of automobiles. Suppose a person who is injured when her car malfunctions brings a design defect claim against the manufacturer. As we saw in Chapter 6, under the prevailing common law rule, the fact that the car was designed in full compliance with federal regulatory standards would not prevent it from being deemed by a jury to be "defectively designed" under the state's products liability law. Yet because of the Supremacy Clause, there remains a separate question that is governed by federal law rather than state common law. It concerns whether the victim's state-law right to obtain redress must give way to the standards set by the federal agency (under the authority granted to it by Congress) because they are properly understood as regulatory "ceilings" rather than floors, such that they *preempt* the operation of state tort law. As there is nothing in the Supremacy Clause beyond its bare edict that federal law stands supreme over conflicting state law, it has fallen to the federal courts—and particularly the U.S. Supreme Court—to determine when state tort law is preempted.

According to the doctrinal framework the Court has developed, it begins with a "presumption against preemption" that is grounded in respect for the enactment and application of tort law as a core exercise of states' police powers. However, the presumption can be overcome in one of two ways—by virtue of an *express* directive from Congress, or by *implication*.

Express preemption occurs when Congress includes in a given statute a specific provision stating that the law is meant to be preemptive of certain aspects of state law. Even in these instances, courts still have a role to play, because preemption clauses tend to be drafted ambiguously. For example, some preemption clauses announce that any regulatory "requirements" set by or under a federal statute nullify conflicting state law "requirements" without specifying whether tort judgments count as state law "requirements." In addition, it is common for Congress to enact statutes that have both a preemption clause and a "savings" clause that overtly *limits* the law's preemptive effect. For example, the Consumer Product Safety Act (CPSA)—which created the CPSC—expressly preempts state legislation and regulations setting standards different than those issued by the CPSC, *yet also* asserts that compliance with CPSC safety regulations "shall not relieve any person from liability at common law ... to any other person." Other statutes contain preemption and savings clauses that are less clear as to how they are meant to interact, thus leaving courts with difficult questions of statutory interpretation.

An important example of express preemption analysis is the U.S. Supreme Court's 1992 *Cipollone* decision, which addressed the effect of a 1969 federal statute requiring cigarette manufacturers to place specifically worded warnings on cigarette packs and in cigarette advertisements about the health risks of smoking.[10] In light of the specificity of Congress's directives, as well as a preemption clause in the statute invalidating more demanding state law "requirements," the Court ruled that the statute was meant to block any and all tort claims against cigarette manufacturers by individual smokers asserting that the manufacturers should have done more to *warn* smokers of the health risks of smoking. Congress, the Court supposed, had chosen the specific warnings that it thought ought to be given and did not want state regulators or courts pushing manufacturers to adopt different or additional warnings. However, *Cipollone* also concluded that Congress did *not* intend the statute to block claims based on certain other theories of liability. For example, it left smokers free to pursue claims alleging that cigarette manufactures had *defrauded* them by deliberately concealing information known to them about the health risks of smoking.

If a federal statute does *not* contain an express preemption provision—or even if it contains such a provision yet a court concludes that the provision's language does not fully specify the impact of the statute on the particular tort rules that a plaintiff seeks to invoke—state law can still be deemed *implicitly preempted*. Implied preemption of this sort comes in three forms.

---

10. Cipollone v. Liggett Group, Inc., 505 U.S. 504 (1992).

First, if the relevant federal and state laws together pose a 'Catch-22'—i.e., create a situation in which an actor literally cannot comply with one without violating the other—the state law will be deemed void. This form of implied preemption, which is known as "impossibility" preemption, has little applicability with respect to possible conflicts between federal law and state tort law. If a federal law *permits* a course of conduct that a state court deems to be tortious, then, *at least with respect to the risk of suffering a legal sanction*, the actor who engages in the conduct simply does not face a 'damned-if-you-do-damned-if-you-don't' situation.

Second, courts will deem state law implicitly preempted when Congress has adopted a regulatory regime with respect to a field of conduct that is so comprehensive as to indicate that Congress meant for this regime to operate exclusively: so-called "occupation-of-the-field" preemption. The Supreme Court's *Davila* decision, discussed above, treats ERISA as having entirely occupied the field with respect to certain employee benefit plans, and hence as preemptive of state law that might otherwise allow tort claims against certain MCOs for erroneous denials of insurance coverage. Congress's provision within a statute of alternative federal remedies to victims whose tort claims stand to be preempted by a statute helps make the case for recognizing this form of implied preemption. As is the case with impossibility preemption, tort defendants are rarely able to invoke occupation-of-the-field preemption.

Third, courts sometimes conclude that state law must be preempted because it functions as an impediment to the proper functioning of particular federal rules and regulations, even though the latter are not part of a comprehensive federal scheme. This "frustration-of-purpose" doctrine is the most important and the most questionable form of implied preemption. The doctrine is questionable because it suggests that the Supremacy Clause confers on federal courts broad authority to nullify the long-standing common law principle that a legal remedy shall be provided to a victim of wrongful conduct whenever they deem it necessary to promote the federal government's nebulous interest in pursuing certain regulatory objectives with a freer hand. It is important because of its attractiveness to sophisticated, repeat-player tort defendants. Instead of having to work to obtain tort reform legislation in all fifty states, or having to run the political gauntlet necessary to obtain a comprehensive alternative federal law regime or a federal statute with an express preemption clause, these actors can instead seek a judicial ruling—ultimately, a ruling from five Supreme Court justices—that an extant piece of regulatory law should block the continued operation of state tort law.

The Rehnquist and Roberts Court clearly have been open to recognizing frustration-of-purpose preemption. The former held that a scheme developed by the Federal Highway Transportation Safety Agency calling for the gradual adoption of air bag technology by U.S. auto manufacturers implicitly preempted negligence and products liability suits by accident victims alleging that manufacturers acted tortiously by failing to install air bags more promptly than the federal regulations required.[11] Meanwhile, the Roberts Court has ruled that when the FDA reviews and approves as safe and effective a new medical device, such as a catheter used to clear clogged arteries, tort suits predicated on the theory that the device should have been differently designed or manufactured are implicitly preempted.[12]

And yet it would be an overstatement to say that the Court in recent years has adopted an unwaveringly pro-defendant stance on the issue of frustration-of-purpose preemption. Indeed, it recently ruled that the FDA's approval of warnings and instructions directed toward medical personnel—which concerned risks associated with a particular technique for the administration of a drug designed to relieve migraine headaches—did not preempt a patient's failure-to-warn claim against the drug's manufacturer.[13] In so ruling, the Court reinstated a jury finding that the inadequate instructions

---

11. Geier v. American Honda Motor Co., 529 U.S. 861 (2000).

12. Riegel v. Medtronic, Inc., __ U.S. __, 128 S. Ct. 999 (2008).

13. Wyeth v. Levine, __ U.S. __, 129 S. Ct. 1187 (2009).

contributed to the improper administration of the drug to the plaintiff, thereby causing her to suffer gangrene at the site of the drug's injection.

13.2.2 Routinization

At the turn of the twentieth century, the great sociologist and philosopher Max Weber presciently observed that modern societies and governments would increasingly place a premium on the sort of orderliness and predictability that is conducive to individuals' planning their lives, to firms' making business decisions, and to the operation of government programs. Writing at the same time, Oliver Wendell Holmes, Jr. correctly foresaw that the future would hold a special place for the "man of economics and the master of statistics." As a body of law that requires often nuanced, context-specific judgments about wrongdoing and responsibility, tort law is in some ways out of synch with this trend. In the United States at least, tort's anomalousness along this dimension is particularly notable because of the important role reserved for lay jurors' judgments—judgments that 'experts' often find to be distorted and even maddening. To someone steeped in statistical analyses of costs and benefits, the practice of having courts and jurors decide—after the fact, in a particular case, in the charged courtroom environment—whether someone acted reasonably or whether a product was defectively designed is exactly the sort of unscientific practice that a rationalized world would abandon. Indeed, workers' compensations systems were adopted in part because they promised to render the cost of employee injuries to employers more predictable and insurable while also delivering compensation to injured employees with less uncertainty, variation, delay, and waste.

At the time they were adopted, workers' compensation laws were presumed by many to constitute an early and important step toward the gradual replacement of tort law with governmental regulatory and compensation regimes organized on more 'rational' and bureaucratic principles. In fact, the "replacement process" has been halting and scattershot, thus leaving the United States with a hybrid system that relies on both regulatory and tort law. This pattern owes a good deal to the alignment of political forces, including the relative wealth and political strength of the plaintiffs' bar. But it also reflects a distinctively American emphasis on individual rights and a distrust of 'big' government. A basic tenet of American constitutional democracy, inherited from the English legal system, is that each person who believes she has been wrongfully injured is entitled to invoke the judicial system and plead her case to a judge and/or jury. Likewise, there is enduring and widespread distrust of the ability of governments to run benefits programs fairly and efficiently, as well as a sense that there is something troubling about programs that place their beneficiaries in the position of supplicants asking for benefits rather than litigants pursuing claims as a matter of right.

Perhaps more in keeping with the American ethos has been a different and very important form of rationalization that has been taking place not at the governmental level, but instead through the interaction of private parties. As it turns out, repeat-player defendants, their insurers, and practicing lawyers usually have an interest in seeing the tort system operate with greater predictability. If defendants are going to incur liability, they prefer it to be predictable. Likewise, liability insurers seek the best possible information about payouts so that they can set premiums at a level that will generate profits. Subject to ethical constraints, plaintiffs' lawyers working on the basis of a contingent fee arrangement look to maximize the amount of the verdict or settlement relative to the number of hours put into a case, which generally favors the prompt resolution of claims.

For these and other reasons, lawyers have increasingly sought to manage the resolution of tort cases privately through pretrial negotiations and settlement. Doing so not only takes the 'wildcard' of the jury out of the picture, but it also significantly reduces judicial control of the case's disposition. In its simplest form, this version of tort litigation involves little more than the filing of a claim by the plaintiff, a failed effort by defense counsel to have it dismissed outright, and then a settlement at an amount equal to the limit of the defendant's liability insurance coverage. As we noted in Chapter 4, for conduct that has allegedly injured many persons, plaintiff and defense lawyers may work together to establish settlement grids or point systems that establish different recoveries for different categories of plaintiffs depending on factors such as age, pre-tort income, and health impairment.

Clearly there is something to be said for these informal modes of dispute resolution. They reduce transaction costs and get money into the hands of plaintiffs more quickly than if their claims were pressed all the way to verdict, judgment, and appeal. Moreover, they can reduce the uncertainty and variation that sometimes accompany court proceedings and jury verdicts, thus giving the parties more control over their own destinies. And, in the case of mass settlements, at least if they are well constructed, a certain amount of 'horizontal' equity among claimants is achieved, as opposed to a situation in which individual juries award different dollar amounts to claimants without any evident rhyme or reason.

And yet the emergence of this mode of processing tort claims also raises potential red flags. Tort claimants often are looking not just for a payment, but also for a sense that their claims are being taken seriously and that they have to some extent been vindicated. A process whereby the plaintiff's lawyer leans on his client to settle quickly at the amount of the defendant's liability insurance coverage often will not provide that sort of satisfaction. Moreover, the absence of judicial supervision over the settlement process increases the chances that lawyers, particularly the plaintiff's lawyer, may succumb to monetary incentives to settle on the cheap rather than represent the best interests of her client.

Finally, at the level of constitutional design and theory, one might worry that the demise of judicial proceedings in favor of private negotiations driven by caps on liability insurance coverage will somewhat weaken the elaborate system of checks and balances that has been regarded in Anglo-American political thought as central to sound political design at least since the common lawyers fought against the absolutist claims of the Stuarts in the early 1600s. To be sure, it would be hyperbolic to suggest that the availability to individuals of a right to pursue claims against putative wrongdoers through the courts is necessary to the maintenance of constitutional democracy. Still, jurists and political actors have long supposed that the right to have one's claims heard and adjudicated is an important component in a system of government that aims to protect against tyranny by, among other things, giving citizens the right to demand certain things of their government. Moreover, the tort system has served the egalitarian purpose of enabling ordinary citizens to call to account even wealthy and politically connected actors, a power that they often lack when dealing with others through markets or democratic political processes. Finally, the resolution of disputes on a purely private, negotiated basis also threatens to undermine tort law as a public practice in which standards of right and wrong are set, and through which consequences for wrongful and injurious conduct are meted out. In its absence, the law may increasingly fail to provide guidance to the citizenry as to how they are obligated to act toward one another.

13.2.3 The Constitutionality of Tort Reform

When state legislatures and Congress enact laws limiting tort liability—e.g., by reducing time periods for suing, by introducing new substantive defenses, by capping damages, or by eliminating entire causes of action—they necessarily affect adversely those plaintiffs who would otherwise have benefited from the rules or principles being reformed. Given that all legislation in the United States is in principle subject to judicial review for its constitutionality, it is natural to ask whether there are any viable constitutional objections to tort reform legislation. (Note that state legislation is reviewable for its compatibly with the relevant state constitution as well as the federal Constitution.) Can it be unconstitutional for a legislature to eliminate or modify a common law rule that, had it been left intact, would have enabled a plaintiff to recover for a tort? In challenging the application of tort reform legislation to their suits, plaintiffs have made arguments to this effect, invoking individual rights guaranteed by the federal Constitution, including the Seventh Amendment's right to a jury trial and the Fourteenth Amendment's Due Process and Equal Protection clauses. In attacking state legislation, plaintiffs have also pointed to rights guaranteed by state constitutions, many of which contain their own jury trial, due process, and equal protection provisions, as well as additional guarantees of separated powers, "open courts," and the right to pursue legal remedies.

There probably are grounds for supposing that the Due Process Clause of the Fourteenth Amendment to the United States Constitution was intended to limit the reasons for which and the means by which a legislature can eliminate certain forms of legal recourse. Nonetheless, since the 1920s, federal courts have consistently applied a toothless standard of review, under which a reform measure is upheld so long as it might possibly advance some imaginable legislative objective, such as that of reducing burdens to economic activity. (Perhaps inconsistently, the same courts have insisted that the Fourteenth Amendment's Due Process Clause affords rights to defendants that limit the power of the states to impose punitive damages on defendants. *See* Chapter 12.)

The record in state courts with respect to challenges based on state constitutional provisions to defendant-friendly tort reforms is more mixed. Although many state high courts have shown the same unwillingness to uphold constitutional challenges to tort reform legislation as shown by federal courts, some have struck down legislation, including damages caps. In doing so, they have suggested that even today, centuries after its inception, tort law has a fundamental role to play in specifying wrongs and providing a means by which victims of those wrongs can obtain recourse against those who have wronged them.

Index

9 780195 373974